15 Tales from Shakespeare

by Charles & Mary Lamb

Revised in modern English by Stuart Varnam-Atkin

翻訳協力
とよざきようこ
•
ナレーター
Stuart Varnam-Atkin
•
録音スタジオ
株式会社1991
•
カバー写真
iStock.com/duncan1890, MicroStockHub, petekarici
•
本文イラスト
Tales from Shakespeare, illus. Rackham (1908)
(https://en.wikisource.org/wiki/Tales_from_Shakespeare,_illus._Rackham_(1908))

以下の写真・イラストはステュウット ヴァーナム-アットキン氏にご提供いただきました (pp.5, 21, 345, 347)

英語で読む
シェイクスピア珠玉の15篇
15 Tales from Shakespeare

原著=チャールズ & メアリー・ラム
リライト=ステュウット ヴァーナム-アットキン

by Charles & Mary Lamb
Revised in modern English by Stuart Varnam-Atkin

IBCパブリッシング

はじめに

シェイクスピアの作品は古典でありながら、現在でも様々な形で取り上げられ、そこで語られたストーリーそのものが、私たちにとっては常識の一部として定着しています。

例えば裏切りと孤独の中で苦しむリア王の姿、妻によって野心をいだくマクベス、さらには、運命のつじつまがちょっとずれたことで恋の旅路が悲劇となるロミオとジュリエットなど、そこで語られる物語は現代人にもしっかりとした声をもって訴えるメッセージがいくつも盛り込まれています。

『ロミオとジュリエット』を例に挙げてみましょう。この不朽の悲劇は、その後、ロシアの作曲家セルゲイ・プロコフィエフの手によって、バレエの名作へと生まれ変わりました。さらに、ジェローム・ロビンズはこの物語を現代に翻案し、舞台をニューヨークに移し、対立する移民グループの確執を息吹を吹き込んだようなバイタリティ溢れる物語に昇華させました。こうして誕生したのが、レナード・バーンスタイン作曲の音楽と融合したブロードウェイ・ミュージカルの名作『ウエストサイド物語』なのです。

このようにシェイクスピアの原作は、様々な形で姿を変えながら、新たなテーマや作品となって私たちを楽しませてくれてもいるのです。

ウィリアム・シェイクスピアはイギリス・ルネッサンスを代表する劇作家であるといわれています。彼が生きた時代は、エリザベス１世によってイギリスが海洋王国として成長した時代でした。ちょうど、日本が安土桃山時代から江戸時代に移行する時期とも重なっています。そんな、世界が大きく変化し、中世が過去のものとなり近代へと移行する時期に活動したのです。

そうした世相を反映してか、イギリスでもちょうど日本で歌舞伎が生まれたように、新たな劇団が生まれ、演劇界が大きく変化していた時代でした。

シェイクスピアはその演劇界で活躍するわけですが、単なる作家としてではなく、劇団の経営をも手がけたビジネスマンとしての一面もあったようです。彼の生涯は不明なところも多いものの、時の王室内の政争とも絡まった、波乱に満ちたものだったようです。音楽家も作家も、貴族がパトロンとなるのがヨーロッパでの芸術活動ではよくあることだったのです。

シェイクスピアの作品が今でも映画やミュージカルなどの新作へのヒントとなるのは、なんといっても古典的な手法のなかに人間の欲や愛憎といった生々しい心のやり取りが盛り込まれたことにあります。私たちにとって、シェイクスピアが生み出した作品は決して古いものではなく、現代人もともすれば陥る心の闇や希望や失望など、時代を超えて変わることのない人間模様がそこに新鮮に描かれているのです。

本書は、そんな人類に共通した常識となった作品の数々を網羅し、優しい英語で楽しむことのできる教養書であり、文学作品集でもあるのです。

IBC編集部

CONTENTS

Introduction 序文 8

The Tempest 23
テンペスト

A Midsummer Night's Dream 43
夏の夜の夢

The Winter's Tale 63
冬物語

Much Ado About Nothing 83
から騒ぎ

As You Like It 103
お気に召すまま

The Merchant of Venice 129
ヴェニスの商人

King Lear 151
リア王

Macbeth 173
マクベス

All's Well that Ends Well 193
終わりよければすべてよし

The Taming of the Shrew 213
じゃじゃ馬ならし

The Comedy of Errors 233
間違いの喜劇

Twelfth Night 253
十二夜

Romeo and Juliet 273
ロミオとジュリエット

Hamlet, Prince of Denmark 299
ハムレット

Othello 323
オセロー

Notes 注釈 344

Acknowledgements 謝辞 364

Word List 367

INTRODUCTION

Once upon a time…

The familiar centuries-old phrase '*Once upon a time…*' conjures up that pleasant feeling of a story about to be told. It's like a storyteller looking around at the expectant faces of the listeners and saying, "Are you sitting comfortably? Then let's begin! This is a story from a long time ago, but it doesn't matter exactly when…" Then we head into whatever world the story wishes to take us: adventures, romances, ghosts, legends, battles, goodness and evil, happiness and sorrow, friendship and discrimination, love and hate…

Once upon a time, storytellers around the world enthralled their audiences as they sat around the fire on dark nights with fairy stories, folktales and legends they had remembered hearing when they were young, and they rewrote them as they performed…

Once upon a time (around 550 years ago) the printing press was invented, and at last versions of all those stories could be produced as books and read, not just narrated…

Once upon another time (around 400 years ago), the English actor and playwright William Shakespeare (1564–1616) rewrote all kinds of old stories into stage plays. They came not only from Britain, but also from Italy, France, ancient Greece and Rome, and the Middle East.

Then once upon a time 200 years later (in December 1806, to be precise), a book was published titled *Tales from Shakespear. Designed for the Use of Young Persons*, with no final 'e' on 'Shakespeare'! It was written by two English writers who were siblings. They were Mary Lamb (1764–1847) and her younger brother Charles (1775–1834). Their mission was to rewrite Shakespeare's plays into stories. The book later became known as *Lamb's Tales from Shakespeare*, or just

序文

むかしむかしその昔……

「むかしむかしその昔……」この何世紀にもわたって親しまれてきた言い回しは、これから物語が語られるというあの心地よい感覚を心に呼び起こす。語り手が、期待に満ちた聞き手の顔を見回して、「皆さん、座り心地は快適ですか？　では始めましょう！　この物語は大昔の話ですが、正確にいつの話かは重要ではありません……」と言うのと同じようなものだ。そして私たちは物語が誘う世界へと向かう。それは、冒険、ロマンス、幽霊、伝説、戦い、善と悪、幸せと悲しみ、友情と差別、愛と憎しみなどなどの世界である……

むかしむかしその昔、世界中の語り手たちは、暗い夜に火を囲んで、自分が幼い頃に聞いたことのあるおとぎ話や民話や伝説を披露し、聞き手を魅了した。そして語りながら物語を書き直していった。

むかしむかしその昔、今から550年ほど前、印刷機が発明され、ようやくそのような物語が本になり、語られるだけでなく読まれるようになった。

むかしむかしそのまた昔、今から400年ほど前、イギリスの役者で劇作家のウィリアム・シェイクスピア（1564-1616）は、あらゆる昔話を戯曲に書き直した。それらはイギリスだけでなく、イタリア、フランス、古代ギリシアやローマ、そして中近東に伝わるものだった。

それから200年後のむかしむかしその昔、正確には1806年12月、*Tales from Shakespear. Designed for the Use of Young Persons*という本が出版された。Shakespeareの末尾のeがなかった！　この本は、姉弟であったふたりのイギリス人作家が書いたものだ。メアリー・ラム（1764-1847）と弟のチャールズ・ラム（1775-1834）である。彼らの役目は、シェイクスピアの戯曲をものがたりに書き直すことだった。本は後に、*Lamb's Tales from Shakespeare*、あるいは単に *Lamb's Tales*『シェイクスピア物語』として知られるようになり、ベスト

Lamb's Tales. It was a bestseller and has been reprinted countless times ever since.

In their *Preface*, the Lambs wrote:

> *The following Tales are meant to be submitted to the young reader as an introduction to the study of Shakespeare. His words are used whenever it seemed possible to bring them in.*

They hoped that the tales would not only encourage young children to use their imagination, but also teach them something about adult emotions, so that later they would better appreciate reading the plays and seeing them performed.

Mary went even further, saying their aim was to produce "easy reading for *very young* children". She was particularly eager to write for young girls who were not allowed into the family library as soon as their brothers, due to the prejudice that girls are slower to understand difficult language than boys. And she chose stories featuring daughters, starting with Miranda in *The Tempest.* She later wrote other children's books and championed the professional rights of women like herself who were skilled at sewing.

Both Charles and Mary suffered with psychiatric issues. In Mary's case they were particularly severe. Charles spent a lot of his life looking after his sister. But when she was well, she was known as a kind, witty and generous woman by their literary friends, including the poet Coleridge. The siblings, neither of whom married, were devoted to each other. When they were writing the *Tales*, they would work on different plays at the same time in the same room. Its production proved to be a great form of therapy for them both.

Their original book covered twenty of Shakespeare's thirty-seven plays. None of the Histories or Roman plays were included. Charles dealt with the six 'Tragedies', and Mary the remaining 14 'Comedies'.

セラーとなった。そして出版以来今日まで数え切れないほど何度も重版されている。

ラム姉弟はまえがきでこう書いている：

The following Tales are meant to be submitted to the young reader as an introduction to the study of Shakespeare. His words are used whenever it seemed possible to bring them in.

姉弟が望んだのは、この物語によって幼い子どもたちが想像力を働かすようになり、大人の感情についても何らかを学びとる、その結果、後々子どもたちが戯曲を読んだり、舞台を見たときにより楽しく理解できることだった。

メアリーはさらに踏み込んで、自分たちの目的は「幼い子供たちのためのやさしい読み物」を作ることだと言った。彼女は特に、女子は男子に比べて難解な言葉の理解が遅いという偏見のせいで、男兄弟たちと同時期に家庭の書斎に入ることを許されなかった、幼い女の子たちのために書こうという気持ちが強かった。それで、娘たちが主人公の物語を選び、まずはミランダが登場する *The Tempest*『テンペスト』から作業を始めた。メアリーは後に他にも児童書を書き、彼女自身のような裁縫の得意な女性の職業上の権利を擁護した。

チャールズもメアリーも精神的な障害を抱えていた。メアリーの場合は特にひどく、チャールズは人生の大半を姉の世話に費やした。とはいえ、体調のよいときのメアリーは、詩人のコールリッジをはじめとする文学仲間には、親切で機知に富む寛大な女性で通っている。姉弟は、どちらも結婚せず、互いに対して献身的だった。*Lamb's Tales* を執筆していた頃は、同じ部屋で同時に別の戯曲に取り組んでいた。この制作過程が、ふたりにとっては優れた治療法であったことがわかっている。

Lamb's Tales は、シェイクスピアの37本の戯曲のうち20本を書き直している。歴史劇やローマ史劇は含まれていない。チャールズは6本の「悲劇」を、メアリーは残る14本の「喜劇」を担当した。戯曲の長さを制限し、年少の読者に

To restrict the length and make them suitable for their young readers, they established a strict policy on what *not* to include. They cut the plays' subplots, comic characters, and overt sexual references.

And now in the 21st century, *my* mission has been to update the language of fifteen of the tales for easier understanding by modern readers of any age. Five of them were originally written by Charles, ten by Mary.

Lamb's Tales has long been valued by adults as well as children for two reasons: as an introduction to the main plots and characters of the plays; and as a reminder of the basic story before you go to see a performance of a play you haven't seen for a long time. However, the style of writing from 200 years ago is extremely hard for most of today's young children to follow and not so easy for adults, either!

My principle aim was to modernize the texts while preserving the essence of the Lambs' editing and writing style and sticking closely to the main storylines. I've removed many of the generalized comments and explanations the Lambs added, such as this line in *A Midsummer Night's Dream*:

Men being always better runners in a long race than ladies.

In some tales they also added spoilers, providing information on what would happen later in the story. I felt they were unnecessary.

I have been less concerned than the Lambs were to retain Shakespeare's own words if they are not so easy to understand today. I've also taken various other liberties, such as adding some famous lines and increasing the amount of dialog.

ふさわしいものにするため、盛り込むべきでないものについて徹底した方針を定めていた。そしてわき筋やコミカルな登場人物、あからさまな性的表現などを削除した。

そして21世紀の今日、私の役目は、*Lamb's Tales*から15本の物語を選び、その言葉を今風にして現代のどんな年代の読者にも理解しやすいように書き直すことである。本書に収めた物語のうち5本はチャールズが、10本はメアリーが書いたものだ。

*Lamb's Tales*は、子どもだけでなく大人にも長く重宝されてきた。そこには二つの理由がある。一つは、戯曲の本筋や主要な登場人物を知るための入門書として、そしてもう一つは、久しぶりに観に行く舞台の基本的なストーリーをおさらいするためのリマインダーとして。しかし、200年前の文体では、今の幼い子どもたちの大半にはとうてい理解しがたく、大人にとってもそう易しいものではない！

私が基本的に目指したのは、ラム姉弟の編集と文体の本質を維持し、主要なストーリーに極めて忠実でありながら、テキストを現代化することであった。*A Midsummer Night's Dream*『真夏の夜の夢』の次の台詞のように、ラム姉弟が付け加えた一般的なコメントや説明の多くは削除した。

Men being always better runners in a long race than ladies.

また、物語によってはネタバレも補足されており、物語の後半で何が起こるかの情報が提供されている。私はそれらは不要だと感じた。

シェイクスピア自身の言葉が現代では理解しにくいことを考慮して、元の言葉を残すことについてはラム姉弟ほどこだわらなかった。ほかにも、有名な台詞を加えたり、会話の量を増やしたりするなど、いろいろと自由に書き直してみた。

Vocabulary

So what kind of problems are there today regarding the vocabulary of Shakespeare from four centuries ago mixed with that of the Lambs from two centuries ago?

First of all, I should point out that the original words of Shakespeare can sometimes be used as they are. For example, these two lines from *Much Ado About Nothing* are still very clear today:

Beatrice: *I love you with so much of my heart that none is left to protest.*

Hero: *And when I lived, I was your other wife. And when you loved, you were my other husband.*

But in many cases, there are either 'archaic' words that are no longer, or rarely, used today or familiar words that had a different meaning in the past. Here's an example from *The Taming of the Shrew*, as written by Mary:

Baptista went to apprize his shrewish daughter of her lover's addresses and sent her in to listen to his suit.

This includes four potentially difficult words: *apprize* (inform), *shrewish* (unpleasant, argumentative), *addresses* (words) and *suit* (marriage proposal). I simplified it to this:

Baptista went to tell Katharine what Petruchio had said, and then sent her in to talk to him.

The word 'suit' appears many times in the *Tales* because there are many 'suitors' hoping to marry young ladies, especially in *The Taming of the Shrew*! The terms 'to woo' and 'to court' also appear a lot.

語彙

では、4世紀前のシェイクスピアの語彙と2世紀前のラム姉弟の語彙の混在にどのような問題があるだろうか？

まず指摘しておきたいのは、シェイクスピアの原語はそのまま使える場合があるということだ。例えば、*Much Ado About Nothing*『空騒ぎ』の次の2行は、現在でも非常にわかりやすい：

Beatrice: *I love you with so much of my heart that none is left to protest.*

Hero: *And when I lived, I was your other wife. And when you loved, you were my other husband.*

しかし、多くの場合、今では使われなくなった、あるいはめったに使われない「古風な」言葉や、よく知られてはいるが昔は異なる意味を持っていた言葉がある。メアリーが書いた*The Taming of the Shrew*『じゃじゃ馬ならし』から例を挙げよう。

Baptista went to apprize his shrewish daughter of her lover's addresses and sent her in to listen to his suit.

この文章には、apprize（知らせる）、shrewish（不機嫌な、論争的な）、addresses（言葉）、suit（求婚）という4つの難しい単語が含まれている。私はこれを次のように平易にした。

Baptista went to tell Katharine what Petruchio had said, and then sent her in to talk to him.

*Lamb's Tales*にはsuit（求婚）という単語が頻繁に出現する。若い女性との結婚を望むsuitors（求婚者）の登場が多いからだ。特に*The Taming of the Shrew*では顕著だ！ to woo（求婚する）やto court（求愛する）という言葉もよく出てくる。

Here's another example from *Much Ado About Nothing*, where the difficulty is the meaning of 'the smallest twine':

Being that I flow in grief/The smallest twine may lead me. (Shakespeare)
I am so grieved that the smallest twine may lead me. (Mary)
I am so unhappy that I will follow the slightest glimpse of hope. (My version)

Here's one more example from *As You Like It*, where the difficulty is 'in sober meaning':

Speakest thou in sober meanings? (Shakespeare)
...asked Ganymede if he spoke in sober meaning. (Mary)
Are you serious? (My version)

Shakespeare's *Speakest thou* simply means 'Are you speaking?' Other archaic words often appear in Lamb as well, such as *five-and-twenty* (5+20=25), *fourscore* (4x20=80), *methinks* (I think), *methought* (I thought), *sallied forth* (went out), *bade him* (ordered him), *broke silence* (began to speak) and *divers suitors* (many suitors). I have tried to identify terms like these that may not be clear today, and modernized them.

Indirect speech v. direct speech

Charles, in particular, believed the plays should be read rather than seen on stage, so he preferred to change dialog from the plays into passages of reported speech. For example, when Hamlet meets his father's ghost, Charles wrote, "the spirit broke silence and told him that he was the ghost of Hamlet's father, who had been cruelly murdered..." Mary was fonder of direct speech, and even apologizes in the *Preface* to "young people not used to the dramatic form of writing" for using it too much!

次は*Much Ado About Nothing*からの別の例で、難しいのはthe smallest twine（極細より糸）の意味である：

Being that I flow in grief/The smallest twine may lead me. (Shakespeare)
I am so grieved that the smallest twine may lead me. (Mary)
I am so unhappy that I will follow the slightest glimpse of hope. (My version)

As You Like It（お気に召すまま）からもう一つ例を挙げると、ここではin sober meaning（本当なの？）が問題だ。

Speakest thou in sober meanings? (Shakespeare)
...asked Ganymede if he spoke in sober meaning. (Mary)
Are you serious? (My version)

シェイクスピアのSpeakest thouは単にAre you speaking?（話してる？）という意味である。他にも、*Lamb's Tales*には古語がよく登場する。例えば、*five-and-twenty*（5 + 20 = 25）、*fourscore*（4 × 20 = 80）、*methinks*（私は思う）、*methought*（私は思った）、*sallied forth*（出かけた）、*bade him*（彼に命じた）、*broke silence*（話し始めた）、*divers suitors*（多くの求婚者）などがある。このような現代では意味が不明瞭な言葉を見極め、今風に書き直した。

間接話法と直接話法

チャールズは特に、戯曲は舞台で見るものではなく読むものだと考えていたので、戯曲の会話を間接話法の一節に書き直すことを好んだ。例えば、ハムレットが父の亡霊に会ったときのことを、“the spirit broke silence and told him that he was the ghost of Hamlet's father, who had been cruelly murdered...”（亡霊は沈黙を破り、自分は無残に殺されたハムレットの父の亡霊だと告げた……）と書いた。一方、メアリーは直接話法を好んだ。それで「脚本形式に慣れていない年少者たち 」に対して、直接話法を多用したことをまえがきで詫びているほどだ。

As an actor and voice artist, I have included more of the plays' dialog, modernized where necessary. I believe it adds interest to storytelling by involving more character voices, such as the words of the weird sisters in *Macbeth* and Hamlet's father's ghost.

Another interesting example is the wonderful romantic conversation when Romeo and Juliet first meet. Shakespeare cleverly wrote it in the form of a 14-line poem (a sonnet). However, Charles decided to stop his version of it half way through, *before* the famous two kisses! Instead, he wrote this very vague sentence to cover the second half of the dialog:

In such like allusions and loving conceits they were engaged when the lady was called away to her mother.

I decided to complete the conversation, including the kisses. I also added some very famous lines which the Lambs cut, but it seemed a shame to leave out. They include *If I were human* (*The Tempest*), *Put out the light* (*Othello*), *If music be the food of love, play on* (*Twelfth Night*), *To be or not to be* and *The rest is silence* (*Hamlet*), and Shylock's monologue on revenge (*The Merchant of Venice*). And I couldn't resist including the famous stage direction *Exit, pursued by a bear* (*The Winter's Tale*).

One other characteristic of Charles' writing especially is his use of long, complicated sentences. Where possible, I have broken them up into several sentences to make them more understandable.

I hope Lamb purists—and Mary and Charles—will forgive me for these minor alterations!

役者で声優の私は、物語の対話を多く採用した。そして必要なところは現代風に書き直した。例えば、マクベスの魔女たちやハムレットの父の亡霊の台詞など、登場人物の声が加わることで、読みがたりに面白みが増すと考えるからだ。

もう一つの興味深い例は、ロミオとジュリエットが初めて出会うときの素晴らしいロマンチックな会話である。シェイクスピアはそれを十四行詩（ソネット）の形式で見事に仕上げた。しかしチャールズは、あの有名な二回のキスの手前でその対話を止めてしまったのだ！　代わりに、対話の後半を描写してこの非常に曖昧な文章を書いている。

In such like allusions and loving conceits they were engaged when the lady was called away to her mother.

私はその二回のキスを生かして会話を完結させることにした。また、ラム姉弟は削除したが、私が付け加えた有名な台詞もいくつかある。採用しないのはもったいないと思えたからだ。*If I were human*（もし私が人間だったら）『テンペスト』、*Put out the light*（灯りを消して）『オセロー』、*If music be the food of love, play on*（音楽が愛の糧であるなら、奏でよう）『十二夜』、*To be or not to be*（生きるべきか死ぬべきか）と *The rest is silence*（あとは沈黙）『ハムレット』、そして復讐に関するシャイロックの独白『ヴェニスの商人』。また、*Exit, pursued by a bear*（熊に追われて退場）という有名な演出『冬物語』も含めずにはいられなかった。

チャールズの文章でもう一つとりわけ特徴的なのは、複雑で長い文章を使っていることだ。私は、それを可能な限り、いくつかの文章に分割して、より理解しやすくした。

ラム愛読者が、そしてメアリーとチャールズのふたりが、これらのちょっとした変更を許してくれることを願っている！

Information

To make the tales a little more reader-friendly, I have added a few words of explanation here and there. These include geographical details, such as where the city of Verona is located in Italy and its distance from Mantua (*Romeo and Juliet*). Another example is the meaning of the all-important *30,000 ducats* in *The Merchant of Venice.* I have indicated they were gold coins, suggesting that 30,000 of them was a huge sum. (It's been calculated that the equivalent value today could be several hundred thousands of dollars.) I also briefly explained about fencing *foils* at the end of *Hamlet* and the meaning of *shrew* in *The Taming of the Shrew.*

Songs

Famous songs appear in several of the plays. I have modernized them a little, but the original Shakespeare versions can also be seen in the Notes at the end. Instead of the owl's *cry* in Ariel's final song of joy in *The Tempest*, I added *Tu-wit, To-who!*, which Shakespeare used in his play *Love's Labours Lost.*

I sincerely hope you will find this version of the Lambs' classic book to be both enjoyable and useful. As for the full stories immortalized in Shakespeare's words, well, I also hope you will be eager to read his plays and see them brought to life on the stage and in movies.

Stuart Varnam-Atkin
Kanagawa, Japan, 2024

参考情報

*Lamb's Tales*を少しでも読みやすくするために、あちこちに二言三言、説明を加えた。例えば、*Romeo and Juliet*『ロミオとジュリエット』に登場するヴェローナという都市がイタリアのどこに位置するのか、またそこからマントヴァまでの距離など、地理的な詳細を含めている。もう一つの例は、*The Merchant of Venice*『ヴェニスの商人』で最も重要な3万ダカットの意味である。私はそれが金貨であること、つまり、それが3万枚というのは多額のお金だということを示唆した(現在の価値に換算すると、数十万ドルになる計算だ)。また、*Hamlet*『ハムレット』の最後に出てくるフェンシングのフルーレや、*The Taming of the Shrew*に登場するshrewの意味についても簡単に説明した。

歌

物語には有名な歌が登場するものもいくつかある。少し現代風に書き直したが、シェイクスピアのオリジナル版も巻末の「注釈」で確認できる。*The Tempest*のエアリエルの最後の喜びの歌では、cryの代わりにTu-wit, To-who!(フクロウのホーホーという鳴き声)を加えた。シェイクスピアはこれを戯曲*Love's Labours Lost*『恋の骨折り損』で使っている。

ラム姉弟の名著を翻案した本書が、楽しく役に立つものであることを私は心から願っている。シェイクスピアの言葉で不朽の名作となった物語の全容については、その戯曲を読み、舞台や映画で命が吹き込まれるのをぜひご覧いただきたい。

ステュウット ヴァーナム–アットキン

神奈川県、2024年

●音声一括ダウンロード●

本書の朗読音声(MP3形式)を下記URLとQRコードから無料でPCなどに一括ダウンロードすることができます。

https://ibcpub.co.jp/audio_dl/0812/

※ダウンロードしたファイルはZIP形式で圧縮されていますので、解凍ソフトが必要です。

※MP3ファイルを再生するには、iTunes(Apple Music)やWindows Media Playerなどのアプリケーションが必要です。

※PCや端末、ソフトウェアの操作・再生方法については、編集部ではお答えできません。付属のマニュアルやインターネットの検索を利用するか、開発元にお問い合わせください。

01

The Tempest

テンペスト

読み始める前に

シェイクスピアの後期の四作品のひとつで、「ロマンス劇」と呼ばれる喜劇。テンペストは嵐という意味。

[登場人物]

Prospero	プロスペロー《前ミラノ大公》
Miranda	ミランダ《プロスペローの娘》
Ferdinand	ファーディナンド《ナポリ王子》
Ariel	エアリエル《空気の精》
Alonso	アロンゾー《ナポリ王》
Caliban	キャリバン《島に住む怪物》
Antonio	アントーニオ《ミラノ大公、プロスペローの弟》
Gonzalo	ゴンザーロー《ナポリ王の重臣》
Sycorax	シコラックス《魔女》

[地名など]

Algiers	アルジェ《アルジェリアの首都》
Milan	ミラノ《イタリアの都市》
Naples	ナポリ《イタリアの都市》

[あらすじ]

弟アントーニオの謀略によってミラノ大公の地位を奪われ、娘ミランダとともにある島に流れ着いたプロスペロー。復讐のために魔術を使って嵐を起こし、アントーニオとナポリ王アロンゾーら一行の船を難破させて島におびき寄せる。

真っ先に海に飛び込み、島に漂着したアロンゾーの息子ファーディナンドは、父は死んだと思い込んでいた。

悲しむファーディナンドは、空気の精エアリアルの計らいでミランダに出会い、すぐさま二人は恋に落ちる。するとプロスペローは、娘への愛が確かなものかどうか試すために、ファーディナンドに難題を与えるのだった。

[総単語数] 4,220語

THE TEMPEST

Once upon a time, there were just two people living on a remote island somewhere west of Italy. One of them was a beautiful teenage girl named Miranda, which means 'worthy of being admired'. The other was her father, Prospero, which means 'fortunate' or 'prosperous'. Miranda had come to the island so young she couldn't clearly remember seeing any human faces besides her father's.

Island life

They lived in a large cave in a rocky cliff near the shore. It was divided into several rooms. One of them Prospero called his 'study', and it was there that he kept his precious books. They were mostly about the magic arts, which was a popular field of study for scholars at that time. He found his knowledge of those wonderful arts to be very useful. It was by a strange chance that he and Miranda had come to this island, which had long been enchanted by a powerful witch called Sycorax. But she had died just before their arrival. Using his magical powers, Prospero released the many good spirits that Sycorax had imprisoned inside the trunks of large trees for refusing to carry out her wicked commands.

After that, those gentle spirits were happy to be obedient to Prospero, regarding him as a great magician. Their leader, named Ariel, was only visible to Prospero. There was nothing very mischievous in the character of the lively little spirit. However, the island had one other inhabitant, called Caliban. He was a strange, ugly creature, much less human in form than like an ape, and Ariel often played tricks on him. Why? Well, it was because Caliban was the son of Ariel's old enemy, the witch Sycorax. After finding him one day in the woods, Prospero had taken him home to his cave, and tried to be kind to him, teaching him how to speak. But Caliban's bad nature, inherited from his mother, would not let him learn anything good or useful. So Prospero employed him more like a slave, fetching wood and doing all the heavy work. At Prospero's order, whenever Caliban was lazy, the invisible Ariel would come and pinch him, and sometimes he would push him into a patch of mud. At other times Ariel would appear in the form of a monkey and make faces at Caliban, or turn into a hedgehog and lie rolling in the way so that Caliban had to jump around to avoid the sharp quills pricking his bare feet.

With powerful spirits like Ariel at his command, Prospero could even control the winds and the ocean waves.

The storm

One day, Prospero suddenly raised a violent storm, which became a raging tempest. As he stood with Miranda on the clifftop, he pointed out a fine, large sailing ship struggling in the wild waves that threatened to swallow it up at any moment.

"See, Miranda… That ship over there is full of people like us."

"It is? Oh, dear Father, if by your magic art you've created this dreadful storm, please take pity on them! Oh, no… Look! The ship is going to be smashed to pieces on the rocks… Those poor souls! They will all drown. If I had your power, I would sink the sea beneath the Earth, rather than let such a good ship be destroyed, with all the precious souls on board her!"

"Calm down, Miranda!" replied Prospero. "There's no need to worry at all. No harm will be done. Believe me. I did raise the tempest, yes, but I've made sure that nobody on the ship will be hurt. And, in fact, I've done all this for *your* sake, my dear child."

"For *my* sake?"

"Yes. Let's sit on this rock for a while and I will explain."

"Well, alright…"

"Now, it's a long story, but I will make it as brief as possible.

Miranda, you don't yet know who you really are, or even where you came from, right?"

"No, I don't."

"And all you know about *me* is that I'm your father and live with you in our poor cave. Can you remember anything from our life before you came here? I doubt it, because you were only three years old."

"I can vaguely remember something…"

"You can? What? Our house, or a person?"

"Well, it seems rather like a dream, but weren't there four or five women looking after me?"

"There were, indeed, and more in fact. And do you remember how you came here?"

"No. That's all I remember."

"I see. Well, twelve years ago, I was the Duke of Milan."

"What? You were the *Duke*?"

"Yes, I was. And you, my only heir, were a princess."

"Oh! So what happened to us?"

"Well, the problem was that I preferred studying to governing. As a result, I often left the management of state affairs to your uncle, my younger brother Antonio—my *wicked* brother as it turned out."

"Wicked?"

"Oh, yes, very wicked! As I buried myself amongst my books and my magic, he began to regard himself as being the duke with all the power.

"I mistakenly gave him the chance of making himself

popular among my subjects, and his bad nature developed his ambition to take my dukedom *from* me. And he managed to do exactly that with the aid of a powerful enemy of mine, Alonso, the King of Naples."

"Oh, how awful! But... why did they let us live?"

"That's a good question. Well, they didn't dare to openly get rid of us because of the great love the people of Milan had for me. Instead, one night, Antonio took us on board a ship and we sailed far out to sea. Then he forced us into a tiny boat, without either a mast or a sail, and left us there, as *he* thought, to die."

"Oh, how terrible!"

"Yes. But we were lucky. Gonzalo, a very kind and loyal lord of the court, had secretly stored on that boat some water, food, and clothes for us both, as well as my precious books, which meant more to me than my dukedom."

"Oh, Father, what a lot of trouble I must have caused you!"

"No, no, my love! You were like a little angel that kept me going. Your innocent smiles helped me face all my troubles. Luckily, the food lasted until we drifted to this island. And ever since then, my chief delight has been to look after you and teach you... and you have been an excellent student!"

"Thank you so much, dear Father. Now please tell me why you caused this storm."

"Well, it's closely connected to the story I've just told you. You see, as a result of this tempest, my two enemies, the King of Naples and my cruel brother, have landed on the island!"

"What?"

"Yes, but enough stories for one day... Now it's time to rest..." Prospero gently touched his daughter on the shoulder with his magic wand, and she fell fast asleep.

Ariel

Ariel had just appeared to give his report on the tempest and what he'd done to all those on board the ship. Although Ariel was invisible to Miranda, Prospero did not want her to see her father apparently talking to thin air!

"Well, my brave spirit, how did you carry out your great mission?"

Ariel gave him a lively description of the storm and the terror on the faces of the sailors and passengers, how Ferdinand, the king's son, was the first to jump into the sea, and how his father thought he saw his dear boy swallowed up by the waves and lost.

"But, in fact, he's quite safe," said Ariel.

"He's sitting in a quiet corner of the island, with his arms folded, sadly lamenting the loss of his father, who he thinks must have drowned. Not one hair on his head was injured, and his fine clothes, although drenched in seawater, now look fresher than they did before!"

"Well done!" said Prospero. "Now I want you to bring that young prince here so that my daughter can see him. But where are the king and my brother?"

"I left them searching for Ferdinand, who they have little hope of finding, of course, thinking they saw him drown. Not one member of the ship's crew is missing, either, although each one thinks *he* is the only one that was saved. As for the ship, it's safe in the harbor."

"Perfectly done so far! But there is much more work to do."

"More work? May I remind you, master, that you have promised me my liberty. I have served you well, and told you no lies, and made no mistakes, and never grumbled..."

"Enough! Don't you remember the torment I freed you from? Have you forgotten that wicked witch Sycorax, bent almost double with age and envy? Where was she born? Tell me!"

"In Algiers."

"Yes. I think I have to remind you of what you seem to have forgotten. For her disgusting witchcraft, Sycorax was banished from Algiers, and left here by some sailors. And because you were a spirit far too delicate to carry out her wicked commands, she shut you up inside a tree, howling. Do you remember who freed you from that torment?"

"It was you, dear master. I beg your pardon! I will continue to obey your commands."

"Good! Do so, and then I will set you free when the time is right."

Prospero told Ariel what else he wanted him to do.

Ferdinand

First, Ariel flew back to the spot where he had left Ferdinand, and he found him still sitting on the grass in the same melancholy pose.

"Young gentleman," said the invisible Ariel, "you must be taken to where the Lady Miranda can see your handsome face. Come, sir, follow me…"

And Ariel began to sing:

Deep in the sea your father lies,
His royal bones changed to coral,
And his eyes now turned to pearls.
Everything fades below the waves,
and changes into something rich and strange.
The spirits of the sea now ring his funeral bell…
Listen! Can you hear them? Ding-dong, bell!

This strange song telling Ferdinand the news of his drowned father immediately roused him from his trance. Amazed, he followed the sound of Ariel's voice. It led him to a place near the entrance to the cave, where Prospero and Miranda, now awake again, were sitting in the shade of a large tree.

"Ah, good," said Prospero and pointed at Ferdinand. "Now, Miranda, what do you think that is over there?"

"Oh… I suppose it must be a spirit. Ah, how it looks around! And what a beautiful creature it is… Is it a spirit?"

"No, my dear. It eats, and it sleeps, and it has senses just like us."

"It does?"

"Yes. This is a young man, and he was on board that ship. He's lost all his companions and is wandering about trying to find them. His face is now somewhat changed by grief, but, yes, I suppose you could describe him as handsome…"

Up to that moment, Miranda had the idea that all men had serious faces and gray beards like her father, so she was delighted with the prince's appearance.

As for Ferdinand, from all the strange sounds he'd been hearing, he was expecting nothing but wonders to appear. Suddenly seeing such a lovely young lady in this deserted place, he imagined he must be on an enchanted island, and she was its goddess.

"I believe I have the great honor of greeting the goddess of this enchanted place…"

"Oh, no, no…" Miranda answered timidly. "I'm not a goddess, just a simple island girl…"

Prospero interrupted her before she could say anything else. He was pleased to find they liked each other so much. In fact, it was obvious they'd fallen in love at first sight. However, he decided it would be best to test Ferdinand's feelings by throwing a few difficulties in their way. So he stepped forward and addressed the prince sternly.

"Young man, I am the lord of this island, and I believe you have come here to take it from me! So, follow me. I will tie your neck and your feet together with rope. You will drink only seawater, and your food will be shellfish, withered roots, and acorn husks."

"Oh, no!" replied Ferdinand, drawing his sword. "I will resist such things until I face an enemy stronger than me!"

Prospero simply waved his magic wand, which fixed Ferdinand to the spot where he stood and made him drop his sword.

"Father, why are you being so rough?" cried Miranda. "Have some pity on this poor man. I will defend him. This is the second man I have ever seen, and to me he seems absolutely pure and honest."

"Silence! What? You want to side with an impostor like him! Foolish girl! You think there are no other fine men in the world, having seen only him and Caliban? Most men excel *him* as much as *he* does Caliban!"

"My feelings are very humble, Father. I have no wish to see a better man."

"Follow me, young man," said Prospero to Ferdinand. "You are powerless to disobey!"

Unaware that magic had deprived him of all power to resist, Ferdinand was astonished to find himself meekly following Prospero into the cave. He looked back at Miranda for as long as he could see her.

"I feel I'm in a dream," he thought, "but surely this strange man's threats and my own weakness won't feel quite so bad if just once a day I can catch a glimpse of her from my prison..."

Log-man

But Prospero didn't keep Ferdinand confined in the cave for long. He soon brought his prisoner out and set him a severe task to perform—carrying and piling up heavy wooden logs. He also told Miranda what was going on. Then he pretended to go into his study, although actually he'd decided to keep an eye on them both secretly.

Now, most princes are not used to doing heavy manual labor, and when Miranda visited Ferdinand he looked as though he was about to die from exhaustion.

"Oh, no!" she cried. "You mustn't work so hard! My father is at his studies, so you are safe for the next three hours. Please take a long rest!"

"Thank you, my dear lady," replied Ferdinand, "but I dare not stop. I must be a patient log-man and finish my task before I can take any rest."

"In that case, sit down here, and *I* will carry your logs for a while!"

Ferdinand certainly wouldn't agree to *that*, and instead they began a long conversation. As a result, Miranda became more of a hindrance than a help, because the log-carrying proceeded very slowly.

Prospero's idea in giving Ferdinand this task was simply to test his affection for Miranda. He was now standing right beside them, invisible, listening to their conversation.

"May I ask your name?" said Ferdinand.

"Well, my father ordered me not to tell you, but... it's Miranda."

"Oh, such a beautiful name! 'Miranda', worthy indeed of being *admired*!"

Prospero smiled at this first instance of his daughter's

disobedience. He had caused her to fall in love suddenly using his magic, so he wasn't at all angry that she showed her love by not obeying him. He was also pleased to hear a long speech from Ferdinand in which he claimed to love Miranda more than all the other ladies he had seen. He explained that they had all had some good points, but *she* was the first one to be perfect in every way.

Miranda replied, "Well, to tell the truth, I don't remember the faces of any other women. Nor have I seen any other men than you and my dear father. So I don't know what people look like out there in the world. But, please believe me when I say that I wouldn't wish to have any companion in the world besides you. In fact, my imagination can't form any shape other than yours that I could like! But I'm afraid I'm forgetting my father's orders and talking too freely..."

Prospero smiled again, and nodded.

"Yes," he thought, "this is going on exactly as I hoped it would. My dear girl will become the Queen of Naples!"

And then, in another fine long speech, Ferdinand told Miranda that he was a prince and the heir to the crown of Naples, and it was possible, although he still prayed it was not true, that he was already the king...and he wanted Miranda to be his queen!

Miranda's eyes filled with tears. "Ah, sir, I am such a simple fool to weep at what I am so very, very thrilled about! But I will answer you in my plain and innocent way. Yes, I will happily be your wife if that is what you wish!"

Prospero decided this was a good moment to appear visible before them.

"There's nothing to fear, my darling child," he said to Miranda. "I have overheard everything, and I approve of all that you have said. And I sincerely apologize, Prince Ferdinand, for treating you so roughly. All your torments were simply my way of testing your love for Miranda, and you have nobly passed that test! To make amends, and as my gift, which your true love fully deserves, please take my daughter to be your wife."

"Thank you so much, sir."

"And please don't smile when I boast that her father believes she is above all praise!"

"I fully agree with you, sir!"

"But now I have some urgent business to attend to. I suggest you two might like to sit down and talk together until I return…"

That was a suggestion Miranda certainly did *not* want to disobey.

The monster

Prospero hurried back to the cave and called Ariel. He quickly appeared, eager to report what he'd done with Antonio and Alonso.

"I left them almost out of their senses with fear at the strange things I'd made them see and hear. When they felt exhausted from wandering about, and famished for want of food, I suddenly set before them a delicious banquet. But just as they were about to start eating, I appeared before them in the shape of a huge and horrible monster with wings, and the feast vanished! Then, to their utter amazement, the 'monster' spoke to them. It reminded them of their cruelty in driving you from your dukedom, and leaving you and your infant daughter to perish out at sea, saying that is why they were suffering such torments now."

"Excellent work!"

"Well, after that, they both repented the terrible injustice they had done to you. I believe their penitence is sincere. And tears ran down the beard of good old Lord Gonzalo. If you saw them now, I think you would feel sorry for them."

"Do you, indeed?"

"I would, master, if I were human."

"Well, if you, Ariel, who are only a spirit, feel pity, surely, as a human being like them, *I* should have some compassion! My vengeance should not go on for ever. Bring them here quickly. I will break my charms over them, and return their senses to normal."

Reunions

Ariel soon returned with Antonio, Alonso and Gonzalo. They had all followed the invisible spirit, wondering at the wild music he played in the air to draw them on to his master. Their senses were so dulled by grief and terror that for a while they didn't recognize Prospero. He first revealed himself to Gonzalo—the lord who had so kindly provided the books and provisions in the open boat—calling him the preserver of his life. And then

Antonio and Alonso began to realize that he was indeed the former Duke who they had treated so badly.

With tears and words of sorrow and true repentance, Antonio implored his brother's forgiveness. Alonso also expressed his sincere remorse for the part he'd played in deposing Prospero. They promised to restore his dukedom.

Prospero forgave them both, and then said to Alonso, "I have a gift in store for you, too."

He opened a door inside the cave and revealed Ferdinand playing chess with Miranda. Nothing could be greater than the joy of the father and the son at this completely unexpected reunion. They both thought the other had been drowned in the tempest.

"Oh, how wonderful!" said Miranda, looking around. "How many noble creatures there are here! And how beautiful humans are! Oh, brave new world that has such people in it!"

"Well," murmured her father, "it's new to *you*!"

Alonso was almost as astonished at the beauty and grace of Miranda as his son had been.

"But who is this?" he asked. "Is she the goddess who parted us, and then brought us back together again . . . "

"No, Father," answered Ferdinand, smiling to find his father had made the same mistake as him when he first set eyes on Miranda.

"She is a mortal like us. However, by some kind of immortal Providence, she has become mine: I chose her to be my wife at a time when I could not ask for your consent, believing you had drowned. She's the daughter of this noble Prospero, the famous Duke of Milan, of whose renown I have heard so much, but had never seen him till now. From him, I've received a new life. He has become like a second father to me, by giving me dear Miranda."

Alonso smiled. "Then I must be *her* father! But how odd it will sound to have to ask my child for forgiveness . . . "

"Well, no more of that right now," said Prospero. "Let's not dwell on our past troubles, since they have ended so happily."

Then Prospero embraced his brother, and again assured him of his forgiveness.

"I now feel," he added, "that some wise and overruling Providence permitted me to be driven from my dukedom so that eventually my daughter could inherit the crown of Naples, as it was by their meeting on this desert island that the king's son fell in love with Miranda."

These kind words were meant to comfort Antonio. But they so filled him with feelings of shame and remorse that he started crying and was unable to speak. Gonzalo also cried to see this happy reconciliation, and prayed for blessings on the young couple.

Prospero now told them that their ship was safe in the harbor with the sailors all aboard, and that he and Miranda would accompany them to Naples the next morning.

"In the meantime," he said, "please partake of the simple refreshments our poor cave can offer. And for your evening's entertainment, I will relate the history of my life from my first landing on this desert island."

He then called for Caliban to prepare some food, and set the cave in order. The guests were astonished at the creature's savage appearance as Prospero explained he was the only attendant he had.

Moving on

As he had promised, Prospero dismissed Ariel from service before leaving the island. The lively little spirit was overjoyed. Although he had been a faithful servant, he longed to enjoy his freedom, to fly uncontrolled through the air like a wild bird, under the green trees and amongst the pleasant fruits and sweet-smelling flowers.

"My dear Ariel, I shall greatly miss you, but you will have your freedom."

"Thank you, dear master. But before you bid farewell, let me attend your ship to Naples with calm seas and good winds. And then, master, when I am free, how merrily I shall live!"

And Ariel burst into a song full of joy:

Where the bee sucks, I will, too,
In a cowslip's flower I'll lie.
I'll crouch when owls Tu-whit, To-who!
And on the back of bats I'll fly.
After summer, merrily, merrily,
Under the blossom on the bough,
Merrily, I will live from now!
Merrily, merrily, merrily!

Prospero was resolved he would give up the magic arts forever, so he broke his wand and tossed his books deep into the ocean. His great hope was that now he could live in peace for the rest of his days. He had been reconciled to his brother and to the King of Naples. All that remained to complete his happiness was to return home to Milan and take possession of his dukedom once again. But first he would witness the wedding of Miranda and Prince Ferdinand, which Alonso promised would be celebrated with great splendor as soon as they all returned to Naples.

And so, under the safe convoy of the spirit Ariel, they departed from the island, leaving behind just Caliban, its original inhabitant, no longer a slave.

02

A Midsummer Night's Dream

夏の夜の夢

読み始める前に

シェイクスピアの作品の中で代表的な喜劇。妖精のいたずらが引き起こすドタバタの恋模様が、最後はハッピーエンドに。

［登場人物］

Hermia	ハーミア《ライサンダーの想い人》
Lysander	ライサンダー《ハーミアの恋人》
Demetrius	ディミートリアス《イジーアスが決めたハーミアの許婚》
Helena	ヘレナ《ハーミアの友人》
Bottom	ボトム《織物職人》
Egeus	イジーアス《ハーミアの父》
Theseus	シーシアス《アテネの領主》
Oberon	オーベロン《妖精の王》
Titania	ティターニア《妖精の女王》
Puck	パック《いたずら好きの妖精》

［地名など］

Athens	アテネ《ギリシャの都市》

［あらすじ］

　昔アテネには、娘の結婚相手を決める権限を父親に与える法律があった。

　ハーミアはライサンダーと恋仲だったが、父親はディミートリアスと娘を結婚させようとしていたため、二人は駆け落ちをして妖精たちが集う森に行くことにする。ハーミアは、その計画を親友のヘレナに打ち明けるが、ヘレナは、それを片思いの相手ディミートリアスに漏らしてしまう。ディミートリアスは駆け落ちを阻止しようと森に入り、ヘレナもそれを追いかけていく。

　森では妖精の王オーベロンが、王妃のティターニアと喧嘩をしていて、ティターニアのまぶたに薬を塗る。それは、「目覚めて最初に見た人を好きになってしまう」という恋の花の汁。妖精のパックが、ライサンダーとディミートリアスにも、この薬を塗ってしまったことから、彼らの恋はもつれ混乱していく。

［総単語数］3,820語

A MIDSUMMER NIGHT'S DREAM

Once upon a time, there was a law in the city of Athens in Greece that gave fathers the power to decide who their daughters should marry. If a daughter refused to marry the man her father had chosen to be her husband, then he could have her put to death or forced to live the rest of her life in a nunnery. Generally speaking, few fathers wanted their daughter to die, however stubborn she might be, so the law was seldom enforced. But it's possible that some parents of young Athenian ladies used the terror of the law as a threat.

A demand for justice

One day, a distinguished courtier named Egeus visited Theseus, the Duke of Athens. He wished to complain that his daughter, Hermia, refused to obey him regarding his choice of her husband. Egeus demanded justice: in other words, he wanted the cruel law to be put into force. The simple background to this was that Egeus wanted Hermia to marry a young man from a noble family named Demetrius. But she refused because she loved another young Athenian gentleman named Lysander.

Theseus ordered Hermia to be brought in and questioned. To excuse her disobedience, she pleaded that Demetrius had previously professed love for her dear friend Helena, and that Helena loved him deeply. But this honorable reason didn't move her stern father at all.

Theseus was a great and merciful prince, but he did not have the power to alter his country's laws. So he told Hermia that she should treat her father as a god.

"But," she replied. "I just wish my father could see with *my* eyes!"

"Rather," replied Theseus, "your eyes should look with *his* sense of judgment. Hermia, I will give you four days to change your mind. At the end of that time, if you still refuse to marry Demetrius, you will be put to death or sent to a nunnery."

Lysander's plan

As soon as Hermia was dismissed from the Duke's palace, she hurried to Lysander and explained the peril she was in. He was greatly shocked to hear this bad news. But then he remembered that he had an aunt who lived some distance from Athens in a place where the cruel law could not be put into force against Hermia. He came up with a plan.

"Tonight, you must quietly escape from your father's house. Let's meet in that delightful wood outside the city where we have so often walked with Helena. Then we'll go together to my aunt's house and get married as soon as possible!"

Hermia happily agreed to this idea. She told no-one about it apart from her good friend Helena. But Helena then did something rather foolish. Even though she was aware it would not benefit herself much, she told Hermia's secret to Demetrius. She was sure that Demetrius would go in pursuit of Hermia. All *she* could do was follow him, a poor kind of pleasure indeed.

A fairy quarrel

The wood in which Lysander and Hermia had planned to meet was the favorite haunt of those little beings known as 'elves' and 'sprites' and 'fairies.' It was there that Oberon and Titania, the King and Queen of the Fairies, held their midnight parties with all their tiny followers.

However, at that time, Oberon and Titania were suffering from a sad disagreement. They could never meet by moonlight in the pleasant shady walks of the wood without quarreling, till all the other fairies would creep into acorn-cups and hide for fear. What was the cause of all this? Well, it was Titania's refusal to give Oberon a little boy, whose mother had been Titania's friend. When the friend died, Titania had stolen the child from its nurse and brought him up in the woods.

Now it just so happened that the night on which Hermia and Lysander were going to meet in the wood, as Titania was out walking with some of her fairy maids-of-honor, she bumped into Oberon attended by his fairy courtiers.

"Oh, ill met by moonlight, proud Titania!" said Oberon.

"Oh, jealous Oberon, is it *you*?" replied Titania. "Fairies, let's leave immediately. I have no desire to talk to *him*!"

"Wait, you hasty fairy!" shouted Oberon. "Why do you get so angry with me, your husband? Just give me that little boy to be my page."

"Oh, calm down!" replied Titania. "Your whole fairy kingdom cannot buy the boy from me." She then rushed away, very angry.

"Well, go your way!" shouted Oberon after her, and then whispered to himself, "But before morning dawns, you will pay for this insult…"

A merry little wanderer

Oberon then sent for his favorite advisor and companion, Puck. Also widely known as Robin Goodfellow, he was a shrewd but naughty sprite, a merry little wanderer of the night.

He played all kinds of practical jokes in the villages around the wood. He would sometimes get into a dairy and skim the milk, plunging his airy little body into the butter churn. Then he would perform a fantastic dance so that the dairymaid would try in vain to change her cream into butter.

He also enjoyed upsetting the young men of the village.

Whenever he played his tricks in the brewery, the ale was spoiled. And sometimes when villagers got together to drink, Puck would jump into the bowl of ale as a roasted crab-apple. Then, when some old granny was about to drink, he would bob against her lips, and she would spill the ale all over her chin. Later, when the same poor old woman was sitting herself down ready to tell a sad story, Puck would slip her three-legged stool from under her, and down she would topple to the floor. And then all the other old gossips would hold their sides in laughter.

A lovers' tiff

"Come here, Puck," said Oberon. "Fetch me some flowers of that little purple pansy which young girls call 'Love-in-Idleness'. If its juice is laid on the eyelids of someone sleeping, the moment they awake they'll fall in love with the very first thing they see! I will drop some on the eyelids of my Titania, and she'll go crazy over whatever she sees when she opens her eyes, even if it's a lion, a bear, or a meddling monkey! And before I remove this charm—which I can do with another flower—I'll make her give me that boy!"

Puck loved any kind of mischief, so he was very amused by his master's intended trick. He flew off at high speed to seek the flower.

As Oberon was waiting Puck's return, he happened to see Demetrius and Helena enter the wood. He went closer, and, invisible, he overheard Demetrius reproaching Helena for following him.

"Where are Lysander and Hermia? Helena, I don't love you, I cannot love you. So stop following me!"

"Oh," replied Helena," I love you all the more for saying that! You see, I'm your pet, Demetrius, your spaniel. Use me like that. The more you ignore me, the more I will follow you. I don't care if you leave me alone or hit me, or try to forget me. Just allow me to *follow* you, even though I don't deserve it…"

"No! I'll run away and hide and leave you to the mercy of the wild animals…"

After many more unkind words from *him*, and gentle protests from *her*, reminding him of his former words of love, Demetrius ran off. Helena ran after him as fast as she could.

Oberon was always sympathetic to true lovers, and felt great compassion for Helena. There was a chance he had seen her there in the wood before, in those happy times when she was loved by Demetrius.

Puck soon returned with the little purple flowers. Oberon said to him, "Take some of these. There has been a sweet Athenian lady here, who is in love with a youth who lacks respect. When you find him sleeping, drop some of this love-juice on his eyelids. But make sure you do it when *she* is near him. Then the first thing he sees when he wakes up will be the despised lady. You will recognize the man by his Athenian clothes."

Puck promised to do it perfectly.

Love-in-Idleness

Then Oberon went quietly and unseen to Titania's fairy bower. It was on a bank, where there grew wild thyme, cowslips, and sweet violets, under a canopy of woodbine, musk-roses and eglantine. Titania always slept some part of the night there. Her blanket was an enameled snakeskin which was quite wide enough to wrap a fairy in.

Oberon found Titania giving orders to her fairies.

"While I sleep, some of you kill the grubs on the musk-rose buds; and some of you fight with the bats for their leather wings to make coats for my elves; and some of you keep watch that the owl that hoots so loud, doesn't come near me. But first, sing me to sleep..."

And they began to sing a pretty lullaby:

You spotted snakes with double tongue,
You prickly hedgehogs, don't be seen!
You newts and lizards do no wrong
And don't come near our Fairy Queen!
Lulla, lulla, lullaby,
Lulla, lulla, lullaby,
No spell, no charm
Do our lady harm!
So, good night, with lullaby,
Lulla, lulla, lullaby.

Once the Queen was fast asleep, the fairies all left her to carry out her orders. Oberon softly crept up and dropped some of the love-juice on Titania's eyelids, saying:

Whatever you see when you awake,
That for your true love you must take!

Confusion

Let's now return to Hermia, who had escaped from her father's house that night to avoid death for refusing to marry Demetrius. When she entered the wood, she found her dear Lysander waiting for her, ready to conduct her to his aunt's house. But before they had passed halfway through the wood, Hermia felt very tired. Lysander took great care of his dear love. He persuaded her to rest till morning on a bank of soft moss. He lay down himself on the ground a little distance away, and they soon fell asleep.

It was there they were found by Puck. He saw a handsome young man in Athenian clothes asleep, and a pretty young lady was sleeping near him. He concluded that this must be the pair Oberon had sent him to seek. And he naturally decided that, as they were alone together, *she* would be the first thing he would see when he woke up. So he poured some of the juice onto Lysander's eyelids and left.

But then something unfortunate happened. Helena had failed to keep pace with Demetrius when he so rudely ran away from her. She soon lost sight of him. As she was wandering about feeling dejected, she arrived at the place where Lysander was sleeping.

"Oh, Lysander!" she said. "Is he asleep... or dead?" She gently touched his shoulder and said, "Lysander, if you're alive, please wake up!"

Lysander opened his eyes, and the love-charm worked at once. He started talking to Helena in terms of deep love and admiration. He said she excelled Hermia in beauty as much as a dove does a raven, and he would happily run through fire for her sweet sake.

Fully aware that Lysander and Hermia were engaged to be married, Helena was very angry to hear herself addressed in that way.

"Oh, you're making fun of me!" she said angrily. "Why was I born to be mocked and scorned by everyone? Isn't it enough that I can never get a sweet look or a kind word from Demetrius? Why are *you* pretending to court me in this awful way? I thought you were a man of true gentleness."

She ran away. Lysander followed her, quite forgetting Hermia, who was still asleep.

More confusion

When Hermia woke up, she was frightened to find herself alone. She wandered about the wood, not knowing what had happened to Lysander, or which way to go to seek him.

In the meantime, Demetrius, still unable to find Hermia and Lysander, had fallen asleep, exhausted by his fruitless search.

Oberon found him. After some careful questioning, he'd learned that Puck had applied the love-charm to the *wrong* Athenian's eyes. Having found the *right* one, Oberon touched the eyelids of Demetrius with the love-juice and left.

When Demetrius woke up, who should he see first but Helena! And like Lysander before, he started to speak to her affectionately.

Just at that moment, Lysander arrived, followed in hot pursuit by Hermia! Lysander and Demetrius, both speaking at the same time, started expressing their great love for Helena. Of course, she was astonished. She could only think that the two men and her once dear friend Hermia were all in a plot together to make fun of her.

Hermia was equally surprised. She couldn't understand why Lysander and Demetrius, who had both previously loved *her*, were now only interested in Helena. To her, it was no joke at all. The two young women, who had always been the dearest of friends, now started shouting at each other.

"Unkind Hermia," said Helena, "did you encourage your fiancé to annoy me with mock praise? And did you ask your other lover, Demetrius, who has been spurning me, to start calling me 'goddess' and 'rare' and 'precious' and even 'celestial'? He hates me! He would never speak to me like that unless you pushed him. I can't believe you could join with those two to scorn your poor friend. Have you forgotten our friendship at school, growing up together like double cherries, scarcely ever parted? How often have we two sat on one cushion, singing a song together, both working on the same embroidery, with our needles working on the same flower. Oh, Hermia, how could you do such a thing?"

"I'm amazed at your passionate words," replied Hermia: "*I* don't scorn *you*. It seems *you* are scorning *me*!"

"I suppose you make mouths at me when I turn my back and wink at each other," said Helena. "If you had any pity or grace or manners, you would not use me like this!"

While Helena and Hermia were arguing, Demetrius and Lysander had gone to fight together in the wood for the love of Helena. When the confused ladies realized the men had left them, they stopped talking and once more wandered wearily around in the wood in search of them.

A thick fog

Oberon and Puck had been listening to the quarrel.

"This is all your fault, Puck," said Oberon. "Did you do this on purpose?"

"Believe me, King of Shadows," answered Puck, "it was all a big mistake. Didn't you tell me I could recognize the man by his Athenian clothes? But, to tell the truth, I'm not sorry it's happened. I think all their confusion makes for excellent sport!"

"Now," continued Oberon, "we heard that Demetrius and Lysander have gone to find a suitable place for a fight. I command you to produce a thick fog, and lead all these quarrelsome lovers astray in the dark so that they can't find each other. I'm sure you can imitate each of their voices! Then with bitter taunts provoke them to follow you, thinking they hear their rival's voice. Do this until they're so weary that they can go no further. And when you find they're asleep, drop the juice of this other flower into Lysander's eyes, so that when he wakes up he'll forget his love for Helena, and return to his old passion for Hermia. Is that clear?"

"Yes!"

"Then the two ladies will both be happy with the man they love, and they will think that all that has gone on was simply a strange dream. Do this quickly, Puck, and I will go and see what sweet love my Titania has found."

Hee-haw!

Titania was still sleeping. Oberon suddenly heard snoring. Nearby, he found a man asleep on the ground.

"Ah, if I'm not mistaken," thought Oberon, "it's Bottom, the Athenian weaver. I've seen him several times wandering around in the wood. Perhaps he lost his way and decided to take a rest. Anyway, Bottom, you are perfect! You shall become my Titania's true love!"

Using his magic, Oberon gently fitted the head of a donkey over Bottom's head. It fit him so well it appeared to have grown on his shoulders. Then Bottom woke up. Unaware of what Oberon had done to him, he got up and went slowly toward the bower where Titania was sleeping.

Titania suddenly opened her eyes and saw him. "Ah, what angel is this? Are you as wise as you are beautiful?"

"Why, lady," said Bottom, "if I am clever enough to find my way out of this wood, I am, yes. Hee-haw!"

"No, do not wish to leave the wood!" said Titania. "I am no ordinary spirit. And I love you! Come here, and I will give you fairies to attend on you."

She then called out to four of her fairies.

"Peaseblossom, Cobweb, Moth, and Mustardseed! Attend on this sweet gentleman. Hop along as he walks and gambol in his sight. Feed him with grapes and apricots, and steal for him the

honey-bags from the bees. Now come, come sit here with me," she said to Bottom, "and let me play with your lovely hairy cheeks, my beautiful donkey! And let me kiss your wonderfully big ears, my gentle joy..."

Bottom wasn't paying much attention to Titania's courtship, but he liked his new attendants. "Where is Peaseblossom?"

"Here, sir."

"Please scratch my head. And where is Cobweb?"

"Here, sir."

"Good Mr. Cobweb, please kill me the red bumblebee on the top of that thistle over there, and bring me the honey-bag. And take care that the honey-bag doesn't break! I should be sorry to have you flooded with honey! Hee-haw! And where is Mustardseed?"

"Here, sir. What do you desire?"

"Nothing, good Mr. Mustardseed, but to help Mr. Peaseblossom to scratch me. Oh, my face seems to be very hairy today. I must go to the barber!"

"My sweet love," said Titania, "what would you like to eat? I have a brave fairy can find the squirrel's hoard and fetch you some fresh nuts."

"Oh, I had rather have a handful of dried peas, hee-haw!" said Bottom, who now had a donkey's appetite. "But, please, ask your people not to disturb me, for I feel like having a nice nap... Hee-haw!"

"Sleep, then, and I will wrap you in my arms. Oh, how I love you! How I *dote* on you!"

When Oberon saw Bottom asleep in the arms of his queen, he revealed himself and reproached her for showering her favors on a donkey. This she could hardly deny, as Bottom was still in her arms, with his donkey's head crowned by her with flowers.

When Oberon had teased her about this for a while, he again demanded the changeling boy. Titania was so ashamed of having been discovered by her lord with her new favorite that she did not dare to refuse him.

Having obtained the little boy he had so long wished for to be his page, Oberon took pity on Titania's disgraceful situation, which he had so merrily arranged. He threw some of the juice of the second flower on to her eyes. Immediately, Titania recovered her senses, and expressed shock at the sight of the strange hairy monster beside her.

Oberon removed the donkey's head from Bottom, and left him to finish his nap with his own fool's head on his shoulders.

The Fairy King and Queen were now perfectly reconciled. Oberon related to her the story of the four Athenian lovers and their midnight quarrels. She agreed to go with him to see the end of their adventures.

Celebration

They found all the lovers sleeping on a grassy plot quite close to each other. To make amends for his former mistake, Puck had carefully arranged to bring them all to the same spot, unknown to one another. He had also removed the charm from Lysander's eyes with the antidote Oberon had given him.

Hermia woke up first. She found her lost Lysander asleep nearby and started wondering at this strange situation. Not long after, Lysander opened his eyes. Seeing his dear Hermia, he recovered his reason which the fairy charm had clouded and his love for Hermia returned as well. They began to talk about the adventures of the night, doubting if those things had really happened. Had they both been dreaming the same bewildering dream?

Helena and Demetrius were also awake by this time. A sweet sleep had quietened Helena's angry spirit. She now listened with delight to the professions of love which Demetrius was making to her. To her great surprise and pleasure, she began to perceive they were sincere.

The night-wandering ladies, now no longer rivals, once more became true friends. All the unkind words which had passed between them were forgiven. Now they calmly discussed what was the best thing to do in their present situation. One thing was soon agreed: now Demetrius had given up all romantic interest in Hermia, he should try to prevail upon her father to revoke the cruel sentence of death. Demetrius was preparing to return to Athens for this purpose, when they were all surprised to see Egeus, Hermia's father. He had come on horseback to the wood in pursuit of his runaway daughter.

When Egeus understood that Demetrius would definitely not marry his daughter, he no longer opposed her marriage to Lysander. He gave his consent that they could be married in four days' time, meaning the same day on which Hermia had been condemned to lose her life. And on that same day Helena joyfully agreed to marry her beloved, and now faithful, Demetrius.

Just visions

The Fairy King and Queen were invisible spectators of this happy ending to the lovers' history, brought about through the good offices of Oberon and Puck. It gave them so much pleasure that they decided to celebrate the approaching weddings with sports and entertainments throughout their fairy kingdom.

And that just about brings us to the end of the story. But Puck would like to say a few final words.

"If you have in any way been upset by this story of we fairies and our silly pranks, and you think it incredible and strange, please think that you have simply been asleep and dreaming. All these adventures were just visions you witnessed in your sleep! I sincerely hope that no-one will be so unreasonable as to be offended in any way by a charming and harmless midsummer night's dream..."

03

The Winter's Tale

冬物語

読み始める前に

シチリア王レオンティーズの嫉妬心から悲劇的なストーリーが始まる。シェイクスピア晩年近くに作られた「ロマンス劇」で、結末はハッピーエンド。

[登場人物]

Leontes	レオンティーズ《シチリア王》
Hermione	ハーマイオニー《リオンティーズの妃》
Perdita	パーディタ《ハーマイオニーとレオンティーズの娘》
Paulina	ポーライナ《ハーマイオニーの友人、アンティゴナスの妻》
Polixenes	ポリクシニーズ《ボヘミア王》
Camillo	カミロー《シチリア王の廷臣》
Florizel	フロリゼル《ボヘミアの王子》
Antigonus	アンティゴナス《シチリア王の側近》
Mamillius	マミリアス《レオンティーズとハーマイオニーの息子》
Doricles	ドリクリーズ《フロリゼルが使った偽名》
Cleomenes	クリオミニーズ《シチリア王の廷臣》
Dion	ダイオン《シチリア王の廷臣》
Emilia	エミリア《ポーライナの侍女》

[地名など]

Bohemia	ボヘミア《現在のチェコ共和国》
Delphi	デルファイ《古代ギリシャの神託所》
Sicily	シチリア《イタリアの島》

[あらすじ]

シチリア王レオンティーズは、友人のボヘミア王ポリクシニーズがシチリアに滞在した折、帰国を引き止める妻のハーマイオニーの言動から突然の嫉妬に駆られ、二人が不義をしていると思い込む。

レオンティーズは生まれたばかりの娘パーディタをポリクシニーズの子だと思いこみ、アンティゴナスに捨ててくるよう命ずる。

ハーマイオニーが罪人として裁判にかけられると、王子は心労で急死。それを知ったハーマイオニーも裁判の途中で倒れてしまう。

やがてハーマイオニーが死んだと聞かされた王は、ようやく自分の過ちに気付き、激しく後悔するのだった。

[総単語数] 4,100語

THE WINTER'S TALE

Once upon a time, the island of Sicily in the Mediterranean Sea was ruled by King Leontes. He and his queen, the beautiful and virtuous Hermione, lived in great harmony. Leontes was so content being loved by that fine lady. But he had just one wish: he wanted to meet again and introduce to Hermione his old schoolmate, Polixenes, King of Bohemia. They had been brought up together from infancy. However, when their fathers died, they were called to reign over their respective kingdoms. As a result, they had not met for many years, although they frequently exchanged gifts and letters.

Old times

But at last, after repeated invitations, Polixenes decided to visit

Sicily. At first, this visit gave nothing but pleasure to Leontes. And Hermione was delighted to meet Polixenes. In the presence of his old friend, Leontes seemed very happy. They talked about old times, remembering their schooldays and youthful pranks. These were all recounted in detail to Hermione, who took a cheerful part in the conversations.

When, after a stay of several months, Polixenes was preparing to go home, Leontes asked Hermione to help persuade him to postpone his departure. And it was then that the good queen's sorrow began. Why? It was because Polixenes refused to stay at Leontes' request, but was won over by Hermione's gentle and persuasive words. He agreed to put off his departure for a few weeks.

Jealousy and escape

Shortly after that, Leontes was suddenly seized with an uncontrollable jealousy. This was very strange because for so long he had known the great integrity and honorable principles of Polixenes. He also knew perfectly well the excellent character of Hermione. But every attention she showed to Polixenes, basically to please Leontes, increased the unfortunate king's jealousy! Far from being a loving and true friend, and the best and fondest of husbands, Leontes became suddenly a savage and inhuman monster.

One day, he sent for Camillo, a loyal lord of his court. He told him of his suspicions and commanded him to poison Polixenes. But Camillo was a good, honest man. He knew well that Leontes' jealousy was not based on the slightest foundation in truth. So, instead of poisoning Polixenes, he went and told him about Leontes' order. They agreed to escape together from Sicily at once.

And so Polixenes, with Camillo's assistance, managed to arrive safely back in his own Kingdom of Bohemia. And from that time, Camillo lived in the king's court and became his chief friend and advisor.

A sad tale...

News of the flight of Polixenes and Camillo enraged the jealous Leontes even more. He headed to the queen's room, where the good lady, who was pregnant again, was sitting with their seven-year-old son Mamillius.

"Come over here, Mamillius," said Hermione. "Tell us a tale!"

"A merry tale or a sad one?"

"That's up to you to decide!"

"Well, a sad tale's best for winter. I have one about sprites and goblins."

"Oh, let's have *that* one, you powerful storyteller! Do your best to scare me with your sprites."

Mamillius began. "Once upon a time, there was a man who lived by a churchyard..."

At that moment, Leontes burst in. He immediately took Mamillius away and sent Hermione to prison.

Mamillius deeply loved his mother. When he saw her so

badly treated, he took it to heart. In the following days, his spirits dropped and he gradually lost his appetite and ability to sleep. It was thought his grief might even kill him.

Then the king decided to send two lords, Cleomenes and Dion, to the temple of Apollo at Delphi in Greece. They were to inquire of the high priestess, known as 'The Oracle', whether or not Hermione had been unfaithful.

A poor little prisoner

Hermione had been in prison just a short time when she gave birth to a daughter. She received a lot of comfort from the sight of her pretty baby, and she said to it, "My poor little prisoner, I am as innocent as you are!"

Hermione's chief friend was the kind-hearted and noble-spirited Paulina. She was the wife of Antigonus, a Sicilian lord. When she heard about the baby, she immediately went to the prison. She said to Emilia, one of Hermione's ladies-in-waiting, "Please tell the good queen, if she can trust me with her little baby, I will take it to the king, its father. There is a chance he may soften at the sight of his innocent child."

"Lady Paulina," replied Emilia, "I will pass your noble offer on to the queen. She was just wondering whether she had any friend who would venture to do just that!"

"And tell her," said Paulina, "that I will speak boldly to the King in her defense."

"May you be forever blessed for your kindness to our gracious queen!"

Hermione was afraid that no one would be brave enough to present the baby to its father. So she joyfully gave her up to the care of Paulina.

Carrying the baby, Paulina tried to force herself into the king's presence, even though her husband, fearing the king's anger, tried hard to stop her. Paulina laid the baby at its father's feet. Then she made a powerful speech to Leontes in defense of Hermione. She reproached him severely for his inhumanity and implored him to have mercy on his innocent wife and child. But Paulina's spirited words only increased Leontes' anger. He ordered Antigonus to take her from his presence.

When Paulina went out, she left the baby, believing that when Leontes was alone with it, he might take pity on its helpless innocence. But she was mistaken. The merciless father at once ordered Antigonus to take the child, carry it on a boat out to sea, and leave it on some deserted shore to perish.

Unlike the good Camillo, Antigonus always obeyed. He immediately did as the King had ordered.

The trial

So firmly was the king persuaded of the guilt of Hermione that he would not wait for the return of Cleomenes and Dion from Delphi. Leontes had her brought to a public trial in front of all the great lords, judges, and nobles of his court. She was still not fully recovered from giving birth and her grief for the loss of her precious baby.

But just as the unhappy queen was standing as a prisoner to receive judgment, Cleomenes and Dion entered the assembly. They presented Leontes the sealed reply from The Oracle of Delphi. He ordered the seal to be broken, and the words of the oracle to be read aloud by a court officer.

"Queen Hermione is innocent. King Polixenes is blameless. Camillo is a true subject. King Leontes is a jealous tyrant. The baby is his, and the King will live without an heir if that which is lost cannot be found."

Leontes reaction was harsh. "There's no truth at all in the oracle! It's a fake invented by the Queen's friends. Let us continue with her trial . . . "

But then a servant rushed in.

"My lord, the King!"

"What is your business?"

"Oh sir, I shall be hated to report the news. The prince, your son, with grief and fear his mother will be sentenced to death . . . is gone."

"What do you mean? Gone?"

"He is dead, my lord."

Leontes staggered. "Oh, Apollo is angry! The gods themselves strike at my injustice!"

Hermione fainted.

"Look down, my lord," said Paulina, "and see what death is doing!"

Pierced to the heart by the awful news, Leontes began to feel pity for his unhappy queen. He ordered Paulina and the other ladies to take her away and use whatever means they could to revive her.

"Apollo," cried Leontes, "pardon my great insult to the oracle! I must renew my bonds with Polixenes, woo Hermione again, and recall good Camillo..."

Then Paulina returned.

"Oh, lords, and thou tyrant, the sweetest, dearest creature, your queen...is dead."

When Leontes heard this, he fell to pieces. He repented his cruelty to her. And now he realized his ill-usage had broken her heart, and he knew she was innocent. He also now believed the words of the oracle were true. He concluded that "if that which is lost cannot be found," meant his baby daughter. She should be his heir, now that Prince Mamillius had gone. He stated he would give his whole kingdom to find his lost daughter!

And so, King Leontes gave himself up to remorse, and passed many years in mournful thoughts, prayer, and repentant grief.

Exit, pursued by a bear...

By chance, the ship in which Antigonus carried the infant princess out to sea was driven by a storm to the coast of Bohemia, which was ruled by the good King Polixenes. Antigonus landed and he decided to leave the child there near the beach.

"Poor baby, your mother appear'd to me in a dream last night. She said, 'Antigonus, since Fate has made you the thrower-out of my baby, there are places remote enough in Bohemia.

Leave her crying there. And because she's believed to have been lost for ever, please name her Perdita. However, because of this unkind act ordered you by my lord, you will never see your wife Paulina again.' Well, maybe a dream means nothing, but I believe Queen Hermione has died and that you are the child of King Polixenes after all. So Apollo wanted you left here on the land of your real father. Ah, the storm is getting worse again… Dear child, I wish you luck! Farewell!"

Hermione had dressed the baby in rich clothes and jewels. Antigonus had pinned a paper to her robe, saying 'Perdita' and some words suggesting she was from a noble family.

But Antigonus never returned to Sicily to tell Leontes where he had left his daughter. Just as he was heading back to the ship, a huge bear came out of the woods…and tore him to pieces.

Perdita

Luckily, the poor, deserted baby was soon found by a shepherd.

"Oh, what have we here? It's a baby! And a pretty one, too. And well-dressed. And there's jewelry and gold! I was told once I'd be made rich by the fairies! This must be fairy gold! Anyway, you can't stay here. Out of pity, I'll take you home with me…"

He was a kind man, and his wife nursed the baby tenderly. They had no idea that 'Perdita' meant 'lost' in Latin, but they liked the sound of the name. However, poverty made them hide the rich prize they had found. They decided to leave that part of the country to avoid discovery. Then, with part of Perdita's jewels, the shepherd bought a big herd of sheep and after that became a wealthy man.

The couple brought up Perdita as their own child, and she just thought she was the shepherd's daughter. As the years passed, she grew up into a lovely sixteen-year-old. She only had a rural education, but somehow the natural grace inherited from her mother shone out in her behavior.

Doricles

King Polixenes had one son, whose name was Florizel. One day, the young prince went out hunting, and near an old shepherd's cottage he happened to see the man's daughter. It was Perdita. Her beauty, modesty, and grace caused him to fall in love with her immediately. After that, in the disguise of a young gentleman called Doricles, he became a regular visitor to the cottage.

But Florizel's frequent absences from court alarmed his father. He ordered his servants to keep an eye on his son. And he soon learned about the shepherd's attractive daughter.

Polixenes then had a meeting with the faithful Camillo who had preserved his life from the fury of Leontes. The king asked him to accompany him on a visit to the shepherd's cottage. Both in disguise, they arrived there just as the sheep-shearing feast was underway. They were complete strangers, but everyone was made welcome. They were invited to walk in and join in the festivities. It was a scene filled with happiness and laughter. Several tables had been prepared for the rustic feast. Some of the young men and women were dancing on the grass in front of the cottage. Others were busy buying ribands and gloves and other party goods from a peddler by the door.

While all this was going on, Florizel and Perdita were sitting quietly in a corner of the garden. They seemed to be more pleased with each other's conversation than interested in taking part in any of the amusements going on around them.

It was impossible for Polixenes to be recognized, as he was so well disguised by a bushy beard and a big floppy hat. So he moved near enough to overhear his son's conversation. He was surprised to hear the simple yet elegant manner in which Perdita chatted to Florizel.

"This is the prettiest low-born girl I ever saw," Polixenes said quietly to Camillo. "Everything she does and says suggests she is almost too noble for this place!"

"Indeed, she is the very queen of curds and cream!" replied Camillo.

"Excuse me, my good friend," said Polixenes to the old shepherd. "Who is that handsome young man talking to your daughter?"

"Ah, they call him Doricles. He says he loves my daughter. And, to speak the truth, there's no way to tell which one of them loves the other best! If young Doricles can win her, she'll bring him something he little dreams of."

"Oh, really?" said Polixenes, and then addressed his son. "Young man, your heart seems full of something that takes your mind off feasting. When I was young, I used to load my love with presents. But you have let the peddler go without buying her anything!"

Completely unaware who he was talking to, Florizel replied, "Well, sir, she does not value such trifles. The gifts which Perdita expects from me are locked up in my heart." Then he turned to her and said, "Perdita, I want this kind old gentleman, who it seems was once himself a lover, to hear what I profess."

"Yes, let me and my friend hear," said Polixenes.

"Please be a witness to a solemn promise of marriage I will make to this girl, Perdita."

"But before that, I have a question. Don't you have a father?"

"I do, but what of it?" replied Florizel.

"Does he know about this?"

"No, he doesn't, nor will he!"

"But I believe a father is the main guest at his son's marriage. What is wrong with him? He can't hear and speak? He can't control his affairs? Is he bedridden? Is he suffering from old age? Has he reverted to childhood?"

"Oh, no, sir. He is in good health and has more strength than most men of his age."

"So surely he should at least be consulted about his family's future?"

"Yes. But, for some reason I cannot tell you, I will not inform him."

"Let him know!"

"No!"

"Please!"

"No, I can't! Please witness our promise of marriage!"

"No, I will *not*!" said the king, throwing off his disguise. "But I will mark your *divorce*, young sir… I can no longer call you my son!"

Polixenes reproached Florizel for daring to contract himself to such a humble girl. He called Perdita 'a shepherd's brat' and a 'sheep-hook,' and other disrespectful names. And if she ever allowed his son to see her again, he threatened he would put her, and her father, to a cruel death.

The king then left them in great anger. He ordered Camillo to follow him with Florizel.

Camillo's scheme

As soon as the king had gone, Perdita said, "Though we're all undone, I was not very afraid. Once or twice, I was about to speak and tell him plainly that the same sun that shines on his palace doesn't hide his face from our cottage, but looks on both homes just the same." Then sorrowfully she added, "But now I have woken from this dream. I will be a queen no more! Leave me, sir. I will just milk my ewes and weep."

The kind-hearted Camillo was charmed with Perdita's spirit and behavior. He could see that the young prince was too deeply in love to give her up at his royal father's command. He suddenly thought of a way to help the lovers and at the same time carry out a favorite scheme that had been brewing in his mind.

Camillo had long known that King Leontes had become truly penitent. And although Camillo was now the close friend of King Polixenes, he could not help wishing once more to see his late royal master and his native home. He therefore proposed to Florizel and Perdita that they should accompany him to the Sicilian court. He would encourage Leontes to protect them until, through Camillo's mediation, they could obtain a pardon from Polixenes and his consent to their marriage.

They happily agreed to this proposal. Camillo promised to deal with everything required for their flight to Sicily. Now a widower, the old shepherd was invited to go along with them, and he took the remainder of Perdita's jewels, her baby clothes, and the paper which he had found pinned to her robe.

Revelations

After a swift and trouble-free voyage, Florizel, Perdita, Camillo and the old shepherd arrived at the Sicilian court. Leontes, who was still mourning the deaths of Hermione, Mamillius, and his lost child, received Camillo with great happiness. And he gave a warm welcome to Prince Florizel. But it was Perdita, whom Florizel introduced as his princess, who seemed to take all Leontes' attention. He could perceive a resemblance between her and Hermione, and that made his grief break out again. He said his own daughter might have been such a lovely creature if he had not so cruelly destroyed her.

"And then, too," he said to Florizel, "I lost the society and friendship of your father. I now desire more than anything to see him again!"

The old shepherd heard how much notice the king had taken of Perdita and that he'd abandoned and lost a baby daughter. He started comparing the time when he found little Perdita, and the jewels and other signs of her high birth. Based on all those details, it was quite possible that Perdita and the king's lost daughter were the same!

Florizel, Perdita, Camillo and the faithful Paulina were all present when the old shepherd told Leontes how he had found the child. He also mentioned having seen a bear seize Antigonus and kill him. He then showed the rich robe in which Paulina remembered Hermione wrapping the baby and the jewel she had tied around Perdita's neck. Finally, he showed the paper bearing Perdita's name. Paulina recognized the handwriting of her husband. There was now no doubt at all that Perdita was indeed Leontes' daughter.

But, oh, what a terrible struggle Paulina had to face, between sorrow for her husband's death and joy that the oracle had been fulfilled and the king's heir, his long-lost daughter, had been found!

A new statue

When Leontes grasped who Perdita really was, he felt great sorrow that Hermione was not alive to see her. For a long time, he could only murmur, "Oh, your mother, your mother!"

Eventually Paulina interrupted this scene that was both

joyful and sad. She told Leontes that in the chapel of her house there was a statue just completed by the famous Italian sculptor, Julio Romano. She described it as a perfect resemblance of the queen.

"And if Your Majesty will go with me and see it, I feel you will almost be ready to think it is Hermione herself!"

And so they all went together. Leontes was anxious to see this likeness of Hermione, and Perdita longed to discover what the mother she had never seen had looked like.

Paulina slowly drew back the curtain which concealed the statue. So perfectly did it resemble Hermione that all the king's sorrow returned. For a long time, he was unable to speak or move. He just gazed at the statue.

"I like your silence," said Paulina. "It shows your amazement. Is not the statue very much like your queen?"

"Oh, yes," replied Leontes. "She stood like this, with such elegance, when I first courted her. And yet, Paulina, her face was not quite so aged."

"But that shows the sculptor's excellence," Paulina replied. "He has made the statue as Hermione would have looked had she been living today. But let me draw the curtain again, or soon you will think it moves!"

"No, leave it," said Leontes. "Ah, I wish I was dead! Look, Camillo, don't you think it seems to breathe? Her eyes seem to have motion in them . . . "

"I must draw the curtain," said Paulina. "You are so carried away, you will persuade yourself that the statue is alive!"

"Oh, sweet Paulina," said Leontes, "I still think breath comes from her. No chisel can cut breath! Please, no-one mock me, for I will kiss her..."

"Oh, no!" said Paulina. "The red paint on her lip is still wet; you will stain your own lips. Let me draw the curtain..."

"No, not for twenty years!"

All this time, Perdita had been kneeling and gazing in silent admiration at the statue. Now she said, "And so long I could stay here, too, looking at my dear mother!"

"Well, either leave the chapel now," said Paulina to Leontes, "or prepare yourself for more amazement. I can make the statue move indeed, and step from the pedestal and take you by the hand. But then you will think that I am assisted by some evil powers, which I insist I am not."

"Whatever you can make her do," said the astonished king, "I am content to see. And whatever you can make her speak, I am content to hear. For I think it is as easy to make her speak as to move..."

Paulina then ordered some slow and solemn music to be played. And then, to everyone's amazement, the statue of Hermione started moving very slowly. It stepped down from the pedestal and threw its arms around Leontes' neck. It then began to speak, praying for blessings on her husband and on her child, the newly found Perdita. Yes, the statue was indeed Hermione herself, the real living queen!

General joy

All those years ago, Paulina had falsely reported Hermione's death to the king. She felt that was the only way to keep her royal mistress alive. Hermione had lived ever since with Paulina, refusing to let Leontes know she was alive until she heard Perdita was found. She had long forgiven Leontes for the injuries which he had done to her, but she could not forgive his cruelty to their baby daughter.

Leontes could scarcely believe such happiness. His dead queen had been restored to life, and his lost daughter had been found! Congratulations and affectionate speeches were heard on all sides. Now the delighted parents thanked Prince Florizel for loving their apparently humble daughter. They also blessed the good old shepherd, for preserving their child. And Camillo and Paulina greatly rejoiced that they had lived to see so good an end to all their faithful services.

And just as if nothing should be missing to complete this strange and unexpected joy, Polixenes himself now appeared at the palace. When he first discovered his son and Camillo had fled, he suspected he would find the fugitives in Sicily. He had pursued them as fast as possible, and happened to arrive at the happiest moment of Leontes' life. When he was told all that had happened, he joined in the general joy. He forgave Leontes the unjust jealousy he had conceived against him, and they again loved each other with all the warmth of their youth. And there was no longer any fear that Polixenes would oppose his son's marriage to Perdita. She was no "sheep-hook" now, but the heiress of the crown of Sicily!

The patient virtues of the long-suffering Hermione had been rewarded at last. She lived many years with her Leontes and her Perdita, the happiest of mothers and of queens. What was lost had indeed been found.

Much Ado About Nothing

から騒ぎ

読み始める前に

二組のカップルが、策略や試練を乗り越えて結ばれる恋物語。シェイクスピアの中期を代表するロマンスコメディ。

［登場人物］

Claudio	クローディオ《フローレンスの貴族》
Hero	ヒーロー《レオナートの娘》
Benedick	ベネディック《パドヴァの貴族》
Beatrice	ベアトリス《レオナートの姪》
Don Pedro	ドン・ペドロ《アラゴン大公》
Leonato	レオナート《メッシーナの知事》
Ursula	アースラ《ヒーローの侍女》
Margaret	マーガレット《ヒーローの侍女》
Don John	ドン・ジョン《ドン・ペドロの異母弟》
Borachio	ボラチオ《ドン・ジョンの家来》
Friar Francis	フランシス神父《修道士》

［地名など］

Arragon	アラゴン《スペインの地方》
Florence	フローレンス《イタリアの都市》
Messina	メッシーナ《イタリアの都市》
Padua	パドヴァ《イタリアの都市》

［あらすじ］

シチリア島メッシーナの知事レオナートの屋敷をアラゴン大公ドン・ペドロ一行が訪れる。レオナートの一人娘ヒーローに一目惚れするクローディオ卿。一方で独身主義者ベネディックはレオナートの姪ベアトリスと会うなり口げんか。

ペドロは、恋を打ち明けられずにいるクローディオをヒーローと結びつけるべく奔走する。また、口げんかに明け暮れているベネディックとベアトリスの縁結びを画策し、ヒーローやレオナートを巻き込んでひと芝居打つことにするが……。

［総単語数］3,940語

MUCH ADO ABOUT NOTHING

Once upon a time, two ladies lived in the Governor's Palace at Messina, the port city on the island of Sicily near the 'toe' of Italy. One of them was Hero, the daughter of Leonato, the Governor. The other was Beatrice, his niece. Beatrice was a lively young woman who loved to amuse her cousin Hero, who had a more serious character. Whatever happened was sure to become a matter of fun for the light-hearted Beatrice.

Benedick and Beatrice

One day, some young gentlemen of high rank in the army passed through Messina. They were returning from a war that had just ended, in which they had distinguished themselves by their great bravery. They went to visit Leonato. Among them were Don Pedro, the Prince of Arragon, and his friend Claudio, who was a lord from Florence. With them was the wild and witty Benedick, a lord from Padua. They had all been in Messina before, and so the hospitable governor could introduce them to his daughter and niece as old friends.

The moment he entered the room, Benedick began a lively chat with Leonato and Don Pedro. Beatrice, who didn't like being left out of any conversation, interrupted Benedick.

"Oh, I'm amazed that you keep talking, Signor Benedick. Nobody is listening to you!"

Now Benedick was as much a rattlebrain as Beatrice, but he was not pleased by this free kind of greeting. He thought it did not become a well-bred lady like Beatrice to be so flippant. He remembered when he was last in Messina, Beatrice would pick him out as the butt of amusing remarks. They were both strong-willed and independent and had always kept up a war of smart banter. And they had always parted mutually displeased with each other! So when Beatrice stopped him in the middle of his chat, he pretended not to have noticed that she was there.

"Oh, my dear Lady Disdain, are you still alive?"

And now war broke out again between them! A long argument began. Beatrice knew Benedick had proved his valor in the war, but she said that she would eat everyone he had killed. He ignored this hint that he was a coward, as he knew he was a brave man. Then, noticing that Don Pedro seemed to enjoy Benedick's conversation, Beatrice called him "the prince's jester." This sarcastic remark sank deeper into Benedick's mind than her other insults. Men with great minds dread being described as a fool or a clown as it may be a little too near the truth!

The modest Hero was silent before all the noble guests. But Claudio was noting how beautiful she had become, and her exquisite grace.

Don Pedro was highly amused listening to the witty banter between Benedick and Beatrice.

"This is a very pleasant-spirited young lady," he whispered to Leonato. "She would be an excellent wife for Benedick!"

"Oh, my lord," replied Leonato, "If they were married just a week, they would talk themselves crazy!"

But the prince did not give up the idea of matching those two smart wits together.

Claudio and Hero

When Don Pedro returned with Claudio from the palace, he found that the marriage he was planning between Benedick and Beatrice was not the only one being considered. Claudio spoke in such glowing terms about Hero that Don Pedro guessed at what was going on in his friend's heart, and he approved.

"So you have an interest in her?" he asked.

"Oh yes, my lord," replied Claudio. "When I was last here in Messina, I saw her only with a soldier's eye. I liked what I saw, but that was it. But now, in this happy time of peace, instead of thinking about war, more delicate thoughts have entered my mind. And they all tell me how attractive young Hero is."

This confession of love greatly impressed Don Pedro. He lost no time in requesting the consent of Leonato to accept Claudio as his son-in-law. Leonato agreed at once, and Don Pedro easily persuaded Hero to consider favorably the suit of the noble Claudio, a lord with many virtues. And Leonato fixed an early date for the celebration of their marriage.

Claudio only had to wait a few days, but he complained of the interval being boring. To make the time seem shorter, Don Pedro proposed a kind of fun pastime: they would invent some clever scheme to make Benedick and Beatrice fall in love with each other! Claudio heartily approved of this whim and Leonato promised them his assistance. Even Hero said she would do whatever she could to help her cousin find a good husband.

Don Pedro came up with a very simple plan. The gentlemen would make Benedick believe that Beatrice was in love with *him*, and Hero and the ladies would make Beatrice believe that Benedick was in love with *her*.

Benedick

Don Pedro, Leonato, and Claudio launched their part of the plan first. They waited for an opportunity when Benedick was quietly seated reading in the sunny palace arbor. Then they put themselves among the trees just behind the arbor, so near that Benedick was sure to hear all they said.

After some idle chat, Don Pedro said, "By the way, Leonato,

what was that you were saying the other day about your niece Beatrice being in love with Benedick? I never thought she'd love anyone!"

"No, nor did I!" answered Leonato. "I think it's wonderful that she dotes on Benedick, who she has always appeared to dislike."

Claudio confirmed this, saying that Hero had told him Beatrice was so in love with Benedick that she would certainly die of grief if he couldn't somehow be persuaded to love her. But Leonato and Claudio both agreed that was impossible as he'd always been very negative toward women, Beatrice in particular.

Don Pedro showed great compassion for Beatrice, saying, "I think Benedick should be told about this."

"But to what end?" said Claudio. "He would only make sport of it and torment the poor lady more!"

"Well, if he did that he should be hung!" said Don Pedro. "Beatrice is such an attractive, virtuous lady, and so wise in everything—apart, that is, from loving Benedick!"

Then he motioned to his companions that they should walk away and leave Benedick to meditate on what he'd overheard.

Benedick had, of course, been listening to their conversation with great interest.

"Is it really possible?" he said to himself. "She *loves* me? She *dotes* on me? Is this some kind of trick? No, it can't be. They were very serious, they have heard it from Hero, and they seem to pity Beatrice. Love? Why, it must be reciprocated! I have never thought of getting married. But when I said I'd die a bachelor, I didn't think I would live to be married! But the world must be peopled! They said Beatrice is attractive and virtuous. That's very true. And wise in everything but loving me. Well, that can be changed! Oh, here she comes… Ah, she's a lovely lady indeed. And I think I can spy some marks of love in her!"

Beatrice came up to him and said, with her usual tartness, "Against my will, I was sent to tell you to come in for dinner."

For the very first time, Benedick replied to her politely. "Oh, Beatrice, that's very kind of you!"

She made some rude comments and left. But Benedick imagined there was some concealed message of kindness behind her words.

"Well," he thought, "if I don't take pity on her, I'm a villain!"

Beatrice

The gentleman having being caught in the net spread for him, it was now the lady's turn.

Hero sent for Ursula and Margaret.

"Good Margaret," she said, "run to the parlor. There you will find my cousin Beatrice talking to Don Pedro and Claudio. Whisper in her ear that Ursula and I are walking in the orchard and that our talk is all about her. Tell her to go quietly into that pleasant arbor, where the honeysuckle forbids the sun from entering."

"Alright, madam," said Margaret. "I will make her come, I promise!"

Hero then took Ursula with her into the orchard.

"Now, Ursula, when Beatrice comes, we will walk up and down this little alley, and our talk must be only of Benedick. When I say his name, you must praise him more than any man deserves! And I will speak to you about Benedick being in love with Beatrice. Oh, she's heading to the arbor! Let's begin . . . !"

As if in answer to something Ursula had commented about Beatrice, Hero said: "No, Ursula. She's much too proud."

"But are you sure," said Ursula, "that Benedick loves Beatrice so deeply?"

"Well, so says Don Pedro and my lord Claudio, and they entreated me to let her know about it. But I persuaded them, if they loved Benedick, never to do that."

"That's right," replied Ursula. "If she found out about his love, she would just mock him!"

"Well, to tell the truth," said Hero, "I have never seen any man—wise, noble, young or handsome—who she was *not* rude about. She once said 'I had rather hear my dog bark at a crow than a man swear he loves me'!"

"Yes, that attitude is not good at all," said Ursula.

"No, but who dares to tell her that? If *I* tried, she would just laugh at me."

"But surely," said Ursula, "she can't be so lacking in good judgment as to refuse so rare a gentleman as Signor Benedick."

"Yes, he has an excellent reputation. Indeed, I would say he's the best man in Italy . . . besides my dear Claudio, of course!"

"Hero gave Ursula a hint that it was time to change the topic. "Madam, your wedding is tomorrow!" said Ursula. "How can I help you?"

"Well, I would like your advice on my clothes. Shall we go in?"

Beatrice had been listening breathlessly to this talk. When Hero and Ursula had gone, she exclaimed, "What is this fire in my ears? Can this be true? Oh, farewell to contempt and scorn, and adieu to my pride! Benedick, love on! I will tame my wild heart to your loving hand..."

Don John

Don Pedro had a half-brother named Don John, who had come along with him to Messina from the war. Very different from his brother in personality, he was a melancholy, discontented man. He hated his brother, and he hated Claudio because he was his friend. As a result, he was determined to prevent Claudio's marriage to Hero, just for the evil pleasure of making Claudio and his brother unhappy. And so he came up with a wicked plan.

He encouraged a man as bad as himself named Borachio to help him, with the offer of a big reward. Don John knew that Borachio had been flirting with Margaret, Hero's maid. His mission was to make Margaret promise to talk to him from her mistress's window that very night after the lady was asleep. Margaret should also dress herself in Hero's clothes. The idea, of course, was to trick Claudio into believing it really was Hero herself.

Don John then went to see his brother and Claudio. He told them that Hero was not as innocent as they thought and that she talked with men from her window at midnight. He offered to take them that night to a place where he was sure they could see this happening for themselves, even though it was the evening before the wedding! They consented to go along with him.

"And if I see any reason tonight why I should *not* marry her," said Claudio, "I will definitely shame her tomorrow at the church!"

"And," Don Pedro added, "I was a kind of go-between, so I will join you to disgrace her."

Don John led them at midnight to a dark place in the orchard where they could see Hero's room. Sure enough, there was a man standing under the window, and a woman looking out of the window and talking to him. Margaret's face was in shadow, but she was wearing the same clothes Hero had worn that day, so Don Pedro and Claudio both believed it was Hero herself.

Nothing could equal the anger of Claudio when he made this discovery. All his love for the innocent Hero was immediately converted into hatred, and he resolved to expose her in the church. Don Pedro agreed, thinking no punishment was too severe for such a wicked young woman who talked to a man from her window the very night before she was to marry the noble Claudio.

A rotten orange

The next day, they all gathered at the church to celebrate the wedding. Claudio and Hero stood before Friar Francis as he began the ceremony. First he spoke to Claudio.

"Count Claudio, have you come here today to marry this lady?"

"No!" replied Claudio.

"Friar," said Leonato, "He's come to be married *to* her. *You* have come to *marry* her!"

"Ah, yes," said the friar. He then looked at Hero. "Lady Hero, do you agree to marry this count?"

"I do."

"Count Claudio, do you know of any reason why this marriage should not proceed?"

Suddenly Claudio burst out in passionate language, proclaiming Hero's guilt.

Shocked by his words, Hero said meekly, "Are you unwell, my lord, that you speak so strangely?"

"Leonato, take your daughter back again," said Claudio, pushing Hero toward him. "I do not want this rotten orange any more!"

Leonato, in the utmost horror, said to Don Pedro, "My lord, why do you say nothing?"

"What should I say?" he replied. "I am dishonored because I linked my dear friend Claudio to such an unworthy woman. Last night at midnight my brother, Claudio and myself all saw her talking to a man at her window."

"This does not look much like a wedding ceremony any more!" said Benedick in astonishment.

"Oh, God!" cried poor Hero, and fainted.

Don Pedro and Claudio stormed out of the church without even bothering to see whether she would recover, and ignoring the distress into which they'd thrown her father.

Friar Francis

Benedick did not leave with them but stayed to help Beatrice, who was trying to revive Hero. "How is she?"

"Almost dead, I think," replied Beatrice, in great agony, for she loved her cousin deeply. And well aware of Hero's virtuous life, she didn't believe a single word of the accusation against her. "Please help, uncle! Benedick! Friar Francis!"

Her poor old father had actually believed the wicked story. To hide her shame, he wished his child might never open her eyes again.

But the friar was a wise man who had observed human nature closely. He had carefully noted Hero's face when she heard herself accused. He first saw a thousand blushes rush into her face, and then an angel-like whiteness removed them, and in her eyes he saw a fire that indicated the error of Don Pedro's story.

"Call me a fool if you wish," he said to Leonato, "but according to my close observation and experience, the sweet lady lies guiltless here because of some awful error."

When Hero had recovered a bit, the friar said to her, "My lady, who was the man you are accused of meeting?"

"I know of no-one!" replied Hero, "Only they know who accused me..." Then, turning to Leonato, she said, "Oh, Father, if you can *prove* that any man has ever talked to me at midnight, or that last night I spoke to anyone, please disown me, hate me, and torture me to death!"

"I believe that Don Pedro and Count Claudio have suffered some serious misunderstanding," said the friar. He then advised Leonato to report that Hero had died from shock. He said her death-like swoon just before they left would make it easy to believe. He also suggested that they should all dress in black, erect a monument for Hero, and carry out all the rites for her funeral.

"But what will this achieve?" asked Leonato.

"Well, first," the friar replied, "the report of her death will change slander into pity. But that is not all the good I'm hoping for. When Count Claudio hears she died the moment she heard his words, his memories of her will sweetly creep back into his mind. Then, if there was ever true love in his heart, he will mourn and wish that he had not accused her, even though he thought his accusation was true."

"Leonato," said Benedick, "take the wise friar's advice. And though you know how well I love Don Pedro and Claudio, I promise I will not reveal this secret to them."

Leonato agreed, and said, "I am so unhappy that I will follow the slightest glimpse of hope."

The kind friar then led Leonato and Hero away to comfort and console them.

Benedick and Beatrice

Beatrice and Benedick remained alone. This was the meeting that their friends, who contrived the merry plot against them, had been looking forward to so much. But those friends were now overwhelmed with trouble, and all thoughts of fun seemed to have been banished forever.

Benedick was the first to speak, rather awkwardly. "Lady Beatrice, have you been crying all this time?"

"Yes, I have, and I will continue to cry."

"I am sure your dear cousin has been falsely accused."

"Ah, how much would the man who could settle the matter deserve my praise!"

"Is there any way for me to show such friendship?" said Benedick. "I love nothing in the world as much as I love you, Beatrice. Is that strange?"

"I could also say I love nothing in the world as much as *you*, Benedick. But don't believe me...and yet it's true. I confess nothing...and I deny nothing. Oh, I am so sorry for my cousin..."

"If you love me, admit it!"

"Oh, Benedick, I love you with so much of my heart that none is left to protest."

"Well, you love me, and I love you. So ask me to do anything for you!"

"Then kill Claudio."

"Kill Claudio? Oh, no... He's my good friend, and I believed he has been tricked!"

"But he's the villain that has slandered, scorned, and dishonored my cousin! Oh, if only I was a *man*!"

"Hear me, Beatrice!"

But she would hear nothing in Claudio's defense, and continued to entreat Benedick to take revenge for her cousin's wrongs.

"Talk to a man from her window?" she said. "What nonsense! Oh, sweet Hero! She has been wronged, slandered, undone… Oh, if only I had a friend who would be a man for my sake! But valor these days seems to have melted into courtesies and compliments. So if I can't be a man by wishing, I'll die a woman by grieving."

"Wait, good Beatrice," said Benedick.

"No, you have no love in you!"

"I swear by this hand that I love you!"

"Use it for my love some other way than swearing by it."

"Enough!" said Benedick. "I will challenge Claudio. I will kiss your hand, and so leave you. By this hand, Beatrice, Claudio will answer for what he has done! Now please go and comfort your cousin…"

Borachio's confession

Meanwhile, Leonato was in the process of challenging Don Pedro and Claudio to answer with their swords for the injury they had done his child.

"She died of grief because of *your* villainy."

"*My* villainy?"

"Yes."

"No, good old man, do not quarrel with us."

Just then Benedick arrived. He also challenged Claudio to fight a duel to answer for the injury he had done to Hero.

"Beatrice has set him on to do this!" whispered Don Pedro.

Claudio might well have accepted Benedick's challenge, but at that moment the justice of Heaven brought better proof of Hero's innocence than the uncertain result of a duel.

A local magistrate appeared with Borachio as a prisoner. He had been overheard talking with one of his companions of the mischief he had been employed to carry out by Don John.

Borachio made a full confession to Don Pedro and Claudio. He told them it was Margaret dressed in her lady's clothes that he had talked to from the window, *not* the lady Hero herself.

Now there was no doubt of Hero's innocence left in the minds of Claudio and Don Pedro. But if any suspicion remained, it would have been removed by the flight of Don John. Hearing his villainy had been detected, he had fled from Messina.

Claudio's heart was sorely grieved when he realized he had falsely accused Hero and caused her death.

"Does what we have just heard not run through your soul like iron?" said Don Pedro.

"Yes," replied Claudio, "while Borachio was speaking, I felt as if I'd taken poison."

The deeply repentant Claudio implored forgiveness of Leonato for the injury he had done his child. He promised that he would endure whatever punishment Leonato wished to give him.

"In that case," replied Leonato, "promise to come to the church tomorrow morning and marry a cousin of Hero's, who is now my heir. In many ways she closely resembles my dear lost daughter."

Claudio said he would gladly marry the lady. But his heart was still full of sorrow, and he passed the night in tears at the tomb Leonato had erected for Hero.

A second wedding

Morning arrived. Don Pedro accompanied Claudio to the church. Friar Francis, Leonato and his niece were already there to celebrate a second wedding. Leonato introduced Claudio to his promised bride. She was wearing a thick veil, so Claudio could not see her face.

"Give me your hand," he said. "Before this holy friar, I declare that I will be your husband, if you will marry me."

"And when I lived, I was your other wife," replied the lady, "and when you loved, you were my other husband!"

She slowly removed her veil to prove she was none other than Leonato's daughter, the lady Hero herself!

"Another Hero!" cried Claudio.

"The former Hero?" cried Don Pedro. "The Hero that was dead!"

"She only died while the slander continued," said her father.

The friar promised them a full explanation of this miracle after the ceremony. But just as he began the marriage service, he was suddenly interrupted by Benedick, who said he wished to be married at the same time to Beatrice!

When they found that they had both been tricked into believing the love of the other, which had never truly existed, Beatrice and Benedick had actually become lovers by the power of a merry joke! Their affection had grown too powerful to be shaken by a serious explanation. Instead, they both offered tongue-in-cheek reasons. Benedick swore to Beatrice that he was only marrying her out of pity because he had heard she was dying of love for him! And Beatrice claimed she only wanted to save his life, for she heard he was very ill and needed a nurse!

So those two wild wits were reconciled and were married right after Claudio and Hero. As for Don John, who had planned the villainy, he was arrested as he tried to fly away, and brought back to Messina. It was a real punishment to that gloomy, discontented man to observe all the joy and feasting going on at the Governor's Palace.

As You Like It

お気に召すまま

読み始める前に

シェイクスピア作品の中で女性主人公が活躍する数少ない物語。
「この世はすべて舞台。男も女もみな役者に過ぎぬ」の名言で有名な喜劇。

［登場人物］

Rosalind	ロザリンド《前公爵の娘》
Ganymede	ギャニミード《ロザリンドの変装名》
Orlando	オーランドー《ド・ボイズ家の末っ子》
Celia	シーリア《公爵の娘》
Aliena	エイリーナ《シーリアの変装名》
Oliver	オリバー《ド・ボイズ家の長男》
Adam	アダム《老僕》
Frederick	フレデリック《公爵》
Rowland de Boys	ローランド・ド・ボイズ《オリバーとオーランドーの父》
Duke Senior	前公爵《フレデリックの兄》
Corin	コーリン《羊飼い》
Charles	チャールズ《レスリング選手》

［地名など］

Arden	アーデン《森》

［あらすじ］

弟に領地を奪われ追放された前公爵は、「アーデンの森」で、家臣や友人たちときままに暮らしていた。前公爵の娘ロザリンドは、叔父の娘シーリアの遊び相手として邸内で暮らしている。

オーランドーは、父の遺産を相続した長兄オリバーにしいたげられている。ある日レスリング大会に出場したオーランドーはロザリンドに出会い、二人は互いにひとめぼれする。オーランドの亡父は追放した兄と親友であることから公爵は不快に思い、同時にロザリンドにも悪感情を抱き、ロザリンドも追放してしまう。

ロザリンドは男装し、シーリアとともに兄妹をよそおって前公爵のいる森に向かう。一方、オーランドーも、兄オリバーの迫害を逃れて森にやってくる。さらに、オーランドを殺すためにオリバーもやってきて……

［総単語数］5,450語

AS YOU LIKE IT

Once upon a time, a usurper named Frederick reigned in one of France's many dukedoms. He had deposed and banished his elder brother, Duke Senior, who was the lawful duke.

The banished duke now lived in the Forest of Arden with a few faithful followers who had put themselves into voluntary exile for his sake. Although their lands and revenues were enriching the usurper, the easy-going life in the forest soon seemed much better than the pomp and splendor of a courtier's life. They were living like old Robin Hood of England! In the summer they lay under the pleasant shade of the large trees, watching the wild deer at play. They grew so fond of the poor dappled animals—the native inhabitants of the forest—that they hated to kill them for venison.

Duke Senior endured the wintry blasts patiently saying, "These chilling winds are real counselors. They don't flatter me, but truly show me my condition. They bite sharply, but their teeth are nothing like as sharp as human unkindness and ingratitude! In adversity, there is always something sweet to be found."

In this way, he learned from everything he observed. He found voices in the trees, books in the streams, sermons in the stones, and good in everything.

Rosalind and Celia

The banished duke had an only daughter, named Rosalind. When he banished her father, Duke Frederick kept her at court as a companion for his own daughter, Celia. The deep friendship between these young ladies was in no way affected by their fathers' disagreement. Celia did her best to make amends to Rosalind for the injustice done to her father with every kindness she could. Whenever Rosalind felt depressed by the situation, Celia tried to console her.

One day, Celia was just saying, "Rosalind, my sweet cousin, please be merry!" when a messenger from the duke entered. A wrestling match was about to begin in the court in front of the palace. If they wanted to see it, they should go at once. Thinking it might amuse Rosalind, Celia agreed to go, and she persuaded her cousin to join her.

The underdog

In those days, wrestling was a very popular sport, even with ladies and princesses. But when Celia and Rosalind arrived, they realized it was likely to provide some tragic sights. Charles, the huge and powerful court champion, who had actually killed many men over the years, was about to wrestle. His opponent was a very young and much smaller man with little experience, and the spectators all feared he would lose his life.

"Ah, welcome, dear daughter and niece!" said Duke Frederick when he saw them. "You may not enjoy this bout, though. Out of pity, I would like to persuade that young man over there not to fight. Why don't you ladies speak to him and see if you can do it?"

They were happy to try. First, Celia entreated the young stranger not to attempt an impossible mission, but he said nothing. Then Rosalind spoke very kindly to him, and with great feeling asked him to consider how much danger he was in. But instead of being persuaded by her to give up, her gentle words had the opposite effect. Now he was determined to distinguish himself in this lovely lady's eyes by showing her his courage! So he refused the ladies' requests, but with such elegant and modest words that they felt even more concerned for him.

He concluded by saying, "I am most sorry to deny such beautiful and considerate ladies anything. But let your fair eyes and gentle wishes go with me to my trial. If I'm defeated, just think that a man was shamed who was never gracious. And if I'm killed, just think there was a man that was willing to die. I won't do my friends any wrong, as I have none to lament me. I shall do the world no injury, for in it I have nothing. I only use up a place in the world which may be better filled when I have emptied it."

The bout began. Celia said she hoped the young stranger would not be hurt, but Rosalind felt much more strongly for him. The friendless state he said he was in, and his wish to die, made her think that he was unfortunate, like herself. She pitied him so much, in fact, and took so deep an interest in the dangerous bout, that you could almost imagine she had fallen in love with him!

The kindness shown by the two noble ladies gave the underdog courage and strength, and he performed wonders. In the end, he completely defeated Charles, who was so hurt that for a while he couldn't speak or move.

Duke Frederick was impressed with the courage and skill shown by the young man. Thinking of taking him under his protection, he asked him his name and parentage.

"My name is Orlando, sir, and I am the youngest son of Sir Rowland de Boys."

Orlando's father had been dead some years, but he had been a true subject and a dear friend of the banished duke. So when Frederick heard his name, his liking for the brave young man immediately disappeared. He hated hearing the name of any of his brother's friends. Even so, he still admired the man's courage. As he walked away in a very bad mood, he said that he wished Orlando had been the son of some other man!

On the other hand, Rosalind was delighted to hear that her new favorite man was the son of her father's old friend.

"My father loved Sir Rowland de Boys," she told Celia. "If I'd known this was his son, I would have added tears to my entreaties!"

The ladies then went up to Orlando. He seemed disappointed by the duke's sudden displeasure, so they spoke kind and encouraging words to him. Just as they left him to go back to the palace, Rosalind suddenly went back to speak to him again. She removed the chain from her neck, and gave it to him, saying, "Please wear this for me. Right now, Fortune isn't smiling on me, or I would have given you a more valuable present!"

Love?

When the ladies were alone, Rosalind continued talking about Orlando. Celia began to realize that her cousin had fallen in love with the handsome young wrestler.

"Cousin," she said, "is it possible that you could fall in love so quickly?"

"My father loved his father dearly."

"I understand that, but does it therefore follow that *you* should love his *son* dearly? In that case, I ought to hate him, for *my* father hated *his* father, but I don't!"

Duke Frederick was in a very bad mood. He had been upset by meeting Sir Rowland de Boys' son, which reminded him that the banished duke had many friends among the nobility. For some time, he'd also been unhappy about Rosalind, his niece. She was widely praised for her virtues and pitied because of her good father's situation. Now his bad feelings erupted like a volcano.

He burst into the room where the ladies were talking. With a look full of anger, he ordered Rosalind to leave the palace at once and follow her father into banishment. Celia pleaded for her, but in vain.

"I have only suffered your cousin to remain here" said her father, "on *your* account!"

"At that time, I didn't ask you to let her stay," replied Celia. "I was too young to value her. But now I know her full worth. For so long we have slept, learned, played, and eaten together. I cannot live without her company!"

"Celia, she's too subtle for you," her father replied. "Her silence and her patience speak to the people, and they pity her. You're a fool to plead for her. When she's gone, you will seem brighter and more virtuous. So say no more in her favor. My decision is final!"

Ganymede and Aliena

Celia realized she could not make her father change his mind. As soon as he had left, she generously resolved to accompany Rosalind. She suggested they should leave the palace that night and go together to look for Rosalind's father in the Forest of Arden.

"But I don't think it's a good idea for two young ladies like us to travel in the fine clothes we're in now!" she said. "I propose that we disguise ourselves by dressing like country girls."

"I think it might give us more protection," Rosalind replied, "if one of us is dressed like a man."

And so it was quickly agreed that Rosalind, who was taller, should wear the clothes of a country youth, and Celia would dress like a country girl. And they decided to say they were brother and sister.

"I will be called Ganymede," said Rosalind. "It's an ancient name suggesting 'freedom'!"

"And I will be Aliena," said Celia. "It means 'stranger' in Latin!"

In these disguises, and taking enough money and jewels to cover their expenses, the two young ladies set out on their long journey. The Forest of Arden was far away, beyond the boundary of the dukedom.

In her manly garb, Rosalind seemed to gain courage. She exerted a cheerful spirit, as if she were indeed Ganymede, the brave, rustic brother of Aliena, the gentle village girl.

The forest

When at last they reached the Forest of Arden, there were no longer any convenient inns with good accommodation like they'd been staying in on the road. They were both desperately in need of food and rest. Ganymede had been cheering along his 'sister' Aliena with pleasant chat and happy remarks all the way. But he now admitted, "I am so tired, I could disgrace this man's apparel and cry like a woman!"

"And I can't go any further!" declared Aliena.

"Come on," said Ganymede. "Let's be strong! We're now near the end of our journey. This is the Forest of Arden."

But fake manliness and forced courage would no longer support them. Yes, they were in the Forest of Arden, but they had no idea where to find Rosalind's father.

Corin the shepherd

And here the travel of the weary ladies might have come to a sad end, lost and starving. But luck was on their side. As they were sitting on the grass, exhausted and with no hope of relief, a young shepherd happened to pass by. Ganymede tried hard to speak in a manly manner.

"Shepherd, if love or gold can bring us any relief in this deserted place, please show us to somewhere we can rest. This young girl, my sister, is so tired from traveling, and fainting for lack of food."

"Well," the man replied, "I'm only a servant to a shepherd, and my master's house is just going to be sold, along with his sheep, so I don't have much to offer you. But if you come with me, you're very welcome to what there is!"

They followed the man, whose name was Corin, the prospect of relief giving them a second wind. They liked the neat little cottage at first sight. They decided they would like to stay there until they could find out where Duke Senior was living. They asked Corin to buy the cottage and the flock of sheep from the shepherd, and they would pay for everything. They would also be happy to employ him as their shepherd and helper.

"Well," said Corin, "if you really like this place and this kind of life, I'd be happy to help you. I'll go and buy it with your gold right away!"

And so Fortune had provided them with a pleasant place to live for a while.

When they were well rested after their journey, they began to like their new way of life. They almost fancied themselves as really being a shepherd and shepherdess! Yet sometimes Ganymede remembered he had once been the Lady Rosalind who had so dearly loved the brave Orlando, the son of old Sir Rowland, her father's friend.

"Oh, I wonder where he is now and whether we will ever meet again? Only time will tell!"

Orlando and Adam

Orlando was very young when Sir Rowland de Boys passed away, and he was left in the care of his eldest brother, Oliver. His father had asked him to give Orlando a good education and provide for him in a way that matched the dignity of their noble family. But Oliver disregarded the commands of his dying father. He never sent his brother to school, but kept him at home, untaught and entirely neglected.

But in his nature and the good qualities of his mind, Orlando closely resembled his father. Even without a proper education, he appeared to be a young man who had been bred with great care. Oliver started envying the excellent personality and dignified manners of his untutored brother. And eventually he decided to destroy him! In an attempt to do just that, Oliver arranged for Orlando to be persuaded to join the palace wrestling match and fight Charles, the famous wrestler who had killed so many men. It was his cruel brother's neglect which made Orlando tell the ladies he was friendless and was willing to die.

When, contrary to Oliver's wicked hopes, Orlando won, Oliver's evil thoughts knew no bounds. His next plan was to burn down the place where Orlando slept. However, he was overheard making his vow by Adam, the old and faithful servant to their father, who loved Orlando because he resembled his father so much. The moment Orlando returned from the palace, Adam rushed out to meet him.

"Oh, my gentle master, my sweet master! Oh, you memory of Old Sir Rowland! Why are you so virtuous? Why do people love you? And how is it that you are so gentle, but also strong and brave? And why would you be so keen to defeat that famous wrestler? You see, your praise has come home before you! But remember that men's good points may become their enemies!"

"Adam, what's the matter?"

"Unhappy boy! Don't come inside. Your wicked and envious brother intends to destroy you by setting fire to this place tonight. I overheard him! The place is doomed. Don't enter!"

"But where else can I go? Can I start begging or become a thief living on the road?"

"I advise you to escape the danger right now. Dear boy, I

know you have no money. But I have five hundred crowns that I saved under your father for when my old body becomes unfit for service. Take that, and God, who feeds the ravens, will look after me in my old age! Here is the gold. I give it all to you. But I am also willing to be your servant. I may have lived for eighty years, but I'm still strong and healthy!"

"Oh, you good old man!" said Orlando, "You are an example of the true service of the good old days. You certainly don't fit the fashion of today where people will only work hard for promotion, not out of duty! Adam, I'm afraid you're pruning a rotten tree that cannot blossom! But, yes, let's go along together, and before your savings are spent, I shall find some means to support us!"

The faithful servant and his beloved master set out together.

A chance encounter

Uncertain which way to head, Orlando and Adam traveled on. And eventually they also found themselves at the Forest of Arden exhausted and hungry. They wandered bravely on, looking for some human habitation, but they couldn't find any.

At last, Adam said, "Oh, my dear master, I think I'm dying from hunger… I can't go any further!" He lay down on the grass, thinking it would be his grave. "Farewell, kind master!"

Seeing Adam in this weak state, Orlando picked him up and carried him under the shelter of a tree.

"Cheer up, Adam! Rest your weary limbs here for a while, and don't talk of dying! I'm sure there must be some kind of wild animals around here. And if one doesn't eat *me*, I will bring it back as food for *you*!"

Adam smiled and nodded. Orlando went in search of food. And then an extraordinary thing happened. By chance, he arrived at that part of the forest where the banished duke lived. He and his friends had just started eating their dinner. The duke was sitting on the grass in the shade of a very large tree.

Suddenly Orlando leapt out from the bushes, sword in hand. Hunger had made him desperate, and his idea was to take some meat by force.

"Eat no more!" Orlando shouted. "I must have some food!"

The duke looked up at him and calmly replied, "Has distress made you so bold or do you simply despise good manners?"

"Distress, yes. I'm dying of hunger!"

"I see. Well, please join us and eat. Welcome to our humble table!"

Hearing him speak so gently, Orlando sheathed his sword and blushed with shame at the rude manner in which he had demanded food.

"Please pardon me, sir," he said. "I thought that all things in this forest would be savage. That is why I was so rough. I don't know what kind of men you are that live under the trees in this wild place, forgetting the creeping hours of time. But, if you have ever seen better days, if ever you have been where church bells have rung, if you have ever sat at a good man's feast, if you have ever wiped a tear from your eyes and know what it is both to pity and be pitied, may my gentle words now move you to do me some human courtesy."

"Well, it's true that we are men who have seen better days," the duke replied, "and although we now live here in this forest, we have all lived in towns and cities, and have all been called to church by holy bells, have all sat at good men's feasts, and from all our eyes we have wiped teardrops caused by pity. So please sit down and take as much refreshment as you need."

"I thank you," replied Orlando. "But I'm not alone. There's a poor old man who has limped after me many, many weary steps out of pure love. He is suffering right now from two sad issues, age and hunger. I cannot touch anything until he is cared for."

"I see," said the duke. "Well, by all means bring him here, and we will eat nothing ourselves until you return."

"Oh, thank you, sir, for your kindness!"

Orlando went off like a doe to find its fawn and give it food. And presently he returned, carrying Adam in his arms.

"Welcome, both of you!" said the duke.

They fed Adam and cheered him up. His strength soon returned.

The duke then asked Orlando about his background. When he discovered that he was the son of his old friend, Sir Rowland de Boys, he said, "Well, well! Good Sir Rowland's son! Yes, I can see a strong likeness! You are truly welcome. I am the duke that loved your father!"

The duke took Orlando under his protection, and he and Adam started living with him and his men in the forest.

Carvings and love poems

Orlando arrived in the forest not so long after Ganymede and Aliena.

One day, when Ganymede and Aliena went out for a walk, they were surprised to find the name 'Rosalind' everywhere. It was carved on some trees, and love sonnets addressed to Rosalind were fastened to others. And just as they were wondering what this could possibly mean, who should they meet but Orlando himself! And they noticed the chain Rosalind had given him was still around his neck.

Of course, it was Orlando who passed his time carving Rosalind's name on the trees and writing sonnets in praise of her beauty. He never imagined that the charming young shepherd Ganymede was really her. But he liked the graceful way he spoke and entered into conversation with him. Ganymede started talking to Orlando about some mysterious person who haunted the forest.

"This lover" said he, "haunts our forest, and is spoiling our young trees by carving 'Rosalind' in their bark! He also hangs love poems on hawthorns, and elegies on brambles, all praising this same Rosalind. If I could just find this lover, I'd give him some good advice that would soon cure him of his love!"

Orlando confessed that *he* was the fond lover writing the poems, and he asked Ganymede to give him the good advice he'd mentioned. Ganymede suggested he should come every day to the cottage where he and his sister lived.

"And then," he said, "I will pretend to be this Rosalind, and

you can pretend to court me in the same manner as you would do if I really *was* Rosalind! Then I will imitate the fantastic ways ladies react to their lovers, until I make you ashamed of your love. That is how I propose to cure you."

The remedy

Orlando didn't have much faith in the effectiveness of this suggested remedy, but he agreed to visit the cottage to fake a playful courtship. He called Ganymede his Rosalind, and every day discussed all the fine words and compliments young men like to use when courting a lady. Ganymede did not, however, seem to be making any progress in curing Orlando of his love.

Orlando regarded it all as a fun kind of game. But at the same time, it did give him the chance to say all the fond things he felt in his heart. It also pleased Ganymede, who enjoyed the secret jest, knowing Orlando's fine love speeches were all addressed to the right person!

The young people passed many pleasant days in this way. Seeing it made Ganymede so happy, the good-natured Aliena let him have his own way. She decided not to remind Ganymede that Rosalind had not yet made herself known to the duke her father. They had learned his location in the forest from Orlando.

Then one day, Ganymede happened to meet the duke and they had a chat. The duke asked about her family. Ganymede replied that he came from as good a family as the duke. This made the duke laugh, for he didn't think the pretty young shepherd boy could have royal blood in him. Seeing the duke look so well and happy, Ganymede was content to put off any further explanation a little longer.

A snake and a lioness

One morning, as Orlando was on his way to visit Ganymede, he saw a man lying asleep on the ground with a large green snake twisted around his neck. Noticing Orlando, the snake glided away among the bushes. Orlando went nearer, and then saw there was a lioness crouching nearby, with her head on the ground. Orlando remembered hearing that lions will not prey on anything dead or asleep. She was presumably waiting for the man to wake up.

Well, it seemed to Orlando as if he had been sent by Providence to save the man from the danger of attack by wild animals. But when he looked closely, he was very surprised to see it was his cruel brother Oliver! For a moment, Orlando was tempted to leave him there as a prey for the hungry lioness. But brotherly affection and his gentle nature soon ended that idea. He drew his sword and attacked the lioness. She tore one of his arms with her sharp claws, but he managed to kill her.

Oliver woke up just in time to see his brother saving him from the fury of a wild beast at the risk of his own life. Feelings of shame and remorse flooded over him. With many tears, he sought Orlando's pardon for the injuries he had done him. Orlando rejoiced to see him so penitent, and readily forgave him. They embraced each other. Oliver had come to the forest bent on chasing down Orlando, but now he was a changed man. From that moment, he loved him with true brotherly affection.

Orlando's arm had stopped bleeding, but he felt too weak to go to Ganymede's cottage.

"Oliver, please go and tell Ganymede, who in sport I call Rosalind, what has happened."

Aliena

Oliver bound up his brother's arm and then set off for the cottage following Orlando's directions. He soon found it. He told Ganymede and Aliena how Orlando had saved his life. Hearing of the danger Orlando had been in, and that he had been injured, Ganymede fainted. When he recovered, he pretended he had faked the swoon in the character of Rosalind.

He said to Oliver, "Tell your brother how well I pretended to faint!"

But Oliver saw by the paleness of his complexion that he really did faint. Wondering at the weakness of the young man, he said, "Well, if you did fake it, fake a man's heart as well."

"Yes," replied Ganymede. "I feel I should have been a woman!"

When Oliver had finished the story of Orlando's bravery and his own lucky escape, he revealed that he was the eldest brother who had so cruelly used him. And he happily told them of their reconciliation.

The sincere sorrow that Oliver expressed for his offenses made a very strong impression on the kind heart of Aliena. In fact, she instantly fell in love with him! When Oliver noticed how much she pitied his distress, he just as suddenly fell in love with *her*!

Oliver made the visit rather long, and when at last he returned to his brother he had many things to tell him. Besides telling him about Ganymede's 'fake swoon' when he heard Orlando was injured, Oliver revealed that he'd fallen in love with the pretty shepherdess Aliena. He said she had been favorable to his suit, even at their first meeting! He talked as if marrying her was almost settled.

"I love her so much, Orlando, that I intend to live here as a shepherd and pass on my estate and house back home to you!"

"Well, you have my consent, of course," said Orlando. "Let your wedding be tomorrow, and I will invite the duke and his friends. Please go and persuade your shepherdess to agree to that. I think she's now alone, because here comes her brother!"

Oliver left in a hurry.

Magic

Ganymede had come to inquire after the health of his injured friend. They started to discuss the amazing mutual love at first sight which had occurred between Oliver and Aliena.

"Yes," said Ganymede, "there's never been anything quite so fast, apart from Caesar's boast 'I came, I saw, I conquered'!"

Orlando said he'd advised his brother to persuade his shepherdess to be married the next day. He added how much he wished he could be married on the same day to his Rosalind.

"How bitter it is," he said, "to see happiness through another man's eyes!"

Ganymede said that if Orlando really loved Rosalind as much as he said he did, he deserved to have his wish granted. Ganymede would ensure that Rosalind appeared in person, and she would be only too willing to marry Orlando. He pretended he could make this unbelievable event happen by the aid of magic, which he had learned since the age of three from an uncle who was a famous magician.

"Are you serious?" said Orlando, only half believing what he'd just heard.

"Oh, yes!" replied Ganymede. "So put on your best clothes, and bid the duke and your friends to *your* wedding as well. If you really want to be married tomorrow to Rosalind, I can guarantee she will be there!"

A double marriage

Oliver had obtained the consent of Aliena, so the next morning at the scheduled time they stood before the duke. Orlando was with them. Everyone was there to celebrate a double marriage, but so far only one bride had appeared. There was a lot of conjecture going on. Most of them thought that Ganymede had been making fun of Orlando.

Hearing that it was his own daughter that was supposed to appear in this strange way, the duke asked Orlando if he believed the shepherd boy could really do what he'd promised. Orlando was just replying that he didn't know what to think, when Ganymede himself appeared and addressed the duke.

"Sir, if I bring your daughter here, will you consent to her marriage to Orlando?"

"I will," he replied, "and I would even if I had whole kingdoms to give her!"

Ganymede then said to Orlando, "And will you marry her if I bring her here?"

"I will," said Orlando, "and I would even if I were the king of all kingdoms!"

Ganymede and Aliena then went out of sight together. In no time at all, Ganymede threw off his male garb, and once more dressed like a woman. He became Rosalind without the power of magic. As for Aliena, she rapidly switched from her country garb into her own rich clothes, and once again became Lady Celia.

While they were gone, the duke said to Orlando, "You know, that shepherd Ganymede somehow reminded me of my daughter Rosalind!"

Orlando said he had also noticed a resemblance.

But they had no more time to wonder how all this would end. At that moment, Rosalind and Celia appeared as themselves in their own clothes. Orlando could not believe his eyes when he saw Rosalind. She was really there!

No longer pretending that she'd arrived there by the power of magic, Rosalind threw herself on her knees before her father and begged his blessing. It seemed so wonderful to all present that she should so suddenly appear, it might well have passed for magic! But Rosalind would no longer trifle with her father. She quickly told him the story of her banishment, and of living in the forest as a shepherd boy, with her cousin Celia passing as her sister.

The duke repeated the consent he had already given to her marriage. And so Rosalind and Orlando de Boys and Celia and Oliver de Boys were married at the same time. Even though their weddings could not be celebrated in the wild forest with any of the usual parade of splendor, there was never a happier wedding day.

But that is not quite the end of the story.

Breaking news

They all sat enjoying eating the feast of venison under the cool shade of the trees. It seemed as though nothing was missing to complete the happiness of the good duke and the newly-weds. But suddenly an unexpected messenger arrived. He told the duke the joyful news that his dukedom had been restored to him!

Frederick, the usurper, had been enraged at the flight of his daughter. He had also heard that every day men of great worth were heading to the Forest of Arden to join the lawful duke. He was very envious that his brother was so highly respected. So Frederick put himself at the head of a large force and advanced toward the forest. He intended to seize his brother and kill him and all his faithful followers.

But once again Providence had stepped in. Just as Frederick entered the forest, he met an old religious man, a hermit. They had a lengthy talk which in the end completely turned Frederick's heart away from his wicked design. He became a true penitent. He resolved to spend the remainder of his days in a religious house. The first act of his penitence was to send a messenger to his brother to offer to restore to him his dukedom, which be had usurped for so long, as well as the lands and revenues of all his faithful followers.

This joyful news, as unexpected as it was welcome, came at a perfect time to raise the wedding festivities to an even higher level. Celia graciously congratulated her cousin on her father's good fortune and wished her every joy. She herself was no longer heir to the dukedom, but she was so happy that Rosalind had now been restored to her rightful role as heir. The love of the two cousins was untainted by any hint of jealousy or envy.

Duke Senior now had the opportunity to reward all his true friends who had stayed with him during his banishment and patiently shared his bad fortune. And they were all delighted to return to peace and prosperity in the palace of their lawful duke.

06

The Merchant of Venice

ヴェニスの商人

読み始める前に

ユダヤ人が差別されていた時代の物語。高利貸しシャイロックはユダヤ人で、キリスト教徒を憎んでいた。「ヴェニスの商人」とはアントーニオを指す。

［登場人物］

Antonio	アントーニオ《貿易商人》
Shylock	シャイロック《ユダヤ人の金貸し》
Portia	ポーシャ《裕福な貴婦人》
Bassanio	バサーニオ《貴族、アントーニオの親友》
Nerissa	ネリッサ《ポーシャの侍女》
Bellario	ベラーリオ《ポーシャの親戚で法律家》
Doctor Balthasar	バルサザー博士《ポーシャの変装名》
Lorenzo	ロレンゾ《シャイロックの娘の夫でアントーニオの友人》
Gratiano	グラシアーノ《アントーニオとバサーニオの友人》

［地名など］

Belmont	ベルモント《ポーシャの住む屋敷》
Rialto	リアルト橋《ヴェニスの橋》
Tripoli	トリポリ《都市》
Venice	ヴェニス《イタリアの都市》

［あらすじ］

舞台はイタリアのヴェニス。資産家の娘ポーシャに求婚するために金が必要なバサーニオは、友人の貿易商人アントーニオから借りようとするが、あいにくアントーニオは持ちあわせがない。そこでアントーニオは悪名高い高利貸しのシャイロックに金を借りに行く。貿易船が戻って来れば借金はすぐに返すことができるのだ。

シャイロックはアントーニオに「無利子で貸す。ただし、期限内に返済できなければ、利子の代わりにお前の体から肉1ポンドを切り取る」という条件を出す。

バサーニオのポーシャへの求婚は成功するが、そこへアントーニオから、貿易船が全部難破し、金を返す期限が切れてしまったという知らせが入る。

［総単語数］4,580語

THE MERCHANT OF VENICE

Once upon a time, a Jewish money-lender named Shylock lived in Venice in Italy. He had made a fortune by lending money at great interest to mostly Christian merchants. Being a hard-hearted man who exacted the payment of the money he lent with severity, Shylock was disliked by many men. One of them was Antonio, a generous Venetian merchant who owned several ships and conducted international trade. Shylock hated Antonio because he would lend money to people in distress and never take any interest from them. And whenever Antonio met Shylock in the commercial center around the famous Rialto bridge, he would strongly reproach him for his hard deals. Shylock would bear the insults with apparent patience, but secretly he thought about revenge.

A noble young friend

Antonio was a very kind and courteous man who seemed to represent the ancient Roman sense of honor. He was greatly liked by his fellow Venetians. But the friend who was nearest and dearest to his heart was Bassanio, a young nobleman. He had only inherited a small patrimony, and had nearly exhausted that by living in a manner that was too expensive for his slender means. Whenever Bassanio wanted money, Antonio gladly assisted him. It seemed as if they had just one heart and one purse between them.

One day, Bassanio came to Antonio and told him that he wished to marry a wealthy lady he dearly loved. Her father, who had recently died, had left her as sole heiress to a large estate. Bassanio explained that when her father was alive he had visited their mansion several times. And every time he saw his daughter, her eyes sent speechless messages that seemed to say he would not be unwelcome as her suitor! But he did not have enough money to give himself a suitable appearance for a suitor of so rich an heiress. So he was visiting Antonio to ask him to add to the many favors he'd already shown him by lending him three thousand gold ducats, a very large sum of money.

"Well, Bassanio, as you know," said Antonio, "my fortunes are all at sea at present, so I cannot raise such money right now. However, I'm expecting some of my ships to come home soon filled with valuable goods. But I can go to Shylock, the rich money-lender, and borrow the money on the credit of those ships."

3,000 ducats

Antonio and Bassanio went together to see Shylock. Antonio asked the Jew to lend him three thousand ducats for three months on any interest he required, to be paid by the cargoes being carried by his ships.

"Three thousand ducats?"

"Yes."

"For three months?"

"Yes."

For a while, Shylock was silent. He was thinking to himself, "Hmm, if I can drag Antonio down just once, I will feed my old grudge against him… He hates us Jews, he lends out money for free, and that reduces my well-earned percentage, which he calls 'interest'. No, I will never forgive him!"

Antonio was waiting a long time for a reply. He was anxious to have the money, so at last he said, "Shylock, did you hear? Will you lend me the money?"

"Signor Antonio," replied Shylock, "on the Rialto you have often railed at me about my money-lending business. I have borne your insults with a patient shrug, for suffering is the badge of we Jews. You have called me an 'unbeliever' and a 'cut-throat dog'. You have spit on my Jewish clothes, and kicked me as if I were a dog. Well, it *now* appears you need my help, and you come to me and you say, 'Shylock, lend me some money.' Does a dog have money? Is it possible that a 'cut-throat dog' would lend three thousand ducats? Shall I bend low and say, 'Oh, sir, you spit on me last Wednesday, and another time you called me dog, and for these kind courtesies I will lend you money?' "

"Well, Shylock," replied Antonio, "I may call you the same things again and spit on you, and spurn you, too. If you are prepared to lend me this money, don't lend it to me as to a *friend*, but rather as to an *enemy*. Then if I fail to repay you, it may be easier to exact the penalty!"

"Oh," said Shylock, "don't get so angry! I want to be friends with you. But I must consider your credit… I understand you have a ship heading to Tripoli, another to India, a third to Mexico, a fourth to England, and other ventures overseas. But ships are only made of wooden boards, and sailors are just men. There are land rats and water rats, there are land thieves and water thieves…'pirates'! Ha-ha… And then there are the dangers of water, winds and rocks… Three thousand ducats, hmm… Well, Antonio, I will forget your insults. I will supply your money and I will take *no* interest."

This apparently kind offer surprised Antonio. Still pretending to be kind, Shylock said, "So, Antonio, you must go with me to a lawyer and there, in merry sport, sign a bond that if you do not repay the money by a certain day three months from now, you will forfeit…a pound of flesh, to be cut off from any part of your body that I wish!"

"I see," said Antonio, swallowing hard. "Alright, I will sign to this bond, and say there is much kindness in Shylock."

"No, Antonio," said Bassanio, "do not sign such a bond for me!"

"Don't worry! Within the next two months, I expect my ships to return with goods worth much more than three thousand ducats! So I will sign the bond."

"Oh," said Shylock, "how suspicious you Christians are! Your own tough deals make you suspect others. Bassanio, if Antonio breaks his bond, what good would it do me? A pound of man's flesh is worth less than that of mutton or beef. I say again, I simply offer this favor in friendship. If he will take it, fine. If he will not, adieu!"

And so Antonio signed the bond, thinking it really was merely in sport.

Revenge

A few days later, Shylock bumped into two of Antonio's merchant friends by the Rialto. Word of the strange bond had traveled around fast.

One of them said, "Shylock, you don't *really* intend to take a pound of flesh, do you? What's that good for?"

"Ha, to bait fish with!" replied Shylock. "And if it will feed nothing else, it will at least feed my revenge. Antonio has disgraced me, laughed at my losses, mocked at my gains, cooled my friends, and heated my enemies. Why? Because I am a Jew. Doesn't a Jew have eyes, hands, senses, affections, passions? We eat the same food, are hurt with the same weapons, are subject to the same diseases, are healed by the same means, and warmed and cooled by the same summers and winters as Christians are. If you prick us, we bleed. If you tickle us, we laugh. If you poison us, we die. And if you wrong us, shouldn't we take revenge? We resemble you in that, too! If a Jew wrongs a Christian, how does he react? Revenge. If a Christian wrongs a Jew, how should he react, following the Christian example? Why, with revenge!"

The rich heiress of Belmont

The rich heiress that Bassanio hoped to marry lived in a fine mansion at a quiet place called Belmont, about fifteen kilometers from Venice. Her name was Portia, and she was a highly intelligent woman of great grace.

Kindly supplied with money by Antonio risking his life, Bassanio set out for Belmont with his friend Gratiano and a splendid train of servants. And he proved successful. Portia quickly consented to accept him as her husband.

Bassanio confessed to Portia that he had no fortune and that all he could boast of was his noble family. But Portia was rich enough not to worry about her husband's lack of wealth. She loved him for his excellent qualities. With a graceful modesty, she replied that she would wish herself a thousand times better-looking, and ten thousand times richer, in order to be more worthy of him. Then she told him she lacked learning and experience, but she was very willing to learn. She would commit her gentle spirit to his direction in all things.

"Yesterday," she concluded, "I was the lady of this beautiful mansion, queen of myself, and mistress over all these servants. But now the house, the servants, and myself are all yours! I give them to you with this ring." She handed Bassanio a ring.

Taking the ring, Bassanio vowed never to part with it. He was overcome with gratitude and wonder at the elegant manner in which the rich and noble Portia accepted a man of his humble means. He could only reply with broken words of love and thanks.

Gratiano and Nerissa, Portia's maid, were present when Portia promised to marry Bassanio. Gratiano wished them joy, and asked their permission for him to be married at the same time.

"With all my heart, Gratiano," said Bassanio, "if you can find a wife!"

Gratiano told them that he loved Nerissa, and that she'd promised to be his wife if her mistress married Bassanio. Portia asked Nerissa if this was true.

"Madam, it is, yes, if you will approve it."

Portia willingly consented.

And Bassanio said, "Then *our* wedding feast will be much honored by *yours* as well!"

A letter from Venice

At this moment, the happiness of the lovers was sadly interrupted by the arrival of a messenger. He had brought a letter from Antonio containing bad news. When Bassanio read the letter, he looked so pale that Portia feared it was to tell him of the death of some dear friend.

"What is the news that has upset you so much?"

"Oh, sweet Portia, here are some of the worst words that ever blotted paper! When I first imparted my love to you, I freely told you that all the wealth I had was in my veins. But I should have told you that I had less than nothing. I was in debt."

Bassanio then told Portia about borrowing money from Antonio, and the bond of a pound of flesh. Then he read Antonio's letter out loud.

"Dear Bassanio, my ships are all lost, and my bond to Shylock is forfeited. Since paying it will surely kill me, I wish I could see you before my death."

"Oh, my dear love," said Portia, "you must go at once! Before this kind friend shall lose one hair by your fault, I will happily give you gold to pay the money twenty times over. As you are so dearly bought, I will dearly love you!"

Portia said Bassanio had to be her husband to give him the legal right to her money. So that afternoon they were married, along with Gratiano and Nerissa. Then the two new husbands set out in great haste for Venice.

They found Antonio already in prison, as the day of payment had passed. Refusing to accept the money Bassanio offered him, Shylock insisted on claiming a pound of Antonio's flesh. The day was appointed to try the shocking case in front of the Duke of Venice. Bassanio waited the outcome in dreadful suspense.

Portia's plan

Portia spoke cheerfully as her husband left, and told him to bring his dear friend Antonio back with him when he returned. But she feared the trial would go badly for Antonio. As soon as she was left alone, she began to consider if there was any way she could help to save his life. She had told Bassanio that she would be governed in all things by his superior wisdom. But now she had to rely on her own power and judgment. She decided to go to Venice and speak in Antonio's defense.

Portia had a relation who was an expert on law, named Bellario. She wrote to him at once, explaining Antonio's case. She asked for his opinion, and requested him to send her the clothes worn by a trial defense lawyer. When the messenger returned, he brought advice from Bellario on how to proceed and all the items that Portia needed.

Portia and Nerissa both dressed up in male clothes and caps to hide their hair. She put on the cap and robes of a defense lawyer and took Nerissa along as her clerk. They set out immediately and arrived in Venice on the very day of the trial.

The trial

The trial was just about to be begin in front of the Duke and the senators in the Senate House, the city's high court of justice. Well disguised by her robes and large wig, Portia entered and presented a letter from Bellario to the Duke. It said that he was prevented by sickness from being there himself to plead for Antonio. He requested that the learned young Doctor Balthasar (which is what he called Portia), his best student from Rome, might be allowed to take his place.

Bellario had added, "He knows my opinion on the case and I cannot commend him enough. I have never known anyone so young to have such an old and wise head!"

The Duke agreed to accept Doctor Balthasar, and the trial began.

Portia looked around the court and saw the merciless Shylock. She also saw Bassanio, who didn't recognize her, standing beside Antonio looking distressed and afraid. The importance of the tough task Portia had given herself gave her courage. She proceeded boldly.

"Is your name Shylock?"

"It is."

"Your suit is unusual, but you have the right by Venetian law to have the forfeit expressed in the bond. Are you Antonio?"

"I am."

"Do you confess to signing the bond."

"I do."

"Then Shylock must be merciful."

"Why?"

"Because the noble quality of mercy drops like gentle rain from heaven. It has a double blessing. It blesses both those that give it and those that receive it. Being an attribute of God himself, it suits kings better than their crowns. We all *pray* for mercy, and we should all *show* it."

"I simply wish to have the penalty written in the bond," Shylock replied.

"Is Antonio unable to pay the money?" asked Portia.

Bassanio then stepped forward and offered the Jew the payment of the three thousand ducats as many times over as he desired. Shylock refused, still insisting on having the pound of flesh. Bassanio begged the learned young lawyer to fudge the law a little to save Antonio's life. Portia answered gravely that once a law was established it could not be altered.

It seemed to Shylock that she was pleading in his favor, and he said, "Oh, wise young judge, I honor you! How much older are you in wisdom than your looks!"

Portia now asked Shylock to let her look at the bond. When she had read it, she said, "This bond is forfeited, and Shylock may lawfully claim a pound of Antonio's flesh near his heart." But then she said to Shylock, "Be merciful. Take the money and I will destroy the bond."

But Shylock intended to show no mercy. "I swear there is no power in the tongue of any man to make me change my mind!"

"In that case, Antonio," said Portia, "you must prepare your chest for the knife."

While Shylock was eagerly sharpening his long knife, Portia said to Antonio, "Do you have anything to say?"

With a feeling of calm resignation, Antonio replied that he had little to say, as he'd prepared his mind to die. Then he said to Bassanio, "Give me your hand, good friend! Farewell! Do not grieve that I have fallen into this misfortune for you. Please give my kind regards to your wife and tell her how much I have loved you!"

"Antonio," Bassanio replied, "I am married to a wife who is as dear to me as life itself. But life, my wife, and all the world are not esteemed more than *your* life. I would be willing to lose everything to deliver you from this devil here."

Although she was moved, Portia could not help murmuring, "If your wife was here, I don't think she would give you thanks for saying that!"

Gratiano, who loved to copy whatever Bassanio did, thought

he should say something as well. In Nerissa's hearing, he said, "And I have a wife whom I protest I love. But I only wish she were in heaven to entreat some power to change the cruel manner of this Jew."

"It's good you wished this behind her back," murmured Nerissa, "or you would have trouble at home!"

Shylock now cried out, impatiently, "We are wasting time! Please pronounce the sentence."

The court went very quiet. All hearts except Shylock's were beating hard, filled with grief for Antonio.

A pound of flesh

Portia asked if the scales were ready to weigh the flesh. Then she said, "Shylock, you must have a doctor standing by, to stop him bleeding to death."

Shylock, whose whole intent was that Antonio *should* bleed to death, said, "It does not say that in the bond."

Portia replied, "You are right, but what of that? It would be good if you could do that out of pity."

To this, all Shylock could reply was, "I cannot find it. It's not in the bond."

"Then," said Portia, "a pound of Antonio's flesh is yours. And you may cut this flesh from off his chest. The law allows it and the court awards it."

Again, Shylock cried, "Oh, wise and upright judge!" He gave his knife another quick sharpen, and looked eagerly at Antonio. "Prepare yourself!"

Bassanio and Gratiano held Antonio tight as Shylock moved over toward him with his knife.

"One moment, Shylock," Portia suddenly said. Shylock stopped and looked at her. "There is something else. This bond gives you no drops of blood. The words expressly are, 'a pound of flesh.' If, in cutting off the pound of flesh, you shed just one drop of Christian blood, your lands and goods will by the law be confiscated to the State of Venice."

It was, of course, impossible for Shylock *not* to shed any blood. So this wise intervention of Portia saved Antonio's life. Everyone in the Senate House breathed a sigh of relief and praised the wisdom of the young lawyer.

Gratiano exclaimed, in Shylock's own words, "Oh, wise and upright judge!"

Finding himself defeated, Shylock said that he would take the money. And Bassanio, rejoicing at Antonio's unexpected deliverance, cried out, "Here it is!"

But Portia stopped him. "Softly, please. There is no hurry. The Jew shall have nothing but the penalty. So prepare, Shylock, to cut off the flesh. But mind you shed no blood. And one more thing: do not cut off either more nor less than one pound exactly. If the scales turn by just the weight of a single hair, you are condemned by the laws of Venice to die, and all your wealth will go to the State."

"Give me my money and let me go," replied Shylock.

"I have it ready," said Bassanio. "Here it is."

Shylock was about to take the money when Portia stopped

him again. "Wait, Shylock! I have yet another hold on you. By the laws of Venice, your wealth is forfeited to the State for having conspired to take the life of one of its citizens. Your life lies at the mercy of the Duke. So, get down on your knees and ask him to pardon you."

Shylock knelt in front of the Duke, his head bowed.

The Duke said, "Shylock, so that you may see the difference of our Christian spirit, I pardon you your life before you ask for it. Half your wealth will go to Antonio, the other half will come to the State."

The generous Antonio then said that he would give up his share of the wealth if Shylock would sign a deed for the money to be given at his death to his daughter and her husband. Antonio knew that Shylock had an only daughter who had recently married, against his consent, a young Christian named Lorenzo, a friend of Antonio's. Shylock had been so upset, he had disinherited his daughter.

Shylock agreed, and said, "I am feeling ill. Let me go home. Send the deed after me, and I will sign it."

"Shylock," said the Duke, "if you repent your cruelty and turn *Christian*, the State will forgive you the fine of the other half of your riches."

Shylock said nothing and left.

Some reward

The Duke now released Antonio and dismissed the court. He then highly praised the wisdom and skill of Doctor Balthasar and invited him home to dinner.

Portia, who was anxious to return to Belmont before her husband, replied, "I humbly thank Your Grace, but I must leave at once."

The Duke turned to Antonio and said, "You should reward this young gentleman, for you are greatly indebted to him."

The Duke and his senators left the court.

Then Bassanio said to Portia, "Most worthy gentleman, my friend Antonio and I have by your wisdom been acquitted of terrible penalties. We beg you to accept the three thousand ducats that was due to the Jew in the bond."

"And," added Antonio, "we shall be indebted to you for ever!"

"They are well paid that are well satisfied," replied Portia. "Having saved you, I am fully satisfied. And so I regard myself as having been well paid! I hope you know me the next time we meet. I wish you well, and so adieu."

Portia could not be persuaded to accept the money. But when Bassanio pressed her to accept some reward, she said, "Give me your gloves, then. I will wear them for your sake! And, for your love, I will take that ring from you. Nothing more."

Bassanio was disturbed by the young man asking him for the only thing he could *not* part with! In great confusion, he replied that it was impossible to give him that ring. It was only a cheap thing, and his wife's gift that he had vowed never to part with. But he would happily search instead for the most valuable ring in Venice.

Portia pretended to be offended. She left the court, saying, "You asked me to beg, but you've proved that beggars can't be choosers!"

"Dear Bassanio," said Antonio, "let him have the ring. Let my love and the great service he has done for me be valued against your wife's displeasure."

Ashamed to appear so ungrateful, Bassanio yielded, and sent Gratiano after Portia with the ring. And then the 'clerk', Nerissa, who had also given her husband a ring, begged *his* ring. Not wishing to be outdone in generosity by Bassanio, Gratiano gave it to her.

As the ladies traveled back to Belmont, they laughed at the prospect of accusing both their husbands of giving away their rings as a present to some woman!

Home again

Having performed such a good action, Portia was in a happy frame of mind when she got home. Her cheerful spirit affected everything she saw. The moon seemed to shine brighter than ever before, and the light coming from her house looked charming.

"That light we can see is from the little candle burning in the hall," she said to Nerissa. "How far it throws its beams! So shines a good deed in a naughty world." And hearing the sound of music, she said, "I also think that music sounds much sweeter at night!"

Portia and Nerissa entered the house, and quickly dressed themselves in their normal clothes to await the arrival of their husbands. They soon came, along with Antonio. Bassanio introduced his dear friend to Portia. All the greetings and congratulations were hardly over when they noticed Nerissa and her husband quarreling in a corner of the room.

"A quarrel already?" said Portia. "What's the matter?"

"Well," Gratiano replied, "it's about a paltry gilt ring that Nerissa gave me, with the simple words 'Love me and leave me not' carved on it!"

"What does the poetry or the value have to do with it?" said Nerissa. "When I gave it to you, you swore that you would keep it till the moment of your death. And now you claim you gave it to a lawyer's clerk! I think you gave it to a woman!"

"No, no," replied Gratiano, "I swear that I gave it to a youth, no taller than yourself. He was the clerk to the young lawyer that saved Antonio's life. He begged it as a fee, and I couldn't deny him!"

"Gratiano," said Portia, "you are to blame for parting with your wife's first gift. I also gave my Lord Bassanio a ring, and I'm sure he wouldn't part with it for all the world!"

Gratiano tried to excuse himself. "But Bassanio first gave his ring to the lawyer, and then his clerk begged my ring!"

Hearing this, Portia pretended to be very angry with Bassanio. "What! You gave away my precious ring? Like

Nerissa, I think some woman now has it!"

Bassanio said he was very unhappy to have offended his dear wife, and added, "No, I swear that no woman has it, but the lawyer who refused the three thousand ducats. He begged to have the ring, and at first I refused. But he went away displeased. Sweet Portia, what could I do? I felt ashamed, and I was forced to send the ring after him. Pardon me, dear wife! Had you been there, I'm sure you would have begged the ring of me to give the worthy lawyer."

"Oh dear!" said Antonio, "I am the unhappy cause of these quarrels."

Portia kindly told Antonio not to concern himself about that.

"You see," continued Antonio, "I lent my body for Bassanio's sake. And only the young man to whom your husband gave the ring saved me from certain death! I am quite sure your lord will never break his faith with you ever again."

"Then you can be his guarantor!" said Portia. "Please give him this ring and tell him to keep it better than the other one."

Antonio handed the ring to Bassanio. He examined it carefully. He was amazed to realize it was the one he had given away. And so Portia explained to him all that she and Nerissa had done. To his great surprise and delight, he discovered that Antonio's life had been saved by the wisdom of his wonderful wife. And, in fact, it was true that both he and Gratiano had given their ring to a woman!

Then some very good news arrived for Antonio. His ships that were believed lost had arrived safely in Venice. So the tragic beginnings of the rich merchant's story could all be forgotten with this unexpected good fortune. And now they were all at leisure to laugh at husbands who could not recognize their own wives and the comical adventure of the rings. Gratiano wrote and sang a merry little jingle:

While I live, I'll fear no other thing
So much as keeping safe Nerissa's ring!

07

King Lear

リア王

読み始める前に

シェイクスピア四大悲劇のひとつで、悲劇の最高峰と評されている。リア王が半狂乱になり嵐の荒野をさまよう場面は壮絶で圧巻。

［登場人物］

Lear	リア王《ブリテン王》
Cordelia	コーデリア《リアの末娘》
Goneril	ゴネリル《リアの長女》
Regan	リーガン《リアの次女》
Caius	カイアス《ケント伯の変装名。リアに仕える》
Earl of Kent	ケント伯《リアの忠臣》
Fool	道化《リア付きの道化師》
Duke of Albany	オルバニー公《ゴネリルの夫》
King of France	フランス王《コーディリアの求婚者》
Duke of Burgundy	バーガンディー公《コーディリアの求婚者》
Duke of Cornwall	コーンウォール公《リーガンの夫》
Edmund	エドマンド《グロスター伯の庶子》
Edgar	エドガー《グロスター伯の嫡子》
Earl of Gloucester	グロスター伯《エドマンドのこと》
late Earl of Gloucester	故グロスター伯《エドガーとエドマンドの父》

［地名など］

Albany	オールバニー《地名》	Dover	ドーバー《港町》
Burgundy	バーガンディ《地名》	Gloucester	グロスター《地名》
Cornwall	コーンウォール《地名》	Kent	ケント《地名》

［あらすじ］

ブリテン王リアは、高齢のため退位するにあたり、3人の娘たちの中で自分への愛情が最も深い者から順番に領土を与えることにする。

長女ゴネリルと次女リーガンは、言葉巧みに王を誉めそやし喜ばせるが、末娘のコーデリアは、父への感謝の気持ちを述べるのみでお世辞を言わない。王は腹を立てて末娘を勘当し、それをかばったケント伯も追放される。

領土を得た途端に本性を現わし王をさげすむ二人の姉娘。リア王は後悔の念にかられ狂いだすのだった。

［総単語数］4,460語

KING LEAR

Once upon a time, there was a King of Britain called Lear. He had three daughters. The eldest one, Goneril, was married to the Duke of Albany. The middle one, Regan, was married to the Duke of Cornwall. The youngest, Cordelia, was still single, but two noble suitors had come to Lear's court in the hope of marrying her. One was the King of France and the other was the Duke of Burgundy.

The younger generation

The old king, who was now over eighty years old, was worn out with age and the fatigue of governing his country. One day, he asked his three daughters to meet him. They all stood around a map of Britain as Lear explained that he had decided to take no further part in the management of state affairs, but to leave it all to the younger generation. Then he would have some time to prepare for his death.

"Tell me, my daughters," he said, "which of you loves me most? I wish to hear from your own lips, so that I can divide the kingdom into such proportions as your affection deserves."

Goneril spoke first.

"Father, I love you more than words can express. You are dearer to me than life and liberty!"

The king was delighted to hear this declaration of her love. Thinking it truly came from her heart, in a fit of fatherly fondness he bestowed on her and her husband one third of the kingdom.

Regan spoke next.

"What my sister said comes short of the love which *I* bear for Your Highness. I find all other joys dead in comparison with the pleasure which I take in the love of my dear king and father."

Lear was delighted to have such loving children. He bestowed a third of his kingdom on her and her husband, equal in size to that which he had given to Goneril.

Then he turned to his favorite, Cordelia, who he called his joy, and asked her what she had to say.

"Nothing, my lord."

"Nothing?" said the king in surprise.

"Nothing."

"Nothing will come of nothing! Speak again."

"I love Your Majesty according to my *duty*, neither more nor less."

"What? Consider carefully what you are saying or it may spoil your fortunes!"

"Dear father, you brought me up and have loved me. I return those duties back as appropriate. I obey you, I love you, and I honor you. But I cannot frame my mouth to such big speeches as my sisters have done, or promise to love nothing else in the world. Why do my sisters have husbands if they say they have no love for anything but their *father*? If I ever get married, I am sure my husband will want half my love and half of my care and duty. I shall never marry like my sisters, to love *only* my father."

"Is this what your heart truly feels?"

"Yes, Father."

"You are so young, but so hard!"

"So young, Father, but honest."

"Then your truth will be your dowry! You are no longer my daughter!"

Cordelia's plainness of speech, which Lear called 'pride', so enraged the king that he divided the third part of his kingdom, which he had reserved for Cordelia, between her two sisters.

He now called Goneril and Regan to him and placed a coronet on each of their heads, investing them jointly with all the power, finances, and operation of government. He only kept for himself the *name* of king. Everything else he gave up, with the one important reservation that he was to be accommodated at each of his daughters' castles with his one hundred knights as attendants, on alternate months.

A true servant

The courtiers were all filled with astonishment and sorrow at the king's ridiculous disposal of his kingdom, guided much more by passion than by reason. But none of them had the courage to speak to the angry king except the Earl of Kent.

He began to say some good words on Cordelia's behalf. But the passionate Lear ordered him to stop on pain of death. However, the good Kent would not give up so easily. He had always been loyal to Lear, honoring him as a king, loving him as a father, following him as a master. He had never even feared to lose his life to save the king. But now that Lear was his own worst enemy, this faithful servant forgot his old principles, and opposed the king to do the king good. He only lacked manners because Lear seemed to have gone mad.

Kent had been a most faithful advisor to the king, and he pleaded with him to follow his advice and change his mind. He said he was sure he was right in believing Cordelia did not love him the least. He told the king that power must not bow to flattery. And Lear's threats could not harm him as his life was already in the king's hands.

Kent's honest words only stirred up the king's anger more. Like a desperate patient who kills his doctor and loves his mortal disease, he banished his true servant.

"I give you five days to make your preparations for

departure. If on the sixth day you are found within the realm of Britain, that moment will be your death."

So Kent said farewell to the king. Before he left, he recommended Cordelia, who had thought so correctly and spoken so discreetly, to the protection of the gods. He told Regan and Goneril he hoped that their big speeches would be followed by deeds of love.

"And so," he said finally, "I bid you all adieu. From now, I'll shape my old ways in a new country."

The suitors

The King of France and the Duke of Burgundy were then called in to say whether or not they wished to continue their courtship of Cordelia, now that she had no fortune.

The Duke of Burgundy declined the match, saying he did not wish to marry her if that was her situation.

But the King of France understood the nature of the fault which had lost her the love of her father—simply her inability to flatter him like her sisters.

"Fairest Cordelia," he said. "You are rich, being poor. Your many virtues are a dowry greater than a kingdom!"

He took Cordelia by the hand and asked her to say farewell to her sisters and her father. Then she would go with him and be his queen and Queen of France, and reign over greater possessions than her sisters.

And so Cordelia took leave of Goneril and Regan with tears in her eyes. She requested them to love their father well and make good their words. They coldly told her not to tell them what to do, for they knew their duty, but to try and keep her husband happy, who had taken her as a free gift from Fortune.

Cordelia departed with a heavy heart. She knew the cunning of her sisters and wished her father was in better hands than she was about to leave him in.

Promises and performance

Cordelia was no sooner gone than the devilish characters of her sisters began to show themselves. It had been agreed that Lear would spend the first month with Goneril. But even before the month was up, he began to find out the difference between promises and performance.

Having got from her father all that he had to give, even to the crown from his head, his wretched daughter began to grudge even those small remnants of royalty the old man had kept to himself. She couldn't bear to see him and his one hundred knights. Every time she met her father she frowned, and whenever he wanted to speak to her, she pretended to be sick to get rid of the sight of him. It was clear she regarded him as a useless burden and his attendants an unnecessary expense. And it was not only her whose expressions of duty to the king loosened. By her example, or perhaps by her instruction, her servants also began to treat him with neglect. They refused to obey his orders or pretended not to hear them.

Naturally, Lear noticed this alteration in his daughter's behavior, but he shut his eyes to it for as long as he could.

Base football player!

Rather than leave Britain, the good Earl of Kent had decided to take the risk of staying in the country as long as there was a chance of him being useful to the king. In the disguise of a servant, all his noble pomp put away, he called himself 'Caius' and offered his services to the king. Not realizing who he was, but pleased with his blunt way of speaking, Lear took Kent into his service.

Caius soon found means to show his fidelity and love to his royal master. Goneril's steward behaved in a rude way to the king, as he was no doubt secretly encouraged to do by his mistress. Lear hit him.

"I will not be struck, my lord!" said the steward. Caius could not endure to hear such an insult to the king.

"Nor tripped, either," said Caius, "you base football player!"

He immediately tripped him up and then pushed him away. As a result of this friendly service, Lear became more attached to his new servant Caius.

The Fool

Kent was not Lear's only friend. It was the custom of kings and great nobles at that time to keep a 'Fool' or 'jester' to entertain them and sometimes to advise them as well. Lear's Fool had clung to the king after he had given away his crown, and his witty sayings kept up Lear's good humor. Sometimes he couldn't resist from jeering at his master for his unwisely uncrowning himself and giving everything away to his daughters. As the

Fool expressed it, those daughters…

For sudden joy did weep.
But I for sorrow sung,
That such a king should play bo-peep
And go the fools among!

With such wild sayings and scraps of songs, of which he had plenty, this pleasant, honest Fool poured out his heart in many a bitter taunt and jest, even in the presence of Goneril herself. He compared the king to a hedge sparrow, the bird who feeds a baby cuckoo (the daughters) until it's old enough, and then has its head bitten off for its pains! He also said that an ass should know when the cart (the daughters) draws the horse (the king); and that Lear was no longer Lear, but just the shadow of Lear. For these free speeches, he was often threatened to be whipped.

The coolness and falling off of respect which Lear had begun to perceive were not all that this foolishly fond father was to suffer from his eldest daughter. She now plainly told him that his stay at her castle was inconvenient so long as he insisted on keeping his one hundred knights. She said it was meaningless and expensive, and only served to fill her court with noisy feasting. She entreated her father to reduce their number and keep only old men about him, like himself.

Lear at first could not believe his eyes and ears that it was his daughter who was speaking to him so unkindly. She had received a coronet from him and yet she would not give him the respect due to his old age and wanted him to get rid of his men. But she persisted in her demands. The old man got very angry and said that she was lying. That was true, for the one hundred knights were all well-behaved, skilled in carrying out their duties, and not given to noisy feasting.

"Ingratitude," said Lear, "is a marble-hearted devil, more hideous in a child than a sea-monster!" And he cursed her terribly, praying she might never have a child, or, if she did, that it might live to return that contempt on *her* which she had shown to *him*. "Then you might feel how much sharper it is than a serpent's tooth to have a *thankless* child!"

Lear ordered his horses to be prepared, for he would go to his other daughter, Regan, with his one hundred knights.

The Duke of Albany, Goneril's husband, began to excuse himself for any share which Lear might suppose he had in the unkindness. But Lear would not hear him finish. In a rage, he ordered his horses to be saddled and set out with his followers for Regan's castle. Lear now realized how small Cordelia's fault, if it was a fault, now appeared in comparison with her sister's, and he started crying. Then he felt ashamed that such a creature as Goneril should have so much power over him as to make him weep.

Regan

Regan and her husband kept their court in great pomp and state at their castle. Lear dispatched Caius with letters to his daughter, so that she could be prepared to welcome him. But

Goneril had already sent letters to her sister, accusing her father of bad behavior and advising her not to accept all the men he was bringing with him. Her messenger arrived at the same time as Caius, and who should it be but the steward Caius had tripped up! Not liking the steward's expression, and suspecting why he was there, Caius began to criticize him and challenged him to a fight. The steward refused. In a fit of passion, Caius beat him soundly, as such a mischief-maker and carrier of wicked messages deserved.

When news of this reached the ears of Regan and her husband, they ordered Caius to be put in the stocks, even though he deserved the highest respect as a messenger from the king her father. So the first thing Lear saw when he entered the castle was his faithful servant Caius sitting in that disgraceful situation.

This was a bad omen of the reception he was to expect. But worse followed when he was told his daughter and her husband were weary from traveling all night and could not see him. He insisted on seeing them in a very angry manner. When, eventually, they came to greet him, who should be with them but the hated Goneril! She had come to tell her story of their father's visit and set her sister against him.

This sight much upset the old man, especially when he saw Regan take her sister by the hand. He asked Goneril if she was not ashamed to look upon his old white beard. Regan advised him to ask for Goneril's forgiveness, go back and live with her peacefully, and dismiss half of his knights. She said he was old and must be led by those that had more discretion than himself.

Lear showed her how preposterous it was to go down on his knees and beg of his own daughter for food and clothing. He argued against such an unnatural dependence, declaring he would never return with her, but stay there with Regan with his one hundred knights. He said her eyes were not fierce like Goneril's, but mild and kind, and he hoped that she had not forgotten that he'd given her half of the kingdom. He added that rather than return to Goneril, with half his men gone, he would prefer to go over to France and beg a wretched pension of the French king, who had married his youngest daughter who had no land at all.

But he was mistaken in expecting kinder treatment from Regan. As if she wanted to outdo her sister, she declared that she thought fifty knights were too many; twenty-five were enough. Nearly heartbroken, Lear turned to Goneril and said in that case he would go back with her. Her fifty was double twenty-five, which meant her love was double Regan's. But then Goneril excused herself, asking him why he needed so many as twenty-five, or even ten, or five, when he could be waited upon by her servants or Regan's servants?

"Why do you need even *one* knight?" added Regan.

It was as if these two wicked daughters were trying to outdo each other in terms of cruelty to their old father, who had been so good to them. It was their ingratitude which pierced the poor king's heart rather than what he would suffer by losing some of his knights. His wits now began to be unsettled.

"You unnatural hags," he said to his daughters, "I will have revenge on you both! Oh, Fool, I shall go mad!"

While Lear was idly threatening what his weak arm could never actually perform, night came on, and with it a loud storm of thunder and lightning with heavy rain. As his daughters were still refusing to admit his knights, Lear said he preferred to encounter the utmost fury of the storm than stay under the same roof as his ungrateful daughters. Saying it was just punishment for their father's behavior, they allowed him to go away in that condition and shut the castle gate on him.

The storm

A very strong wind was blowing and the rain was increasing as the old man went out to combat with the elements. They were less sharp to him than his daughters' unkindness. For many miles around, there was hardly a bush on that bleak heath. So Lear was exposed to the full fury of the storm in the dark night. As he wandered around, he defied the winds and the thunder.

"Blow, winds, and crack your cheeks! Rage! Blow! Fire, spit! Rain, spout!"

He bid the winds to blow the earth into the sea, or swell the waves of the sea till they drowned the earth, so that nothing would remain of any such ungrateful animal as Man.

The king was now left with no other companion besides his poor Fool.

"Oh," said the Fool, "please ask your daughters' blessing! This is a night that pities neither the wise man nor the fool!"

He did his best to joke about misfortune, and when the king started taking off his clothes, the Fool said, "Oh, it is a naughty night to swim in!"

But he that has a little tiny wit,
With heigh ho, the wind and the rain,
Must make content with his fortunes fit,
Though the rain it comes down every day!

The once great monarch was found in this awful state by his ever-faithful servant Caius.

"Alas, sir, are you here? Creatures that love the night don't love nights like this! This dreadful storm has driven all the beasts to their hiding places. Man's nature cannot endure such affliction or fear."

Lear rebuked him and said such lesser evils were not felt when there was a greater malady. When the mind is at ease, the body has leisure to be delicate, but the tempest in his mind had taken away all feeling from his senses but that which beat at his heart. And then he spoke of filial ingratitude. He said it was just like your mouth biting your hand for lifting food to it.

But Caius continued saying that the king should not stay out in the open air. Eventually, he persuaded him to enter a little wretched hovel out on the heath. The Fool went in first and suddenly ran back out terrified, saying that he had seen a spirit named Tom. But this spirit proved to be nothing more than a poor beggar who had crept into there for shelter, and had frightened the Fool with his talk about devils.

Seeing the beggar in so wretched a plight, the king, who had nothing but a blanket to cover his body, believed he must be a father who had given away everything to his daughters. Only having unkind daughters, he thought, could bring a man to such a wretched state.

Dover and France

From this and many other wild words, Caius realized that the king was not in his perfect mind, and that his daughters' ill-usage had really made him go mad. Now the loyalty of the Earl of Kent could show itself in a more essential service than he had so far found the opportunity to perform. With the assistance of some of the king's knights who remained loyal he had the king removed at daybreak to Dover Castle in Kent, where he had many friends and great influence.

Kent himself quickly embarked for France. He hurried to the court of Cordelia, and in moving terms described to her the pitiful condition of her royal father. He also vividly reported the inhumanity of her sisters. With many tears, Cordelia entreated her husband to give his permission for her to go to England with a sufficient power to subdue those cruel daughters and their husbands and restore the old king to his throne. He granted her request. She soon set forth and landed with the royal French army at Dover.

Having by some chance escaped from his guardians, Lear was found wandering about in the fields near Dover by some of Cordelia's men. He was in a pitiable condition, singing aloud to himself. On his head was a crown which he had made himself from straw, nettles and other weeds he had picked up in the corn-fields.

Cordelia earnestly wished to see her father. But her doctors advised her to wait, until by sleep and the operation of herbs which they would give him, he was restored to a more stable condition. By the aid of those skillful physicians—to whom Cordelia promised all her gold and jewels for the speedy recovery of her father—Lear was soon in a fit state to see his daughter.

Reunion

The reunion of father and daughter was a moving sight indeed. Lear struggled between his joy at seeing again his once darling child and his shame at receiving such kindness from the daughter he'd cast off for so small a fault. Both these passions mixed in his half-crazed brain with the remains of his malady. At times he could hardly remember where he was or who it was that so kindly kissed him and spoke to him.

"I am a very foolish old man, eighty or more! And I fear I may not be in my perfect mind. Do not laugh at me, for I think this lady is my child, Cordelia…"

"And so I am, I am!"

And then Lear fell on his knees to beg pardon of his child. And she kneeled as well to ask a blessing of him. She told him that it did not become a king to kneel, but it was *her* duty, for she was his child. And she said she kissed him to kiss away all her sisters' unkindness, and that they should be ashamed of themselves to turn their kind old father with his white beard out into the cold air. Her enemy's dog, even though it had bitten her, would have been allowed to stay by her fire on such a night as that and warm itself!

She told her father how she had come from France to bring

him assistance. He said that she must forget and forgive, for he was old and foolish and didn't know what he did. He added she surely had a great reason *not* to love him, but her sisters had none. But Cordelia replied that she had no more reason than they had.

Monsters

Meanwhile, those monsters of ingratitude, the two sisters who had been so false to their old father, could hardly have been expected to prove more faithful to their own husbands. They soon grew tired of showing even the appearance of duty and affection, and openly showed they had fixed their loves upon another man. It happened that the object of their guilty loves was one and the same. It was Edmund, the illegitimate son of the late Earl of Gloucester. By his treachery, he had succeeded in disinheriting his brother Edgar, the lawful heir, from his earldom, and was now earl himself. A wicked man, he was a fit object for the love of such wicked creatures as Goneril and Regan.

It so happened that around this time the Duke of Cornwall, Regan's husband, died. She immediately declared her intention of marrying the Earl of Gloucester. This aroused the jealousy of her sister, to whom the earl had many times professed his love. Goneril was so jealous, in fact, she found a way to kill her sister by poison. But her guilt was revealed, and she was imprisoned by her husband, the Duke of Albany. Her guilty passion for the earl had also reached his ears. In a fit of disappointed love and rage, she soon put an end to her own life. In this way, the justice of Heaven at last overtook the two wicked daughters.

Prison

Cordelia's good deeds would have seemed to deserve a positive conclusion. But it is an awful truth that innocence and goodness are not always successful in this world. The armed forces which Goneril and Regan had sent out under the command of the Earl of Gloucester were victorious over the French army. Cordelia was thrown in prison at the insistence of the cold-hearted earl, who did not like anyone to stand between him and the vacant British throne. And she ended her life in prison. Her father did not long survive her.

Before the king died, the good Earl of Kent, who had attended his old master's steps all the way from his daughters' ill-usage to the sad period of his decay, tried to make him understand that it was he who had followed him under the name of Caius. But Lear's care-crazed brain could not comprehend how Kent and Caius could be the same person. So Kent thought it needless to trouble him with more explanations at such a time. Not long after his master's death, the faithful servant soon followed the king to the grave.

And so ends the tragic story of King Lear and his three daughters. As for what happened to Britain *after* that, well, just a couple of spoilers, perhaps... The judgment of Heaven soon overtook the evil Earl of Gloucester: his treasons were discovered, and he was slain in single combat with his brother Edgar, the lawful earl... Goneril's husband, the Duke of Albany, who had never encouraged his wife in her actions against her father, and was not connected with Cordelia's death, ascended the throne...

But those are other stories...to be told next time!

Macbeth

マクベス

読み始める前に

マクベスは妻と謀って主君を暗殺し王位に就くが、地位を失う恐怖から次々と罪を重ね、自ら破滅の道をたどっていく。シェイクスピア四大悲劇のひとつ。

［登場人物］

Macbeth	マクベス《ダンカン王の臣下で、スコットランドの将軍》
Lady Macbeth	マクベス夫人《夫マクベスを叱咤して悪行を重ねさせる》
Banquo	バンクォー《スコットランドの将軍で、マクベスの友人》
Macduff	マクダフ《スコットランドの貴族、ファイフの領主》
Duncan	ダンカン王《スコットランド王》
Malcolm	マルカム《ダンカンの長男》
Donalbain	ドナルベイン《ダンカンの次男》
Witches	（3人の）魔女《マクベスとバンクォーに予言をする》
Weird sisters (=Witches)	
Fleance	フリーアンス《バンクォーの息子》

［地名など］

Birnam Wood	バーナムの森《重要な舞台となる場所》
Cawdor	コーダー《地名》
Dunsinane	ダンシネーン《地名》
Fife	ファイフ《地名》
Glamis	グラミズ《地名》

［あらすじ］

スコットランドの将軍マクベスと友人のバンクォーは、荒野で3人の魔女に出会う。魔女はマクベスに「万歳、コーダーの領主」「万歳、いずれ王になるお方」と呼びかけ、バンクォーには「王にはなれないが、子孫が王になる」と予言し消える。そこへスコットランド王・ダンカンの使者が現れ、マクベスが新しくコーダーの領主に任命されたと言う。魔女の言葉通りとなったことに2人は驚き、次は王になるという予言にマクベスは希望を膨らませる。

マクベスが妻にその話をすると、妻はマクベスにダンカンを殺害させ、マクベスは予言どおり王になった。しかし罪の呵責からか精神は不安定になり、王位を守るために暴政を続けていくが……。

［総単語数］3,980語

MACBETH

Once upon a time, when Duncan the Meek reigned as King of Scotland, there was a great lord, or 'thane', called Macbeth. Closely related to the king, he was held in great esteem for his valor and conduct as a warrior. He had recently been involved in defeating a rebel army, assisted by Norwegian troops. Our story begins as he was returning from that great battle accompanied by his friend Banquo, another Scottish general.

Hail, Macbeth!

As they made their way across a wild area of heath, they were suddenly stopped by the strange appearance of three figures. They resembled women, but had beards.

"What withered skins and wild clothes!" said Banquo. "They don't look like inhabitants of the Earth, and yet they are on it!"

Macbeth addressed them.

"Speak if you can. What are you?"

"Hail, Macbeth, thane of Glamis!" said one of them.

Macbeth was a little startled to find himself known by such creatures, but much more when the second one also saluted him.

"Hail Macbeth, thane of Cawdor!"

He had no right to that title. Then the third one spoke.

"Hail, Macbeth, who will be king!"

Such a prophetic greeting amazed him, as he knew that he could have no hope of succeeding to the throne while the king's sons lived.

Then Banquo spoke.

"If you can look into the future and say which grain will grow and which will not, speak to me as well."

"Hail, Banquo, lesser than Macbeth and greater!"

"Hail, Banquo, not so happy, but much happier!"

"Hail, Banquo, who will breed kings but not reign yourself!"

Then they vanished into thin air, making the two generals believe they were witches.

As the two men stood pondering on this strange happening, messengers from the king arrived. They announced that they were empowered to confer upon Macbeth the title of 'Thane of Cawdor'. Macbeth was astonished. It miraculously corresponded with the prediction of the witches! For a few moments he stood wrapped in amazement, unable to speak.

Then he turned to Banquo and said, "Don't you hope that your children will be kings, when what the witches promised *me* has so wonderfully come true?"

"Well, *that* hope," answered Banquo, "might encourage *you* to aim at the throne! But often these ministers of darkness tell us trivial truths to trick us into deeds of great consequence."

But the wicked suggestions of the witches had sunk too

deep into the mind of Macbeth to allow him to attend to the warnings of the good Banquo. From that time on, he bent all his thoughts on how to help the second prediction become reality—himself sitting on the throne of Scotland.

The king's visit

Macbeth arrived home, and was welcomed by his wife. He immediately told her about the strange predictions of the weird sisters and how they had partly come true. Lady Macbeth was a determined, ambitious woman. She cared not much by what means she and her husband could achieve greatness. She eagerly pointed out that killing the king was an absolutely necessary step to the fulfillment of the witches' prophecy. Macbeth hesitated at the thought of blood being shed like that, but his wife did her best to overcome his reluctance to consider it.

King Duncan made it a habit to pay friendly visits to his nobles. And it so happened that he decided to visit Macbeth's Dunsinane Castle to honor Macbeth for his triumphal success in battle. He was attended by his two sons, Malcolm and Donalbain, and a host of thanes and other attendants.

The castle was pleasantly situated, and the air about it was sweet. Proof of this could be found in the many nests which swallows had built under all the jutting parts of the building. The air is always pure where swallows breed.

The king very much liked the place, and also the attentions and respect of his hostess, Lady Macbeth. She was a woman who had the skill of covering treacherous plans with a smile.

She could look like an innocent flower, while she was really the deadly serpent beneath it. The king was unusually pleased with his reception. He was very tired after his long journey, but before he retired to his room he made presents to his principal officers. He also sent a valuable diamond to lady Macbeth in thanks for her hospitality. Then he went to bed. As usual, two grooms slept near him as bodyguards.

The milk of human kindness

It was the middle of the night, when over half the world of Nature seems dead, when wicked dreams enter men's sleeping minds, and when only wolves and murderers are active. This was the time when Lady Macbeth was plotting the murder of the king. She did not want to commit such an awful deed herself, but she feared her husband's nature. It was perhaps too full of the milk of human kindness to commit murder. She knew him to be ambitious, but also very careful, and not prepared for that height of crime which sometimes accompanies great ambition. She had won him over to consent to the murder, but she doubted his resolution. She feared that the natural tenderness of his character would emerge and prevent the action.

So with her own hand armed with a dagger, she went quietly up to the king's room. She had taken care to ply the grooms with lots of wine so that they slept fully intoxicated, neglecting their charge to protect the king. Duncan was lying there in a sound sleep. There was something in his face which reminded her of her father, and she suddenly lacked the courage to proceed.

She went back down to confer with her husband. As she had feared, his resolution had started to weaken. He considered that there were several strong reasons against the deed. In the first place, *he* was not only a subject, but a close relative of the king. And that day he had been his *host*, whose duty it was, by the laws of hospitality, to shut the door against murderers, not to use the knife himself! Then he'd recalled how just and merciful a king Duncan had been, how kind to his subjects, and how loving to his nobility, in particular himself. Such kings are the peculiar care of Heaven, and their subjects are doubly bound to revenge their deaths. Besides, by the favors of the king, Macbeth stood high in the opinion of all sorts of men, and how much would those honors be stained by the reputation of so foul a murder?

In these mental conflicts, Lady Macbeth found her husband inclining toward canceling the plan. But she was a woman not easily shaken from her evil aims. She began to pour words into his ears which infused a portion of her own spirit into his mind. She produced reason after reason why he should not shrink from what he had decided to do: how easy it was; how soon it would be over; and what the action of one short night would give to all their future nights as royalty! Then she started tossing contempt on his change of purpose. She accused him of fickleness and cowardice. She declared that she had breastfed a child, and knew how tender it was to love the baby that milked her. But, while it was smiling at her face, she would have plucked it from her breast and dashed its brains out if she had *sworn* to do it, just as he had *sworn* to perform the murder! Then, she added, how easy it was to lay the guilt of the deed on the drunken grooms. The passion of her words overcame Macbeth's negative feelings. He once more summoned up courage to carry out the bloody business.

Sleep no more!

Taking the dagger in his hand, Macbeth softly stole up in the dark to the room where Duncan lay. As he went, he suddenly thought he saw another dagger in the air, with the handle toward him, and on the blade and at the tip of it there were drops of blood… But when he tried to grasp it, it was nothing but air, a mere illusion proceeding from his own hot brain and the business he had in hand.

He shook off his fear and entered the king's room. He wasted no time but quickly dispatched the old man with one stroke of his dagger. Just then, one of the sleeping grooms laughed in his sleep, and the other cried "Murder!", which woke them both. But they said a short prayer, one of them said "God bless us!" and the other answered "Amen". Then they both went back to sleep. Macbeth, who had stood listening to them, tried to say 'Amen' himself, but though he had the most need of a blessing, the word stuck in his throat.

Again he thought he heard a voice, which cried "Sleep no more! Macbeth has murdered sleep, the innocent sleep that nourishes life. Sleep no more. Glamis has murdered sleep, and therefore Cawdor will sleep no more, Macbeth will sleep no more!"

With such horrible images and sounds in his head, Macbeth returned to his wife. He came in so distracted a state that she reproached him with his want of firmness. She began to think he'd failed and that the deed was *not* accomplished. But then she saw the blood on his hand and she sent him at once to wash it off. She took Macbeth's bloody dagger and went upstairs again to stain the cheeks of the grooms with blood...

Suspicion

Morning came, and with it the discovery of the murder by Macduff, the Thane of Fife, who had just arrived at the castle to greet the king. Macbeth and his wife made a great show of grief and the proofs against the grooms were strong. Even so, suspicion soon began to fall on Macbeth. The reasons for *him* to carry out the awful deed were so much stronger than the poor grooms could possibly have had.

Duncan's sons soon fled. Malcolm, the elder brother, sought refuge in the English court. His younger brother, Donalbain, escaped to Ireland. Malcolm should have succeeded his father, so the throne was left empty. Macbeth, as the next in line, was therefore crowned king. The prediction of the weird sisters had become reality.

Although placed so high, Macbeth and his queen could not forget the other prophecy that, though Macbeth would be king, the children of Banquo would be kings after him. The thought of this, and that they'd defiled their hands with blood and done such a great crime only to put Banquo's sons on the throne, greatly disturbed them. They decided to make the predictions void by killing both Banquo and Fleance, his son.

For this purpose they organized a great feast, to which they invited all the chief thanes, including Banquo and his son. Macbeth had arranged that on the way to the castle Banquo would be attacked by hired assassins. Banquo was indeed stabbed to death, but in the scuffle in the dark, Fleance managed to escape.

The feast

At the feast, the queen, whose manners were very pleasant and royal, played the hostess with such grace and attention that the guests were all impressed. Macbeth talked freely with the thanes and other nobles and then stood up to give a toast. He said he was happy that all those who were honorable in Scotland were there under his roof together, apart from his good friend Banquo, who he hoped had a good reason for being absent!

As Macbeth spoke these words, the ghost of Banquo suddenly entered the room, drifted across, and sat down on Macbeth's chair. Macbeth was basically a bold man—and could have faced the devil without trembling—but at this horrible sight his cheeks turned white with fear, and he stood quite still with his eyes fixed on the ghost. His queen and all the nobles, who couldn't see the ghost, thought he was staring at an empty chair. They took it for some temporary kind of fit. The queen reproached him, whispering that it was only the same fancy which had made him see the dagger in the air. But Macbeth continued to see the ghost, and ignored everybody. Then he addressed it with distracted words.

"No, you can't say I did it! Don't shake your bloody head at me! Your blood is cold! Go away!"

The queen, fearing their dreadful secret would be disclosed, in great haste apologized to the guests. She excused Macbeth's behavior as a disorder he was often troubled with. Then she asked everyone to leave and wished them all goodnight.

Such dreadful fancies were now disturbing Macbeth. Both he and the queen suffered from terrible nightmares. But the blood of Banquo troubled them far less than the escape of Fleance. They saw him as the father to a line of kings who would keep their own posterity off the throne. With these miserable thoughts they found no peace. Macbeth decided to seek out the weird sisters once more, and discover the worst from them.

Something wicked

He headed to a cave on the heath. Knowing by foresight of his coming, they were engaged in preparing their dreadful charms, by which they conjured up infernal spirits to reveal the future to them. Their horrid ingredients included toads, the eye of a newt, the toe of a frog, the wool of a bat, the tongue of a dog, the leg of a lizard, the wing of an owl, the scale of a dragon, the tooth of a wolf, the throat of a shark, the mummy of a witch, the finger of a dead child, the root of the poisonous hemlock, and leaves of the yew tree that roots itself in graves. All these were tossed into a huge cauldron to boil. When it grew too hot, it was cooled with the blood of a baboon. By these charms they could call the infernal spirits to answer their questions.

One of the witches suddenly chanted, "By the pricking of my thumbs, something wicked this way comes! Who knocks?"

It was Macbeth.

"You secret, black and midnight hags, please answer my questions."

"Speak!"

"Demand!"

"We'll answer!"

They asked him whether he would prefer to have his doubts resolved by them or by their masters, the spirits. Not at all daunted by the dreadful bubbling cauldron, he boldly answered, "Where are they? Let me see them." And so they called up three spirits.

The first one appeared in the form of a head wearing a helmet.

"Unknown power," said Macbeth, "please tell me…"

"He knows your thoughts," interrupted a witch. "Just listen and say nothing!"

"Macbeth!" said the spirit. "Beware Macduff, the thane of Fife!"

"Thank you for your warning. One word more…"

"He has gone. Here's another…"

The second spirit appeared in the form of a bloody child.

"Macbeth! Be bloody, bold and determined. Scorn the power of men, for none of woman born can harm you!"

"Then live, Macduff!" cried Macbeth. "I have no need to fear you. But I will make doubly sure. You will not live!"

The third spirit appeared in the form of a crowned child holding a tree. "Macbeth! Be proud and strong like a lion. You will never be defeated until Birnam Wood shall come to Dunsinane."

"Well, that can never happen!" cried Macbeth. "Who can move the wood from its earth-bound roots? Oh, sweet predictions! Good! I see I shall live the full length of my natural life, and not be cut off by a violent death. But my heart throbs to know one thing. Tell me, if you can. Will Banquo's issue ever reign in this kingdom?"

"Seek to know no more!" said all three witches.

Here the cauldron sank into the ground, and music was heard. Eight shadows, like kings, passed by Macbeth, the last one bearing a glass which showed the figures of many more. Then came the ghost of bloody Banquo, who smiled at Macbeth, and pointed at the line of kings. Then the apparitions disappeared.

With a sound of soft music and some dancing, the witches made a show of duty and welcome to Macbeth, and then vanished.

From that moment, Macbeth's thoughts were all bloody and terrible.

Out, out, brief candle

The first thing Macbeth heard when he left the cave was that Macduff had fled to England. He had gone to join the army which was forming against him under Malcolm, the late king's eldest son. Their aim was to displace Macbeth and set Malcolm, the lawful heir, on the throne. Stung with rage, Macbeth attacked Macduff's castle, killed his wife and children, and extended the slaughter to everyone related to Macduff.

These and other similar deeds alienated all the great Scottish nobles from him. Some of them fled to join Malcolm and Macduff, who were now approaching with a powerful army. The rest secretly wished them success, though they would take no active part for fear of Macbeth. Everybody now hated and suspected the tyrant. Nobody loved or honored him. He began to envy the condition of Duncan—against whom treason had done its worst—who slept soundly in his grave. Neither steel or poison, domestic malice or foreign levies, could hurt him any longer.

While all these things were going on, the queen, who had been the sole partner in his wickedness, and in whose arms he could sometimes seek brief relief from the nightmares, suddenly died. It was believed she had taken her own life, unable to bear public hate and the remorse of her guilt.

"Tomorrow, and tomorrow, and tomorrow..." murmured Macbeth when he heard the news. "Out, out, brief candle. Life's but a walking shadow, a poor player that struts and frets his hour upon the stage and then is heard no more. It is a tale told by an idiot..."

Macbeth was left alone, without a soul to love or care for him, or a friend to whom he could confide his wicked intentions. He grew careless of life, and wished for death himself.

The moving wood

But the steady approach of Malcolm's army roused in him what remained of his old courage, and he was determined to die "with armor on my back." The hollow promises of the witches had filled him with a false confidence.

He clearly remembered the spirits saying that 'none of woman born' could hurt him, and that he would never be defeated 'until Birnam Wood shall come to Dunsinane'. So he shut himself up in his castle, which was strong enough to defy a siege, and sullenly waited for the approach of Malcolm.

Suddenly a guard came to him, pale and shaking with fear, almost unable to report what he had seen. He claimed that as he stood upon his watch from the top of the castle, he looked toward Birnam Wood, and it appeared that all the trees had started to *move*!

"You liar!" cried Macbeth. "If what you say is *wrong*, I'll hang you alive from a tree till famine kills you! But if your tale is *true*, you can do the same to me."

Macbeth's resolution was weakening fast. He now began to doubt the predictions of the spirits. He had been told not to fear until Birnam Wood came to Dunsinane, and now the wood was moving!

"But if what you say is true, then let us all arm and go out to fight. There is no running away or staying here. Ah, I begin to be weary of the sun, and wish my life would end!"

With these desperate words, he went out to meet Malcolm's army, which had now come right up to the castle walls.

A charmed life

The mystery of the illusion which had given the guard the idea of the wood moving is easily solved. As his army was marching through Birnam Wood, not far from Macbeth's castle, the skillful general Malcolm had an excellent idea. He instructed all his soldiers to cut off a bough and carry it in front of them, as a way to conceal the true numbers of his force as they advanced. It was the appearance of this forward march of the soldiers from a distance that had frightened the guard. In a sense rather different from the way Macbeth had understood them, the words of the spirit had come true, and one great support of his confidence disappeared.

And now severe fighting began. Though feebly supported by those who called themselves his friends—but in reality hated the tyrant and were inclined to join Malcolm and Macduff—Macbeth fought with extreme rage and valor, cutting down all who approached him. Then he came to the place where Macduff was fighting. Remembering the caution of the spirit, Macbeth tried to turn back. But Macduff, who had been seeking him through the whole fight, stopped him. He shouted foul reproaches at Macbeth for the murder of his wife and children. Macbeth, whose soul was charged enough with that family's blood already, was not eager to fight. But Macduff urged him on, calling him a tyrant, a murderer, a hell-hound, and a villain.

Then Macbeth remembered the words of the spirit. Smiling confidently, he said to Macduff, "You're wasting your effort! You might as well be cutting the air with your sword as trying to make me bleed. I bear a charmed life, which will not yield to one of woman born!"

"Oh, forget your charm," replied Macduff, "and let that lying spirit you have served tell you that Macduff was never born of a woman in the normal way, but born by caesarean section!"

"Cursed be the tongue that tells me that!" said the trembling Macbeth, feeling his last hold on confidence give way. "And let men in future never believe the lies of witches and spirits! They just deceive us with their riddles which have double meaning, and while they seem to keep their promise, disappoint our hopes with a different meaning. Macduff, I will *not* fight with you!"

"Then stay alive!" said the scornful Macduff. "We will put you on display, as men show monsters, with a painted board on which we will write 'Here you can see a tyrant!'"

"Never!" said Macbeth, whose courage had suddenly returned with despair. "I will not live to kiss the ground before young Malcolm's feet, and to be baited by the curses of the rabble. Though Birnam Wood has come to Dunsinane, and you who was not 'born of woman' is opposed to me, I will fight to the end…"

With these frantic words, Macbeth threw himself upon Macduff. After a severe struggle, Macduff overcame him and stabbed him to death. He cut off the tyrant's head and presented it to the new lawful king. From that moment, the young Malcolm took upon himself the government of Scotland, which he had so long been deprived of by the stratagems of the usurper Macbeth. He ascended the throne of Duncan the Meek with the enthusiastic approval of all the Scottish nobles and the people. "The King is dead! Long live the King!"

And that is the end of the tragic story of Macbeth. But you may be wondering what happened to Fleance, Banquo's son. Well, to cut a very long story very short, his descendants would eventually become a long line of monarchs who later sat on the Scottish throne, ending with James the Sixth of Scotland and the First of England, under whom the two crowns of Scotland and England were united.

All's Well that Ends Well

終わりよければすべてよし

読み始める前に

結末はハッピーエンドにみえるが、なんとなくすっきりしない。「ダークコメディ（暗い喜劇）」「問題劇」などと呼ばれる作品のひとつ。

［登場人物］

Helena	ヘレナ《主人公、伯爵夫人の侍女》
Bertram	バートラム《ロシリオン伯爵》
Diana	ダイアナ《未亡人の娘》
Widow of Florence	フローレンスの未亡人
Lafeu	ラフュー《老貴族》
King of France	フランス王
Gerard de Narbon	ジェラード・ド・ナーバン《有名な医者、ヘレナの父》
Countess of Roussillon	ロシリオン伯爵夫人《バートラムの母親》

［地名など］

Florence	フローレンス《イタリアの都市》
Roussillon	ロシリオン《フランスの地名》

［あらすじ］

父を亡くしてロシリオン伯爵の地位を継いだバートラムは、フランス国王に仕えるためパリへ出立する。両親と死に別れ、バートラムの母の世話になっているヘレナは、バートラムにひそかな想いを寄せていたので、別れを悲しんだ。

身分は低いが、優れた医師を父にもつヘレナは、亡父から受け継いだ秘伝の処方箋を持っている。フランス国王が不治の病にかかっていると聞き、ヘレナはその薬で王の病を治すことを口実に、本当はバートラムに会いたい一心でパリへ向かう。

ヘレナは「治すことができなければ死刑に。うまくいったら夫を選ぶ権利を」という約束で王を治療し、見事成功。約束通り、バートラムを夫に選んだ。しかし、傲慢なバートラムは自分と身分がつりあわないヘレナを拒否し、パリを出て軍隊へ入ってしまう。

［総単語数］4,300語

ALL'S WELL THAT ENDS WELL

Once upon a time in the south of France, a nobleman named Bertram had just acquired the title of Count of Roussillon following his father's death. The King of France had been very fond of his father, so he sent for Bertram to go immediately to the royal court in Paris. He intended to provide the young Bertram with his special favor and protection. The king was an absolute monarch, so an invitation to court was a royal command, which nobody could disobey.

Bertram goes to Paris

Bertram was living with his mother, the widowed countess. One day, Lafeu, an elderly lord of the French court, arrived to conduct him to Paris. Parting with her dear son, the countess felt she was burying her husband a second time, but she dared not keep him even one day more. The king was waiting! So she gave orders for Bertram's instant departure.

Lafeu tried to comfort the countess for the loss of her late lord and her son's sudden absence.

"The king is so kind," he said, "that you will find him to be like a husband to you and a father to your son."

He then told the countess that the king had fallen into a sad illness, which his doctors believed to be incurable.

"I'm very sorry to hear that," said the countess. "If only the father of Helena, my young attendant, was still alive! I'm sure *he* could have cured His Majesty."

Then she briefly told Lafeu about Helena's background. She was the only daughter of the famous physician, Gerard de Narbon, who had recommended his daughter to her care just before he died. So the countess had taken Helena under her protection. She praised her virtuous character and many excellent qualities inherited from her father. While the countess was speaking, Helena cried in sad silence. The countess gently reproved her for grieving too much for her father's death.

Bertram now came to wish his mother farewell. The countess parted from him with tears and her blessing.

"Bertram, please follow in the footsteps of your fine father! Love all people, but only trust a few. Do wrong to no-one!" Then she commended him to Lafeu's care. "My good lord, please advise him well, for he's an inexperienced courtier!"

Bertram's last words were spoken to Helena, simply wishing her happiness and asking her to look after his mother well.

Helena

When Helena had wept in silence, her tears were not for her father… She had loved him greatly, but now she had a deeper love for the man she was about to lose, Bertram. Helena had long loved him, but she had to remember that he was now the Count of Roussillon, descended from one of France's most ancient families. *His* ancestors had all been noble; *hers* had not. She was of humble birth. And so she looked up to the high-born Bertram as her dear lord, and dared not form any hope to live other than as his servant. That's how she would live and die. So great the distance seemed between his height of dignity and her lowly fortunes that she said to herself, "I may love a particularly bright star, and think to marry it, but he is so far above me!"

His absence filled her eyes with tears and her heart with sadness. Although she loved without hope, yet it had been of some comfort to her to see him every day at Roussillon. She would sit and look at his dark eyes, his arched eyebrows, and the curls of his hair until she seemed to draw his portrait on the tablet of her heart. That heart was capable of remembering every line of the face she adored.

When her father died, he left Helena his medicines of rare and well-proved power. Based on deep study and long experience, he had collected almost infallible remedies. Among them was a medicine for the disease which the King was suffering from. Its efficacy had been proved. Before hearing Lafeu's explanation, Helena had felt so humble and so hopeless. But as soon as she heard about the illness, an ambitious project began to form in her mind: to go to Paris herself and undertake the king's cure! But although Helena possessed the important medicine, the king and all his doctors thought there was no remedy for his disease. They were unlikely to give credit to a poor uneducated woman if she offered to perform a cure. Even so, she strongly believed that the good medicine was sanctified by all the luckiest stars in Heaven to advance her fortune, even to the high dignity of becoming Count Roussillon's wife… But, anyway, she had to *do* something. "Our remedies can be found in ourselves," she thought.

The countess

Shortly after Bertram left, the countess was informed by her steward that he'd overheard Helena talking to herself. From some words she uttered, he understood she was in love with Bertram and was thinking of following him to Paris. The countess dismissed the steward with thanks, and asked him to tell Helena she wanted to speak to her. What she had just heard reminded her of days long past when her love for Bertram's father had begun.

"So it was with me when I was young," she said to herself. "Ah, love is a thorn that belongs to the rose of youth!"

While she was meditating on the romantic errors of her own youth, Helena entered.

"Ah, Helena, you know I am a mother to you."

"You are my honorable mistress," replied Helena.

"You are my *daughter*," said the countess. "And I am your *mother*. Why do you look so pale at my words?"

Alarmed and confused, Helena was afraid the countess suspected her love for Bertram, and she replied, "Pardon me, madam, but you are *not* my mother, the Count Roussillon is *not* my brother, and I am *not* your daughter."

"And yet, Helena, you *could* be my daughter-in-law. I think that is what you intend to be, and that's why the words 'mother' and 'daughter' disturb you. Helena, do you love my son?"

"Good madam, pardon me," said Helena, now very afraid.

"I said, do you love my son?"

"Don't you love him, madam?"

"Helena, don't give me such an evasive answer! Come on, admit your feelings!"

On her knees now, Helena replied, "Yes, I love your son."

Feeling both shame and terror, she implored the pardon of her mistress, and noting the sense she had of the great inequality between their fortunes, she said Bertram did not know she loved him. The countess then asked Helena whether she intended to go to Paris. Helena admitted that idea had formed in her mind when she heard Lafeu speak of the king's illness.

"Is that your *real* motive for wishing to go?" said the countess. "Is it? Tell me the truth!"

"My lord your son made me think of it," replied Helena in all honesty. "Otherwise, Paris and the king and the medicine may not have remained in my mind."

The countess heard the whole of this confession without saying a word either of approval or of blame. But she closely questioned Helena on the probability of the medicine being useful to the king. She found that it was the one *most* prized by Gerard de Narbon, and that he had given it to his daughter on his deathbed. The countess remembered the solemn promise she had made with regard to Helena. She realized Helena's plan might be the unseen workings of Providence to save the king and lay the foundation of the future fortunes of Gerard de Narbon's daughter. So she gave Helena free leave to pursue her own way and generously furnished her with ample means and suitable attendants.

And so Helena set out for Paris with the blessings of the countess and her kindest wishes for her success.

Helena goes to Paris

Soon after Helena arrived in Paris, she obtained an audience with the king thanks to the assistance of Lord Lafeu. She had many difficulties to overcome, for the king was not easily persuaded to try the medicine offered him by this young lady. But she told him she was the daughter of Gerard de Narbon, with whose fame the king was well acquainted. She explained that the precious medicine contained the essence of all her father's long experience and skill. And she boldly offered to give up her own life if it failed to restore his Majesty to perfect health within two days.

The king at length consented to try it, with the condition that if he did *not* recover in two days' time, she would lose her life.

"I agree, Your Majesty," replied Helena. "But if I *succeed*, what then?"

"Make your demand."

"Please promise to give me the choice of any nobleman in France—apart from your royal sons, of course—to be my husband."

"I agree. Here is my hand..."

Choosing a husband

Helena's belief in the power of the medicine proved correct. Before two days had passed, the king was restored to perfect health. Delighted, he assembled all the young noble bachelors of his court together, in order to confer the promised reward to his fair physician. He invited Helena to choose one to be her husband. It didn't take Helena very long to choose, as among the young lords she saw Bertram.

"This is the man, Your Majesty," she said. "Count Roussillon, I dare not say I *take* you, but I *give* myself and my service into your guiding power for the rest of my life!"

"Why, then, young Bertram," said the king, "take her to be your wife."

"My *wife*, Your Majesty! Please allow me to choose my wife with my own eyes!"

"Do you know what she has done for me?"

"I do, my good lord. But she is a poor physician's daughter, brought up at my father's charge, and now living entirely dependent on my mother's generosity."

"Is her humble status your problem?" asked the king. "I can easily increase that. Status depends not on blood but on what people *do*! Good is good without any name. She is young, wise and beautiful..."

"But I cannot love her, Your Majesty, and I will not try to do it!"

When Helena heard these words of rejection, she said to the king, "I am glad that you have recovered, Your Majesty. But please forget my fee."

But the king would not allow his royal command to be so slighted. The power of bestowing his nobles in marriage was one of the many privileges of the King of France.

"No," he said. "Proud boy, take her hand! You are unworthy of this good gift. Obey my will or I will throw you away from my care forever!"

"Pardon, Your Majesty," said Bertram. "I will take her hand."

So that very day Bertram was married to Helena. To Bertram, it was a forced and uneasy marriage. And it was not promising for poor Helena. She had acquired the noble husband she had risked her life to obtain. But her husband's *love* was not a gift the King of France had the power to bestow.

Helena was no sooner married than Bertram asked her to apply to the king for his leave of absence from the court. She soon brought him the king's permission for his departure.

Bertram told her that he was not prepared for this sudden marriage, it had unsettled him, and she should not be surprised at what he wanted to do. She was shocked to realize he intended to leave her. He ordered her to go home to his mother.

When Helena heard this unkind command, she replied, "All I can say to this is that I am your most obedient servant."

Her humble words did not move the haughty Bertram to pity his gentle wife. He left without even saying farewell.

A letter

So back to Roussillon went Helena. She had accomplished the two aims of her journey: she'd saved the life of the king and she'd married her great love, the Count Roussillon. But she returned to her noble mother-in-law a dejected woman. And as soon as she entered the house, she received a letter from Bertram which almost broke her heart.

The good countess received her with a warm welcome, as if she had been her son's own choice and was a lady of high status. She spoke kind words to comfort Helena for her son's unkind behavior in sending his wife home alone on her bridal day. But this gracious reception failed to cheer up the sad mind of Helena.

"Madam, my lord is gone, forever gone!"

She then read out some words from Bertram's letter:

> *When you can get the ring from my finger, which will never come off, then you can call me husband. But as for 'Then' I say 'Never'!*

"This is such a dreadful sentence!" said Helena.

The countess begged her to be patient, and said, "Now Bertram has gone, you will be my only child. You deserve a husband that twenty such rude boys as Bertram would serve, and hourly call you 'mistress'!"

But the considerate mother failed to soothe the sorrows of her daughter-in-law.

Helena still had her eyes fixed on the letter, and cried out in an agony of grief, "*Until I have no wife, there is nothing for me in France!*"

"Are those words in the letter?"

"Yes . . ."

When she was alone again, Helena hastily cooked up another plan.

"Come, night; end, day! And in the dark, like a thief, I'll steal away!"

Pilgrimage

The next morning Helena had gone. She left a letter to be delivered to her mother-in-law after her departure, explaining the reason for her sudden absence. In the letter she told her that she was very upset at having driven Bertram from France and his home. To atone for her offense, she would undertake a pilgrimage to the shrine of St. Jaques le Grand. She ended by asking the countess to tell her son that the wife he so hated had left his house forever.

When he left Paris, Bertram went to Florence, and there

became an officer in the Duke of Florence's army. After a successful war, in which he distinguished himself by many brave actions, Bertram received letters from his mother. They contained the welcome news that Helena would not disturb him any more. As he was preparing to return home, he had no idea that Helena herself, dressed in her pilgrim's clothes, had just arrived in Florence.

Many pilgrims passed through Florence on their way to St. Jaques le Grand. Helena heard that a hospitable widow welcomed female pilgrims to stay in her house. Helena went there at once, and the widow gave her a courteous welcome and offered to show her around the sights of that famous city. She also said that if Helena would like to see a presentation of the duke's army, she could take her to a place where she would have a full view of it.

"And you will see a countryman of yours," said the widow. "His name is Count Roussillon, and he has done worthy service in the duke's wars." Helena needed no second invitation when she learned that Bertram was to be there.

A secret visit

So Helena accompanied the talkative widow to the event. And, sure enough, Bertram the hero was on display. It was a bitter-sweet pleasure to see her dear husband's face again.

"Don't you think he's handsome?" said the widow.

"Well, yes, I do!" replied Helena.

On the walk back to the house, the widow's chat was all

about Bertram. She told Helena the story of his marriage, and how he'd deserted the poor lady his wife and joined the duke's army to avoid living with her. Helena listened patiently to this account of her own misfortunes. But there was more to the history of Bertram than she was aware. The widow began another story about Bertram's new love, and every word cut deep into Helena's heart.

Although Bertram was not happy with the marriage forced on him by the king, it seemed he was not totally avert to romance. Since he'd been stationed with the army in Florence, he'd fallen in love with Diana, the daughter of the widow who was Helena's hostess. Every night, he would come under her window and serenade her love, with music of all sorts and songs composed in praise of her beauty. And his greatest hope was that she would allow him to visit her secretly after her mother had gone to bed. However, Diana could by no means be persuaded to grant this improper request. And knowing him to be a married man, she didn't encourage him. She had been well brought up by her prudent mother, who was descended from the noble Capulet family.

All this the widow told Helena, praising the high principles of her discreet daughter, which she claimed to be entirely due to the excellent education and good advice *she* had given her! She added that Bertram had been particularly eager for Diana to admit him to her room that night, as he was leaving Florence early the next morning.

It naturally upset Helena to hear all this, but it stimulated her sharp mind to come up with another plan to recover her truant lord. First, she revealed to the widow that she was in fact Helena, Bertram's deserted wife. She then requested her kind hostess and daughter to allow the secret visit from Bertram to take place, but to allow *her* to pretend to be Diana. She explained that her chief motive was to get a ring from his finger. He had told her that if ever she succeeded in the impossible mission of possessing it he would acknowledge her as his wife. The two kind ladies promised to assist her. They were partly moved by pity for the unhappy, forsaken wife and partly won over by the purse of gold Helena offered them.

During the day, Helena also made sure that the news she had *died* reached Bertram. She was hoping that he would then think himself free to make a second choice and propose marriage to her in her guise as Diana. If she could obtain that promise and the ring, she was sure she could make some future good come of it.

The exchange of rings

That night, after the widow had retired to bed, Bertram was finally admitted into Diana's dark room. And Helena was there ready to receive him. The flattering compliments and passionate love talk he addressed to her were indeed precious sounds to her ears, even though she knew they were intended for Diana.

Bertram had never appreciated just how smart Helena was. If he had, then perhaps he would not have been so regardless of her. Moreover, seeing her every day, he had entirely overlooked her beauty. And it was impossible he could notice her wit, because she felt such reverence for him, mixed with love, that she'd always been silent in his presence! But now her future fate, and the happy ending of her love projects, seemed to depend on her leaving a favorable impression on his mind.

She exerted all her powers to please him. The simple grace of her lively conversation and the endearing sweetness of her manners so charmed Bertram that he made a solemn promise to be her husband, and to love her forever. Helena eagerly hoped this was prophetic of the real affection he would feel when he learned it was his own wife, the despised Helena, whose conversation had so delighted him.

Helena then begged the ring from his finger as a token of his vow, and he willingly gave it to her. In return, she gave him a ring which had been a present from the King of France. Before dawn broke, she sent Bertram away. Shortly after, he set out on his journey toward his mother's house.

Helena then asked the widow and Diana to accompany her to Paris, their further assistance being necessary to fully accomplish the plan she'd formed. When they arrived, they found the king had left to visit the Countess of Roussillon. Helena and the two ladies followed the king as fast as they could...

Reunions in Roussillon

The king was still in perfect health. His gratitude to Helena who had saved him was so lively in his mind that the moment he saw the Countess of Roussillon he began to talk about her.

He called her a precious jewel that was lost by her son's folly.

"It is all past," said the countess. "Your Majesty, please regard it as the rebellion of youth."

"My good lady, I have forgiven and forgotten all."

But the good-natured Lafeu, who had traveled there with the king, could not stand that the memory of his favorite Helena should be so lightly passed over.

"This I must say," he said, "The young lord greatly offended Your Majesty, his mother, and Helena. But to himself he did the greatest wrong of all. He has lost a wife whose beauty astonished all eyes, whose words captivated all ears, and whose perfection made all hearts wish to serve her."

"Yes," said the king, "Praising what is lost makes the remembrance dear."

Bertram now arrived and presented himself before the king. He expressed deep sorrow for the injuries he'd done to Helena. For his late father's and his admirable mother's sake, the king pardoned him and restored him once more to his favor.

But suddenly the gracious countenance of the king clouded over. He had just noticed that Bertram was wearing the ring which he had given to Helena. And he remembered clearly that Helena had called all the saints in Heaven to witness that she would never part with that ring unless she sent it to the king when something very bad happened to her.

The king immediately asked Bertram how he came to have that ring. Bertram told an unlikely story of a lady throwing it to him out of a window, and he denied ever having seen Helena since the day of their marriage. Knowing Bertram's dislike of his wife, the king feared he had killed her, and he ordered his guards to seize Bertram.

"I am enveloped in dismal thoughts," said the king, "as I fear the life of Helena was snatched away by foul means!"

At this moment, Diana and her mother rushed in and presented a petition to the king. It begged His Majesty to exert his royal power to compel Bertram to marry Diana, as he had made her a solemn promise of marriage. Fearing the king's anger, Bertram denied making any such promise. Then Diana produced the ring which Helena had given her to confirm the truth of her words. She said she had given Bertram the ring he was then wearing, in exchange for that one, at the time he vowed to marry her.

On hearing this, the king ordered the guards to seize her as well. Her account of the ring differed from Bertram's, so the king's suspicions seemed to be confirmed. He said that if they did not confess how they came by Helena's ring they would both be put to death. Diana requested her mother might be permitted to bring in the jeweler from whom she got the ring. Her request was granted and she went out, and presently returned, leading in Helena herself…

There were gasps all around the room.

Finding Helena was still living, the good countess, who loved her with a mother's affection, felt a huge sense of relief and delight.

The king could hardly believe it was really Helena. "Is this indeed the wife of Bertram?" he said, filled with surprise and joy.

"No, Your Majesty," replied Helena, "it is only the shadow of a wife you see; the name, but not the thing."

"No, both, both!" cried out Bertram. "Oh, Helena, I beg your pardon!"

"Oh, my eyes smell onions," cried Lafeu. "I think I'm going to cry..."

"Oh, my lord," said Helena, "when I impersonated this fair lady, I found you amazingly kind. And look, here is your letter!" Then she read out in a joyful tone those words she had once repeated so sorrowfully. "'*When you can get the ring from my finger...*' It was to *me* you gave the ring, so it is *done*! Bertram, will you be mine, now you are doubly won?"

"If you can *prove* that you were the lady I talked with that night," Bertram replied, "I will love you dearly for ever..."

That was not a difficult task, as it was the reason the widow and Diana had gone there with Helena. Diana reported what had happened. The king was very pleased with her for the friendly assistance she had rendered Helena, who he so truly valued for the service she had done him. He promised Diana also a noble husband and said he would provide her dowry! Helena's story had given him a hint that it was a suitable reward for kings to bestow on fair ladies when they performed notable services.

Helena had at last found that her father's legacy was indeed sanctified by the luckiest stars in Heaven. She was now the beloved wife of her dear Bertram, the daughter-in-law of her noble mistress, and herself the Countess of Roussillon.

So, as the smiling King of France himself commented, "All's well that ends well!"

10

The Taming of the Shrew

じゃじゃ馬ならし

読み始める前に

陽気な恋のかけひきを描く初期の喜劇。Shrewはネズミの一種で、耳障りな声で鳴くことから「口やかましい女」の代名詞となっている。

[登場人物]

Katharine	キャサリン《バプティスタの長女、じゃじゃ馬》
Kate	ケイト《キャサリンの別名》
Petruchio	ペトルーチオ《キャサリンの求婚者》
Baptista	バプティスタ《裕福な商人、キャサリンとビアンカの父》
Bianca	ビアンカ《バプティスタの次女》
Lucentio	ルーセンシオ《ビアンカの求婚者》
Vincentio	ヴィンセンシオ《ルーセンシオの父》
Hortensio	ホーテンシオ《ペトルーチオの古い友人》

[地名など]

Padua	パドヴァ《イタリアの都市》
Pisa	ピサ《イタリアの都市》
Verona	ヴェローナ《イタリアの都市》

[あらすじ]

富豪の娘キャサリンは美人だが、勝ち気で怒りっぽく、手におえないじゃじゃ馬むすめ。結婚相手がなかなか見つからない。そこへ、妻になる人を探しているペトルーチオが現れ、持参金欲しさにキャサリンに求婚する。

縁談が成立すると、ペトルーチオは「じゃじゃ馬ならし作戦」を始めた。キャサリンに食べ物も睡眠も与えない、召使いを怒鳴り散らして乱暴な態度をとる、キャサリンが何か言っても、聞き違えたふりをしてまともに取り合わない——ペトルーチオの作戦は、キャサリンを上回るほどのあらあらしい言動をすることだった。

キャサリンは次第に、ペトルーチオにさからわないことが最善策と悟り、従順でおとなしい女性に変わっていく。

[総単語数] 3,790語

THE TAMING OF THE SHREW

Once upon a time, in the Italian city of Padua, not far from Venice, there lived a rich gentleman called Baptista. He had two daughters. The elder one, Katharine, was a young woman of such an uncontrollable spirit and fiery temper, that she was widely known as 'Katharine the Shrew'. At that time, the term 'shrew' referred to a bad-tempered, noisy woman like her. It seemed very unlikely, indeed impossible, that any man would ever be found who was bold enough to marry her. On the other hand, many men were eager to marry her gentle younger sister, Bianca. Baptista was blamed by them a lot for postponing his consent to *her* marriage. But he insisted it would not happen until her elder sister was safely off his hands!

The man from Verona

One day, however, a gentleman named Petruchio came to Padua from Verona with the specific aim of finding a wife. He was not at all discouraged by the reports he heard of Katharine's temper. When he also learned she was rich and good-looking, he resolved to marry her and 'tame' her into a meek and obedient wife, just like he would tame a hawk or a dog!

And nobody was more suitable than Petruchio to take on that mighty task. He was a smart, witty, good-tempered man. And he knew well how to pretend to be passionate and angry when he actually felt perfectly calm. He could laugh at his own fake anger, for he was naturally easy-going.

One of Bianca's suitors said to Petruchio, "We will be most grateful if you succeed! Perhaps you should 'break the ice' by talking to her father first."

And so Petruchio went to court Katharine the Shrew. First, he visited her father.

"Sir, I have come to ask your permission to woo your gentle daughter Katharine. Having heard about her modesty and mild behavior, I came all the way from Verona hoping to marry her!"

Although Baptista wanted Katharine married as soon as possible, he had to confess she was not quite the woman Petruchio had described. This was proved at that moment by her music teacher rushing into the room. He complained that Katharine had hit him on the head with her lute for criticizing her playing.

When Petruchio heard this, he said, "Oh, she's a bold

woman indeed! That makes me love her even more. I long to have a chat with her. I am a very busy man, Signor Baptista. I cannot come every day to woo her. You knew my father, I believe. Well, he has died, and left me as the heir to all his lands and goods. Please tell me, if I obtain your daughter's love, what dowry you will give with her."

Baptista thought Petruchio's manner was rather blunt for a lover. However, he was so eager to get Katharine married, he replied that he would give twenty thousand crowns for her dowry, and half his estate after his death. And so the rather odd match was quickly agreed on. Baptista went to tell Katharine what Petruchio had said, and then sent her in to talk to him.

First meeting

While he waited, Petruchio considered what style of courtship he should use.

"Hmm... I think I'll talk to her with some spirit when she comes in. If she starts getting angry, I'll tell her that she sings as sweetly as a nightingale. If she frowns, I'll say she looks as fresh as roses newly washed with dew. If she remains silent, I'll praise the eloquence of her words. And if she asks me to leave, I'll give her thanks as though she'd asked me to stay with her for a week..."

And then the stately Katharine entered the room.

"Ah, good morning, Kate, for I hear that is your name."

"Really?" she replied sharply. "Well, maybe your hearing is bad? All those who speak about me call me Katharine."

"No, you're lying! You're called just Kate, and Bonny Kate, and sometimes even Kate the Cursed. But, Kate, you are the prettiest Kate in the world, my super-dainty Kate. And therefore, Kate, hearing your mildness and virtues and beauty praised everywhere, I have come to ask you to marry me!"

It was a strange kind of courtship. With her loud and angry words, Katharine showed just why she had gained the name of 'Shrew,' while Petruchio continued to praise her sweet and courteous words.

At last, Petruchio heard her father coming, and said, "Sweet Katharine, let us stop this idle chat! Your father has consented that you shall be my wife, your dowry is agreed on, and, whether you are willing or not, I *will* marry you!"

Baptista entered. Petruchio told him his daughter had received him kindly, and that she'd promised to marry him the next Sunday. This Katharine denied at once, saying she would rather see him *hanged* on Sunday. She reproached her father for wishing to marry her to such a crazy roughneck as Petruchio. Petruchio asked her father to ignore her angry words. He explained that the two of them had agreed she should *seem* reluctant in front of him, but as soon as they were alone she was very fond and loving.

And he said to Katharine, "Give me your hand, Kate. I will now go to Venice to buy clothes for our wedding. Father, please provide the feast and invite all the guests. I will be sure to bring rings and gorgeous clothes, so that my Katharine will look perfect! And so, kiss me, Kate, for we will be married on Sunday!"

The wedding day

The following Sunday, all the wedding guests assembled. However, Petruchio did not appear... They all had to wait...and wait... Katharine wept from anger, believing Petruchio had only been making fun of her.

But then suddenly he appeared. He had brought none of the bridal finery he had promised her. Nor was he dressed like a bridegroom, but was wearing strange, messy, dirty clothes, as if he meant to make a sport of the serious wedding business. His servant and the horses on which they rode were also dressed strangely. But Petruchio refused to change into something more suitable. He said Katharine was to be married to *him*, and not to his *clothes*. It was impossible to argue with him, so they all went into the church.

Petruchio continued behaving in the same crazy way. When the priest asked him if Katharine should be his wife, he swore so loud that everyone was shocked. The priest dropped his book. As he stooped down to pick it up, the wild bridegroom gave him such a push that down went the priest and his book again. And all the time they were being married, Petruchio stamped his feet and swore so much that even the high-spirited Katharine trembled and shook with fear.

Once the ceremony was over, while they were still in the church, Petruchio called for some wine. It was brought. He then loudly toasted everyone's health and kissed Katharine so loudly that the whole church echoed. There had never been such a ridiculous marriage ceremony!

Baptista had prepared a splendid marriage feast. But as they were all leaving the church, Petruchio took hold of Katharine, and said he would carry her home at once. He thanked everyone for observing his marriage to his sweet, patient wife. Neither his father-in-law, or the angry Katharine, or anyone else, could make him change his mind. Petruchio claimed a husband's right to treat his wife as he pleased, and away he hurried, carrying Katharine. No-one dared to stop him.

Petruchio placed his wife on a very old, thin horse, specially chosen for the purpose. He and his servant rode on similar horses. The three of them traveled slowly along the rough and muddy tracks. And whenever Katharine's horse stumbled, Petruchio swore at the poor animal.

Home, sweet home!

At long last, after the tiring journey, during which Katharine had heard nothing but Petruchio shouting at his servant and the horses, they arrived at his house. Petruchio welcomed her kindly to her new home. But he declared that she should neither sleep nor eat that night.

The table was spread, and supper soon served. But Petruchio pretended to find some fault with every dish, and threw all the food on the floor. He said he did this out of love for Katharine. He did not want her to eat anything that was not properly cooked.

When the weary and hungry Katharine finally retired to rest, Petruchio found some problems with the bed. He threw

the pillows and bedclothes all around the room, so she was forced to sit down in a chair. But whenever she dozed off, she was immediately woken up by the loud voice of her husband screaming at the servants for making his wife's bridal bed so badly.

The poorest service

The next day, Petruchio continued with the same plan. He still spoke kind words to Katharine. But if she attempted to eat, he found fault with everything placed in front of her. He threw the breakfast on the floor just as he had done the supper. And the proud Katharine was reduced to begging the servants to secretly bring her some morsels of food. But, as instructed by Petruchio, they replied that they dared not give her anything behind their master's back.

"Ah," she said to herself, "did he marry me to *starve* me to death? Beggars that come to my father's door are given food. But I, who have never had to ask for anything in my whole life, am starved for want of food, giddy for want of sleep, and kept awake with shouting! And what annoys me most is that he claims he does it in the name of *love*!"

Petruchio came in. Not intending to starve her, he had brought her a small portion of meat.

"Ah, how fares my sweet Kate? Here, my love, see how kind I am! I've prepared your meat myself. I'm sure this kindness deserves some thanks... What, not a word? You don't like my meat, eh? So all the effort I've taken was to no purpose?"

He ordered a servant to take the dish away.

Extreme hunger, which had greatly reduced Katharine's pride, made her say, "Please leave it..."

But Petruchio wanted more than that. "The poorest service receives *thanks*, and so will mine before you touch that meat."

Reluctantly, Katharine murmured, "Thank you."

Petruchio smiled. He urged her to enjoy the small meal, saying, "I hope it will do your gentle heart good, Kate. Please eat! And now, my honey love, we will return to your father's house and have a good time, with silken coats and caps and golden rings, with ruffs and scarves and fans and beads and amber bracelets."

The tailor and the haberdasher

To make Katharine believe he really intended to give her those things, Petruchio called in a tailor and a haberdasher. They brought the new dress and fashionable hat he had ordered for her.

The haberdasher first presented a cap, saying, "Here is what you ordered, sir."

"Hmm," said Petruchio, "it looks like it was molded on a pudding bowl, and it's no bigger than a walnut shell, a baby's cap! Take it away and make it bigger!"

"Oh, no," said Katharine, "I will have this one. It's the latest fashion for gentlewomen to wear caps like this!"

"When *you* are gentle," replied Petruchio, "you shall have one, too, but not till then."

The meat Katharine had eaten had revived her fallen spirits a little, and she said, "I hope I'm allowed to speak, and I will speak. I am not a child or a baby. Better men than you have let me say what's on my mind; and if you can't, you should stop up your ears!"

"What you say is true," replied Petruchio. "It's a miserable little cap, like a silken pie! And I love you for not liking it."

"Love me or love me not, I *like* this cap, and I will have this one or none."

"Do you want to see your dress now?" said Petruchio, still pretending not to understand her.

The tailor showed her the lovely dress he had made for her. Petruchio intended her to have neither the cap nor the dress, so he found fault in it.

"Oh, Heaven! What kind of stuff is this! Do you call this a sleeve? It's like a small cannon, carved up and down like an apple tart! It's all snip and nip and cut and slash!"

"Sir, you asked me to make it according to the latest fashion," said the tailor.

"And I have never seen a better-fashioned dress," said Katharine.

This was enough for Petruchio. With fierce words and furious gestures, he drove the tailor and the haberdasher out of the room. (However, he secretly arranged to pay the craftsmen for their fine work, and apologized for his strange behavior.)

Then he turned to Katharine, and said, "Well, Kate, I think we can visit your father's house in these simple garments we're wearing now. You see, it's the *mind* that makes the body rich. Honor appears in the meanest clothes, just like the sun breaking through the darkest clouds. Is the jay more precious than the lark because its feathers are more beautiful? Oh, no, good Kate."

And then he ordered his horses to be made ready.

"Let's see... It's now seven o'clock in the morning, so we should get there in time for dinner."

"Actually," said Katharine, "it's two o'clock in the afternoon, and it will be suppertime before we get there."

Before he could take her to see her father, Petruchio wanted her to agree to everything he said. He spoke as if he were lord even of the sun and could command the hours of the day.

"When we leave here," he said, "it will be whatever o'clock I say it is! You are still arguing with me, Kate! So, we will *not* go there today!"

On the road...

The next day, Katharine forced herself to practice her newly found obedience. Petruchio would not allow her to go to her father's house until he had made her forget the idea of contradicting him.

At last they set out. But even as they traveled, Katharine felt she was in constant danger of being turned back again.

At noon, Petruchio suddenly said, "Oh, how brightly the moon is shining today!"

"The moon?" replied Katharine. "It's the sun, not moonlight."

"But I say it's the *moon* that shines so bright."

"I *know* it's the *sun* that shines so bright."

"Kate," said Petruchio, stopping his horse, "it will be the moon, or the stars, or whatever I say it is, before I will travel to your father's house."

He looked as if he was about to head back home again.

But Katharine was no longer the Shrew. She said, "Oh, let us keep going, now that we have come so far! It will be the sun, or the moon, or whatever you please! And even if you want to call it a *candle*, I promise it will be a candle for me as well!"

Petruchio wanted proof, so he repeated, "I say it's the moon."

"I *know* it is the *moon*!" replied Katharine.

"You lie. It's the blessed sun."

"Then it's the blessed sun. But sun it is not when you say it is not! Whatever you will have it named, so it is, and so it ever shall be for me, too."

And so they continued on their journey to Padua. Petruchio wanted to see if Katharine's attitude would last, so when they met an old gentleman on the way he addressed him as if he was a young woman.

"Greetings, young lady! Katharine, have you ever seen a lovelier young woman? What pleasant red and white cheeks, and eyes like two bright stars!" He spoke to the old man again, saying, "Oh, lovely girl, once more greetings to you!" And he said to his wife, "Sweet Kate, please embrace her for her beauty's sake!"

Katharine immediately agreed with her husband's opinion, and said to the old man, "Young and budding virgin, you are so lovely and fresh and sweet. Where do you live and where are you going? Your parents must be so happy to have such a nice child!"

"Kate," said Petruchio. "I hope you haven't gone mad! This is an old and wrinkled man, and not a young girl, as you say he is."

"Oh, please pardon me, sir," she said immediately. "The sun

has so dazzled my eyes that everything I see looks green! Now I can tell you are a gentleman. I hope you will pardon me for my awful mistake."

"Yes, please forgive us both!" said Petruchio. "May I ask which way you are traveling? We shall be glad of your company if we are going the same way."

"Good sir, and you, my merry lady," the old gentleman replied, "our strange encounter surprised me! My name is Vincentio, I come from Pisa, and I am going to visit my son Lucentio who lives in Padua."

Then Petruchio realized Vincentio was the father of the young gentleman who was about to be married to Bianca, Baptista's younger daughter. He made the old man very happy by telling him about the charming and wealthy wife his son would have.

They journeyed on pleasantly together until they reached Baptista's house. Many guests were assembling to celebrate the wedding of Bianca and Lucentio. Baptista had willingly consented to the marriage once Katharine was off his hands.

The wedding feast

Baptista welcomed them warmly to the wedding feast. Another newly married couple were present: Petruchio's old friend Hortensio and his wife, who was a wealthy widow.

Lucentio and Hortensio could not avoid making sly comments hinting at the shrewish character of Petruchio's wife. The fond bridegrooms seemed highly pleased with the mild characters of the ladies *they* had both chosen. They laughed at Petruchio for his less fortunate choice.

Petruchio took little notice of their jokes until the ladies retired from the table after dinner. Then he noticed Baptista himself joining in the laughter against him. When Petruchio stated that his wife would surely prove more obedient than theirs, her father said, "Sadly, my son-in-law Petruchio, I fear you've got the least obedient one of all."

"Well," said Petruchio, "I disagree! And to prove that I'm speaking the truth, let each one of us husbands send for his wife. He whose wife is most obedient, and comes at once, will win a wager which we will propose."

The other two husbands willingly consented to this bet. Each one of them was confident that his loving wife would prove more obedient than the headstrong Katharine. They proposed a wager of twenty crowns. But Petruchio only laughed. He said he would bet that much on his hawk or his hound, but he'd bet twenty times as much on his wife. So Lucentio and Hortensio raised the wager to a hundred crowns each.

Lucentio offered to go first. He sent his servant to ask Bianca to come to him.

But the servant soon returned and said: "Sir, my mistress says she is busy and cannot come."

"What?" said Petruchio, laughing. "She's *busy* and can't come? What kind of an answer is that for a wife to give?"

Then they all laughed at him, and said it would be well if Katharine did not send him a *worse* answer.

Next it was Hortensio's turn. He said to his servant, "Go and entreat my wife to come to me."

"Oh, yes," said Petruchio. "*Entreat* her! Then she will surely come!"

"I'm afraid, Petruchio," said Hortensio, "that *your* wife will never be entreated!"

However, his servant returned without his mistress.

"What? Where is my wife?"

"Sir, my mistress says you must be playing some kind of joke and therefore she will not come. Instead, she bids *you* go to *her*."

"Oh, worse and worse!" cried Petruchio. And then he sent his servant, saying, "Go to your mistress and tell her I *command* her to come to me."

They had scarcely had time to think she would never obey an order like that when Baptista exclaimed in amazement. "Here she comes!"

Katharine entered the room and said meekly to Petruchio, "What do you require of me, dear husband?"

"Where are your sister and Hortensio's wife?"

"They're sitting chatting by the fireplace."

"Go and fetch them here!" said Petruchio. "And if they refuse, hit them!"

Away went Katharine to perform her husband's command.

"Oh, here is a wonder indeed!" said Lucentio.

"And so it is," said Hortensio. "What does this mean, Petruchio?"

"Oh, it means peace, and love, and a quiet life, and, to be

short, everything that is sweet and happy."

Overjoyed to see Katharine's reformation, Baptista said: "Now, good Petruchio! You have won the wager, and I will add another twenty thousand crowns to her dowry, just as if she were another daughter, for she is so changed!"

"Well," said Petruchio, "I will win the wager better yet, and show more signs of her new virtue and obedience."

Katharine returned with the two other wives.

"Ah, here she comes," continued Petruchio, "bringing your obstinate wives as prisoners to her womanly persuasion! Katharine, I don't think that cap of yours suits you at all! Take it off and throw it on the floor!"

Katharine instantly took off her cap and threw it down.

"Oh!" said Hortensio's wife, "I hope *I* will never have to do anything so silly!"

And Bianca said, "What kind of foolish duty do you call this?"

"I wish *your* sense of duty were as foolish!" said her husband. "The wisdom of your sense has cost me a hundred crowns!"

"Well, the more fool you," replied Bianca, "for laying money on my duty!"

"Katharine," said Petruchio, "Please tell these stubborn women what duty they owe their lords and husbands."

To the wonder of everyone present, the reformed Shrew spoke eloquently in praise of a wife's duty of obedience as she had practiced it by submitting to Petruchio's will.

"I'm ashamed," she said, "that we women are so simple that

we offer war when we should kneel for peace; or seek for rule and supremacy when we have a duty to serve, love and obey our husbands."

Katharine once more became famous. But this time it was not as the Shrew, but as the most obedient and duteous wife in Padua.

The Comedy of Errors

間違いの喜劇

読み始める前に

シェイクスピア最初期の作品で、瓜二つの2組の双子が取り違えられることから起こる混乱を描いた喜劇。シェイクスピアの劇の中ではもっとも短い。

［登場人物］

Aegeon　イージオン《シラクサの商売人》

Antipholus of Ephesus　兄アンティフォラス（エフェソスのアンティフォラス）《イージオンの息子》

Antipholus of Syracuse　弟アンティフォラス（シラクサのアンティフォラス）《イージオンの息子》

Dromio of Ephesus　兄ドローミオ（エフェソスのドローミオ）《兄アンティフォラスに仕える》

Dromio of Syracuse　弟ドローミオ（シラクサのドローミオ）《弟アンティフォラスに仕える》

Adriana　エイドリアーナ《兄アンティフォラスの妻》

Luciana　ルシアーナ《エイドリアーナの妹》

Adriana's cook　料理女《兄ドローミオの妻》

Menaphon　メナフォン公《有名な軍人。エフェソス公のおじ》

Duke of Ephesus　エフェソス公《エフェソスの領主》

Abbess　尼僧院長

［地名など］

Ephesus　エフェソス《古代都市》

Epidamnum　エピダムヌス《古代都市》

Syracuse　シラクサ《古代都市》

［あらすじ］

双子のアンティフォラス兄弟とその召使いの双子ドローミオ兄弟は、幼い頃に事故でそれぞれが離れ離れになってしまい、兄同士、弟同士が敵対する国に分かれて暮らしていたが、父イージオンと暮らしていた弟アンティフォラスは弟ドローミオと共に、兄探しの旅に出る。

兄たちが住むエフェソスにやってきた二人は、街のあちこちで兄と間違われ、間違いが間違いを生み、大騒ぎに。

［総単語数］4,590語

THE COMEDY OF ERRORS

Once upon a time in Ancient Greece, the cities of Syracuse and Ephesus were on very bad terms with each other. Ephesus had made a cruel law ordaining that if any merchant from Syracuse was seen in Ephesus he would be put to death unless he could pay one thousand marks.

Aegeon's story

One day, an old merchant of Syracuse named Aegeon, was discovered in the streets of Ephesus, and brought before the Duke. He was ordered either to pay the heavy fine or receive the death sentence, as the law stated. But Aegeon had no money to pay the fine. But before pronouncing the sentence of death on him, the Duke requested him to tell the story of his life, and also explain why he'd dared to enter Ephesus, knowing the great risk.

Aegeon said that he was not afraid to die, for sorrow had made him weary of living. But relating the events of his unfortunate life was an even heavier sentence! However, he began.

"I was born in Syracuse, and brought up to be a merchant. I married a lady, with whom I lived very happily. However, I had to go to Epidamnum on the Adriatic Sea, and I was detained there by my business for six months. Finding I would have to stay there even longer, I sent for my wife. Well, as soon as she arrived, she gave birth to two sons. And what was very strange was that they were twins who both looked exactly the same. It was impossible to distinguish one from the other!

"By chance, a poor woman in the inn where my wife was lodging also had identical twins at the same time. She and her husband were very poor, so I bought the two boys and brought them up to attend on my sons.

"Our sons were fine boys, and my wife was very proud of them. But after a while, she felt homesick. Every day she said she wanted to return home to Syracuse and eventually I agreed to take her, although I was not very willing. So, one terrible day, we got on board a ship bound for home. But we had not sailed far from Epidamnum when a dreadful storm blew up. It continued with such violence that the sailors, seeing no chance of saving the ship, all crowded into the lifeboat to save their own lives. They left us alone on the ship! Can you believe it?

We every moment expected the storm would kill us.

"As I'm sure you can imagine, the non-stop weeping of my wife and the cries of our pretty boys filled me with terror. I didn't fear death myself, but all my thoughts were concentrated on finding some way to save them. I tied my younger son to the end of a small mast, such as sailors provide for storm conditions. At the other end, I tied the younger of the other twins. I showed my wife how to fasten the other children to another mast. So she had the care of the two elder children, and I had the care of the younger two. Without that preparation, I think we would all have drowned, as the ship soon split on a mighty rock and was dashed to pieces.

"Clinging to those slender masts, our heads were all supported above the waves. But I was unable to assist my wife, who, with the other children, was soon separated from me. But at least I saw them picked up by a fishing boat. Having seen them rescued, I focused on struggling with the wild waves to preserve the two boys.

"At length, we were also picked up by a ship. Luckily, I knew the sailors, and they gave us a kind welcome and assistance and landed us safely at Syracuse. But since that sad hour I have no idea what happened to my wife and the two other boys.

"When my son reached the age of eighteen, he began to wonder about the fate of his mother and brother. He often asked me if he could go with his servant in search of both their brothers. At first, I was unwilling to give my consent. I was anxious to hear news of my lost wife and son, of course, but I didn't want to risk losing my *other* son. But eventually I let them go.

"It's now seven years since my son left me, and for five years I have been traveling in search of him. I've been to the far corners of Greece and around the countries of Asia, but no success. On my way home, I landed here in Ephesus, unwilling to miss any place where *he* might have landed.

"This day must end this story of my life. But I could die happy if only I was assured that my wife and sons are still alive…"

Here poor Aegeon ended the account of his misfortunes. The Duke felt great pity for this unfortunate father and would have liked to freely pardon him. But he said his oath and dignity did not allow him to alter the law. The strict letter of the law required instant death. However, instead of dooming Aegeon immediately, the Duke said he would give him the whole day until sunset to try and beg or borrow the money to pay the fine.

This one day of grace did not seem much of a great favor to Aegeon, who knew nobody in Ephesus. And there seemed to him little chance that any stranger would lend, or give him, one thousand marks. Feeling helpless and with little hope of any relief, Aegeon left the presence of the Duke in the custody of a jailer.

The boys from Syracuse

Besides being exactly alike in all respects, Aegeon's sons were both named Antipholus. And the two twin servants were also both named Dromio. Antipholus of Syracuse happened to arrive at Ephesus with *his* Dromio the very same day as his father. Being another Syracusian merchant, he was in the same danger. But, by good fortune, he met a friend who told him the peril an old merchant of Syracuse was in that very day, and advised Antipholus to pretend to be from Epidamnum. Antipholus agreed. He was sorry to hear one of his own countrymen was in danger, never imagining that the old merchant was actually his father.

The other son of Aegeon, who we can refer to as Antipholus of Ephesus, had actually been living in Ephesus for twenty years. He was now a rich man, so he could easily have paid the money to save his father's life. But he knew nothing about his father. He was so young when he was saved with his mother by the fishermen. He had no recollection of either his father or his mother. In fact, to the great grief of his unhappy mother, the fishermen had taken the two boys away from her, intending to sell them.

Antipholus and Dromio were first sold by them to Menaphon, a famous warrior who was the Duke of Ephesus' uncle. He took the boys with him when he went to Ephesus to visit his nephew. The Duke took an instant liking to young Antipholus and took over his care. When Antipholus grew up he was made an officer in the Duke's army. He distinguished himself by his great bravery in the wars, and even saved his patron's life. The Duke rewarded Antipholus by marrying him to Adriana, a rich lady of Ephesus. And he was living with her and his servant Dromio when his father arrived in the city.

Antipholus of Syracuse

When Antipholus of Syracuse parted with his friend, he gave his servant Dromio some money to carry to the inn where he intended to dine. He said he would walk about to view the city and observe the manners of the people.

Dromio of Syracuse was a pleasant man. Whenever Antipholus felt dull or depressed, Dromio would entertain him with jokes and funny stories. So the master and his servant spoke more freely to each other than was normal. After Dromio had left, Antipholus stood for a while remembering his solitary wanderings in search of his mother and his brother. Nowhere had he heard any news of them.

"Ah," he said to himself, unhappily, "I'm like a drop of water in the ocean which loses itself in the wide sea as it seeks to find its fellow drop... As I've sought my lost mother and brother, I think I've lost myself as well!"

While he was meditating on his travels, Dromio returned. Surprised that he'd come back so soon, Antipholus asked him where he'd left the money. He failed to realize it was not his own Dromio, but the twin brother that lived in Ephesus!

"My mistress sent me to tell you to come home for dinner," Dromio replied. "The chicken's burnt, the pig's falling from the spit, and everything will be cold if you don't come home soon! That's why my mistress is so hot!"

"Forget the jokes," said Antipholus, irritated. "Where did you leave the money?"

Dromio just repeated that his mistress had sent him.

"*What* mistress?" said Antipholus.

"Why, your wife, sir!" replied Dromio.

"I don't have a wife!" said Antipholus angrily. "Just because I sometimes chat casually with you, you think you can freely make fun of me! I am not in a light mood right now. Where is the money? We're strangers here, Dromio. How dare you trust my money with anybody?"

Dromio now thought Antipholus was joking, so he replied in a cheerful manner. "Please, sir, save the jokes until you're eating your dinner. My only order was to fetch you home to dine with my mistress and your sister-in-law."

Now Antipholus lost all patience with Dromio, and hit him. Dromio ran home and told his mistress that his master had refused to come to dinner and claimed that he had no wife!

Adriana, the wife of Antipholus of Ephesus, was very angry to hear this. She had a jealous nature and thought her husband must have meant that he loved another woman more than her. She began to fret and say unkind things about him. Her sister Luciana, who lived with them, tried in vain to talk her out of her groundless suspicions.

Antipholus of Syracuse headed straight to the inn, where he found his own Dromio. The money was safe! He was about to chide Dromio for his bad jokes, when the angry Adriana suddenly appeared. Not for a moment doubting it was her husband in front of her, she began to reproach him.

"Why do you look strangely at me and frown?" she said. "I am no longer Adriana or your wife? There was a time you said that unless *I* spoke, words were not music to your ears, unless *I* looked at you, nothing pleased your eyes, unless *I* touched your hand, no touch was welcome, and unless *I* carved, no meat tasted delicious! So how comes it, husband, that I've lost your love?"

"Who do you think you're talking to, madam?" said the astonished Antipholus. "I don't know you!"

In vain he tried to tell her he was not her husband and that he'd only been in Ephesus a couple of hours. But she insisted on him going home with her. At last, Antipholus gave up arguing and went with her to what was, unknown to him, his brother's house. He dined there with Adriana and her sister, the one calling him 'husband' and the other 'brother-in-law'! The confused Antipholus thought he must have got married to her in his sleep, or it was all just a dream. And Dromio, who had followed them, was no less surprised, for the cook—who was actually his brother's wife—also claimed him for her husband.

Antipholus of Ephesus

As Antipholus of Syracuse was dining with his brother's wife, his brother, Adriana's real husband, returned home to dinner with his servant Dromio. But the servants would not open the door, because their mistress had ordered them not to admit anybody. When they kept knocking, saying they were Antipholus and Dromio, the servants just laughed. They said Antipholus was already at dinner with their mistress and Dromio was in the kitchen. Antipholus was very angry, and surprised to be told some man was dining with his wife. At last, he and Dromio had to give up and go away.

When Antipholus of Syracuse finished his dinner, he was perplexed that the lady still insisted on calling him 'husband'. And he heard that the cook also claimed Dromio as *her* husband! Antipholus really disliked the fiery Adriana, although he did find her sister Luciana very attractive. Dromio was certainly not very keen on the cook. So they escaped from the house as soon as possible.

But the moment Antipholus of Syracuse left the house, he was met by a goldsmith, who addressed him as 'Antipholus' and gave him a gold chain. Antipholus said it did not belong to him. But the goldsmith insisted he had made it according to *his* order. The man left, leaving Antipholus holding the chain. Antipholus immediately ordered Dromio to take his things on board a ship, *any* ship! He had no wish to stay a moment longer in a place where he had such weird adventures. He suspected he had been bewitched!

Arrests

The goldsmith who had given the chain to the wrong Antipholus was arrested immediately after for a sum of money he owed. Antipholus of Ephesus happened to go to the place where the arrest was happening. When the goldsmith spotted Antipholus, he asked him to pay for the gold chain he had just delivered to him, as it amounted to nearly the same sum as that for which he'd been arrested. Naturally, Antipholus denied he'd received the chain. The goldsmith insisted that he'd given it to him just a few minutes before. They argued for a long time, both thinking they were right. At last, the officer took the goldsmith away to prison for the debt he owed. But the goldsmith insisted that Antipholus should *also* be arrested for stealing the chain! So they were both taken away to prison together.

A nation of witches

On his way to prison, Antipholus of Ephesus happened to meet Dromio of Syracuse. He ordered him to go to his wife, Adriana, and tell her to immediately send the money for which he'd been arrested. Dromio was surprised that his master should send him back to the strange house where they'd dined, and from which they'd been in such a haste to depart. But he did not dare to reply, even though he'd come to tell his master that the ship was ready to sail. He saw that Antipholus was in a very serious mood.

Dromio headed back, grumbling to himself. "Why do I have to go back to that awful place where the awful cook claims me for a husband? But I have to go, for servants must always obey their masters' commands!"

Luckily, Adriana gave him the money without any fuss. As Dromio was returning, he bumped into his master, Antipholus of Syracuse. Antipholus was still rather stunned by the surprising incidents he had experienced. His brother was well known in Ephesus, so nearly every man he met in the streets greeted him warmly. Some offered him money which they said they owed him, some invited him to go and visit them soon, and some thanked him for his kindness, all mistaking him for his brother! A tailor even showed him some silks he had bought for him, and insisted upon measuring him for some clothes. Antipholus began to think he was in a nation of sorcerers and witches.

His bewildered thoughts were in no way relieved by Dromio asking him how he escaped from the officer who was taking him to prison, and giving him the purse of gold which Adriana had sent to pay off the debt. This talk totally confused Antipholus.

"Dromio is also affected," he thought, "and we are wandering around here surrounded by illusions. Oh, some blessed power please deliver us from this place!"

Then a woman came up to him, called him 'Antipholus', told him he'd dined with her earlier, and asked him for the gold chain which she said he'd promised to give her. Antipholus now lost all his patience. He called her a sorceress, denied he had ever promised her a chain or dined with her, or had even seen her face before that moment. But the woman persisted in her claims and added that she'd also given him a valuable ring. If he would not give her the chain, then she insisted on having her own ring back again.

Antipholus got quite frantic. Calling her a witch, he denied all knowledge of her and everything she claimed. Then he ran away, leaving her astonished at his words and his wild looks.

Lunacy

The woman had fallen into the same mistake as all the others, taking him for his brother, who had actually done everything she had accused his brother of doing! She began to think Antipholus had gone crazy. She decided to go and report this to Adriana.

But while she was talking to her, her husband appeared, with the jailer, to get the purse of money to pay off the debt. Of course, it had already been sent with Dromio and delivered to the wrong Antipholus!

Adriana believed the story about her husband's madness must be true: he'd reproached her for shutting him out of his own house; he'd protested all through dinner that he was not her husband; and he'd claimed he'd never been in Ephesus till that day. She was is no doubt that he was completely crazy. She gave the money to the jailer, who then released Antipholus. Adriana ordered her servants to tie her husband up with rope, and take him to a dark room. Then she sent for a doctor to come and cure him of his lunacy. Needless to say, Antipholus hotly denied this false accusation. But his rage only confirmed them in the belief that he was crazy. And when Dromio persisted in telling the same story, they tied him up as well and took him away along with his master.

Not long after that, a servant came to tell Adriana that Antipholus and Dromio must have broken loose and escaped, because they were both walking at liberty in the next street. Adriana ran out to fetch him home, taking several servants with her to tie him up again. Her sister joined them. When they arrived at the gates of the convent in the neighborhood, they saw Antipholus and Dromio.

Antipholus of Syracuse was still feeling confused. The chain the goldsmith had given him was hung around his neck, and the goldsmith was reproaching him for denying that he had it and refusing to pay for it. Antipholus was protesting that the goldsmith had freely handed him the chain that morning, and since then he hadn't seen the goldsmith again.

Then Adriana rushed up to him and claimed him as her lunatic husband who'd escaped from his keepers! Her servants approached him with rope in their hands. Antipholus thought fast. He ran into the convent with Dromio, and begged the abbess to give them shelter.

The abbess then came out herself to inquire into the cause of the disturbance. She was a venerable lady of great wisdom and she wished to carefully judge the situation before she gave up the man who had sought protection. So she strictly questioned Adriana about the story she had heard of her husband's supposed madness.

"What is the cause of this sudden issue of your husband?" she asked. "Has he lost his wealth at sea? Or has his mind been disturbed by the death of some dear friend? Or perhaps he has fixed his affections on some other lady than you, his wife, and *that* has driven him to this state?"

"None of those, except, perhaps, the last," replied Adriana. "I have long thought the love of some other woman was the cause of his frequent absences from home."

"Ah, then you should have reprehended him for that."

"Why, I did!"

"I see," said the abbess, "but perhaps not enough."

Adriana was eager to convince the abbess that she had said enough to Antipholus on this subject. "It was the constant theme of our conversation. In bed, I wouldn't let him sleep for speaking of it. At meals, I wouldn't let him eat for speaking of it. When I was alone with him, I talked of nothing else. And in company, I gave him frequent hints of it. All my talk was about how vile and bad it was for him to love any woman more than me!"

Having drawn this full confession from the jealous Adriana, the abbess said, "And I believe *that* is why your husband is mad. The venomous clamor of a jealous woman is a more deadly poison than a mad dog's tooth! It seems his sleep was disturbed by your railing, so no wonder his head is light. And his meat was sauced with your scolding. Unquiet meals lead to bad digestion, and that has also driven him into this fever. And you say his leisure time was disturbed by your brawling. Being barred from the enjoyment of society and proper rest and recreation, what could follow but melancholy and despair? In other words, it is your jealous fits that have made your husband mad."

Luciana wanted to excuse Adriana, saying that she always reprehended her husband *mildly*, and she said to her sister, "Why do you hear all these rebukes without saying anything?"

But the abbess had made Adriana so plainly perceive her fault that she could only say, "She has showed me exactly what I am!"

Although ashamed of her conduct, Adriana still insisted on having her husband given back to her. But the abbess would allow no-one to enter her convent. Nor would she deliver up the unhappy man to the care of the jealous wife. She had decided to use gentle means for his recovery. She went back inside and ordered her gates to be closed.

Sunset

During the course of this eventful day, in which so many errors had happened because of the likeness of the two sets of twin brothers, old Aegeon's day of grace had been passing away. It was now nearly sunset, the time he was doomed to die if he could not pay the money. The place of his execution was near the convent. He arrived there with several officers just as the abbess went back inside. The Duke was attending in person, so that if anyone offered to pay the money, he would be present to pardon Aegeon.

Adriana suddenly stopped the melancholy procession, and cried out to the Duke for justice. She told him that the abbess had refused to deliver up her crazy husband to her care. But while she was speaking, her real husband and Dromio, who had managed to escape from the dark room, appeared. He, too, demanded justice from the Duke, complaining that his wife had confined him on a false charge of lunacy, and explaining how he had broken free. Adriana was very surprised to see her husband there when she thought he was inside the convent.

Seeing his son, Aegeon concluded it must be the son who had

left him to go in search of his mother and his brother. With a feeling of great relief, he felt sure that his dear son would readily pay the money for his ransom. So he spoke to Antipholus in words of fatherly affection, with the hope that he would be released.

"Excuse me, sir, but are you Antipholus and is this your servant Dromio?

"I am, yes, and he is."

"I am sure you remember me?"

"No. I never saw you in my life before!"

"Ah, maybe grief and the anxieties I have suffered have altered my appearance. But don't you recognize my voice?"

"No, I don't."

"Dromio, don't *you*?"

"No, sir."

"Oh, Antipholus, please tell me you are my son!"

"I have never seen my father."

"But we parted seven years ago in Syracuse! Maybe you are ashamed to acknowledge your father in his misery..."

"I have never been to Syracuse!"

"And I can vouch for him," said the Duke. "These past twenty years he has not been to Syracuse!"

Then suddenly the convent gates opened and out came the abbess with the other Antipholus and the other Dromio.

Adriana gasped when she saw two husbands and two servants!

And now all the strange errors, which had so perplexed them

all, could be sorted out clearly. When the Duke saw the two Antipholuses and the two Dromios so exactly alike, he at once reckoned correctly the cause of all of these seeming mysteries. He vividly remembered the story Aegeon had told him that morning, and he said these men must be his two sons and their twin servants.

But now an unexpected joy completed Aegeon's history. In the morning his tale had been full of sorrow. But now, under the sentence of death, and just before the sun went down, it was brought to a happy conclusion... The venerable abbess revealed that she was the long-lost wife of Aegeon and the fond mother of the two Antipholuses!

She explained to the amazed audience how the fishermen had taken Antipholus and Dromio away from her. She had then entered a nunnery, and by her wise and virtuous conduct she was at length made the abbess of that convent. And in discharging the rites of hospitality to an unhappy stranger she had unknowingly protected her own son!

The outburst of joyful congratulations and affectionate greetings between the long-separated parents and their children made them for a while forget that Aegeon was still under sentence of death... When they calmed down a little, Antipholus of Ephesus offered the Duke the ransom money for his father's life. But the Duke refused to take the money. Instead, he freely pardoned Aegeon.

The Duke then went with the abbess and her newly found husband and children into the convent. He was eager to hear the happy family saga in detail with the blessed ending of their adverse fortunes there in Ephesus.

The two Dromios also had their joyous greetings and congratulations. Each one of them pleasantly complimented the other on his good looks, and was well pleased to see his own handsome person in his brother!

Adriana had profited so well by the good counsel of her mother-in-law that she never again cherished unjust suspicions or was jealous of her husband.

Antipholus of Syracuse married the fair Luciana, the sister of his brother's wife.

As for the good old Aegeon, he lived happily in Ephesus for many years with his wife and sons.

But the unraveling of the perplexities did not entirely remove every possibility of errors happening in the future. And so comical blunders would sometimes happen to remind them all of their past adventures. One Antipholus and one Dromio could so easily be mistaken for the *other* Antipholus and Dromio. All things considered, it made for a very pleasant and entertaining comedy of errors.

12

Twelfth Night

十二夜

読み始める前に

クリスマスシーズンの終わりを告げる十二夜のために書かれたと考えられているが、ストーリーに十二夜に関わるようなシーンはない。副題のWhat You Willは、「あなたのお好きなように」という意味。

[登場人物]

Viola	ヴァイオラ《主人公》
Cesario	シザーリオ《ヴァイオラの変装名》
Olivia	オリヴィア《イリリアの伯爵令嬢》
Sebastian	セバスチャン《ヴァイオラの双子の兄》
Orsino	オーシーノ公爵《イリリアの公爵。オリヴィアに求婚》
Antonio	アントーニオ《セバスチャンの友人》
Feste	フェステ《伯爵家の道化》

[地名など]

Illyria	イリリア《架空の国》
Messaline	メサリーン《架空の国》

[あらすじ]

双子の兄妹セバスチャンとヴァイオラは、男女の服装の違いがなければ見分けがつかないほどそっくりだった。ふたりは旅の途中、乗っていた船が難破し離れ離れになってしまう。

妹のヴァイオラは、たどりついたイリリア国で、少年に変装してオーシーノ公爵に仕えることにする。オーシーノ公爵は伯爵家の令嬢であるオリヴィアに求婚しているが受け入れてもらえず、つらい胸の内をヴァイオラに打ち明けるが、ヴァイオラもまた、オーシーノ公爵に恋をしていた。

ヴァイオラの気持ちも知らずオーシーノ公爵は、自分がいかにオリヴィアを愛しているかを伝えてほしいとヴァイオラを使いに出すが、オリヴィアは少年の姿のヴァイオラにひとめぼれ。

同じ頃、漂流しているところを別の船の船長に助けられた兄のセバスチャンもイリリア国に上陸していた。セバスチャンと男装のヴァイオラは見分けがつかなかったため、騒動になる。

[総単語数] 3,790語

TWELFTH NIGHT
OR
WHAT YOU WILL

Once upon a time, the country of Illyria on the Adriatic Sea near eastern Italy was ruled by a lovesick lord called Orsino. He was lovesick because of his long and unsuccessful suit to a lady who despised him and refused to even meet him. For the love of this lady who treated him so unkindly, the noble Orsino started giving up all the sports and exercises he used to love. He stopped meeting the wise and learned lords he used to associate with. And he listened only to the sounds of soft music, gentle airs, and passionate love-songs. His favorite expression was, "If music be the food of love, play on, and give me excess of it!"

Twins

Sebastian and his sister Viola, a young gentleman and lady of Messaline in Italy were twins. From their birth they resembled each other so much that they could only be told apart by their clothes.

One day, while on a sea voyage together, the ship hit a rock in a violent storm off the coast of Illyria. Only a few members of the crew escaped with their lives. The captain and some of the sailors reached land safely in a small boat. They had taken Viola with them. But instead of rejoicing at her own deliverance, she started lamenting Sebastian's loss. The captain comforted her. He told her that he had seen her brother tie himself to a strong mast when the ship broke up, and he saw him carried along above the waves. This account gave Viola some hope that Sebastian had survived.

Viola and the captain

She now started wondering what she was going to do in a strange country so far from home. She asked the captain if he knew anything about Illyria.

"Aye, I know it very well," replied the captain. "I was born less than three hours' walk from this place."

"Who governs Illyria?" asked Viola.

"Oh, a noble duke called Orsino."

"Ah, yes, I remember my father mentioning that name. I think he said he was a bachelor."

"And he still is, or at least he *was* just a month ago when

I was here. There was a lot of gossip about him being in love with Lady Olivia. She's a very virtuous woman who was the daughter of a count who died one year ago. Olivia was left to the protection of her brother, but *he* soon died as well. They say she is still in mourning for her dear brother, and refuses to spend any time with men."

Viola, who was so worried about her brother, said she wished she could live with this lady who so tenderly mourned a brother's death. She asked the captain if he could introduce her to Olivia, saying she would willingly serve her. But he replied that would be a tricky thing to do, as Lady Olivia wouldn't admit anybody into her house, not even Duke Orsino himself.

Then Viola came up with another idea: she would put on men's clothes and serve the Duke as a page! She knew it would be a strange thing for her to try and pass for a boy. But she was a young woman alone in a foreign land, and it might keep her safe.

The captain had showed a friendly concern for her welfare, so she told him her plan. He was happy to help her. She gave him some money and asked him to buy her some suitable items of clothing. She decided to have them made of the same color and in the same fashion her brother Sebastian wore. And when she eventually dressed in her manly garb she looked exactly like him!

Cesario and Orsino

The captain had previously done some business for the Illyrian court. Having transformed the pretty Viola into a charming young gentleman, he managed to get her presented to Orsino under the new name of Cesario. The Duke was very pleased with the words and grace of this handsome youth, and he made Cesario one of his pages at once. Viola fulfilled her duties as Cesario so well, she soon became Orsino's favorite. It was not long before Orsino was spending most of the day chatting with young Cesario. And he soon confided the whole history of his love for Lady Olivia to him.

But Viola was not very happy to realize that *she* was suffering for the love of Orsino all that he told her *he* endured for Olivia! She was very surprised that Olivia could have such little interest in her wonderful lord. She thought no woman could avoid admiring him deeply! As Cesario, she gently hinted to Orsino that it was a pity he should love a lady who was so blind to his qualities.

"If a lady were to love you, my lord," she said, "as much as you love Lady Olivia, would you tell her you couldn't love her in return, and she would have to be content with that answer?"

"Ah," replied Orsino, "I don't think it's possible for any woman to love as much as I do! No woman's heart is big enough to hold so much love."

Viola could not help thinking this was not quite true.

"Ah, but I know, my lord," she said.

"What do you know, Cesario?" said Orsino.

"I know very well how much love women can have for a man. They're as true of heart as we are. My father had a daughter loved a man, as I perhaps, if I were a woman, would love your lordship!"

"And what is her story?" asked Orsino.

"A complete blank, my lord. She never told him of her love. She pined away, sitting like Patience on a monument, smiling at Grief."

"Did this lady die of her love?"

Viola could only give an evasive answer. She had created a story about her own secret love and silent grief!

Seven years...

While they were talking, a gentleman who the Duke had sent to Olivia came in.

"My lord," he said, "I was not admitted in to see the lady. But one of her maids gave you this answer. For the next seven years, even the sky will not see her face. She will walk like a nun, veiled, watering her room with tears in memory of her dead brother."

"Oh, what a fine heart she has!" exclaimed the Duke. "Cesario, I have already told you all the secrets of my heart. So please go to Lady Olivia's house. Refuse to be denied access! Stand at her door and tell her your foot will grow there until she lets you in!"

"And if I do get to speak to her, my lord, what then?"

"Oh, then unfold to her the passion of my love. Explain at length my dear sincerity. You can act out my woes in front of her! I'm sure she will listen to you more than to someone too serious."

So away went Viola. Naturally she was not very willing to woo a lady to become the wife of the man she wished to marry herself. But she faithfully carried out her probably impossible mission. Olivia was soon told that a young man was outside who insisted upon being allowed in to see her.

"I told him that you were sick," said Olivia's servant. "He said he knew you were, and that is why he has come to speak to you. Then I told him that you were asleep. He seemed to know that, too, and said that was also why he must speak to you. What can I say to him, my lady? He refuses to go away, and seems determined to speak to you, whether you want to or not."

Olivia was curious to see who this arrogant messenger might be. She was sure he came from the Duke because of his persistence. She decided to put on her veil and let him come in out of curiosity.

Cesario and Olivia

As Viola entered the room, she put on as much of a manly air as possible. She tried to sound like a courtier.

"Most radiant, exquisite, and matchless beauty, I pray you tell me if you are the lady of this house. I should be sorry to cast away my speech to the wrong person. Not only is my speech well written and poetic, I have also taken great pains to learn it by heart."

"Where do you come from, sir?" said Olivia.

"I can say little more than that I have studied," replied Viola.

"Are you a comedian?"

"Oh, no, and yet I am not quite the part I play. Are you indeed the lady of this fine house?"

"I am."

"Good lady, please let me see your face."

Despite being such a haughty beauty, Olivia actually wanted to show her face. Why? Because at first sight she had fallen for the humble page called Cesario!

"Have you any commission from your lord to negotiate face-to-face?" Olivia asked. And then, completely forgetting her decision to go veiled for seven years, she drew her veil to one side, saying, "But for you I will draw the curtain and show you the picture. Is it not well painted?"

"Oh, it is beauty truly mixed," Viola replied. "The red and white of your cheeks is provided by Nature's clever hand! You are the cruellest lady living if you take these graces to the grave and leave the world no copy."

"Oh, sir," replied Olivia, "I will not be so cruel. The world can have a list of my beauties: two lips, red; two gray eyes with lids; one neck; one chin; and so forth. Were you sent here to praise me?"

"Ah, now I see what you are. You are beautiful but you are too *proud*. My lord Orsino loves you with adoration and with tears, with groans that thunder love, and sighs of fire!"

"Your lord," replied Olivia, "knows what I think of him. I cannot love him. He is virtuous, yes. I know him to be noble and of high estate, of fresh youth. Everyone proclaims him well-educated, courteous, and valiant, but I cannot love him. He could have accepted this long ago."

"If I loved you as much as my master does, I would build a willow cabin at your gates, and call out your name. I would write complaining sonnets on Olivia, and sing them in the dead of the night. Your name should sound among the hills, and I would make Echo, the gossip of the air, cry out 'Olivia!' And you would take pity on me!"

"Hmm, you could progress far!" said Olivia. "What is your background?"

"Above my fortunes, yet I am doing well. I am a gentleman."

Olivia now reluctantly dismissed Viola, saying, "Go back to your master and tell him I cannot love him. Tell him to send no more messages... unless *you* come again, Cesario, to tell me his reaction."

"Farewell, fair Cruelty!" said Viola and left.

Softly, softly...

As soon as Viola had gone, Olivia repeated Cesario's words in her head, "Above my fortunes, yet I am doing well. I am a gentleman."

And she said aloud, "Yes, I will be sworn he is; his speech, his face, his limbs, his actions, and his spirit plainly show he is a gentleman... How I wish the messenger was the Duke! What? I feel this young man's perfections are taking hold of me! Not too fast, Olivia, softly, softly..."

She immediately sent a servant running after Cesario with

a diamond ring, pretending he had left it with her as a present from Orsino, and she had no interest in the ring or him. She included the message that he should return tomorrow to hear the reasons. She hoped the ring would give Cesario some hint of her feelings.

Indeed, it did make Viola suspect something, as she knew that Orsino had not sent a ring. She began to recall that the lady's looks and manner had expressed admiration, and she guessed that Olivia had fallen in love with her!

"I am the man!" she said. "Poor lady, she might as well love a dream. I see now that disguise is wicked, for it has caused Olivia to breathe fruitless sighs for me, as *I* do for Orsino!"

A simple old song

Viola returned to Orsino's palace, and related to her lord her lack of success, repeating Olivia's command that he should trouble her no more. Yet still the Duke persisted in hoping that the gentle Cesario would in time be able to persuade her to show some pity. And so he asked him to visit her again the next day. In the meantime, to pass away the tedious afternoon, he asked Feste the jester to sing a song he liked.

"Good Cesario," he said, "when I heard this song last night, I felt it relieved my passion a lot. It's just a simple old song that spinsters and knitters enjoy when they sit in the sun, and the young weavers chant it. It's silly, but I like it, for it tells of the innocence of love in the old days."

Come away, come away, Death,
And by sad cypress trees may I be laid;
Fly away, fly away, breath,
I am slain by a fair cruel maid.
My shroud of white with yew, prepare!
My death no one so true can share.
Not a flower, not one flower sweet,
On my black coffin let there be strewn:
No-one, not one friend greet
Me where my bones are thrown.
A thousand, thousand sighs to save,
Lay me, oh lay me where?
Where sad true lovers cannot find my grave
To weep their pity there!

Viola understood the words of the song well. It described the pain of unrequited love. Her sad looks expressed exactly what it was about. Orsino noticed.

"Cesario," he said, "I think that although you're so young, your eyes have looked upon some face that they dearly love. Am I right?"

"Yes, my lord," replied Viola.

"And what kind of woman, and of what age is she?"

"About your age and with the same complexion, my lord."

Orsino smiled to hear that the fair young boy loved a woman so much older than himself, with a dark complexion! He had no idea that she was really talking about *him*.

The second visit

When Viola made her second visit to Olivia she had no difficulty gaining access to her. Servants soon discover when their ladies delight to converse with handsome young messengers. The instant Viola arrived the gates were thrown wide open, and the duke's page was shown into Olivia's room with great respect.

When Viola told her that she had come again to plead on her lord's behalf, the lady said, "I asked you never to speak of him again. However, Cesario, I would prefer you to plead a different suit."

Olivia soon explained herself more plainly. She openly confessed her love for Cesario. When she saw the mix of displeasure and confusion on Viola's face, she said, "Oh, how beautiful is the contempt and anger of his lip! Cesario, by the roses of the spring, by honor, and by truth, I love you. I have neither the wit nor the reason to hide my passion."

But Olivia wooed in vain. Viola hastened from her presence, threatening she would never go again to plead Orsino's love. The only reply she could make to Olivia's words was a resolution never to love any woman!

Saved by a stranger

No sooner had Viola left Olivia's house than her valor was tested. A gentleman who was another rejected suitor of Olivia had learned how she now favored the duke's young messenger. He challenged Cesario to fight a duel. What should poor Viola do? Maybe she looked like a man on the outside, but she had a woman's heart underneath and was even afraid to look on her own sword!

When she saw her formidable rival advancing toward her with his sword drawn, she was tempted for a moment to confess that she was a woman. But suddenly relief from her terror and the shame of such a confession appeared out of nowhere! A passing stranger spoke to her opponent as if he had long known Cesario and was his dearest friend.

"If this young gentleman has caused you any trouble, sir, I will accept the fault myself, and if you have offended him, I will defy you on his behalf!"

But before Viola had time to thank him or ask the reason for his kind and brave interference, some officers of the peace appeared.

"We arrest you in the Duke's name to answer for an offense committed some years ago!"

"Ah, this comes from trying to find you!" the man said to Viola. "And now I must ask you for my purse. I'm upset much more for what I cannot now do for you than about whatever happens to me! But you look amazed…"

His words did indeed amaze Viola. She protested that she didn't know him, nor had she ever received a purse from him. But for the kindness he had just shown her she offered a small sum of money, most of what she possessed. Now the stranger charged her with ingratitude and unkindness.

"I snatched this youth you see here from the jaws of death!" he said. "And for his sake alone I came here to Illyria and have fallen into this danger."

The officers were not interested in hearing their prisoner's complaints. They hurried him away, saying, "What's all that to us?" But he kept shouting, "Sebastian, you have disowned your best friend!"

He was taken away too fast for Viola to ask for an explanation. But she immediately thought that this mystery might have come from her being mistaken for her brother! And she began to cherish hopes that it was indeed Sebastian's life this man had preserved.

Antonio

And so indeed it was. The stranger, whose name was Antonio, was a ship's captain. He had pulled the exhausted Sebastian up onto his ship when he was spotted floating on the mast to which he'd fastened himself in the storm. They soon became such good friends that Antonio said he would accompany Sebastian wherever he went. So when Sebastian expressed a desire to visit Orsino's court in Illyria, Antonio joined him. However, he knew his life would be in danger if anyone knew he was there. Why? Because many years before he had seriously wounded Duke Orsino's nephew in a sea fight. And that was the offense for which he had just been arrested.

Antonio and Sebastian had landed together just a few hours before Antonio met Viola. He had given his purse to Sebastian, wanting him to use it freely if he saw anything he wanted to buy in the market. He told him he would wait at the Elephant Inn while Sebastian went to view the town. But when Sebastian didn't return at the appointed time, Antonio had reluctantly gone out to look for him.

Two halves of an apple

Meanwhile, a priest confirmed to Orsino that his page had robbed him of the treasure he prized above his life: Cesario had married Olivia! Thinking his dream had ended, Orsino was bidding farewell to his faithless mistress, and the 'young dissembler', her husband, as he called Viola. He was just warning Cesario never to come in his sight again, when a miracle occurred! Another Cesario entered, and addressed Olivia as his wife.

"One face, one voice, one set of clothes, but two people!" cried the amazed Duke.

"Most wonderful!" cried Olivia.

"Like two halves of an apple!" said Antonio, forgiven by Orsino at Viola's request and released from prison.

This new Cesario was in fact Sebastian, and he really had been Olivia's husband for the past two hours. When everyone's wonder at the twins had died down a little, the brother and sister began to question each other. Viola could scarcely believe that her brother was alive, and Sebastian could scarcely believe that the sister he had supposed drowned was standing in front of him dressed like a man! It took a while for Cesario to persuade him that she was indeed Viola, his sister!

Reunited

Eventually, all the errors caused by the identical appearance of the twins were cleared up. They laughed at Olivia for the pleasant mistake she had made in falling in love with a woman. And Olivia was quite contented when she found she had in fact married the brother rather than the sister.

Olivia's marriage brought the hopes of Orsino to an end, and his fruitless love seemed to have vanished away. But all his thoughts were now fixed on the fact that his favorite page, young Cesario, had changed into a charming woman. As he looked at Viola with great attention, he remembered how handsome he had always thought Cesario was. He concluded that Viola would look very beautiful in women's clothes. And then he remembered how often Viola, as Cesario, had said she loved him! At the time, he thought they were just the dutiful words of a faithful page. But now he guessed that something much more was meant. He also recalled many of her pretty sayings, which had been like riddles to him. It didn't take him long to decide he wanted Viola to be his wife.

"Cesario—I mean Viola!—a thousand times you have told me that you would never love a *woman* like me! For all the faithful service you have given me with your soft and tender breeding, and since you have called me 'master' so long, I trust you will now agree to be not only your master's mistress, but also Orsino's true Duchess! Please give me your hand…"

Viola was certainly not going to refuse him!

Olivia observed that Orsino was now offering to Viola the heart she had so ungraciously rejected. She invited everyone to enter her house. She also asked the priest who had married her to Sebastian that morning to perform the same ceremony for Viola and Orsino.

And so the twin brother and sister were both married on the same day. The storm and the shipwreck which had separated them turned out to be the means to bring them to great good fortune. Sebastian was now the husband of the rich and noble countess, Lady Olivia. And Viola was now the Duchess of Illyria, the wife of Orsino, who was no longer a lovesick Duke.

Romeo and Juliet

ロミオとジュリエット

読み始める前に

今日までオペラ、映画、バレエなど、数多くの作品が生み出されており、日本ではアニメにもなった。シェイクスピアの最も有名な悲劇のひとつ。(☜p.4)

［登場人物］

Romeo	ロミオ《主人公。モンタギューの息子》
Juliet	ジュリエット《主人公。キャピュレットの娘》
Friar Lawrence	ロレンス神父《修道士》
Paris	パリス伯爵《貴族の青年》
Nurse	乳母《ジュリエットの世話係》
Tybalt	ティボルト《ジュリエットの従兄》
Mercutio	マーキューシオ《ロミオの友人》
Benvolio	ベンヴォーリオ《ロミオの従兄弟、ロミオの友人》
Lord Capulet	キャピュレット卿《キャピュレット家の家長》
Lady Capulet	キャピュレット夫人《キャピュレットの妻》
Lord Montague	モンタギュー卿《モンタギュー家の家長》
Lady Montague	モンタギュー夫人《モンタギューの妻》
Prince	ヴェローナの太守
Rosaline	ロザライン《ロミオが最初に恋する女性》

［地名など］

Mantua	マントヴァ《イタリアの都市》
Verona	ヴェローナ《イタリアの都市》

［あらすじ］

モンタギュー家の息子ロミオとキャピュレット家の娘ジュリエットは、仮面舞踏会で出会い恋に落ちる。両家は昔から対立しいがみあっていたが、お互いがその敵対する家の出身だとわかっても二人の気持ちは変わらなかった。

二人はロレンス神父に頼んで密かに結婚式を挙げるが、その帰り道、ロミオはジュリエットの従兄ティボルトを殺してしまい、追放されてマントヴァへ。一方、ジュリエットは父の選んだ相手と結婚させられることになってしまう。両家の仲直りを願うロレンス神父は一計を案じ、ジュリエットに42時間だけ死んだようになる薬を渡した。

［総単語数］5,620語

ROMEO AND JULIET

Once upon a time, in the city of Verona in northern Italy, the two main noble families were the Capulets and the Montagues. The longstanding quarrels between them had grown so strong that they involved even distant members of both families and all those who worked for them. If, for example, a Montague servant met a Capulet servant by chance, there would be strong insults and sometimes even a fight leading to bloodshed. This situation disturbed the happy peace of Verona's streets.

The Capulet party

One day, Lord Capulet decided to hold a great party, to which many fair ladies and noble guests were invited. Anyone was welcome to attend as long as they were *not* from the Montague family. Now it so happened one of those attending was Rosaline, the beautiful young woman loved by Romeo, the son of Lord Montague. It would obviously be dangerous for a Montague like him to be seen at the event. But his good friend Benvolio persuaded him to go disguised by a mask.

"You can compare *her* face with others that I will show you, and then you will realize your 'swan' is really just a 'crow'!"

Romeo didn't believe that at all. However, for the love of Rosaline, he was persuaded to go. He was a sincere and passionate lover. He lost his sleep for love and preferred being alone to think about Rosaline. Unfortunately, she ignored him and showed no affection. That's why Benvolio hoped to cure his friend by introducing a diversity of ladies.

So Romeo, Benvolio, and their friend Mercutio went masked to the Capulet party. Lord Capulet welcomed them and urged them to dance. He seemed light-hearted and merry.

"Back in the good old days, you know, I used to wear a mask myself and whisper tales in fair lady's ears! Oh, yes! Ha-ha! Come, musicians, play! Make room, and dance, girls, dance!"

The musicians started playing and the dancing began.

Romeo was suddenly struck by the great beauty of one of the young ladies. He asked a servant who she was, but he didn't know.

"Oh," murmured Romeo, "she shines brighter than the torches! She hangs upon the dark cheek of the night like a rich jewel. Her beauty is too dear for this world! She's like a snowy white dove among crows. Did my heart really love till now? I have never seen true beauty until tonight… "

Tybalt

Romeo's words were overheard by Tybalt, Lord Capulet's nephew, and he recognized the voice immediately. Tybalt had a fiery temperament and could not endure a Montague gate-crashing the party under cover of a mask. He got very angry, and was about to strike Romeo with his sword. But his uncle stopped him. He would not allow Tybalt to do any injury to Romeo, both out of respect to his guests and because Romeo behaved like a gentleman and was known in Verona as a fine and well-bred young man. Forced to be patient against his will, Tybalt restrained himself. But he swore that the vile Montague would at another time pay dearly for being at the party.

Two blushing pilgrims

When the lady stopped dancing, Romeo noted where she was standing, and walked slowly over toward her. Then, in a very gentle way, he took her by the hand. He murmured that he regarded her hand as a holy shrine, and if he was treating it with disrespect by touching it, his lips like two blushing pilgrims would tenderly kiss it to make amends.

"Good pilgrim," she answered, "your devotion is too courtly. Saints have hands which pilgrims may touch. Palm to palm is the pilgrim's kiss."

"But don't saints and pilgrims both have lips?" said Romeo.

"Yes, lips to use for prayer."

"Oh, then, my dear saint, hear my prayer by letting lips do what hands do, so that I will not despair."

"Saints do not move to grant prayers."

"Then do not move..." Romeo kissed her gently. "And so my sin is swept *away*."

"But now *my* lips have taken your sin."

"In that case, return it!" said Romeo, and kissed her again.

"Oh, you kiss so sweetly!" she replied.

At that moment, the lady's nurse appeared and said her mother was waiting for her. She left at once. Romeo immediately asked the nurse who her mother was, and discovered that the young lady he was so much struck with was none other than Juliet, the daughter and heir to Lord Capulet, the great enemy of the Montagues!

This greatly worried Romeo, but it could not change his heart. And Juliet had suddenly been overcome with the same passion for *him* that he had conceived for *her*. So she was also greatly worried when she learned from her nurse that the gentle young man who spoke so well was a Montague. Could she really love an enemy her family would wish her to hate?

It was now around midnight, and Romeo and his companions decided to leave.

The orchard

But a few minutes later, Romeo suddenly left his friends. Unable to stay away from the place where he'd left his heart, he climbed over the wall of the orchard at the back of Juliet's house. It was not long before Juliet appeared on the balcony above him. Her great beauty seemed to Romeo to shine out like the light of the sun at dawn. The moon, shining down with its faint light, appeared to be pale with grief at the superior brightness of this new sun. As Juliet leant her face on her hand, Romeo dearly wished he was a glove on it, so that he could touch her cheek!

Thinking she was all alone, Juliet sighed deeply, and then spoke aloud.

"Ah, poor me!"

Delighted to hear her voice again, Romeo murmured, "Oh, speak again, bright angel! Being above me, you are like a winged messenger from heaven!"

Unaware of being overheard, and full of the new passion which that night's adventure had given birth to, Juliet called upon her lover by name.

"Oh Romeo, Romeo, why are you 'Romeo'? Go against thy Montague father and refuse thy name, for my sake! And if you can't, be my sworn love, and I will no longer be a Capulet…"

Romeo wanted to say something, but he also wished to hear more, so he remained silent.

"It is only your name that is my enemy," Juliet continued. "You would be the same person even if your name was different. What's 'Montague'? It's not a hand, or foot, or arm, or face, or any other part of a man. Oh, Romeo, please be some other name! What's in a name, anyway? The thing we call a 'rose' would smell as sweet by any other name! And so would Romeo, if he was not called 'Romeo'. Give up your name and I am yours!"

Hearing these loving words, Romeo could no longer refrain from speaking.

"Yes, call me but 'Love' and I will no longer be called Romeo!"

Juliet was briefly alarmed to hear a man's voice from the garden below.

"Who are you hidden in the dark listening to my thoughts?"

"I know not how to tell you, as my name is your enemy!"

"My ears have not yet drunk a hundred of your words, but I know you are Romeo. But you are in great danger! If any of my family find you there it will be death for you, being a Montague!"

"Oh," said Romeo, "I think there's more danger in *your* eye than in twenty of *their* swords! If you look kindly on me, I'm safe. And night's cloak will hide me. If not, it's better for my life to be ended by their hate than for it to go on without *your* love!"

"But how did you get in?" asked Juliet.

"With love's light wings, I flew over the wall, which cannot hold love out!"

Unseen by Romeo, Juliet blushed as she realized the truth of her love for Romeo. She wished she could recall her words, but that was impossible. She knew she should have behaved properly, keeping her lover at a distance, so that he would not think her too easily won! But there was no chance of that now.

Romeo had heard a confession of her love from her own mouth, when she never dreamed that he was listening. So, with an honesty which the novelty of her situation excused, she confirmed the truth of what he'd already heard.

"Fair Montague, gentle Romeo, pardon me for expressing my passion so boldly! And if you love me, say so sincerely…"

"Juliet, I swear by the moon…"

"Do not swear by the moon, it changes so quickly."

"What shall I swear by, then?"

"Do not swear at all! This is all too fast, like the lightning that disappears so soon. So, my sweet, good night! And may this bud of love become a beautiful flower when we next meet."

Romeo wanted to exchange a vow of love with her at once. Juliet said she'd already given him hers before he asked for it, but she'd happily take it back for the pleasure of giving it again.

"My love is as boundless and as deep as the sea," she said.

At this moment, Juliet was called in by her nurse, who thought it time for her to be in bed. Juliet told Romeo to wait.

She soon returned and said, "If your love is indeed honorable, and your purpose is indeed marriage, I will send a messenger to you at nine o'clock tomorrow to fix the time for our marriage. Then I will lay all my fortunes at your feet and follow you throughout the world!"

Juliet was repeatedly called by her nurse, and went in and came back, and went in and came back… Eventually, she said, "Romeo, a thousand times good night! Parting is such sweet sorrow…"

Friar Lawrence

It was already dawn when they parted, and Romeo was too full of thoughts of Juliet and that beautiful meeting to be able to sleep. Instead of going home, he headed straight to the nearby monastery to talk to Friar Lawrence, his good friend and advisor.

The friar was already up working in the herb garden. Seeing young Romeo awake so early, he guessed correctly that he had not been to sleep, but had been kept awake by some youthful romance. But he wrongly guessed at the lady involved, thinking it would be Rosaline.

When Romeo revealed his new passion for Juliet, and requested the assistance of the friar to marry them that very day, the holy man lifted up his eyes and hands in amazement at the sudden change in Romeo's affections.

"Ah, now I see that young men's love does not truly lie in their hearts, but only in their eyes!"

"But, Father, you have often told me off for loving Rosaline."

"For *doting* on her, not for *loving*!"

"But Juliet agrees entirely to our shared love!"

The friar agreed to some extent to Romeo's reasons. He was hoping that a marriage between Juliet and Romeo might be a happy way to bring an end to the ancient strife of their families. He was, in fact, a friend to both families and had often tried to stop their quarrelling. Moreover, he was very fond of young Romeo, and could deny him nothing, so he agreed to hold their marriage ceremony. Now was Romeo blessed indeed.

The joining of hands

Juliet heard of the plan from the messenger she had sent as promised. She made sure to arrive early at the monastery, where the friar joined the hands of the young Capulet and the young Montague in holy matrimony.

Juliet hurried home as soon as the ceremony was over. There she waited impatiently for night to come, when Romeo had promised to meet her in the orchard. Her nurse was preparing a rope ladder for him to climb up to Juliet's 'bird's nest'! The

time until then seemed as tedious to Juliet as the night before a big festival seems to a child that has got new clothes it eagerly wants to put on...

Swordfight at noon

That same day, around noon, Benvolio and Mercutio, Romeo's friends, were out walking through the streets of Verona. Suddenly they bumped into a Capulet group led by the fiery Tybalt, the man Mercutio called 'the prince of cats', who had wanted to fight with Romeo at the party.

As soon as he saw Mercutio, Tybalt accused him of associating with Romeo, a Montague. Mercutio, who had as much youthful fire in him as Tybalt, replied sharply. In spite of all Benvolio could say to calm the two men down, a quarrel was developing. And just at that moment, Romeo appeared. Tybalt immediately turned to him and called him a villain.

Tybalt was the last person Romeo wished to quarrel with. He was a relative of Juliet and she was very fond of him. Besides, Romeo had never really entered into the family quarrel, being by nature wise and gentle. So he tried to reason with Tybalt.

"Good Capulet," he began, "a name that I regard as dearly as my own. Please leave me alone!"

Tybalt, who hated all Montagues, would hear no reason, and drew his sword. Mercutio, unaware of Romeo's secret motive for wanting peace with Tybalt, did not like Romeo's calm reply. He, too, drew his sword. Romeo tried to stop him, but it was no good. Tybalt and Mercutio began to fight. Suddenly, as Romeo and Benvolio tried in vain to part the swordsmen, Mercutio fell to his death, stabbed under Romeo's arm by Tybalt.

Romeo could no longer hold his temper.

"Tybalt, take back that insult 'villain', or you will join Mercutio's soul!"

They fought until Tybalt was stabbed to death by Romeo.

This deadly broil occurred in the middle of Verona at noon, and the news of it quickly brought a crowd to the spot. Among them were the Lords Capulet and Montague, with their wives. The Prince himself, who was related to Mercutio, soon arrived on horseback. He was determined to enforce the law strictly against those responsible.

Benvolio was ordered to explain what had happened. He kept as near to the truth as possible without giving injury to Romeo, and he softened the part his friends had taken in it.

Lady Capulet, in deep grief for the loss of Tybalt, demanded strict justice on his murderer, and told the Prince to ignore Benvolio's biased story. Little did she realize that she was arguing against her new son-in-law. On the other hand, Lady Montague pleaded for Romeo's life, arguing, with some reason, that Romeo had done nothing worthy of punishment in taking the life of Tybalt, who had just murdered Mercutio.

The Prince was unmoved by the passionate claims of the two women. After careful considering the facts, he pronounced his sentence on Romeo: he was to be banished from Verona.

Heavy news

This was very heavy news for young Juliet. She had been a bride for just a few hours and now seemed divorced forever! When the news reached her, she at first raged against Romeo, who had killed her dear cousin. She called her husband many strange names, showing the struggle in her mind between her love and her resentment: "Beautiful tyrant, angelical devil, dove-feathered raven, a lamb with a wolf's nature, a snake's heart hidden under a flowering face!"

But in the end love triumphed. The tears she had shed in grief for Romeo killing her cousin turned to teardrops of joy that her husband, who Tybalt had tried to kill, was still alive. Then came fresh tears of grief for Romeo's banishment.

The friar's advice

After the fight, Romeo had quickly taken refuge in the monastery. And it was there that he heard the Prince's sentence, which seemed far worse than death. To him, there was no world outside Verona's walls, no life out of sight of Juliet. Heaven was there, where Juliet lived, and everywhere beyond was purgatory, torture, hell.

Friar Lawrence tried to find words of consolation. But the frantic Romeo refused to listen. He tore out his hair and threw himself on the ground, saying he was measuring out his own grave.

Then a message from his dear Juliet arrived and that calmed him down a little. The friar took the opportunity to talk about the weakness Romeo had displayed.

"You killed Tybalt, yes, but will you also kill yourself, and kill your dear lady, who lives only for your life? The law has been lenient to you, pronouncing only banishment instead of death. Remember that Tybalt intended to kill you! And Juliet is alive and, unbelievably, has become your dear wife. So, all those things considered, you should be most happy. And do not ignore all these blessings, Romeo, for those who despair die miserable."

When Romeo had calmed down, the friar advised him that he should go that night and secretly say goodbye to Juliet. Then he should travel immediately to the city of Mantua, about forty-five kilometers away. He should stay there until the friar found a suitable occasion to reveal the marriage, which might be a joyful means of reconciling their families. Then he had no doubt the Prince would decide to pardon Romeo, and he could return with twenty times more joy than the amount of grief with which he left! The good friar promised to send Romeo letters from time to time, updating him on the situation at home.

Romeo was convinced by this wise advice, thanked the friar, and said he would go to Juliet, stay with her that night, and then journey alone to Mantua at daybreak.

"I would happily stay here longer, Father, but a joy beyond joy awaits me! Farewell."

Unwelcome daybreak

That night, Romeo passed with his dear wife as planned, gaining admission to her bedroom via the orchard. It was a time of great joy. But the delight the two lovers took in each other's company was sadly tinged by the fatal adventures of the past day and the prospect of parting. The unwelcome daybreak seemed to come too soon.

"It's not yet dawn!" said Juliet. "That is only the song of the nightingale, not the lark! Believe me, love."

"No, my dear," replied Romeo, "it's the lark, the herald of the morning! Night's candles are burned out and daylight stands tiptoe on the misty mountain tops. I must be gone, and live; or stay, and die."

Romeo left his dear wife with a heavy heart, promising to write to her from Mantua every hour of the day. He climbed down from her balcony, and stood looking up from below. In the sad state of mind in which she was, he appeared to her eyes as someone dead at the bottom of a grave. But then he was gone, for it would be death for him to be found within the walls of Verona after daybreak. This was the beginning of the tragedy of the pair of star-crossed lovers.

The Count of Paris

Romeo had not been gone many days before the Lord Capulet proposed a match for Juliet. Unaware that she was already married, the husband he had chosen for her was Count Paris. He was a young nobleman who would have been a worthy suitor if she had never met Romeo.

The terrified Juliet was in a sad and confused state following her father's offer. She came up with various excuses: she was too young to marry; Tybalt's recent death had left her too weak to show any joy; and it was not right for the Capulets to celebrate a wedding so soon after his funeral. She pleaded every possible reason against the wedding besides the true one. But her father was deaf to all her excuses, and he ordered her to prepare for her marriage to Paris the next Thursday. Capulet believed he had found her a fine, rich husband that any young woman in Verona would joyfully accept. He would not accept that her shyness, as he understood her excuses, could go against her own good fortune.

Juliet meets the friar

In this state of mind, Juliet visited Friar Lawrence, who was always a wise counselor at times of distress. He asked her if she was willing to undertake a desperate kind of remedy. She replied that with her own dear husband still living, she would prefer to be buried alive rather than marry Paris!

The friar instructed her to go home, appear to be happy, and give her consent to marry Paris. Then, the night before the marriage, she should drink the contents of a small bottle which he then gave her. He explained that for forty-two hours after drinking the potion she would appear cold and lifeless. When her bridegroom came to fetch her in the morning, she would appear to have died. Then she would be taken, uncovered on a carriage, to be buried in her family vault. If she could forget her fear, and consent to this terrible trial, she would be sure to awake in forty-two hours, just as she would from a dream. And before that the friar would let Romeo know what had happened, and he would come at night and take her at once to Mantua.

Love, and the fear of marrying Paris, gave Juliet the strength to undertake this awful adventure. She took the bottle from the friar, saying she would observe his directions, and thanked him.

On her way from the monastery, she met the young Count Paris, and promised to become his bride. This was joyful news to Lord Capulet and his wife. Juliet had upset her father greatly by refusing the Count, but now that she had agreed to be obedient, she was once again her father's darling. Suddenly their house was full of hustle and bustle as the preparations were made. No expense was spared to make it the greatest wedding Verona had ever seen.

The potion

Wednesday night arrived. The time had come to drink the friar's potion. Juliet was naturally worried that the friar might have given her poison to avoid being blamed for marrying her to Romeo. But he had always been known as a very holy man, and she trusted him completely. Then she began worrying about waking up before the time that Romeo was to come for her. Would the terror of the place, full of Capulet bones, and Tybalt lying there in his bloody shroud, drive her crazy?

She remembered all the stories she'd heard of ghosts haunting family vaults. But then her love for Romeo and her aversion for Paris returned. She desperately swallowed the potion and fell unconscious.

Young Paris came early the next morning with musicians to wake up his bride. But instead of a living Juliet, her bedroom presented the terrible sight of her lifeless body. His hopes were destroyed! His bride had been divorced from him even before their hands were joined.

Confusion rapidly spread through the house. It was very sad to hear the mourning of Lord and Lady Capulet. They only had this one loving child to rejoice in, and cruel death had snatched her from their sight.

Now all the things planned for the colorful marriage festival were changed into preparations for a black funeral. The wedding feast would now have to serve as a sad burial feast, the bridal hymns were changed into solemn songs, and the cheerful instruments to melancholy bells. The flowers that would have been thrown in the bride's path would now serve to surround her body. Instead of a priest to marry her, a priest was needed to bury her. She was carried to the family vault just as the friar had described.

The news travels to Mantua

Bad news, which tends to travel faster than good news, now brought the grim story of Juliet's death to Romeo in Mantua. Sadly, it arrived *before* the messenger who had been sent from

Friar Lawrence to tell Romeo that it was only a mock funeral and that Juliet would lie alive in the tomb for a short while, waiting for him to come to release her from that dreary place.

The day before, Romeo had been unusually happy and light-hearted. But then he dreamed that he was dead and that Juliet came and found him, and breathed such life into him with kisses on his lips that he revived and became an emperor! So when the messenger came from Verona, he was sure it was to confirm some good news. But in fact it was the exact opposite: Juliet was dead, and he could never revive her with kisses. He ordered horses to be got ready at once, as he was determined to return to Verona that night to see his wife in her tomb.

Mischief quickly enters the mind of a desperate man, and Romeo remembered a poor shop selling medicines and drugs that he had passed in Mantua. From the poor appearance of the man there, who looked famished, and all the empty boxes on dirty shelves, Romeo had thought, "If a man were to need poison, which by Mantuan law it is a death penalty to sell, here lives a poor wretch who would sell it."

Romeo immediately went to the shop. The owner refused at first, but when Romeo offered him gold, he could not resist. He sold Romeo a poison which, he said, would quickly kill even someone with the strength of twenty men.

Return to Verona

Romeo set out for Verona with the poison, intending to drink it and be buried by Juliet's side. He reached the city at midnight, and soon found the churchyard in the midst of which was the ancient Capulet vault. He was carrying a lantern, a spade, and a crowbar. Just as he started to break open the door of the vault, he was interrupted by a voice.

"Stop that, you vile Montague! Condemned villain, I arrest you! You must come with me and die!"

It was the young Count Paris, who had come to leave flowers for Juliet and weep at her tomb. He had no idea what interest Romeo might have in the dead. But he did know that Romeo was a Montague and suspected he had come to do some shameful thing to the bodies. He wanted to arrest him as a criminal who was condemned to die by the laws of Verona if he were found within the walls of the city.

"Well, I must die, yes," replied Romeo. "But do not tempt a desperate man, good youth! Leave me alone! I warn you I'm armed. Don't put another sin, your death, on my head. Go home and live!"

But the Count refused his warning, and tried to seize him. Romeo resisted, they fought, and Paris fell.

"Ah, I'm dying! Please lay me with Juliet in the vault..."

By the light of his lantern, Romeo realized it was Count Paris he had stabbed. On his way from Mantua, he had learned that Paris was due to marry Juliet. Realizing that they had both suffered misfortune, Romeo told the dying Paris he would bury him in "a triumphant grave", meaning Juliet's.

Then Romeo opened the door of the vault...

Ah, dear Juliet

And there lay Juliet in all her beauty, as though death had no power to change one feature. She lay still fresh and blooming, just as she had fallen to sleep after swallowing the potion.

"Oh, my love! My wife! Ah, dear Juliet... Death, that has sucked the honey of your breath, has had no power yet upon your beauty."

Nearby lay Tybalt in his bloody shroud.

"Forgive me, cousin!" said Romeo. "I am about to do you a favor by putting your enemy to death!"

Romeo took his last leave of his wife's lips, kissing them gently.

"Here will I start my everlasting rest, and shake off from my weary body the burden of my unlucky stars. Eyes, look your last! Arms, take your last embrace. Lips, give your final kiss..."

And then he gulped down the poison. It was real and fatal, unlike the potion which Juliet had swallowed, the effect of which was just ending. She was about to wake up to complain that Romeo was late coming...or that he had come too soon.

Friar Lawrence

The time had arrived at which the friar had promised Juliet she would wake up. He had learned that, by some unlucky chance, the letters he had sent to Mantua had never reached Romeo. He rushed to the churchyard, carrying a pickax and a lantern, to let her out. But he was shocked to find a light already burning inside the Capulet vault, to see swords and blood at the entrance, and then to find the lifeless bodies of Romeo and Paris.

Before he had time to imagine how these fatal accidents had occurred, Juliet started coming out of her trance. When she saw the friar, she remembered where she was, and why.

"Oh, kind friar," she murmured, "where is my husband?"

But, hearing a noise outside, the friar said, "Some greater power has thwarted our plan. Romeo lies next to you, dead, and Paris too... We must leave this place of death at once. I will take you to a nunnery. The watchmen are coming... I cannot stay here!"

"You can go, Father, but I will stay!" cried Juliet.

And Friar Lawrence ran away.

"What's this in my true love's hand?" said Juliet. "A small bottle. Ah, poison, I see, has taken you from me. Haven't you left even one friendly drop to help me follow you? Then I will kiss your lips. Maybe some poison is left on them... Oh, Romeo, your lips are warm..."

Then she heard the sound of many people approaching. She quickly unsheathed her small dagger... She stabbed herself and died beside her true love, saying, "Oh, happy dagger!"

Alarm...

The city's night watchmen started arriving. Count Paris's servant had witnessed the fight between his master and Romeo, and raised the alarm. It spread fast among the citizens, who ran up and down the streets of Verona shouting, in great confusion, "Paris! Romeo! Juliet!"

The uproar brought Lord Montague and Lord Capulet

hurrying from their beds, along with the Prince, to find out what all the noise was about. A huge crowd gathered outside the Capulet vault.

The friar had been seized by the watchmen as he left the churchyard, trembling, sighing, and crying suspiciously. The Prince ordered him to report all he knew about those strange and terrible accidents.

And there, in the presence of the Lords Montague and Capulet, Friar Lawrence faithfully related the story of their children's fatal love. He told how Romeo was Juliet's husband and Juliet his dear wife, and explained the part he had played in the marriage, hoping it might end the long quarrels between their families. He said that before he could find an opportunity to reveal their marriage, another match had been suggested for Juliet. To avoid a second marriage, she had swallowed the sleeping potion he gave her, and everyone thought she had died. He reported how he had written to Romeo to come and meet Juliet when she woke up, but by an unfortunate chance the letters had not reached him. Beyond all this, the friar could not continue the story. When he came to deliver Juliet from that place of death, he found Count Paris and Romeo already dead.

The remaining details were supplied by the Count's servant who had seen Paris and Romeo fight, and by Romeo's servant who came with Romeo from Mantua carrying a letter to be delivered to Romeo's father in the event of his death. The Prince read the letter. Romeo confirmed the friar's story regarding his marriage to Juliet, implored his parents to forgive him, admitted buying the poison from a poor Mantuan man, and expressed his intent to go to the vault to die next to Juliet.

All this made it clear that the friar had not been directly involved in any of the deaths. They were the unintended result of his well-meant plans.

The strife ends

The Prince turned to the lords.

"Capulet! Montague! See what your hate has led to! Heaven has killed your joys."

And the old rivals, no longer enemies, agreed to bury their long strife in their children's graves.

"Oh, brother Montague," said Capulet, "give me your hand. I can demand no more."

"But I can give you more than that," replied Montague. "I will order a statue of pure gold of the true and faithful Juliet. As long as Verona survives, no work of art will be more treasured for its richness and workmanship."

"And I shall erect another statue of Romeo to go beside it," said Capulet, "to honor those two poor sacrifices of our ancient quarrels!"

In that way, those poor old lords, although it was too late, tried hard to equal each other in good deeds.

And so ends the tragic tale of Verona's famous 'star-crossed lovers'. But still today people flock to 'Juliet's House' in the city and touch her statue, hoping to have good fortune in love.

14

Hamlet, Prince of Denmark

ハムレット

読み始める前に

「生きるべきか死ぬべきか、それが問題だ」という台詞は、しばしば引用される有名なフレーズ。人生の意味や死生観について哲学的に問いかけ、悲劇の傑作と言われている。

［登場人物］

Hamlet	ハムレット《デンマーク王国の後継者》
Claudius	クローディアス《デンマーク王、ハムレットの叔父》
Gertrude	ガートルード《デンマーク王妃、ハムレットの母》
King Hamlet	先王ハムレット《先代のデンマーク王。ハムレットの父》
Ghost	亡霊《先王ハムレットの亡霊》
Horatio	ホレイショー《ハムレットの親友》
Ophelia	オフィーリア《ハムレットの恋人、ポローニアスの娘》
Laertes	レアティーズ《オフィーリアの兄》
Polonius	ポローニアス《デンマーク国王の重臣。オフィーリアとレアティーズの父》

［地名など］

Elsinore	エルシノア《デンマークの城》
Troy	トロイア《古代都市》
Wittenberg University	ヴィッテンベルク大学《ハムレットが学んだ大学》

［あらすじ］

デンマーク王が急死し、王の弟クローディアスが王妃と結婚、王に即位した。父の死と母の早い再婚で、王子ハムレットは憂いに沈んでいた。

ある日、従臣から、夜になると父の亡霊がエルシノアの城壁に現れるという話を聞き、確かめに行ったハムレットはそこで父の亡霊に会う。そして父がクローディアスに毒殺されたことを知り、復讐を決意するのだった。

やがてハムレットは、クローディアスが父を暗殺した証拠を掴むが、自分と王妃との会話を隠れて盗み聞きしていた宰相ポローニアスを、王と間違えて刺殺してしまう。ポローニアスの娘で、ハムレットの恋人であったオフィーリアは、悲しみのあまり気が狂い、川に入り溺死……復讐のなかで悲劇が続いていく。

［総単語数］5,050語

HAMLET, PRINCE OF DENMARK

Once upon a time, the popular King Hamlet ruled Denmark with Queen Gertrude. But suddenly one day the king was found dead in the garden of Elsinore Castle where they lived. The official report released by his brother Claudius was that he'd been bitten by a venomous snake. Then, less than two months later, Gertrude married her brother-in-law and he became King Claudius. This was regarded by many Danes as a strange act of *indiscretion*, or lack of *feeling*, or worse. Claudius in no way resembled his late brother in the qualities of his person or his mind. He was as *unattractive* in his looks as he was *unworthy* in character. As a result, suspicions arose in the minds of some. Had he done away with his brother to marry his widow and become king instead of young Prince Hamlet, the dead king's son and lawful successor to the throne?

The young prince

The action of his mother made a huge impression on Hamlet. He was a student at Wittenberg University in Germany, and he rushed home when he heard of his father's death. He had loved his father deeply and worshipped his memory. Possessing a fine sense of what was correct behavior, he was very upset about his mother's conduct. Between grief for his father's death and shame for his mother's marriage, he sank into a deep depression. He lost all his mirth and his good looks. His love of books disappeared, along with his interest in exercise and sports. He grew weary of the world. It now seemed to him like an unweeded garden, where all the healthy flowers were withered and only weeds remained.

Being excluded from the throne was a bitter wound and a great indignity to Hamlet. But what took away his cheerful spirits most was the fact that his mother seemed to have forgotten his father already. King Hamlet had been a kind and gentle husband, and she had always appeared to be a loving and obedient wife. And yet within two months she had married again! And not only that... She had married his *uncle*, which was an unlawful marriage in Denmark. And what made it even worse was the indecent haste with which it was all completed, as well as the bad character of the man she'd chosen to be the partner of her throne and bed.

Gertrude and Claudius tried hard to divert Hamlet in some way, but it was in vain. He still appeared in court dressed all in black, as though mourning his father's death. He even wore black on the day Gertrude married again, and refused to join in any of the festivities on what he regarded as a disgraceful day.

What also troubled Hamlet was the uncertainty about his father's death. He seriously doubted the deadly snake story. He suspected that it was Claudius himself who had been the snake—in other words, he had murdered his brother for the crown. Could that be true? What should he think about his mother? Had *she* been involved in the murder in any way? These issues continually distracted him.

A ghostly figure

Then one day, Horatio, Hamlet's closest friend and fellow student at university arrived in Elsinore.

"Oh, I am so glad to see you, Horatio," said Hamlet. "But why are you here?"

"I came to see your father's funeral."

"I think it was to see my mother's wedding."

"Ah, yes, it did follow hard very soon!"

"A terrible day, Horatio!"

"He was a good king."

"Yes, a good man. We shall not see his like again. But I can clearly picture him now in my mind!"

"But I think I saw him last night..."

"What? Who?"

"The king, your father."

"My father?"

"Let me explain. On two successive nights at midnight, the men on the rooftop watch saw a ghostly figure who looked just like your father. From head to foot, it was wearing the same suit of armor as King Hamlet wore. It looked pale, with an expression more of sadness than of anger. They were very scared, of course, and secretly told me. So last night I joined them on the watch. Sure enough, the figure appeared again. Even its black beard streaked with silver was just like your father's."

"Did you speak to it?"

"I did, yes. But it said nothing. Once it lifted up its head as if it were about to speak, but at that moment the cock crew and it shrank away in haste and vanished."

"Oh, this is very strange, Horatio!"

"But it's true. I felt it was my duty to let you know about it."

"Indeed, yes, thank you. But this troubles me. What could it mean? I think I will join the watch myself tonight. If it appears again, I'll speak to it. Maybe it will talk to me. Horatio, please tell no-one else about this."

"My lips are sealed."

Hamlet waited impatiently for night to come.

Remember me...

At eleven o'clock, Hamlet went up to the castle roof with Horatio. It was a bitterly cold night. They walked around to keep warm. Then suddenly Horatio whispered that the figure was coming.

At the sight of his father's ghost, Hamlet was struck with sudden surprise and fear. At first he called on the angels of Heaven to defend them, for he didn't know whether the spirit was good or bad, whether it came for good or evil. But gradually his courage returned. The ghost gazed at Hamlet sadly as if he wanted to have a conversation with him. It did in every respect look like his father, so Hamlet could not help speaking to him.

"Hamlet, King, Father!" he cried. "Why have you left your grave to come again and visit the Earth in the moonlight? Is there something I can do to give you peace?"

The ghost beckoned to Hamlet that he should go with him to a place where they could be alone. Horatio feared it could be an evil spirit who would tempt Hamlet to leap into the sea or somehow drive him crazy. But Hamlet was determined to take the risk. He cared too little about life to fear losing it. He followed after the ghost...

When they were alone together, the spirit spoke.

"I am the ghost of your father, Hamlet. I have come to tell you that I was cruelly murdered!"

"Murdered?"

"Yes. One afternoon, as was my custom, I was sleeping in the castle garden. But I was not bitten by a snake. My evil brother Claudius crept up and poured the juice of poisonous henbane into my ears. It raced through my veins, heating up my blood and spreading a crust all over my skin. So, I was cut off from my crown, my queen, and my life, by my brother's hand... *He* was the snake!"

"So it *was* my uncle!" cried Hamlet.

"Hamlet," continued the ghost, "if you did ever love your father, revenge his foul murder! But do not in any way hurt your mother. Leave her to Heaven's judgement and the stings and thorns of her conscience. Ah, dawn is coming... Adieu, adieu, Hamlet. Remember me..."

As the ghost vanished, Hamlet promised to observe its requests.

A mad resolution

As soon as Hamlet was left alone, he made a solemn resolution. He would instantly erase everything in his memory, all that he had ever learned from books or observation. He would let nothing live in his brain but the memory of what the ghost had told him and requested him to do. He only told the details of the conversation to Horatio. And he asked both him and the guards to say nothing to anyone about what they had seen.

Hamlet was worried that the terror he had felt might drive him mad. If that happened, it might put his uncle on his guard and suspect Hamlet was planning something. Hamlet decided that from that moment he would pretend to be really and truly mad. He reckoned his uncle would then think he was not capable of doing anything dangerous.

So Hamlet began to behave wildly and to dress and speak strangely. He did this so well that Gertrude and Claudius were both deceived. They concluded that his love was the cause and they thought they knew who was the object of his passion.

Ophelia

Before his father's death, Hamlet had dearly loved Ophelia, the daughter of Polonius, the king's chief counselor in affairs of state. He had sent her letters and rings, and sought her love in an honorable way. She had believed all his vows. But the melancholy into which he'd fallen had made him neglect her. Now, as he pretended to be mad, he decided it would be better to treat her unkindly, and even rudely.

But rather than reproach him, Ophelia persuaded herself that it was nothing but some kind of depression that was affecting him. She compared his once noble mind to sweet bells which are capable of producing the loveliest music, but produce only a harsh and unpleasant sound when roughly handled.

Although Hamlet's focus on revenge did not go well with such an idle passion as love, there were moments when he felt he was treating gentle Ophelia too harshly. So he wrote her a letter full of passion, which matched with his supposed madness, but was mixed with gentle touches of affection. This suggested that a deep love for her still remained in his heart. He told her to doubt the stars were fire, and to doubt that the sun moved, but never to doubt that he loved her.

Ophelia dutifully showed this letter to her father, and he thought himself bound to show it to the king and queen. Gertrude was hoping that Ophelia was indeed the cause of Hamlet's wildness, and that her beauty and virtues might happily restore him to his normal self.

But Hamlet's sickness lay deeper than she thought, and was

not so easily cured. His determination to revenge his father's murder would give him no rest until it was accomplished. Every hour of delay seemed to neglect his father's commands. But how to do it was no easy matter. Claudius was constantly surrounded by guards or with Gertrude. And the fact that the usurper was his mother's husband also blunted the edge of his purpose. The mere act of killing someone was in itself revolting to as gentle a person as Hamlet. His melancholy also weakened his ability to act.

He thought long and hard about life and death, including his own.

"To be . . . or not to be? That is the question . . . "

Moreover, Hamlet could not help having doubts as to whether the ghost he had seen really *was* his father's spirit. Maybe it was the Devil, who could take any form he pleased and wanted to take advantage of Hamlet's weakness to drive him to carry out murder?

He decided he needed more solid grounds for action than just seeing a ghost that might have been an illusion.

Priam and Hecuba

While Hamlet was in this frame of mind, a familiar troupe of traveling actors arrived at Elsinore. Hamlet had seen them perform many times, and he welcomed his old friends. He suddenly remembered a certain tragic speech that he had long been fond of. It described the death of old Priam, King of Troy, and the grief of Hecuba his queen. Hamlet requested the leader of the troupe to perform it.

The actor willingly agreed, and presented it in a very lively manner: the cruel murder of the feeble old king; the destruction of his city by fire; the mad grief of the old queen, running barefoot up and down the palace, with a piece of cloth on her head instead of a crown, and wearing just a blanket snatched up in haste instead of a royal robe...

The performance drew tears from all those watching, who imagined they could see the actual scene. Even the actor himself delivered the words with a broken voice and real tears.

This started Hamlet thinking. "Hmm, this actor works himself into a passion with a fictional speech. He can weep for someone he's never seen, Hecuba, who's been dead for many centuries! So how dull *I* am in contrast! *I* have a real motive for passion—a dear father murdered—and yet I am so little moved that my desire for revenge seems to be asleep!"

As he was thinking about actors and acting, and the powerful effects a good play representing real life can have on an audience, he remembered an interesting case in the past. Seeing a murder story performed on stage, an actual murderer was so affected by the power of the scene and the similarity of circumstances that he immediately confessed his own crime!

"Yes," thought Hamlet, "I will ask these actors to perform something like my father's murder in front of my uncle. I can give them some extra lines to learn. I will carefully watch what effect it has on him. From his reaction, I may be able to gather with more certainty if he was the murderer or not. The play's the thing to catch the conscience of the king!"

The Mousetrap

And so Hamlet asked the actors to prepare the play and then present it in the Great Hall that evening in front of the King and Queen. The play was titled *The Mousetrap*. It was based on the murder in Vienna of a duke named Gonzago. His wife's name was Baptista. Lucianus, the duke's nephew, poisoned him in his garden in order to take over his dukedom, and shortly after became Baptista's lover.

Claudius, of course, had no idea that a trap had been laid for him. He happily attended with Gertrude and the whole court. Horatio and Hamlet sat where they could easily observe the King.

The play opened with a conversation between Gonzago and his wife, in which the lady made strong protestations of love. She ensured him that if he died before her she would never marry a second husband. She said she might be cursed if she took a new husband, and added that the only women who did that were wicked ones who had killed their first husband.

Hamlet noticed his uncle's face go pale when he heard this. But when Lucianus came on and poisoned Gonzago, who was sleeping in the garden, the strong resemblance to his own wicked act hit Claudius's conscience hard. He could take no more. He suddenly called for lights, saying he was not feeling well, and abruptly left the hall. The play was stopped.

Now Hamlet had seen enough to be satisfied that the words of the ghost were true! He felt a rush of relief and joy.

"Horatio," he said, "I will take the ghost's words for a thousand pounds!"

A bloody deed

But before he could decide exactly how to carry out his revenge, he was sent for by his mother to visit her in her private room.

"Well," he thought, "I will be tough with her, but not unkind..."

In fact, Claudius had asked her to tell her son how much his recent behavior had displeased them both. He also wanted to know everything that was said at their meeting. However, he felt that the report of a mother might avoid some of her dear son's words, words which *he* should hear. And so Polonius, the old counselor of state, was ordered to hide behind the hangings in the queen's room. There, unseen, he could hear the whole conversation. This plan suited Polonius perfectly, as he loved acquiring knowledge in a cunning way.

As soon as Hamlet arrived, he said, "Now, Mother, what's the matter?"

She immediately began to complain strongly about his behavior, referring to Claudius as 'your father'.

"Hamlet, you have greatly offended your father!"

"Mother," replied Hamlet at once, "*you* have greatly offended *my* father."

"That is an idle answer!" said Gertrude sharply.

"As good as your wicked comment deserved!"

"Have you forgotten who it is you're speaking to?"

"Ah, I wish I could forget! You are the queen, your husband's brother's wife; and you are my mother. I wish you were *not* what you are!"

"Well Hamlet, if you are going to show me so little respect, I'll send for someone to whom you *can* speak. Your uncle, perhaps?"

But now he had her alone, Hamlet would not let her go until he had tried to bring her to some sense of her wicked life. Taking her by the wrist, he held her fast, and made her sit down.

Frightened by his earnest manner, she cried out; "What are you going to do? Murder me? Help, help!"

And a voice came from behind the hangings. "Help, help the Queen!"

"What?" cried Hamlet. "A rat?" Thinking it was Claudius, he drew his sword and stabbed through the hangings where the voice came from, just the way he would have stabbed a rat.

"Oh, I am killed!" said the voice. Then there was silence.

"Oh, what have you done?" cried Gertrude.

"I don't know. Is it the King?"

But when Hamlet dragged the body out, he realized the spy had been Polonius.

"Oh, you wretched intruding fool! Now you know how dangerous it is to be too busy! Farewell!"

"Oh!" exclaimed Gertrude. "What a rash and bloody deed!"

"A bloody deed, yes, mother," replied Hamlet, "almost as bad as yours, to kill a king, and marry his brother."

"To kill a king?"

"Yes, that's what I said!"

Hamlet had gone too far to stop there. He was now in the

mood to speak plainly to his mother, and he did. In moving terms, he described her great offense in being so forgetful of his father, as in marrying so soon his brother and reputed murderer.

"After the vows you made to your first husband, such an act is enough to make all vows of women suspect and religion just a form of words! You have done a deed that the Heavens blush at, and the Earth is sick of you because of it..."

Then he showed her two pictures, the one of his father, the other of his uncle. He begged her to see the difference.

"Oh, what grace was on the brow of my father," he said, "and how he looked like a god: the curls of Apollo, the forehead of Jupiter, the eye of Mars, and a posture like Mercury! This man was your husband!"

And then he showed her the man who had replaced him, Claudius.

"How like some plant disease, he looks! And this man blasted away his brother!"

Gertrude was ashamed that Hamlet had turned her eyes inward on her soul in this way. She could now see how black and unnatural it was. Hamlet asked her how she could continue to live with that man who had murdered her first husband and seized the crown like a thief.

But just as he said this, the ghost of his father entered the room.

"Oh!" cried Hamlet, in great terror. "Protect me, heavenly guards! Why have you come again?"

"Ah, he's mad!" said Gertrude, who could see nothing.

"To remind you of the revenge you promised me, but seem to have forgotten," said the ghost. "But speak to your confused mother, Hamlet, or the grief and terror she is suffering will kill her…"

The ghost vanished. His mother had been terribly frightened to hear her son conversing, as it seemed to her, with nothing. She thought he had really gone mad.

"Look over there!" cried Hamlet. "Father in his armor…"

But Gertrude could still see nothing.

Hamlet tried to beg her not to flatter her wicked soul by thinking that rather than her offenses it was his madness that had brought his father's spirit back. And he asked her to feel his pulse, which was beating calmly, not like a madman's. He begged her, with tears in his eyes, to confess to Heaven and repent the past. As for the future, she should avoid the company of the king and stop behaving as a wife to him. She promised to follow his directions.

"So, goodnight, Mother. I have to be cruel only to be kind!"

And now Hamlet looked at the body of Polonius, the father of Ophelia who he had so dearly loved.

"I do repent this deed…" he said as he dragged the body out of the room.

Bound for England

The unfortunate death of Polonius gave Claudius a good reason to send Hamlet out of the country. He would willingly have put him to death, fearing him as being very dangerous. However, he was worried about the reaction of the people of Denmark, who loved Hamlet. And Gertrude doted on her son. So, under the pretense of providing for Hamlet's safety, and to avoid being called to account for Polonius's death, the subtle king arranged for him to be taken on board a ship bound for England. He was in the care of two courtiers, who carried letters to the English court, which at that time paid tribute to Denmark. The letters requested that—for totally invented reasons—Hamlet should be put to death as soon as he landed.

Suspecting some treachery, however, Hamlet, secretly got at the letters at night. He skillfully erased his own name, and replaced it with the names of the two courtiers. Then, unnoticed, he resealed the letters and put them back where they belonged.

Soon after that, the ship was attacked by pirates. A sea fight began, during which Hamlet, anxious to show his valor, boarded the pirate vessel with sword in hand. His own ship sailed away in a cowardly manner, leaving Hamlet to his fate. The two courtiers continued on their way to England, unaware that they were about to deliver their own death sentence.

The pirates had the prince in their power. But they showed themselves to be generous enemies. When they realized just who their prisoner was, they hoped that he might do them some good turn at court if they treated him well. So they were happy to set Hamlet on shore at the nearest Danish port.

Hamlet immediately wrote to Claudius, informing him of

the strange chance which had brought him back home, and saying that he would present himself before His Majesty the following day.

Sweets to the sweet

But the first thing he saw as he approached Elsinore Castle was a sad sight indeed. It was the funeral of the young and beautiful Ophelia.

Ever since Polonius's death, her mind had flipped. The fact that her father should die a violent death at the hands of the prince she loved was just too much for the tender girl to take. She grew distracted, and started wandering about giving flowers to the ladies of the court, saying they were for her father's burial. And she sang songs about love and death as if she had no clear memory of what had happened to her.

Near the castle, there was a willow tree with boughs hanging down over a small stream. Ophelia went there one day when nobody was watching her. She had been making a garland of daisies and nettles, flowers and weeds all mixed together. She clambered up on to a willow bough to hang it, the bough snapped, and she was thrown into the water with her garland. For a while, her clothes bore her up. She chanted scraps of old tunes as though she was quite unaware of her situation, or as if that was her natural element. But before long her heavy wet clothes dragged her down from her melodious singing to a muddy and miserable death.

It was her funeral led by her brother Laertes that was in progress when Hamlet arrived. The King and Queen and the whole court were present. Hamlet quickly understood what all the show meant, but he stood on one side, not wishing to interrupt the ceremony.

As the Queen threw flowers into the grave, she said, "Sweets to the sweet! I hoped to have decked your bridal bed, sweet girl, not to have thrown them in your grave. You should have been my Hamlet's wife..."

Hamlet heard Laertes wish that violets might spring from his sister's grave. Then he saw him leap into the grave, frantic with grief, and order the attendants to pile a mountain of soil upon him, so that he could be buried with her. Hamlet's love for Ophelia came back to him at that moment. He couldn't bear to see her brother showing so much grief, as he thought he loved Ophelia better than forty thousand brothers.

Even more frantic than Laertes, he leapt into the grave. Laertes, recognizing Hamlet as the man responsible for both his father's and his sister's deaths, grabbed him by the throat until the attendants rushed over to part them.

After the funeral, Hamlet excused his hasty act, explaining that he couldn't bear anyone outdoing him in a show of grief for fair Ophelia's death. For the moment, the two noble young men seemed reconciled.

The death of a sparrow

But as a result of Laertes' grief and anger, Claudius came up with a plan to destroy Hamlet. He urged Laertes, under the cover of peace and reconciliation, to challenge Hamlet to a friendly trial of fencing skill. Hamlet accepted, and a day was appointed for the match. All the court was to be present and large bets were placed, as both Hamlet and Laertes were known to excel at fencing.

Horatio talked to Hamlet just before the match.

"I fear you will lose, my lord!"

"No, I don't think so. I've been practicing hard recently.

But even so, I do feel a bit uneasy today…"

"Do you want me to say you're not feeling well and would prefer to cancel the match?"

"No, no. We cannot go against Fate. Even the death of a sparrow is ruled by Fate. If it is now, then it will not be in the future. If it is not to be in the future, it will be now. And if it is not now, it will definitely come… Being ready is the important thing, Horatio!"

The match

Everyone assembled in the Great Hall of the castle for the fencing match. The laws of fencing required the use of blades called 'foils'. They were all of equal length and their points were blunted to avoid injury. But the king had ordered Laertes to prepare one blade with a sharp poisoned point. When the time came to select the foils, Hamlet chose one without suspecting any treachery. He confirmed that all the foils were the same length with the referee, but he did not check Laertes' weapon.

At first Laertes fenced lightly, allowing Hamlet to gain 'a hit'. Claudius praised him loudly and drank to his success, placing a big bet on the outcome. There were a few more equal bouts and then another 'hit' by Hamlet. But as they were taking a short break, Laertes suddenly made a deadly thrust at Hamlet from behind with his poisoned weapon…and gave him a mortal blow.

Hamlet was shocked when he realized he was bleeding. Very angry, but not fully understanding the treachery, he managed to exchange his own blunt weapon for Laertes' deadly one. And with one thrust from Hamlet, Laertes was caught in his own trap.

At that instant, Gertrude cried out and fell from her chair to the floor. But she had not fainted at seeing the blood, as Claudius claimed… Inadvertently, she had drunk from a tankard infused with a deadly poison which the king had prepared for Hamlet if he asked for a drink. It was a backup plan in case Laertes failed to kill Hamlet. But Claudius had not warned Gertrude to leave the tankard alone…

"The drink, the drink!" she cried. "Oh, my dear Hamlet, I am poisoned!"

And she died.

"Lock all the doors!" shouted Hamlet, horrified. "Treachery! Who is to blame for this?"

"Hamlet, I am the traitor," murmured Laertes. "You're holding the poisoned weapon that has killed us both. I'm a victim of my own deadly plan! You have less than half an hour to live, as no medicine can cure you now. Forgive me, Hamlet… Your mother was poisoned as well. The king, the king's to blame…"

Those were his last words.

Hamlet looked at the foil in his hand. "Ah, maybe there is still some poison left on it!"

He staggered over to his uncle and thrust the blade into his heart. Then he grabbed the poisoned tankard and forced it to the king's mouth.

"Here, you damned murderous Dane, drink this! Follow my mother!"

The king collapsed, dead.

Feeling his breath fading and his life departing, Hamlet turned to his dear friend Horatio, who had been a spectator of this awful tragedy.

"I am dead, Horatio! But you are alive... Please tell this story to the world...

"No, I will drink the poison and go with you!"

"No, no... Only *you* know the whole, true story."

Horatio nodded, his eyes filling with tears.

"Ah," said Hamlet, "the powerful poison is working fast... Adieu, Horatio... The rest is silence..."

And Hamlet died.

"Now cracks a noble heart!" said Horatio. "Good night, sweet prince, and flights of angels sing you to your rest!"

There were many tears shed that day. Hamlet was a kind and gentle prince who had been greatly loved for his many noble qualities. And if he had lived, he would surely have proved a very complete King of Denmark.

Othello

オセロー

読み始める前に

オセローは妻の不貞を疑い、自ら破滅していく。「四大悲劇」のひとつ。
「嫉妬」がテーマになっており、登場人物の心理が明快で、悲劇のなかではわかりやすい内容とされている。

［登場人物］

Othello	オセロー《ヴェニスの軍人でムーア人》
Desdemona	デズディモーナ《オセローの妻》
Brabantio	ブラバンショー《デズデモーナの父》
Cassio	キャシオー《オセローの副官》
Iago	イアーゴー《オセローの旗手》
Emilia	エミリア《イアーゴーの妻、デズディモーナの侍女》
Montano	モンターノ《将校》
Barbara	バルバラ《デズディモーナの母の侍女》

［地名など］

Cyprus	キプロス《島》
Venice	ヴェニス《イタリアの都市》

［あらすじ］

ヴェニスの軍人でムーア人のオセローは、美しいデズディモーナと愛し合う。しかし、デズディモーナの父ブラバンショーに反対されたふたりは、誰にも知らせずにこっそりと結婚する。

勇敢な軍人でヴェニス人に信頼されていたオセローは、トルコ軍が攻め入るキプロス島へ行くことになり、デズディモーナを伴い戦場へ行く。

オセローの部下イアーゴーは、自分を差し置いて副官に昇進した同輩のキャシオーを妬んでいた。また、キャシオーを引き立てているオセローも憎んでいた。イアーゴーは、二人を陥れようと、キャシオーがデズディモーナと密通しているとオセローに告げ口する。さらに真実味が増すように、オセローがデズディモーナに送ったハンカチを盗んでキャシオーの部屋に置く。

嫉妬にかられたオセローはイアーゴーにキャシオーを殺すように命じ、自ら破滅への道をたどるのだった。

［総単語数］4,540語

OTHELLO

Once upon a time, in the city of Venice in northern Italy, there was a rich senator named Brabantio. He had a beautiful and gentle daughter named Desdemona. She was sought after by many handsome, fair-skinned Venetians, both for her excellent qualities and for her wealth. But none of them attracted her. She was much more interested in the *minds* of people than in their looks or the color of their skin. In fact, she had chosen for the object of her affections a dark-skinned Moor from North Africa, called Othello. Her father was very fond of him and often invited him to their house.

Tales of a soldier and traveler

Othello lacked nothing which would recommend him to the

affections of a great lady. He was a brave soldier. As a result of his service in wars against the Turks, he'd risen to the rank of general in the Venetian army. He was highly esteemed and trusted by the state.

He had also traveled widely. Desdemona loved to hear him tell the stories of his adventures. He would run through them all the way from his earliest memories: battles, sieges and encounters; the dangers he'd been exposed to on land and at sea; his hairbreadth escapes, such as when he marched up to the mouth of a cannon; and how he'd been taken prisoner by the enemy and was sold to slavery, but managed to escape.

To all these accounts, he would add his description of the strange things he had seen in other countries: the vast wildernesses and romantic caverns, quarries, rocks and mountains whose heads are always in the clouds; the cannibals who are man-eaters; and the people in Africa whose heads do grow beneath their shoulders. These traveler's tales so grabbed Desdemona's attention that if she were called away at any time by some household matter, she would finish it as fast as possible and rush back, greedy to hear more of his stories.

One day, when Othello had some free time, Desdemona asked him to tell her the whole story of his life. Up to then, she had only heard bits and pieces. He consented, and made her cry several times when he described the hardships of his youth. When he finished, she sighed and said it was all very strange and sad, and she wished she hadn't heard it. Yet she also wished that heaven had made her such a man! Then she thanked him, and said that if he had a friend who loved her, he had only to teach him how to tell the same story, and that would make her love him!

Following this hint, Othello felt free to speak more openly of his love, saying, "I think you love me for the dangers I have faced, and I love you that you feel sorry for me!"

And taking advantage of this golden opportunity, Othello gained the consent of the generous Desdemona to marry her in secret.

Magic spells and witchcraft?

Brabantio had left his daughter free to choose her own husband. He naturally expected her, as a noble young Venetian lady, to choose a wealthy man of the rank of senator, or something like that. But he was deceived. Desdemona loved Othello, and devoted her heart to *his* valiant parts and qualities. But, because of the Moor's background and fortune, Brabantio would never accept him as his son-in-law.

Their private marriage could not be kept a secret for long. Sure enough, it soon reached Brabantio's ears. At once, he appeared at a solemn council of the Senate to accuse Othello of using magic spells and witchcraft to seduce his daughter and marry her without his consent.

It so happened that just at that time, the State of Venice had immediate need of Othello's service. News had arrived that a large Turkish fleet was heading toward the island of Cyprus. Its aim was to regain the strong Mediterranean base from

Venice, which was currently controlling it. In this emergency situation, the State turned its eyes to Othello. He was the only commander Venice deemed adequate to lead the defense of Cyprus. So Othello was summoned to the Senate for two reasons: as a candidate for important state business; and charged with offences which by the laws of Venice could mean his death!

The age and character of Brabantio deserved a patient hearing from the Duke and the serious assembly. But the angry father conducted his accusation wildly, producing mere possibilities as proofs. So when Othello was asked to defend himself, he only had to tell them the simple tale of the course of his love. He did it so eloquently and honestly that the Duke, who was chief judge, had to admit that the story would have won his own daughter! The 'spells' which Othello had used were clearly no more than the honest art of a man in love; and the only 'witchcraft' he had used was the ability to tell a soft tale to win a lady!

Desdemona herself then appeared in court and confirmed all that Othello had said.

Then her father said, "Daughter, in this room, can you see the person to whom you most owe obedience?"

"Dear Father," replied Desdemona, "To *you*, I owe great respect and thanks for my life and education. But I can see a divided duty. Here stands my husband. And the same amount of duty my mother showed to *you*, more than to her father, I feel I am due to show *him*."

"Then God be with you!" said Brabantio. "Moor, I here give

you with all my heart that which, if you did not have it already, I would with all my heart keep from you... my daughter! Duke, I have finished. Please move on to the urgent affairs of state."

That issue finished, Othello said he was ready to manage the war in Cyprus. The hardships of military life were as natural to him as food and rest are to other men. As for Desdemona, she said she placed her husband's honor before the idle pleasures of a newly-married couple, and cheerfully consented to his going. But, at the same time, she made a request to go with him, and this was accepted.

The new lieutenant

Othello and Desdemona had just landed in Cyprus when news arrived that a tempest had dispersed the Turkish fleet. So the island was safe from any immediate attack. However, the war Othello was personally to suffer was about to begin.

Among all Othello's friends, no one possessed more confidence than Michael Cassio. A young soldier from Florence, he was cheerful, charming, handsome and eloquent. In fact, he was just the type of man who might alarm jealousy in an older man who had married a young and beautiful wife. Othello was certainly much older, but he was as free from jealousy as he was noble; he did not behave badly himself, and he did not suspect others of doing it.

In fact, Cassio had been a sort of go-between in Othello's love affair with Desdemona. Othello had feared he lacked those soft parts of conversation which please ladies, but his friend

Cassio was the opposite. As a result, Cassio would sometimes go courting on behalf of Othello. So it was not surprising that the gentle Desdemona loved and trusted Cassio almost as much as she did Othello. Marriage of the couple had not made any difference in their behavior to Cassio. He often visited their house. His free way of talking was a pleasant change to that of Othello, who was generally more serious. And Desdemona and Cassio would talk and laugh together, just as they did when he went courting for Othello.

A net

Othello had lately promoted Cassio to be his lieutenant, the general's right-hand man, a position of great trust. The promotion had greatly upset Iago, an older officer who thought *he* had a much better claim to the position. He would often ridicule Cassio as being fit only for the company of ladies, a man who knew no more about the art of war than a girl. Basically, Iago hated Cassio. He also hated Othello for favoring Cassio, and for a ridiculous suspicion that the Moor was too fond of his wife, Emilia.

"The Moor," thought Iago, "has such a free and open nature, he believes men are honest if they just appear to be. He's as easy to lead by the nose as a donkey!"

Iago started developing a horrid scheme of revenge, which would involve Cassio, Othello, and Desdemona. He had studied human nature deeply, and he knew that of all the torments which can afflict a man's mind, the pain of jealousy has the sharpest sting. He decided it would be an exquisite plot of revenge if he could succeed in making Othello jealous of Cassio. It might even end in the death of Cassio or Othello, or both. He didn't care.

"I shall make a net to capture them all!"

Welcome to Cyprus!

At five o'clock in the afternoon in Cyprus, a herald made a big announcement: "Regarding the news of the enemy fleet's dispersal, our valiant General Othello has requested everyone to rejoice until the hour of eleven tonight! Moreover, we will celebrate his recent marriage. It is a time for feasting, making merry, dancing, and bonfires! May Heaven bless this island and our noble General!"

The wine flowed freely, and many toasts were made to Othello and Desdemona.

Cassio was in charge of the guard that night. There was an order from Othello to keep the newly-arrived soldiers from drinking too much. He didn't want any fights to start to frighten or upset the residents.

But that night, Iago set in motion his evil plan. Saying it was a sign of loyalty and love for the General, he encouraged Cassio to drink, a terrible fault for an officer on guard. Cassio resisted for a while, but he could not hold out for long against the apparent honesty of the tricky Iago. Glass after glass was drunk, and Iago even started singing.

"Oh, let our tankards clink, clink!
Soldiers are men, so let them all drink,
And let our tankards clink, clink, clink!"

"An excellent song, indeed!" said Cassio.

"Yes, I learned it in England, where they are much stronger at drinking than the Danes or the Germans or the Dutch!"

Then Cassio began to praise Desdemona, toasting her many times, and declaring she was a most exquisite lady.

At last, the liquid enemy Cassio put into his mouth and drank seemed to steal his brains. Iago had arranged a man to insult Cassio. Immediately, swords were drawn, and a good officer called Montano, who tried to stop the fight, was wounded. Then a riot began, with Iago cunningly spreading the alarm. This caused the castle bell to be rung to announce some major problem. It woke Othello, who quickly dressed, rushed to the scene of the action, and questioned Cassio on the cause of all the noise.

Cassio had sobered up a bit, but he was too ashamed to reply. At first, Iago pretended to be reluctant to accuse Cassio, but he was forced into it by Othello, who wanted to know the truth. So Iago gave an account of the whole matter, leaving out his own part in it. But while he seemed to reduce Cassio's offence, he actually made it seem greater than it was.

Othello was a strict observer of discipline. He felt he had no choice but to remove the position of lieutenant from Cassio.

In this way, the first part of Iago's scheme succeeded. He had made a fool of Cassio, his hated rival, and pushed him from his position. But he planned to make another use of the adventure of that disastrous night.

My reputation!

The shocked and sober Cassio lamented to Iago, who he regarded as a friend, that he should have been so stupid as to behave like an animal.

"Oh, Iago, I have lost my reputation! How could I possibly ask Othello to give me my position back? He will tell me I was drunk and despise me! Oh, you invisible spirit of wine, I call you the devil!"

Iago pretended to make light of the situation, saying that he, or any other man living, might be drunk sometimes. Cassio should make the best of a bad situation.

"The General's wife is now the general! He will listen to anything she says. So you should ask her to mediate with him on your behalf. She's very free and kind and has an obliging character. I'm sure she'll help you and put you back in his good books! That will surely paper over this temporary crack in your relationship and make it stronger than ever!"

"Hmm, you advise me well, honest Iago."

"From my love and kindness!"

"I will ask her tomorrow to help me."

Desdemona mediates

Cassio did just as Iago had advised him. He talked to

Desdemona, and she promised him that she would plead with her husband.

"Be merry, Cassio! I would rather die than give up your cause!"

Desdemona immediately set about her task in earnest. Othello was deeply upset about Cassio, but found it difficult to put off his wife's pleas. He asked for some delay, saying it was too soon to pardon him. Desdemona insisted that it should be that night, or the morning after, or the next morning, but no more. Then she explained how full of regret and humbled poor Cassio felt, and his offence surely did not deserve so sharp a punishment. Othello still hung back.

"What!" she said, "I have so much to do to plead for Cassio? He is Michael Cassio, who came courting for you! I count this but a small thing to ask of you. Now I see that whenever I mean to test your love, I should ask about something more important!"

Othello could not deny such a plea. He promised to receive Cassio back in favor.

I don't like that...

By chance, Othello and Iago had entered the room where Cassio had been imploring Desdemona's help just as was leaving by the opposite door.

"Hmm, I don't like that..." murmured Iago, as if to himself.

At the time, Othello took no particular notice of what Iago said. And the discussion with Desdemona had put it out of his head. But he suddenly remembered it afterwards. For after Desdemona had left, Iago asked Othello whether Cassio, when Othello was courting his lady, knew about his love.

"Of course he did, from the beginning to the end. He often went between us. Why do you ask?"

Iago knitted his brow, and said, "Indeed!"

"*Indeed*, yes," said Othello. "Isn't Cassio honest?"

"*Honest*, my lord?"

"Yes, honest!"

"Well, as far as I know."

"Iago, what are you thinking?"

"*Thinking*, my lord?"

"Stop echoing me! What do you mean? What did you not like when we came into this room? If you love me, tell me what's on your mind!"

"You know I love you, my lord."

"I think you do, yes."

Iago went on to say what a pity it would be if any trouble should arise because of Othello's imperfect observations; that it would *not* be good for him to know *all* Iago's thoughts; and that people's good names should *not* be taken away for slight suspicions.

And when Othello's curiosity was raised by these hints, Iago said, "Oh, beware, my lord, of jealousy. It is the green-eyed monster which mocks the meat it feeds on!"

"Jealousy? Oh, misery!" cried Othello. "But why? My wife feeds well, loves company, is free of speech, sings, plays music, and dances well. When someone has virtue, these are all virtuous qualities. I must see before I doubt, and I must have proof when I doubt."

Sounding relieved, Iago declared that he had no actual proof. However, he advised Othello to observe Desdemona's behavior well when Cassio was around. Iago said he knew much more about the ways of Italian ladies than Othello did: in Venice, wives let everyone see the pranks they dared not show their husbands!

"Remember, my lord, she deceived her father in marrying you, and kept it so secret he believed it was *witchcraft*!"

Othello was moved by this argument, which brought the matter home to him. Yes, if she had deceived her father, she might also deceive her husband. Iago begged pardon for having upset Othello so much. Othello was shaken with inward grief at Iago's words, but begged him to continue.

With many apologies, Iago said he was unwilling to produce anything against Cassio, his friend. But then he came strongly to the point: he reminded Othello how Desdemona had refused many suitable Venetian matches and married him, a Moor. That proved her to have a strong will. But when her better judgment returned, maybe she would reconsider her choice? He ended by advising Othello to postpone forgiving Cassio a little longer. In the meantime, he should note how eagerly Desdemona pleaded on Cassio's behalf.

Innocent until proved guilty

The conversation ended with Iago advising Othello to regard his wife as innocent until he had more proof. Othello promised to be patient. But from that moment, he never again enjoyed peace of mind. Not all the sleeping pills in the world could restore to him that sweet rest which he had enjoyed just yesterday. And his occupation now sickened him. He no longer took delight in military business. His spirits used to be roused by the sight of troops and banners, and his heart would leap at the sound of a drum, or a bugle, or a neighing warhorse. He seemed to have lost all the pride and ambition of a soldier.

At times he believed Desdemona to be honest, but at others he decided she wasn't. At times he thought Iago truthful, but at others he decided he wasn't. Then he wished that he knew nothing about it; he was no worse for her loving Cassio, so long as he was ignorant!

Then one day, torn apart by these mixed thoughts, he grabbed Iago by the throat. He demanded him to prove Desdemona's guilt or he would kill him for lying. Iago feigned indignation that his honesty was in question. He asked Othello if he had sometimes seen Desdemona holding a handkerchief spotted with strawberries. Othello answered that it had been his very first gift to her.

"Well, today I saw Michael Cassio wipe his face with it," said Iago.

"If that is true..."

"If that is true, my lord, it is *proof*!"

"Oh, blood, blood!" growled Othello. "I will not rest till revenge swallows them up. First, as a token of your loyalty, Iago, I expect Cassio to die within the next three days. As for that fair devil, my wife, I will devise some swift means of death for her. Iago, *you* are now my lieutenant!"

The spotted handkerchief

To a jealous man, trifles as light as air can become mighty proofs. The story of the handkerchief was enough proof for Othello to condemn Cassio and Desdemona. But he never asked *how* Cassio had come to have it. In fact, Desdemona had not given it to Cassio as a present. She would never have wronged Othello by giving his present to another man. Both Cassio and Desdemona were innocent of any offence against Othello. But Iago's wife had often been asked by Iago to steal Desdemona's precious handkerchief. Why, she didn't know. Then, one day, she found the handkerchief on the floor by chance and decided to have the embroidery copied. Iago saw it and insisted on her giving it to him. Innocently, she did. Unknown to her, his plan was to drop it in a place where Cassio was sure to find it.

Later that day, Othello, pretending he had a headache, asked Desdemona to lend him a handkerchief to tie around his forehead. She did.

"Not this small one," said Othello, "but that large spotted one I gave you."

"I'm not carrying it today."

"What?" said Othello, "that is a big fault indeed. An

Egyptian witch gave that handkerchief to my mother. She told her that while she kept it, it would make her very attractive, and my father would love her. But if she ever lost it or gave it away, my father would loathe her as much as he had loved her. My mother gave it to me before she died, and told me to give it to my wife if I ever married. I did so, as you remember, so please take great care of it!"

"Is that history true?" said the frightened Desdemona.

"Oh, yes, it's true. It's a magical handkerchief made by a fortune-teller who had lived for two hundred years. The silkworms that provided the silk were sacred, and it was dyed in ancient dye from Egyptian mummies!"

Having heard all this, Desdemona was ready to die with fear. She had lost the handkerchief, and now feared she had lost her husband's love as well. Othello continued his demand to see it.

"Fetch it! Let me see it!"

Desdemona desperately tried to divert her husband from his serious mood.

"Well, of course I can do that, but I don't want to right now. Ah, I see now... This is a trick to stop my plea for Cassio! Please let him be welcomed again..."

"The handkerchief, the handkerchief!" cried Othello and rushed out of the room.

It was at that moment that Desdemona, unwillingly, began to suspect that her husband was jealous. What had she done to cause it? Then she accused *herself* for accusing *him*. She imagined it must be some bad news from Venice that had made him angry.

And she said to herself, "Men are not gods, and in marriage we shouldn't expect the same care as they showed us on our wedding day."

A weed

When Othello and Desdemona met again, he accused her more plainly of loving another man. But he did not say who it was. Then he started to weep.

"Oh no!" said Desdemona, "Why are you crying?"

Othello told her he could bear all sorts of evil with strength and patience—poverty, disease, or even disgrace. But her infidelity had broken his heart.

"Oh, you are a *weed* that looks so fair and smells so sweet... I wish you had never been born!"

And he left.

Willow, willow...

The innocent Desdemona was so shocked at Othello's untrue suspicion that she suddenly felt very tired. She only desired Emilia to prepare her bed, using the same sheets as on her wedding night.

"And if I die before you, Emilia, shroud me in one of those sheets."

"Please don't talk like that," replied Emilia.

"My mother," continued Desdemona, "had a maid called

Barbara who was deeply in love. But the man she loved forsake her. She used to sing an old song that expressed her fortune. And she died singing it. Tonight, that song won't leave my mind. I feel like hanging my head on one side, and singing it like poor Barbara did...

The poor soul sighed by a sycamore tree,
Her hand on her heart, and her head on her knee,
Sing willow, willow, willow:
The fresh streams ran by, and murmur'd her moans;
Her tears they fell, and soften'd the stones;
Sing willow, willow, willow...
I call'd my love false; but what said he then?
If I court other women, you'll lie with more men!
Sing willow, willow, willow:
And so, get thee gone; good night..."

Put out the light...

Desdemona went to bed expecting Othello to follow her soon. When he finally came, she was fast asleep. His mind was full of his terrible plan to kill her.

"That is the cause, that is the cause, but I cannot name it!"

But when he gazed down at her, he realized he could never shed her blood or scar her skin, which was whiter than alabaster.

"Yet she must die, or she'll betray other men! Put out the candle's light, and then put out *her* light... But if I quench the candle, I can easily relight it if I change my mind. But once I have put out *your* light, Desdemona, it can never be relit... When I have pluck'd the rose, I cannot make it grow again... It will surely wither. Ah, I will smell it on the tree..."

Othello kissed her.

"Oh, such sweet breath! It almost persuades me to change my mind. One more kiss, one more..."

He kissed her again.

"Now I must weep cruel tears... But just one more kiss, and this the final one..."

He kissed her again.

"Oh, she's waking up!"

When Desdemona saw his rolling eyes, she knew something very bad was about to happen. Othello told her to prepare for death, and say her prayers, for he would not kill her soul. As Desdemona lay at his mercy, she begged for compassion. She wanted to know what she had done wrong. And then Othello named Cassio and the spotted handkerchief which he claimed she had given him. As the guiltless lady once again tried to clear herself, Othello suddenly would hear no more. He seized her pillow, and stifled her until she stopped breathing.

A terrible discovery

Moments later, Cassio was brought into the house, wounded and bleeding. The man ordered by Iago to kill Cassio had failed, so Iago killed *him* to prevent discovery. But in the man's pockets were found letters which clearly proved Iago's guilt and

Cassio's innocence. Cassio had come to beg pardon of Othello, and to ask how he had offended him so much that he'd ordered Iago to murder him.

This discovery hit Othello like a stroke of lightning. He now realized that he was no better than a murderer and that poor Desdemona had always been faithful.

"I have loved not wisely, but too well. And now I have discovered the truth, my eyes drop tears as fast as Arabian trees drop their gum."

He could no longer live after such a terrible discovery. He immediately seized his Spanish sword, stabbed himself, fell across the body of his dear wife, and died.

These rash acts raised feelings of both horror and amazement. Othello had held such a great reputation, and till Iago's evil plan began, he was a loving husband.

All Othello's merits and valiant acts were remembered and duly honored. Nothing now remained but to put the full power of the law in force against Iago: he was executed. Then word of the lamentable death of the renowned General Othello was sent to the State of Venice by the new Governor of Cyprus, Michael Cassio.

NOTES

1. The Tempest

Mary closely followed the main Prospero/Miranda/Ferdinand story line. She included Caliban, but removed all his lines. The comic scenes were cut, so the drunken butler Stephano and the jester Trinculo do not appear, nor the dancing spirits.

Here are Shakespeare's original versions of the two songs:

Full fathom five thy father lies;
Of his bones are coral made;
Those are pearls that were his eyes:
Nothing of him that doth fade,
But doth suffer a sea-change
Into something rich and strange.
Sea-nymphs hourly ring his knell:
Hark! now I hear them—Ding-dong, bell.

Where the bee sucks, there suck I;
In a cowslip's bell I lie:
There I crouch when owls do cry.
On the bat's back I do fly
After summer merrily.
Merrily, merrily shall I live now
Under the blossom that hangs on the bough.

2. A Midsummer Night's Dream

Shakespeare set the play in Greece, but Robin Goodfellow (Puck) was a familiar British folklore spirit since ancient times. He was well known for his naughty tricks and for encouraging good housekeeping.

Mary focused on the four young lovers and the fairies. She cut the comical scenes of the local craftsmen who have a try at amateur dramatics and only referred to the character Bottom as 'a foolish clown'.

注釈

1. テンペスト

メアリーは、主要人物のプロスペロー、ミランダ、ファーディナンドのストーリーラインに忠実に従った。キャリバンを登場させたが、彼の台詞はない。コミカルなシーンはカットされ、酔っぱらいの執事ステファーノと道化師トリンキュローは登場しない、踊る妖精も然り。

テンペストに登場する劇中歌2曲のシェイクスピアの原文は次のとおりだ。

Full fathom five thy father lies;
Of his bones are coral made;
Those are pearls that were his eyes:
Nothing of him that doth fade,
But doth suffer a sea-change
Into something rich and strange.
Sea-nymphs hourly ring his knell:
Hark! now I hear them—Ding-dong, bell.

Where the bee sucks, there suck I;
In a cowslip's bell I lie:
There I crouch when owls do cry.
On the bat's back I do fly
After summer merrily.
Merrily, merrily shall I live now
Under the blossom that hangs on the bough.

2. 夏の夜の夢

シェイクスピアはこの戯曲をギリシャを舞台にしたが、ロビン・グッドフェロー（パック）は古来イギリスの民間伝承でおなじみの妖精である。パックは、いたずら好きだが家事を立派にこなす妖精としてよく知られている。

メアリーは4人の若い恋人たちと妖精に焦点を当てた。アマチュア演劇に挑戦する地元の職人たちのコミカルなシーンはカットし、ボトムを「愚かな道化」とだけ言及している。私は、彼を織工のボトムとして復帰させた。シェイクスピアと同じ

I reinstated him as Bottom the weaver. Like Shakespeare, Mary used the word 'ass', which has the double meaning of 'fool', but I decided to change it to today's more familiar 'donkey' and let Bottom go 'hee-haw', as many actors do on stage.

Mary based the storyteller's words she included at the end on Puck's final speech to the audience in the play. I thought it more fun to let Puck have the last word.

Here is Shakespeare's original version of the lullaby for Titania:

You spotted snakes, with double tongue,
Thorny hedgehogs, be not seen;
Newts and blind-worms do no wrong;
Come not near our fairy queen:
Philomel, with melody,
Sing in our sweet lullaby;
Lulla, lulla, lullaby; lulla, lulla, lullaby;
Never harm, nor spell, nor charm,
Come our lovely lady nigh;
So, good night, with lullaby.

3. The Winter's Tale

Only a few minor characters are missing from Mary's version, such as the young shepherd, Bohemian shepherdesses, and the pedlar Autolycus.

I added the dialog when Mamillius starts telling his winter's tale, Antigonus' dream of Hermione, and the famous stage direction 'Exit, pursued by a bear.'

4. Much Ado About Nothing

Mary decided to cut Dogberry, the amusing leader of the city's citizen police force who arrests Borachio by chance.

I added dialog from the play in a few places, such as the start of the first wedding ceremony and some of Beatrice and Benedick's conversations.

ように、メアリーはfoolの意味もあるass(=donkeyロバ)を使ったが、私はそれを現在より馴染みのあるdonkeyに変えて、舞台で多くの俳優がやるようにボトムにhee-hawとロバのバカ笑いを発してもらうことにした。

メアリーは、パックが戯曲の最後で観客に語りかけるスピーチをもとに、語り手が語りかける言葉で締めくくった。私は、パックに最後のスピーチをさせる方が面白いと思った。

以下は、シェイクスピアが書いたティターニアのための子守唄の原文である。

You spotted snakes, with double tongue,
Thorny hedgehogs, be not seen;
Newts and blind-worms do no wrong;
Come not near our fairy queen:
Philomel, with melody,
Sing in our sweet lullaby;
Lulla, lulla, lullaby; lulla, lulla, lullaby;
Never harm, nor spell, nor charm,
Come our lovely lady nigh;
So, good night, with lullaby.

3. 冬物語

メアリーのバージョンから欠けている登場人物は、若い羊飼い、ボヘミアの羊飼いの女たち、行商人のオートリカスなど、ほんのわずかな脇役だけだ。

私は、マミリアスが自分の冬の物語を語り始めるときの対話、アンティゴナスがハーマイオニーを夢見る場面、そして有名な舞台演出「熊に追われて退場」を付け加えた。

4. から騒ぎ

メアリーは、たまたまボラチオを逮捕した街の市民警察の愉快なリーダー、ドグベリーをはずすことにした。

私は、ところどころに戯曲の対話を加えた。最初の結婚式の始まりや、ベアトリスとベネディックの会話の一部などである。

Trivia: 'Much ado about nothing' is today a common expression meaning 'more excitement and fuss than something deserves'. So 'nothing' basically means 'nothing important'. In Shakespeare's time, however, the word 'nothing' in the play's title had several meanings, and was pronounced 'noting'. So, besides 'nothing' (as it's always pronounced today) it could mean 'noting' things in the sense of 'paying attention' (noting someone's beauty or noting what other people say and do) and also 'eavesdropping' (overhearing), which is central to the plot.

5. As You Like It

Mary included most of the play's main characters, apart from the jester Touchstone and the cynical Jacques, who makes the famous 'Seven Ages of Man' speech. Also missing are Silvius, Phoebe, and Audrey, who are involved in a romantic subplot.

I added a few interesting lines such as Orlando calling himself 'a rotten tree' and the mention by Ganymede of Julius Caesar's famous boast 'I came, I saw, I conquered'. Shakespeare's version of that is 'I came, saw, and overcame.'

Trivia: Although the play is supposed to be set in France, perhaps in the Forest of Ardennes, the Forest of Arden was in England, near Stratford-upon-Avon, so it was very familiar to Shakespeare. And the surname of his mother's family was Arden. The play also mentions deer and eating venison. The story goes that the young Shakespeare was caught poaching deer in a nobleman's park near Stratford.

6. The Merchant of Venice

Mary concentrated on the main Shylock/Antonio/Bassanio/Portia storyline. She cut various minor characters, such as the Gobbos (father and son), Jessica, Lorenzo, merchants and Tubal. Also missing are Portia's suitors who appear in the casket scenes, always interesting on stage but not essential to the story.

トリビア：Much ado about nothingは、今日、「大騒ぎするほどのことではない」を意味する一般的な表現になっている。つまり、nothingは基本的に「たいしたことではない」を意味する。しかしシェイクスピアの時代には、戯曲のタイトルにあるnothingにはいくつかの意味があって、notingと発音されていた。つまり、今日の発音どおりのnothing「たいしたことではない」という意味の他に、誰かの美しさに注目する、また他の人の言動に注目するなどのpaying attention（注目する）という意味、またeavesdropping（立ち聞きする）という意味があったのだ。この物語のあらすじの中核となるのがこの後者の意味である。

5. お気に召すまま

メアリーは、この戯曲の主要登場人物のほとんどを登場させたが、道化のタッチストーンと、有名なSeven Ages of Man（人生の七幕劇）の演説をする皮肉屋のジェイクイーズは除いている。また、ロマンチックなわき筋に絡むシルヴィウス、フィービー、オードリーも登場しない。

私は、興味深い台詞をいくつか付け加えた。自分のことを「腐った木」と呼ぶオーランドーの台詞、ジュリアス・シーザーが豪語した台詞I came, I saw, I conquered（私は来た、私は見た、私は征服した）に関するギャニミードの台詞などだ。ちなみにシェイクスピア版では、これがI came, saw, and overcameとなっている。

トリビア：この戯曲の舞台はフランス、おそらくアーデンの森とされているが、アーデンの森はイングランドのストラットフォード・アポン・エイボンの近くにあり、シェイクスピアにとっては非常になじみ深い場所だった。シェイクスピアの母の姓はアーデンだった。劇中では、鹿や鹿肉を食べることにも触れている。シェイクスピアは若い頃ストラトフォード近郊の貴族の公園で鹿を密猟して捕まったという逸話がある。

6. ヴェニスの商人

メアリーは主要人物のシャイロック、アントーニオ、バサーニオ、ポーシャのストーリーラインに集中した。ゴボ爺さんと息子、ジェシカ、ロレンゾ、商人たち、テューバルなど、さまざまな脇役をカットした。また、小箱のシーンに登場するポーシャの求婚者たちも登場しない。舞台ではいつも面白いが、物語に絶対必要というわけではない。

I reduced the number of times Mary described Shylock as ‘cruel’ or ‘evil’. I added Shylock’s famous ‘To bait fish’ monologue and his ‘pi-rates’ joke.

The original words of Portia’s famous speech on mercy at the trial begin like this:

The quality of mercy is not strain’d,
It droppeth as the gentle rain from heaven
Upon the place beneath: it is twice blest;
It blesseth him that gives and him that takes:
’Tis mightiest in the mightiest: it becomes
The throned monarch better than his crown;

7. King Lear

Charles’ version is nearly all written in indirect speech, but I added some dialog based on Shakespeare’s words. The main character missing is the Earl of Gloucester (Edmund and Edgar’s father), and Edgar is only mentioned briefly. Rather than saying Edmund was an ‘illegitimate son’, Charles used ‘natural son’.

Kent uses the insult ‘base football player’: In Shakespeare’s time, football was a wild, dangerous game. It was regarded as being very low-class (‘base’). Kent was put in ‘the stocks’, an ancient form of outdoor punishment in which the feet were restrained by boards, and the punished person could be abused publicly.

‘To play bo-peep’ in the Fool’s song means to be a like a child playing the game called ‘peekaboo’.

Here are the original words of the songs:

For sudden joy did weep,
And I for sorrow sung,
That such a king should play bo-peep
And go the fools among.

私は、メアリーがシャイロックを「残酷」とか「邪悪」と描写した回数を減らした。そしてシャイロックの有名なTo bait fish（魚を餌で釣る）の独白とpi-ratesの冗談（piratesをpie-ratsと発音）を追加した。

裁判でのポーシャの有名な慈悲に関するスピーチの原文は以下のように始まる。

The quality of mercy is not strain'd,
It droppeth as the gentle rain from heaven
Upon the place beneath: it is twice blest;
It blesseth him that gives and him that takes:
'Tis mightiest in the mightiest: it becomes
The throned monarch better than his crown;

7. リア王

チャールズのバージョンはほとんどが間接話法なので、私はシェイクスピアの原語に基づいた対話を増やした。出現しない主な登場人物はグロスター伯（エドマンドとエドガーの父親）で、エドガーはほんのわずかしか登場しない。チャールズは、エドマンドをillegitimate son（私生子）と言わずに、natural sonと表現している。

ケントはbase football player（下層階級のサッカー競技者）という侮辱的な言葉を使っている。シェイクスピアの時代、フットボール（サッカー）は野性的で危険な、非常にbase（下層階級）のゲームだとみなされていた。ケントはthe stocksにさらされた。the stocksとは、足かせなどで足を拘束した木製の枠で野外に置かれた古代のさらし台である。罪人は人前で罵倒された。

道化の歌にあるTo play bo-peepとは、peekaboo（いないいないバー）という遊びをしている子供のようだという意味である。

以下はこの戯曲の二つの歌の原語である。

For sudden joy did weep,
And I for sorrow sung,
That such a king should play bo-peep
And go the fools among.

He that has and a little tiny wit—
With hey, ho, the wind and the rain—
Must make content with his fortunes fit,
For the rain it raineth every day.

8. Macbeth

Charles includes more dialog than he did in *King Lear.* However, I changed some of his indirect speech back to direct speech and added some well-known words, such as the conversation with the witches and Macbeth's reaction to his wife's death.

The witches use the ancient term of greeting 'Hail!'. Today it's used in the sense of respecting someone, and also 'to hail a taxi'!

'The King is dead! Long live the King!' This traditional proclamation indicating the throne is never empty originated in France in the 15th century (*Le roi est mort, vive le roi!*). It is often parodied for newspaper headlines. It was not in Charles' version, but it seems very appropriate.

Superstition: Productions of *Macbeth* on stage are believed to be jinxed by accidents, so actors refer to it as 'The Scottish Play.'

Trivia: It's been suggested that all the strange ingredients of the witches' brew—such as 'eye of newt'—are actually common names for flowers! The Elizabethan audience would have understood that kind of wordplay. Shakespeare grew up in the countryside, and was very familiar with plant names.

9. All's Well that Ends Well

This fairy-tale story includes a 'rags-to-riches' theme rather like the ancient Cinderella story. It includes one of Shakespeare's favorite plot devices—the exchange of rings—and magic medicine! Characters missing from Mary's cleverly edited text include the Clown and Parolles, Bertram's cowardly companion. Dialog from the play has been added in several places, such as when the King orders Bertram to marry Helena.

He that has and a little tiny wit—
With hey, ho, the wind and the rain—
Must make content with his fortunes fit,
For the rain it raineth every day.

8. マクベス

チャールズはKing Lear『リア王』よりも対話を増やしている。しかし、私は彼の間接話法の一部を直接話法に戻し、魔女との会話や妻の死に対するマクベスの反応など、よく知られた台詞を付け加えた。

魔女は古代の挨拶Hailを使う。今日では、誰かに敬意を表する意味で使われるほか、to hail a taxi（タクシーを呼ぶ）という意味でも使われる！

The King is dead! Long live the King!（国王崩御！　国王万歳！）。王位が決して空位ではないことを示すこの伝統的な表現は、15世紀のフランスで始まった*Le roi est mort, vive le roi!* に由来する。新聞の見出しによくパロディとして使われる。チャールズのバージョンには登場しなかったが、私にはこの表現の採用は非常に適切だと思われた。

迷信：舞台でマクベスが上演されると事故が起こるというジンクスがあるため、役者たちはマクベスをThe Scottish Play（スコットランド劇）と呼ぶ。

トリビア：eye of newt（イモリの目）など、魔女のスープに使われる一風変わった材料はすべて、実は一般的な花の名前だと言われている！　エリザベス朝時代の観客はそのような言葉遊びを理解していたのだろう。シェイクスピアは田舎で育ち、植物の名前にとても詳しかった。

9. 終わりよければすべてよし

このおとぎ話には、昔話のシンデレラ物語のようなrags-to-riches（玉の輿）のテーマが含まれている。シェイクスピアお気に入りの筋立てのひとつである指輪の交換や魔法の薬も登場する！　メアリーの巧みに編集されたテキストから消えた登場人物には、道化と、バートラムの臆病な仲間パローレスがいる。国王がバートラムにヘレナとの結婚を命じる場面など、戯曲の台詞がところどころ加えられている。

'All's well that ends well' is now a common idiom for when something ends in a good way after various difficulties have been overcome.

Trivia: This is the only Shakespeare play besides *Macbeth* in which the first words are spoken by a woman.

10. The Taming of the Shrew

Mary did not include the characters Tranio, Biondello, and Gremio (another of Bianca's suitors), and Grumio, Petruchio's servant, appears but doesn't speak. She avoided the scenes with lots of chatting on the street.

Trivia: I added the first recorded use of the phrase 'to break the ice'. Shakespeare cleverly used it not only with today's meaning of 'to start a conversation', but also as a reference to 'breaking' Katharine's 'icy' temperament.

And if you break the ice and do this feat

11. The Comedy of Errors

This Shakespeare farce about merchants and family bonds is still very popular. Theatre audiences always enjoy understanding better than the characters on stage what is going on and who is really who! Mary did an excellent job distinguishing the confusing characters clearly on paper. But I changed her use of 'slaves' for the two Dromios to 'servants', which seems to me more appropriate, even though one of them was actually sold.

'A comedy of errors' has become an idiom for an event or a series of events made ridiculous by the number of mistakes made.

The 1938 musical *The Boys from Syracuse* (music by Richard Rodgers) was based on the play.

The 'mark' was a coin dating back to medieval times. It was used in many countries, especially in Germany, where marks were only replaced by euros in 1999.

All's well that ends well(終わりよければすべてよし)は、様々な困難を乗り越えたのち物事が良い形で終わることを表す慣用句として定着している。

トリビア:シェイクスピアの戯曲の中で、最初の言葉が女性によって語られるのは、Macbeth『マクベス』の他にはこの作品だけである。

10. じゃじゃ馬ならし

メアリーは、トラーニオ、ビオンデロ、グレミオ(ビアンカのもう一人の求婚者)以外の主要登場人物をすべて登場させた。ペトルーチオの召使いのグルーミオは登場するが、喋らない。メアリーは賢明にも、路上での数多くのおしゃべりのシーンを避けた。

トリビア:私は、break the ice(口火を切る)を採用した。というのは、このフレーズはこの戯曲で初めて活字になったものだからだ。

シェイクスピアはこのフレーズを、今日の「会話を始める」という意味だけでなく、キャサリンの「冷淡な」気性を「なおす」という意味で巧みに使っている。

And if you break the ice and do this feat

11. 間違いの喜劇

商人たちと家族の絆を描いたこのシェイクスピアの茶番劇は、今でもとても人気がある。劇場では、観客はいつも、何が起こっているのか、本当は誰が誰なのか、舞台上で混乱している登場人物よりもよく理解できるので、この芝居を楽しんでいる！　メアリーは、混乱しがちな登場人物を本の中で見事に描き分けている。しかし、彼女が二人のドローミオに対して使ったslaves(奴隷)を、私はservants(召使)に変更した。実際に一人は売られたという意味ではslavesが正確ではあるが。

A comedy of errorsは、ミスが多くてばかばかしくなる出来事や一連の出来事を表す慣用句になっている。

1938年のミュージカルThe Boys from Syracuse『シラキュースから来た男たち』(音楽：リチャード・ロジャース)は、この戯曲を基に作られた。

Mark(マルク)は中世にさかのぼる硬貨で、多くの国で使用され、特にドイツでは好まれたが、1999年にユーロに取って代わられた。

Trivia: Shakespeare's shortest play, with 1,787 lines. The longest is *Hamlet*: 4,042 lines.

12. Twelfth Night; or, What You Will

Mary focused on the Orsino/Viola/Olivia triangle relationship. That meant losing the many comical elements of the play. So the popular characters Maria, Sir Andrew Aguecheek, Sir Toby Belch, and Malvolio, are missing, and Feste the jester only appears to sing one song. Actually, it was those characters who were responsible for the title 'Twelfth Night', which is now celebrated on January 6th as the end of the Christmas festival. It used to be a day for chaos and wild parties like those loved by Sir Toby and his friends, but not by the Puritan character Malvolio. It's also likely that the play was first performed on Twelfth Night.

Feste's song begins with 'cypress', and cypress trees have been symbols of mourning since ancient times, so they're often seen in cemeteries. Yew trees are also mentioned. They represent 'eternity' to Christians and are also commonly found in churchyards and cemeteries. The song refers to the ancient custom of burying some yew shoots with a body. Here are the original lyrics:

Come away, come away, Death,
And in sad cypress let me be laid;
Fly away, fly away, breath,
I am slain by a fair cruel maid.
My shroud of white stuck all with yew, O prepare it!
My part of death no one so true did share it.
Not a flower, not a flower sweet,
On my black coffin let there be strewn:
Not a friend, not a friend greet
My poor corpse, where my bones shall be thrown.
A thousand thousand sighs to save, lay me O where
Sad true lover never find my grave, to weep there!

トリビア：シェイクスピアの最も短い戯曲で、台詞数1,787。最も長いのはHamlet『ハムレット』で4,042。

12. 十二夜

メアリーは、オーシーノ公爵とヴァイオラとオリヴィアの三角関係に焦点を当てた。そのため、この戯曲のコミカルな要素を多分に失うことになった。それで、人気キャラクターのマライア、サー・アンドルー・エイギュチーク、サー・トービー・ベルチ、マルヴォーリオがいなくなり、道化のフェステは1曲を歌うためだけに登場する。実は、Twelfth Night『十二夜』というタイトルの由来となったのはこれらの登場人物たちであり、現在ではクリスマスの祝祭の最終日1月6日に祝う。かつてはサー・トービーとその友人たちが大好きだった無礼講でどんちゃん騒ぎの一日だったが、清教徒のマルヴォーリオはそういうのを嫌った。この戯曲が最初に上演されたのも十二夜だったようだ。

フェステの歌はcypress（イトスギ）で始まるが、cypressは古来より弔いの象徴であり、墓地でよく見かける木だ。yew（イチイ）の木も登場する。キリスト教徒にとって「永遠」を表す木であり、一般に教会の庭や墓地で見られる。この歌は、イチイの新芽を亡骸と一緒に埋葬するという古くからの慣習を歌っている。以下はオリジナルの歌詞である。

Come away, come away, Death,
And in sad cypress let me be laid;
Fly away, fly away, breath,
I am slain by a fair cruel maid.
My shroud of white stuck all with yew, O prepare it!
My part of death no one so true did share it.
Not a flower, not a flower sweet,
On my black coffin let there be strewn:
Not a friend, not a friend greet
My poor corpse, where my bones shall be thrown.
A thousand thousand sighs to save, lay me O where
Sad true lover never find my grave, to weep there!

13. Romeo and Juliet

In Charles' version of this tragic tale, no major characters are missing, although most of Benvolio's and Mercutio's lines are cut.

Some of the vocabulary I cut includes derogatory terms such as *blackamoor* and *Ethiope*.

I added the second half of the famous first kisses dialog (see Introduction). Here is the original dialog. It's a 14-line sonnet, with a typical ABAB CDCD EFEF GG rhyme scheme:

If I profane with my unworthiest hand
This holy shrine, the gentle fine is this:
My lips, two blushing pilgrims, ready stand
To smooth that rough touch with a tender kiss.

Good pilgrim, you do wrong your hand too much,
Which mannerly devotion shows in this;
For saints have hands that pilgrims' hands do touch,
And palm to palm is holy palmers' kiss.

Have not saints lips, and holy palmers too?
Ay, pilgrim, lips that they must use in prayer.
O, then, dear saint, let lips do what hands do;
They pray, grant thou, lest faith turn to despair.

Saints do not move, though grant for prayers' sake.
Then move not, while my prayer's effect I take.

14. Hamlet, Prince of Denmark

Characters missing from include the Gravediggers, Osric, Fortinbras, and Rosencrantz and Guildenstern only briefly appear but are not named.

There is very little dialog in Charles' version. I added some famous lines such as *To be or not to be* and *The readiness is all.*

Here is Gertrude's original description of Ophelia's death:

13. ロミオとジュリエット

この悲劇的な物語のチャールズ版では、ベンヴォーリオとマーキューシオの台詞がほとんどカットされてはいるが、主要な登場人物の欠落はない。

私が削除した語彙には、blackamoorやEthiopeといった蔑称がある。

有名なファーストキスの台詞の後半を追加した(「序文」を参照)。以下が対話のの原文である。14行のソネットで、典型的なABAB CDCD EFEF GGの押韻形式である。

If I profane with my unworthiest hand
This holy shrine, the gentle fine is this:
My lips, two blushing pilgrims, ready stand
To smooth that rough touch with a tender kiss.

Good pilgrim, you do wrong your hand too much,
Which mannerly devotion shows in this;
For saints have hands that pilgrims' hands do touch,
And palm to palm is holy palmers' kiss.

Have not saints lips, and holy palmers too?
Ay, pilgrim, lips that they must use in prayer.
O, then, dear saint, let lips do what hands do;
They pray, grant thou, lest faith turn to despair.

Saints do not move, though grant for prayers' sake.
Then move not, while my prayer's effect I take.

14. ハムレット

登場しないのは、墓堀人たち、オズリック、フォーティンブラス、そしてローゼンクランツとギルデンスターンは少しだけ登場するが、名前は出てこない。

チャールズのバージョンにはほとんど対話がない。私は、To be or not to be(生きるべきか死ぬべきか)やThe readiness is all(覚悟こそがすべてだ)といった有名な台詞をいくつか付け加えた。

以下は、ガートルードがオフィーリアの死を描写した原文である。

There is a willow grows aslant a brook,
That shows his hoar leaves in the glassy stream;
There with fantastic garlands did she come
Of crow-flowers, nettles, daisies, and long purples
That liberal shepherds give a grosser name,
But our cold maids do dead men's fingers call them:
There, on the pendent boughs her coronet weeds
Clambering to hang, an envious sliver broke;
When down her weedy trophies and herself
Fell in the weeping brook. Her clothes spread wide;
And, mermaid-like, awhile they bore her up:
Which time she chanted snatches of old tunes;
As one incapable of her own distress,
Or like a creature native and indued
Unto that element: but long it could not be
Till that her garments, heavy with their drink,
Pull'd the poor wretch from her melodious lay
To muddy death.

And here is part of the conversation between Horatio and Hamlet just before their fatal fight at the end of the play:

HORATIO
If your mind dislike any thing, obey it: I will
forestall their repair hither, and say you are not
fit.
HAMLET
Not a whit, we defy augury: there's a special
providence in the fall of a sparrow. If it be now,
'tis not to come; if it be not to come, it will be
now; if it be not now, yet it will come: the
readiness is all: since no man has aught of what he
leaves, what is't to leave betimes?

There is a willow grows aslant a brook,
That shows his hoar leaves in the glassy stream;
There with fantastic garlands did she come
Of crow-flowers, nettles, daisies, and long purples
That liberal shepherds give a grosser name,
But our cold maids do dead men's fingers call them:
There, on the pendent boughs her coronet weeds
Clambering to hang, an envious sliver broke;
When down her weedy trophies and herself
Fell in the weeping brook. Her clothes spread wide;
And, mermaid-like, awhile they bore her up:
Which time she chanted snatches of old tunes;
As one incapable of her own distress,
Or like a creature native and indued
Unto that element: but long it could not be
Till that her garments, heavy with their drink,
Pull'd the poor wretch from her melodious lay
To muddy death.

そして、これは戯曲の最後に起こる宿命の闘いの直前のホレイショーとハムレットの会話の一部である。

HORATIO
If your mind dislike any thing, obey it: I will
forestall their repair hither, and say you are not
fit.
HAMLET
Not a whit, we defy augury: there's a special
providence in the fall of a sparrow. If it be now,
'tis not to come; if it be not to come, it will be
now; if it be not now, yet it will come: the
readiness is all: since no man has aught of what he
leaves, what is't to leave betimes?

15. Othello

Charles compressed the story neatly, sometimes switching the order of scenes. He also decided to have the handkerchief stolen, not found by chance, but I went back to what happened in the play. He cut the character of Roderigo and greatly reduced Emilia's dialog.

I cut some of the terms referring to Othello's skin color which could be regarded today as derogatory: *complexion*, *unsuitableness*, etc.

Here is Shakespeare's version of the *Willow Song:*

The poor soul sat sighing by a sycamore tree,
Sing all a green willow:
Her hand on her bosom, her head on her knee,
Sing willow, willow, willow:
The fresh streams ran by her, and murmur'd her moans;
Sing willow, willow, willow;
Her salt tears fell from her, and soften'd the stones;
Sing willow, willow, willow;

Sing all a green willow must be my garland.
Let nobody blame him; his scorn I approve,—
I call'd my love false love; but what said he then?
Sing willow, willow, willow:
If I court moe women, you'll couch with moe men!

15. オセロー

チャールズは、時にはシーンの順序を入れ替えながら、物語を巧みに要約した。またハンカチは偶然発見されたものではなく、盗まれたものにした。だが、私はその筋書きを元の戯曲どおりに戻した。チャールズはロデリーゴという登場人物をカットし、エミリアの台詞を大幅に減らした。

私は、今では軽蔑的とみなされるオセロの肌の色に言及した語彙のいくつかを削除した。complexion（肌の色）、unsuitableness（不似合い）などだ。

以下はシェイクスピア版の*the Willow Song*（柳の歌）である。

The poor soul sat sighing by a sycamore tree,
Sing all a green willow:
Her hand on her bosom, her head on her knee,
Sing willow, willow, willow:
The fresh streams ran by her, and murmur'd her moans;
Sing willow, willow, willow;
Her salt tears fell from her, and soften'd the stones;
Sing willow, willow, willow;

Sing all a green willow must be my garland.
Let nobody blame him; his scorn I approve,—
I call'd my love false love; but what said he then?
Sing willow, willow, willow:
If I court moe women, you'll couch with moe men!

Acknowledgements

It was, of course, William Shakespeare himself and those formidable siblings Charles and Mary Lamb who did all the basic work for this book. I trust my version has not made them turn in the grave!

A stimulating companion as I worked on it was Dame Judi Dench's fascinating *Shakespeare: The Man who Pays the Rent* (Penguin Michael Joseph, 2023). It reminded me of the vital perspectives of actors and directors, as well as the fact that we all continue to benefit in so many ways from Shakespeare's words.

I remain ever grateful to my parents who introduced me to the wonderful world of his plays, not only via *Lamb's Tales*, but also by taking me to see the likes of Judi Dench, Helen Mirren, Ian Holm, Patrick Stewart and David Warner performing at the RSC in Stratford-upon-Avon in my youth.

I also owe a great deal to Anthony Trott and Michael Parslew, my English teachers at King Edward's School, Birmingham, who further instilled in me a love of Shakespeare, both in the classroom and on stage.

My sincere thanks to Kyoko Kagawa, Hirohide Sugiyama and the editors at IBC, to everyone at Studio 1991, and to Yoko Toyozaki for her painstaking translation of the Introduction and Notes.

Stuart Varnam-Atkin

Kanagawa, Japan, 2024

謝 辞

本書の出版にあたってその土台となる仕事をしたのはすべて、言うまでもなく、ウィリアム・シェイクスピア本人、そして優れた姉弟、チャールズ・ラムとメアリー・ラムである。私の翻案が彼らの霊を動揺させていなければ幸いだ！

本書の執筆中によい刺激をくれたのは、デイムの称号のあるジュディ・デンチの魅力的な著書、*Shakespeare: The Man who Pays the Rent* (Penguin Michael Joseph, 2023)である。おかげで、私たちは誰もがシェイクスピアの言葉から常に多くの恩恵を受けているという事実の他に、俳優や演出家たちのきわめて重要な考え方を再認識することになった。

シェイクスピアの戯曲の素晴らしい世界に誘ってくれた両親には、今でも感謝している。Lamb's Talesに触れる機会を与えてくれただけでなく、若い頃によくストラトフォード・アポン・エイボンのRSC（ロイヤル・シェイクスピア・カンパニー）の劇場に連れて行ってくれた。ジュディ・デンチ、ヘレン・ミレン、イアン・ホルム、パトリック・スチュワート、デヴィッド・ワーナーらが舞台に立っていた。

また、バーミンガムのキング・エドワード・スクールで、教室と舞台の両方で私のシェイクスピアに対するさらなる熱意を植え付けてくれたふたりの英語教師、アントニー・トロットとマイケル・パーズリューにも大いに恩恵を受けている。

IBCの賀川京子さん、杉山博英さん、編集者の方々、スタジオ1991の皆さん、そして序文と注釈を丹念に翻訳してくれた豊崎洋子さんにも心から感謝する。

ステュウット ヴァーナム–アットキン

神奈川県、2024年

Word List

・本文で使われている全ての語を掲載しています（序文、注釈と謝辞を除く）。

・語形が規則変化する語の見出しは原形で示しています。不規則変化語は本文中で使われている形になっています。

・一般的な意味を紹介していますので、一部の語で本文で実際に使われている品詞や意味と合っていないことがあります。

・品詞は以下のように示しています。

名 名詞	代 代名詞	形 形容詞	副 副詞	動 動詞	助 助動詞	前 前置詞	接 接続詞	間 間投詞
冠 冠詞	略 略語	俗 俗語	熟 熟語	頭 接頭語	尾 接尾語	記 記号	関 関係代名詞	

A

□ **a** 冠 ①1つの, 1人の, ある ②～につき

□ **abandon** 動 ①捨てる, 放棄する ②(計画などを)中止する, 断念する

□ **abbess** 名 (女子の)大修道院長

□ **ability** 名 ①できること, (～する)能力 ②才能

□ **able** 形 ①《be – to ～》(人が) ～することができる ②能力のある

□ **aboard** 副 船[列車・飛行機・バス]に乗って

□ **about** 副 ①およそ, 約 ②まわりに, あたりを 前 ①～について ②～のまわりに[の] **be about to** まさに～しようとしている, ～するところだ **be worried about** (～のことで)心配している, ～が気になる[かかる] **bring about** 引き起こす **hear about** ～について聞く **set about** ～に取り掛かる **speak about** ～について話す **walk about** 歩き回る **wonder about** ～について知りたがる **worry about** ～のことを心配する

□ **above** 前 ①～の上に ②～より上で, ～以上で ③～を超えて 副 ①上に ②以上に **above all** 何よりも

□ **abruptly** 副 不意に, 突然, 急に

□ **absence** 名 欠席, 欠如, 不在

□ **absent** 形 不在の, 欠けた, 欠席[欠勤]した

□ **absolute** 形 ①完全な, 絶対の ②無条件の ③確実な

□ **absolutely** 副 ①完全に, 確実に ②《yesを強調する返事として》そうですとも

□ **accept** 動 ①受け入れる ②同意する, 認める

□ **access** 名 ①接近, 近づく方法, 通路 ②(システムなどへの)アクセス

□ **accident** 名 ①(不慮の)事故, 災難 ②偶然

□ **accommodate** 動 ①収容する ②適合させる, 合わせる

□ **accommodation** 名 ①収容能力, 宿泊設備 ②適合, 適応

□ **accompany** 動 ①ついていく, つきそう ②(～に)ともなって起こる ③伴奏をする

□ **accomplish** 動 成し遂げる, 果たす

□ **accomplished** 形 ①完成した ②(技量に)優れた, 熟達した

□ **according** 副《– to ～》～によれば[よると]

□ **account** 名 ①計算書 ②勘定, 預金口座 ③説明, 報告, 記述 動 ①《– for ～》～を説明する, ～(の割合)を占める, ～の原因となる ②～を…とみなす **on someone's account** (人)のために

□ **accusation** 名 非難, 告訴, 告発

□ **accuse** 動《– of ～》～(の理由)で告訴[非難]する

□ **accused** 形 告発された, 非難された

□ **achieve** 動 成し遂げる, 達成する, 成功を収める

□ **acknowledge** 動 (～として, ～を)認める

□ **acorn** 名 ドングリ

□ **acorn-cup** 名 ドングリの殻斗(かくとう)《ドングリの実が落ちた後に残る, 帽子のような形状をした部分》

□ **acquainted** 形 (…に)精通して, (人と)知り合いで, 知り合って

□ **acquire** 動 ①(努力して)獲得する, 確保する ②(学力, 技術などを)習得する

□ **acquit** 動 無罪にする, 放免する, 免じる

□ **across** 前 ～を渡って, ～の向こう側に, (身体の一部に)かけて 副 渡って, 向こう側に

□ **act** 名 行為, 行い 動 ①行動する ②機能する ③演じる

□ **action** 名 ①行動, 活動 ②動作, 行為 ③機能, 作用

□ **active** 形 ①活動的な ②積極的な ③活動[作動]中の

□ **actor** 名 俳優, 役者

□ **actual** 形 実際の, 現実の

□ **actually** 副 実際に, 本当に, 実は

□ **Adam** 名 アダム《老僕》

□ **add** 動 ①加える, 足す ②足し算をする ③言い添える

□ **address** 名 ①住所, アドレス ②演説 動 ①あて名を書く ②演説をする, 話しかける

□ **adequate** 形 十分な, ふさわしい, 適切な

□ **adieu** 名 別れ《フランス語》間 さようなら《フランス語》

□ **admirable** 形 賞賛に値する, 見事な

□ **admiration** 名 賞賛(の的), 感嘆

□ **admire** 動 感心する, 賞賛する

□ **admission** 名 ①入場(許可), 入会, 入学, 入社 ②入場料

□ **admit** 動 認める, 許可する, 入れる

□ **ado** 名 から騒ぎ, 騒動

□ **adoration** 名 崇敬, 熱愛, 憧れ

□ **adore** 動 崇拝する, あこがれる

□ **Adriana** 名 エイドリアーナ《兄アンティフォラスの妻》

□ **Adriatic Sea** アドリア海

□ **advance** 名進歩, 前進

□ **advantage** 名有利な点［立場］, 強み, 優越 **take advantage of** ～を利用する, ～につけ込む

□ **adventure** 名冒険 動危険をおかす

□ **adverse** 形逆の, 反対の

□ **adversity** 名逆境, 不運,

□ **advice** 名忠告, 助言, 意見

□ **advise** 動忠告する, 勧める

□ **advisor** 名忠告者, 助言者, 顧問

□ **Aegeon** 名イージオン《シラクサの商売人》

□ **affair** 名①事柄, 事件 ②《-s》業務, 仕事, やるべきこと **affairs of state** 政務

□ **affection** 名愛情, 感情

□ **affectionate** 形愛情のある, 優しい

□ **affectionately** 形愛情を込めて

□ **afflict** 動悩ます, 苦しめる

□ **affliction** 名（心身の）苦痛

□ **afraid** 形①心配して ②恐れて, こわがって **I'm afraid** 残念ながら～, 悪いけれど～

□ **Africa** 名アフリカ《大陸》

□ **after** 前①～の後に［で］, ～の次に ②《前後に名詞がきて》次々に～, 何度も～《反復・継続を表す》副後に［で］ 接（～した）後に［で］ **after a while** しばらくして **after all** やはり, 結局 **after that** その後 **look after** ～の世話をする, ～に気をつける **run after** ～を追いかける

□ **afternoon** 名午後

□ **afterwards** 副その後, のちに

□ **again** 副再び, もう一度

□ **against** 前①～に対して, ～に反対して, （規則など）に違反して ② ～にもたれて

□ **age** 名①年齢 ②時代, 年代 **old age** 老後

□ **aged** 形①年を取った ②《the –》年寄りたち, 老人

□ **ago** 副～前に **long ago** ずっと前に, 昔

□ **agony** 名苦悩, 激しい苦痛

□ **agree** 動①同意する ②意見が一致する **agree on** ～について合意する **agree with**（人）に同意する

□ **ah** 間《驚き・悲しみ・賞賛などを表して》ああ, やっぱり

□ **aid** 名援助（者）, 助け 動援助する, 助ける, 手伝う

□ **aim** 動①（武器・カメラなどを）向ける ②ねらう, 目指す 名ねらい, 目標

□ **air** 名①《the –》空中, 空間 ②空気,《the –》大気 ③雰囲気, 様子 **open air** 戸外, 野外

□ **airy** 形①空気のような, 風当たりのよい ②軽やかな, 気軽な ③非現実的な, うわべだけの

□ **alabaster** 名雪花石こう, アラバスター《鉱物。彫刻の素材などに用いられる》

□ **alarm** 名①警報, 目覚まし時計 ②驚き, 突然の恐怖 動①はっとさせる ②警報を発する

□ **alarmed** 形～に驚いて, 不安で 動alarm（不安にさせる）の過去形

□ **alas** 間ああ《悲嘆・後悔・恐れなどを表す声》

□ **Albany** 名オールバニー《地名》

□ **ale** 名エール《ビールの一種》

□ **Algiers** 名アルジェ《アルジェリアの首都》

□ **Aliena** 名エイリーナ《シーリアの変装名》

□ **alienate** 動疎遠にする, 遠ざける

□ **alike** 形よく似ている 副同様に

□ **alive** 形①生きている ②活気のある, 生き生きとした

□ **all** 形すべての, ～中 代全部, すべて（のもの［人］）名全体 副まったく, すっかり **above all** 何よりも **after all** やはり, 結局 **all kinds of** さまざまな, あらゆる種類の **all over** ～中で, 全体に亘って, ～の至る所で **all the time** ずっと, いつも, その間ずっと **all the way** ずっと, はるばる, いろいろと **by all means** なんとしても, ぜひとも **for all** ～にもかかわらず **not at all** 少しも～でない **not ～ at all** 少しも［全然］～ない **over all** 全体にわたって **with all** ～がありながら **with all one's heart** 心から

□ **alley** 名路地, 裏通り, 小道

□ **allow** 動①許す,《– … to ～》…が～するのを可能にする, …に～させておく ②与える

□ **almost** 副ほとんど, もう少しで（～するところ）

□ **alone** 形ただひとりの 副ひとりで, ～だけで **leave ～ alone** ～をそっとしておく

□ **along** 前～に沿って 副～に沿って, 前へ, 進んで **along with** ～と一緒に **carry along** 持ち運ぶ **come along** ①一緒に来る, ついて来る ②やって来る, 現れる ③うまくいく, よくなる, できあがる **go along** ～に沿って行く, （人）について行く **go along with** ～に同調する

□ **Alonso** 名アロンゾー《ナポリ王》

□ **aloud** 副大声で, （聞こえるように）声を出して

□ **already** 副すでに, もう

□ **alright** 副よろしい, 申し分ない（= all right）

□ **also** 副～も（また）, ～も同様に 接その上, さらに

□ **alter** 動(部分的に)変える, 変わる
□ **alteration** 名変更, 手直し
□ **alternate** 動交替する, 交互に起こる
□ **although** 接～だけれども, ～にもかかわらず, たとえ～でも
□ **always** 副いつも, 常に **not always** 必ずしも～であるとは限らない
□ **am** 動～である, (～に)いる[ある]《主語がIのときのbeの現在形》
□ **amaze** 動びっくりさせる, 驚嘆させる
□ **amazed** 形びっくりした, 驚いた
□ **amazement** 名びっくりすること, 驚愕
□ **amazing** 形驚くべき, 見事な
□ **amazingly** 副驚くほどに, 驚いたことに
□ **amber** 名琥珀(色)
□ **ambition** 名大望, 野心
□ **ambitious** 形①大望のある, 野心的な ②熱望して
□ **amen** 間アーメン
□ **amend** 動①品行を改める, 改心する ②(法律などを)改正する **make amends** 償いをする
□ **among** 前(3つ以上のもの)の間で[に], ～の中で[に]
□ **amongst** 前の間に[を・で]
□ **amount** 名①量, 額 ②《the –》合計 動(総計～に)なる
□ **ample** 形十分な, 豊富な, 広大な
□ **amuse** 動楽しませる
□ **amused** 形面白がっている
□ **amusement** 名娯楽, 楽しみ
□ **amusing** 形楽しくさせる, 楽しい
□ **an** 冠①1つの, 1人の, ある ②～につき
□ **ancestor** 名①祖先, 先祖 ②先人
□ **ancient** 形昔の, 古代の
□ **and** 接①そして, ～と… ②《同じ語を結んで》ますます ③《結果を表して》それで, だから **and so** そこで, それだから, それで **and so forth** など, その他 **and yet** それなのに, それにもかかわらず
□ **angel** 名①天使 ②天使のような人
□ **angelical** 形天使の, 天使に関する
□ **angel-like** 形天使のような
□ **anger** 名怒り 動怒る, ～を怒らせる
□ **angrily** 副怒って, 腹立たしげに
□ **angry** 形怒って, 腹を立てて **get angry** 腹を立てる
□ **animal** 名動物 形動物の
□ **announce** 動(人に)知らせる, 公表する
□ **announcement** 名発表, アナウンス, 告示, 声明
□ **annoy** 動いらいらさせる[する]
□ **another** 形①もう1つ[1人]の ②別の 代①もう1つ[1人] ②別のもの **at another time** 別の折に **one another** お互い **yet another** さらにもう一つの
□ **answer** 動①答える, 応じる ②《– for ～》～の責任を負う 名答え, 応答, 返事 **in answer to** ～に応じて
□ **antidote** 名解毒剤
□ **Antigonus** 名アンティゴナス《シチリア王の側近》
□ **Antipholus of Ephesus** 兄アンティフォラス(エフェソスのアンティフォラス)《イージオンの息子》
□ **Antipholus of Syracuse** 弟アンティフォラス(シラクサのアンティフォラス)《イージオンの息子》
□ **Antonio** 名アントーニオ《①ミラノ大公, プロスペローの弟(テンペスト) ②貿易商人(ヴェニスの商人) ③セバスチャンの友人(十二夜)》
□ **anxiety** 名①心配, 不安 ②切望
□ **anxious** 形①心配な, 不安な ②切望して
□ **any** 形①《疑問文で》何か, いくつかの ②《否定文で》何も, 少しも(～ない) ③《肯定文で》どの～も 代①《疑問文で》(～のうち)何か, どれか, 誰か ②《否定文で》少しも, 何も[誰も]～ない ③《肯定文で》どれも, 誰でも **any time** いつでも **at any moment** 今すぐにも **if any** もしあれば, あったとしても **in any way** 決して, 多少なりとも **not in any way** 少しも[全く]～ない **not ～ any more** もう[これ以上]～ない
□ **anybody** 代①《疑問文・条件節で》誰か ②《否定文で》誰も(～ない) ③《肯定文で》誰でも
□ **anyone** 代①《疑問文・条件節で》誰か ②《否定文で》誰も(～ない) ③《肯定文で》誰でも
□ **anything** 代①《疑問文で》何か, どれでも ②《否定文で》何も, どれも(～ない) ③《肯定文で》何でも, どれでも 副いくらか **anything but** ～のほかは何でも, 少しも～でない **anything else** ほかの何か
□ **anyway** 副①いずれにせよ, ともかく ②どんな方法でも
□ **apart** 副①ばらばらに, 離れて ②別にして, それだけで **apart from** ～を除いては
□ **ape** 名サル, 類人猿
□ **Apollo** 名アポロ《ギリシャ神話の太陽神》

□ **apologize** 動謝る，わびる
□ **apology** 名謝罪，釈明
□ **apparel** 名衣服，服装
□ **apparent** 形明らかな，明白な，見かけの，外見上の
□ **apparently** 副見たところ～らしい，明らかに
□ **apparition** 名幻，亡霊
□ **appear** 動①現れる，見えてくる ②(～のように)見える，～らしい
□ **appear'd** 動 appearedの古い綴り
□ **appearance** 名①現れること，出現 ②外見，印象
□ **appetite** 名①食欲 ②欲求
□ **apple** 名リンゴ
□ **apply** 動①申し込む，志願する ②あてはまる ③適用する
□ **appointed** 形(日時・場所などが)指定された，約束の **be appointed to** ～に任命される
□ **appreciate** 動①正しく評価する，よさがわかる ②価値[相場]が上がる ③ありがたく思う
□ **approach** 動①接近する ②話を持ちかける 名接近，(～へ)近づく道
□ **appropriate** 形①適切な，ふさわしい，妥当な ②特殊な，特有の 動①割り当てる ②自分のものにする，占有する
□ **approval** 名①賛成 ②承認，認可
□ **approve** 動賛成する，承認する
□ **apricot** 名アンズ
□ **Arabian** 形アラビア(人)の
□ **arbor** 名あずまや，木陰の休み場所
□ **arched** 形弓なりの，弓なりに曲がった
□ **Arden** 名アーデン《森》
□ **are** 動～である，(～に)いる[ある]《主語がyou, we, theyまたは複数名詞のときのbeの現在形》 名アール《面積単位。100平方メートル》
□ **area** 名①地域，地方，区域，場所 ②面積
□ **argue** 動①論じる，議論する ②主張する
□ **argument** 名①議論，論争 ②論拠，理由
□ **Ariel** 名エアリエル《空気の精》
□ **arise** 動①起こる，生じる ②起きる，行動を開始する ③(死から)よみがえる ④(風が)たつ
□ **arm** 名①腕 ②腕状のもの，腕木，ひじかけ ③《-s》武器，兵器 動武装する[させる]
□ **armed** 形武装した
□ **armor** 名よろい，かぶと，甲冑
□ **army** 名軍隊，《the –》陸軍
□ **arose** 動 arise(起こる)の過去
□ **around** 副①まわりに，あちこちに ②およそ，約 前～のまわりに，～のあちこちに **jump around** 跳び回る **look around** まわりを見回す **show ~ around** ～を案内して回る **walk around** 歩き回る，ぶらぶら歩く
□ **arouse** 動(感情などを)起こす，刺激する
□ **Arragon** 名アラゴン《スペインの地方》
□ **arrange** 動①並べる，整える ②取り決める ③準備する，手はずを整える
□ **arrest** 動逮捕する 名逮捕
□ **arrival** 名①到着 ②到達
□ **arrive** 動到着する，到達する **arrive at** ～に着く **arrive in** ～に着く
□ **arrogant** 形尊大な，傲慢な，無礼な，横柄な
□ **art** 名芸術，美術 **art of** ～術
□ **as** 接①《as ～ as …の形で》…と同じくらい～ ②～のとおりに，～のように ③～しながら，～しているときに ④～するにつれて，～にしたがって ⑤～なので ⑥～だけれども ⑦～する限りでは 前①～として(の) ②～の時 副同じくらい 代①～のような ②～だが **as a result** その結果(として) **as a result of** ～の結果(として) **as ~ as one can** できる限り～ **as ~ as possible** できるだけ～ **as far as** ～と同じくらい遠く，～まで，～する限り(では) **as for** ～に関しては，～はどうかと言うと **as good as** ～も同然で，ほとんど～ **as if** あたかも～のように，まるで～みたいに **as it turned out** 後でわかったことだが **as long as** ～する以上は，～である限りは **as much as** ～と同じだけ **as soon as** ～するとすぐ，～するや否や **as such** ～など **as though** あたかも～のように，まるで～みたいに **as to** ～に関しては，～については，～に応じて **as usual** いつものように，相変わらず **as well** なお，その上，同様に **as well as** ～と同様に **as you know** ご存知のとおり **be known as** ～として知られている **just as** (ちょうど)であろうとおり **pass as** ～として通す **see ~ as ...** ～を…と考える **so ~ as to ...** …するほど～で **so long as** ～する限りは **such as** たとえば～，～のような **such ~ as ...** …のような～ **the same ~ as ...** …と同じ(ような)～
□ **ascend** 動上がる，上る
□ **ashamed** 形恥じた，気が引けた，《be – of ～》～が恥ずかしい，～を恥じている
□ **Asia** 名アジア
□ **ask** 動①尋ねる，聞く ②頼む，求める **ask ~ if** ～かどうか尋ねる
□ **asleep** 形眠って(いる状態の) 副眠って，休

止して **fall asleep** 眠り込む, 寝入る **fast asleep** ぐっすり眠っている

□ **ass** 名 ①ロバ ②ばか ③けつ, 尻

□ **assassin** 名 暗殺者

□ **assemble** 動 ①集める, 集まる ②組み立てる

□ **assembly** 名 ①集合, 集めること, 会合 ②組み立て ③下院, 議会

□ **assist** 動 手伝う, 列席する, 援助する

□ **assistance** 名 援助, 支援

□ **associate** 動 ①連合[共同]する, 提携する ②～を連想する ③交際する 名 仲間, 組合員 形 連合した

□ **assured** 形 保証された, 確実な, 自信のある

□ **astonished** 形 驚いた

□ **astonishment** 名 驚き

□ **astray** 形 (道などに)迷った, はずれた 副 迷って, 正しい道からそれて

□ **at** 前 ①《場所・時》～に[で] ②《目標・方向》～に[を], ～に向かって ③《原因・理由》～を見て[聞いて・知って] ④～に従事して, ～の状態で **at a distance** 少し離れて **at a time** 一度に, 続けざまに **at another time** 別の折に **at any moment** 今すぐにも **at first** 最初は, 初めのうちは **at first sight** 一目見て **at last** ついに, とうとう **at least** 少なくとも **at leisure** 暇で, ゆっくり **at length** ついに, 長々と, 詳しく **at long last** やっとのことで **at once** すぐに, 同時に **at one's command** 思いのままに **at one's mercy** ～のなすがままになって **at present** 今のところ, 現在は, 目下 **at that moment** その時に, その瞬間に **at that time** その時 **at the end of** ～の終わりに **at the risk of** ～の危険をおかして **at the sight of** ～を見るとすぐに **at the time** そのころ, 当時は **at times** 時には

□ **Athenian** 形 アテナイ人の

□ **Athens** 名 アテネ《都市名》

□ **atone** 動 償う, あがなう

□ **attached** 動 attach (取りつける) の過去, 過去分詞 形 ついている, 結びついた, 《be - to ～》～に未練[愛着]がある

□ **attack** 動 ①襲う, 攻める ②非難する ③(病気が) おかす 名 ①攻撃, 非難 ②発作, 発病

□ **attempt** 動 試みる, 企てる 名 試み, 企て, 努力

□ **attend** 動 ①出席する ②世話をする, 仕える ③伴う ④《- to ～》～に注意を払う, 専念する, ～の世話をする

□ **attendant** 形 つき添いの, 伴う 名 つき添い人, 案内係, アテンダント

□ **attention** 名 ①注意, 集中 ②配慮, 手当て, 世話 間《号令として》気をつけ

□ **attitude** 名 姿勢, 態度, 心構え

□ **attract** 動 ①引きつける, 引く ②魅力がある, 魅了する

□ **attractive** 形 魅力的な, あいきょうのある

□ **attribute** 動 起因すると考える, (～の)せいにする 名 特性, 属性

□ **audience** 名 聴衆, 視聴者

□ **aunt** 名 おば

□ **aversion** 名 (強い)反感, 嫌悪

□ **avert** 動 ①避ける, 防ぐ ②(～から)そむける

□ **avoid** 動 避ける, (～を)しないようにする

□ **await** 動 待つ, 待ち受ける

□ **awake** 動 ①目覚めさせる ②目覚める 形 目が覚めて

□ **awaken** 動 ①目を覚まさせる, 起こす, 目覚める ②《- to ～》～に気づく

□ **award** 動 (賞などを)与える, 授与する 名 賞, 賞品

□ **aware** 形 ①気がついて, 知って ②(～の)認識のある

□ **away** 副 離れて, 遠くに, 去って, わきに 形 離れた, 遠征した **blast away** 吹き飛ばす **carry away** 運び去る **cast away** 投げ捨てる **come away** ～から離れて行く **far away** 遠く離れて **fly away** 飛び去る **give away** ただで与える, 贈る, 譲歩する, 手放す **go away** 立ち去る **pass away** 過ぎ去る, 終わる, 死ぬ **pine away** やつれる **push away** 押しのける, 押しやる **put away** 片づける, 取っておく **right away** すぐに **run away** 走り去る, 逃げ出す **run away from** ～から逃れる **send away** 追い払う, 送り出す, ～を呼び寄せる **stay away from** ～から離れている **steal away** ～をこっそり盗み去る **take away** ①連れ去る ②取り上げる, 奪い去る ③取り除く **take someone away** (人)を連れ出す **throw away** ～を捨てる; ～を無駄に費やす, 浪費する **turn away** 向こうへ行く, 追い払う, (顔を)そむける, 横を向く **walk away** 立ち去る, 遠ざかる

□ **awful** 形 ①ひどい, 不愉快な ②恐ろしい 副 ひどく, とても

□ **awkwardly** 副 ①ぎこちなく ②きまり悪そうに

□ **aye** 間 はい, 賛成

B

□ **baboon** 名 ヒヒ《動物》

□ **baby** 名 ①赤ん坊 ②《呼びかけで》あなた 形 ①赤ん坊の ②小さな

□ **bachelor** 名 ①独身男性 ②学士

□ **back** 名 ①背中 ②裏, 後ろ 副 ①戻って ②後ろへ[に] 形 裏の, 後ろの 動 後ろへ動く, 後退する **bring back** 戻す, 呼び戻す, 持ち帰る **come back** 戻る **come back to** ～へ帰ってくる, ～に戻る **give back** (～を) 返す **go back to** ～に帰る[戻る], ～に遡る, (中断していた作業に) 再び取り掛かる **hang back** ためらう **look back at** ～に視線を戻す, ～を振り返って見る **put back** (もとの場所に) 戻す, 返す **take back** ①取り戻す ②(言葉, 約束を) 取り消す, 撤回する **turn back** 元に戻る

□ **background** 名 背景, 前歴, 生い立ち

□ **backup** 形 予備[代替]の 名 ①後援者, 支持するもの ②予備, 代替え

□ **bad** 形 ①悪い, へたな, まずい ②気の毒な ③(程度が) ひどい, 激しい

□ **badge** 名 バッジ, 記章

□ **badly** 副 ①悪く, まずく, へたに ②とても, ひどく

□ **bad-tempered** 形 不機嫌な, 怒りっぽい

□ **bait** 動 ①誘惑する, おびき寄せる ②いじめる 名 えさ, おとり, 誘惑

□ **balcony** 名 ①バルコニー ②桟敷, 階上席

□ **banish** 動 追放する, 追い払う

□ **banished** 形 追放された

□ **banishment** 名 国外追放, 流刑, 追放

□ **bank** 名 ①銀行 ②堤防, 岸 動 ①(銀行と) 取引する ②積み上げる

□ **banner** 名 旗, 垂れ幕, 大見出し

□ **banquet** 名 宴会, ごちそう

□ **Banquo** 名 バンクォー《スコットランドの将軍で, マクベスの友人》

□ **banter** 名 気さくな会話, からかい, 冷やかし

□ **Baptista** 名 バプティスタ《①裕福な商人, キャサリンとビアンカの父 (じゃじゃ馬ならし) ②劇中劇に登場する人物 (ハムレット)》

□ **bar** 名 ①酒場 ②棒, かんぬき ③障害(物) 動 かんぬきで閉める

□ **Barbara** 名 バルバラ《デズディモーナの母の侍女》

□ **barber** 名 理髪師, 床屋

□ **bare** 形 裸の, むき出しの 動 裸にする, むき出しにする

□ **barefoot** 形 はだしの, 素足の

□ **bark** 名 ①ほえる声, どなり声 ②木の皮 動 ほえる, どなる

□ **base** 名 基礎, 土台, 本部 動《-d on ～》～に基礎を置く, 基づく 形 ①卑劣な ②生まれが卑しい **base football player**「卑しい行為をする人物」の意

□ **basically** 副 基本的には, 大筋では

□ **Bassanio** 名 バサーニオ《貴族, アントーニオの親友》

□ **bat** 名 ①コウモリ ②(野球の) バット 動 バットで打つ

□ **battle** 名 戦闘, 戦い 動 戦う

□ **be** 動 ～である, (～に) いる[ある], ～となる 助 ①《現在分詞とともに用いて》～している ②《過去分詞とともに用いて》～される, ～されている

□ **beach** 名 海辺, 浜

□ **bead** 名 数珠玉,《-s》ビーズ[のネックレス]

□ **beam** 名 ①長い角材, 梁 ②光線 ③輝き 動 ①光を発する ②顔を輝かせる ③(光などを) 発する

□ **bear** 動 ①運ぶ ②支える ③耐える ④(子を) 産む 名 ①熊 ②(株取引で) 弱気 **bear up** 耐える, 持ちこたえる

□ **beard** 名 あごひげ

□ **bearing** 名 ①態度 ②関係 ③《-s》ベアリング, 軸受け

□ **beast** 名 ①動物, けもの ②けもののような人, 非常にいやな人[物]

□ **beat** 動 ①打つ, 鼓動する ②打ち負かす 名 打つこと, 鼓動, 拍

□ **Beatrice** 名 ベアトリス《レオナートの姪》

□ **beautiful** 形 美しい, すばらしい 間 いいぞ, すばらしい

□ **beauty** 名 ①美, 美しい人[物] ②《the –》美点

□ **became** 動 become (なる) の過去

□ **because** 接 (なぜなら) ～だから, ～という理由[原因]で **because of** ～のために, ～の理由で

□ **beckon** 動 ①招く, 手招きする ②合図する

□ **become** 動 ①(～に) なる ②(～に) 似合う ③become の過去分詞

□ **bed** 名 ①ベッド, 寝所 ②花壇, 川床, 土台 **go to bed** 床につく, 寝る

□ **bedclothes** 名 寝具

□ **bedridden** 形 (病気などで) 寝たきりの

□ **bedroom** 名 寝室

□ **bee** 名 ミツバチ

□ **beef** 名 牛肉

□ **been** 動 be (～である) の過去分詞 助 be

(～している・～される)の過去分詞 **have been to** ～へ行ったことがある **have never been to** ～に行ったことがない

□ **before** 前 ～の前に[で], ～より以前に 接 ～する前に 副 以前に **before long** やがて, まもなく **the night before** 前の晩

□ **beg** 動 懇願する, お願いする **I beg your pardon.** ごめんなさい。失礼ですが。もう一度言ってください。

□ **began** 動 begin(始まる)の過去

□ **beggar** 名 乞食, 物貰い

□ **begin** 動 始まる[始める], 起こる

□ **beginning** 名 初め, 始まり

□ **begun** 動 begin(始まる)の過去分詞

□ **behalf** 名 利益 **on behalf of** ～のために, ～に代わって

□ **behave** 動 振る舞う

□ **behavior** 名 振る舞い, 態度, 行動

□ **behind** 前 ①～の後ろに, ～の背後に ②～に遅れて, ～に劣って 副 ①後ろに, 背後に ②遅れて, 劣って **leave behind** あとにする, ～を置き去りにする

□ **being** 名 存在, 生命, 人間 **human being** 人, 人間

□ **belief** 名 信じること, 信念, 信用

□ **believe** 動 信じる, 信じている, (～と)思う, 考える

□ **bell** 名 ベル, 鈴, 鐘 動 ①(ベル・鐘が)鳴る ②ベル[鈴]をつける

□ **Bellario** 名 ベラーリオ《ポーシャの親戚で法律家》

□ **Belmont** 名 ベルモント《ポーシャの住む屋敷》

□ **belong** 動《– to ～》～に属する, ～のものである

□ **beloved** 名 最愛の人 形 最愛の, いとしい

□ **below** 前 ①～より下に ②～以下の, ～より劣る 副 下に[へ]

□ **bend** 動 ①曲がる, 曲げる ②屈服する[させる] **bend ～ double** ～を二つに折る

□ **beneath** 前 ～の下に[の], ～より低い 副 下に, 劣って

□ **Benedick** 名 ベネディック《パドヴァの貴族》

□ **benefit** 名 ①利益, 恩恵 ②(失業保険・年金などの)手当, 給付(金) 動 利益を得る, (～の)ためになる

□ **bent** 動 bend(曲がる)の過去, 過去分詞 形 ①曲がった ②熱中した, 決心した 名 (生まれつきの)好み, 傾向

□ **Benvolio** 名 ベンヴォーリオ《ロミオの従兄弟, ロミオの友人》

□ **Bertram** 名 バートラム《ロシリオン伯爵》

□ **beside** 前 ①～のそばに, ～と並んで ②～と比べると ③～とはずれて

□ **besides** 前 ①～に加えて, ～のほかに ②《否定文・疑問文で》～を除いて 副 その上, さらに

□ **best** 形 最もよい, 最大[多]の 副 最もよく, 最も上手に 名《the –》①最上のもの ②全力, 精いっぱい **do one's best** 全力を尽くす

□ **bestow** 動 (名誉などを)授ける

□ **bet** 動 賭ける 名 賭け, 掛け金(の対象)

□ **betray** 動 裏切る, 背く, だます

□ **better** 形 ①よりよい ②(人が)回復して 副 ①よりよく, より上手に ②むしろ

□ **better-fashioned** 形 より良く仕立てられた, より洗練された

□ **better-looking** 形 より魅力的な

□ **between** 前 (2つのもの)の間に[で・の] 副 間に

□ **beware** 動 用心する, 注意する

□ **bewildered** 形 当惑した, 頭が混乱した

□ **bewildering** 形 まごつかせる, ひどく困惑させる

□ **bewitch** 動 (人・物に)魔法をかける, (魔法で～を)言いなりにする, (魅力で人を)とりこにする

□ **beyond** 前 ～を越えて, ～の向こうに 副 向こうに

□ **Bianca** 名 ビアンカ《バプティスタの次女》

□ **biased** 形 偏見のある, 偏った, 先入観にとらわれた

□ **bid** 動 ①(競売・入札などで)値をつける, 入札する ②(トランプなどでせり札を)宣言する ③述べる, 告げる 名 ①付け値, 入札 ②(トランプなどで)宣言, ビッド

□ **big** 形 ①大きい ②偉い, 重要な 副 ①大きく, 大いに ②自慢して

□ **bigger** 熟 **be no bigger than** ～ほどの大きさだ

□ **bird** 名 鳥

□ **Birnam Wood** バーナムの森《重要な舞台となる場所》

□ **birth** 名 ①出産, 誕生 ②生まれ, 起源, (よい)家柄 **give birth** 出産する **give birth to** ～を生む

□ **bit** 動 bite(かむ)の過去, 過去分詞 名 ①小片, 少量 ②《a –》少し, ちょっと ③(情報量単位の)ビット **bits and pieces** こまごました物

□ **bite** 動かむ, かじる 名かむこと, かみ傷, ひと口

□ **bitten** 動bite (かむ) の過去分詞

□ **bitter** 形①にがい ②つらい 副①にがく ②ひどく, 激しく 名①にがさ ②苦しみ ③《-s》苦味ビール, ビターズ

□ **bitterly** 副激しく, 苦々しく

□ **bittersweet** 形悲喜こもごもの, 甘く切ない

□ **black** 形黒い, 有色の 名黒, 黒色

□ **blade** 名①(刀・ナイフなどの) 刃 ②(麦・稲などの) 葉 ③(オールの) 水かき, ブレード

□ **blame** 動とがめる, 非難する 名①責任, 罪 ②非難

□ **blameless** 形欠点のない, 文句のつけられない

□ **blank** 形①白紙の, からの ②うつろな, 単調な 名空白, 空虚

□ **blanket** 名毛布 動毛布でくるむ

□ **blast** 名突風, ひと吹き 動①爆破する ②演奏する **blast away** 吹き飛ばす

□ **bleak** 形荒涼とした, わびしい

□ **bleed** 動出血する, 血を流す [流させる]

□ **bleeding** 形出血する **bleeding to death** 失血死

□ **bless** 動神の加護を祈る, ～を祝福する

□ **blessed** 形祝福された, 恵まれた

□ **blessing** 名①(神の) 恵み, 加護 ②祝福の祈り ③(食前・食後の) 祈り

□ **blew** 動blow (吹く) の過去

□ **blind** 形①視覚障害がある, 目の不自由な ②わからない ③盲目的な 動①目をくらます ②わからなくさせる 名①《the -》視覚障害者 ②ブラインド

□ **blood** 名①血, 血液 ②血統, 家柄 ③気質 間怒りや苦痛の表現

□ **bloodshed** 名流血 (の惨事), 殺害

□ **bloody** 形血だらけの, 血なまぐさい, むごい 副ひどく

□ **blooming** 動bloom (咲く) の現在分詞 形花の咲いた, 花盛りの

□ **blossom** 名花 動開花する

□ **blot** 動汚す

□ **blow** 動①(風が) 吹く, (風が) ～を吹き飛ばす ②息を吹く, (鼻を) かむ ③破裂する ④吹奏する 名①(風の) ひと吹き, 突風 ②(楽器の) 吹奏 ③打撃 **blow up** 破裂する [させる]

□ **blunder** 名大失敗, へま 動へまをやらかす, やり損なう

□ **blunt** 形鈍い, ぶっきらぼうな 動鈍くする [なる]

□ **blush** 動顔を赤らめる 名①赤面 ②赤色, バラ色

□ **blushing** 形赤らんでいる, 照れている

□ **board** 名①板, 掲示板 ②委員会, 重役会 動①乗り込む ②下宿する **on board** (乗り物などに) 乗って, 搭乗して

□ **boast** 動自慢する, 誇る, 鼻にかける 名自慢 (話), 誇り

□ **boat** 名ボート, 小舟, 船 動ボートに乗る [乗せる], ボートで行く

□ **bob** 動軽くぶつかる, ちょっかいを出す

□ **body** 名①体, 死体, 胴体 ②団体, 組織 ③主要部, (文書の) 本文

□ **bodyguard** 名ボディーガード, 護衛

□ **Bohemia** 名ボヘミア《現在のチェコ共和国》

□ **boil** 動①沸騰する [させる], 煮える, 煮る ②激高する 名沸騰

□ **bold** 形①勇敢な, 大胆な, 奔放な ②ずうずうしい ③派手な ④(文字が) 太字の

□ **boldly** 副大胆に, 厚かましく

□ **bond** 名①縛るもの, ひも ②結びつき, 結束 ③《-s》束縛 ④契約, 約定 ⑤保証 (人・金), 担保 ⑥債券, 公債, 社債, 債務証書 ⑦接着, 接着剤 動①担保に入れる, 債券に振り替える ②保証人になる, 保証する ③接着する [させる], 結合する

□ **bone** 名①骨, 《-s》骨格 ②《-s》要点, 骨組み 動(魚・肉) の骨をとる

□ **bonfire** 名(祝祭日などの) 大かがり火, たき火

□ **Bonny Kate** 美しいケイト, 愛らしいケイト

□ **book** 名①本, 書物 ②《the B-》聖書 ③《-s》帳簿 動①記入する, 記帳する ②予約する

□ **bo-peep** 名いないいないばあ

□ **Borachio** 名ボラチオ《ドン・ジョンの家来》

□ **bore** 動①bear (耐える) の過去 ②退屈させる ③穴があく, 穴をあける 名退屈な人 [もの], うんざりすること

□ **boring** 形うんざりさせる, 退屈な

□ **born** 動**be born** 生まれる 形生まれた, 生まれながらの

□ **borne** 動bear (負う, 耐える) の過去分詞

□ **borrow** 動借りる, 借金する

□ **both** 形両方の, 2つともの 副《both ～ and … の形で》～も…も両方とも 代両方, 両者, 双方

□ **bother** 動悩ます, 困惑させる 名面倒, いざ

こざ，悩みの種

□ **bottle** 名瓶，ボトル 動瓶に入れる［詰める］

□ **Bottom** 名ボトム《織物職人》

□ **bough** 名大枝

□ **bought** 動buy（買う）の過去，過去分詞

□ **bound** 動①bind（縛る）の過去，過去分詞 ②跳びはねる ③境を接する，制限する 形①縛られた，束縛された ②《－for ～》～行きの 名境界（線），限界 **be bound to** きっと～する，～する義務がある **know no bounds** 際限がない

□ **boundary** 名境界線，限界

□ **boundless** 形限りない

□ **bout** 名（ボクシングなどの）試合，一勝負，競争

□ **bow** 動（～に）お辞儀する 名①お辞儀，えしゃく ②弓，弓状のもの **bow to** ～に屈服する

□ **bower** 名あずまや，木陰の休息所，木陰

□ **bowl** 名どんぶり，わん，ボウル 動ボウリングをする，ボールを転がす

□ **box** 名①箱，容器 ②観覧席 ③詰所 動①箱に入れる［詰める］ ②ボクシングをする

□ **boy** 名①少年，男の子 ②給仕

□ **Brabantio** 名ブラバンショー《デズデモーナの父》

□ **bracelet** 名ブレスレット

□ **brain** 名①脳 ②知力

□ **bramble** 名イバラ《植物》

□ **brat** 名がき，子ども

□ **brave** 形勇敢な 動勇敢に立ち向かう **brave new world** 素晴らしい新世界

□ **bravely** 副勇敢に（も）

□ **bravery** 名勇敢さ，勇気ある行動

□ **brawl** 動（公衆の面前で）騒々しくけんか［口論］する

□ **break** 動①壊す，折る ②（記録・法律・約束を）破る ③中断する 名①破壊，割れ目 ②小休止 **break loose**（人が監禁状態から）逃げ出す **break open**（金庫などを）こじ開ける **break out** 発生する，急に起こる，（戦争が）勃発する **break through** ～を打ち破る **break up** ばらばらになる，解散させる

□ **breakfast** 名朝食

□ **breaking news** 最新ニュース，ニュース速報

□ **breast** 名胸，乳房 動（～を）胸に受ける，立ち向かう

□ **breast-fed** 動breast-feed（（乳房から赤ん坊に）乳を飲ませる）の過去分詞形

□ **breast-feed** 動（乳房から赤ん坊に）乳を飲ませる

□ **breath** 名①息，呼吸 ②《a－》（風の）そよぎ，気配，きざし

□ **breathe** 動①呼吸する ②ひと息つく，休息する

□ **breathlessly** 副ハラハラしながら，息せき切って

□ **bred** 動breed（産む）の過去，過去分詞

□ **breed** 名品種，血統 動①（動物が子を）産む，繁殖する ②（人が子を）育てる

□ **breeding** 名しつけ，繁殖，飼育

□ **brew** 動①（茶・コーヒーなどを）いれる ②（あらし・陰謀などが）起こる

□ **brewery** 名（ビールなどの）醸造所

□ **bridal** 形花嫁の，婚礼の

□ **bride** 名花嫁，新婦

□ **bridegroom** 名花婿，新郎

□ **bridge** 名橋 動橋をかける

□ **brief** 形①短い時間の ②簡単な 名要点，概要

□ **briefly** 副短く，簡潔に

□ **bright** 形①輝いている，鮮明な ②快活な ③利口な 副輝いて，明るく

□ **brightly** 副明るく，輝いて，快活に

□ **brightness** 名①明るさ，輝き ②鮮やかさ ③聡明

□ **bring** 動①持ってくる，連れてくる ②もたらす，生じる **bring about** 引き起こす **bring back** 戻す，呼び戻す，持ち帰る **bring home** 家に持ってくる **bring～home to someone**（人）に～をはっきりと認識させる **bring out**（物）をとりだす，引き出す，（新製品など）を出す

□ **Britain** 名大ブリテン（島）

□ **British** 形①英国人の ②イギリス英語の 名英国人

□ **broil** 名けんか，口論，騒ぎ

□ **broke** 動break（壊す）の過去

□ **broken** 動break（壊す）の過去分詞 形①破れた，壊れた ②落胆した

□ **brother** 名①兄弟 ②同僚，同胞

□ **brother-in-law** 名義理の兄（弟）

□ **brotherly** 形（愛情・親切心などが）兄弟の，兄弟らしい

□ **brought** 動bring（持ってくる）の過去，過去分詞

□ **brow** 名ひたい，まゆ（毛） **knit one's brow** 眉を寄せる

□ **bubbling** 形（ブクブクと）泡立つ

☐ **bud** 名芽, つぼみ 動芽を出す, つぼみをつける

☐ **budding** 形①芽を出しかけた ②新進の, 世に出始めた

☐ **bugle** 名(通例軍隊で使われる)ラッパ

☐ **build** 動建てる, 確立する 名体格, 構造

☐ **building** 名建物, 建造物, ビルディング

☐ **built** 動build (建てる)の過去, 過去分詞

☐ **bumblebee** 名マルハナバチ《昆虫》

☐ **bump** 名①衝突(の音) ②こぶ, 隆起 動①ドスン[バン]と当たる ②ぶつかる, ぶつける **bump into** (人)とばったり出会う, 鉢合わせする

☐ **burden** 名①荷 ②重荷 動荷[負担]を負わす

☐ **Burgundy** 名バーガンディ《地名》

☐ **burial** 名埋葬

☐ **burn** 動燃える, 燃やす, 日焼けする[させる] 名やけど, 日焼け **burn out** 燃え尽きる

☐ **burnt** 動burn (燃える)の過去, 過去分詞 形焼いた, 焦げた, やけどした

☐ **burst** 動①爆発する[させる] ②破裂する[させる] 名①破裂, 爆発 ②突発 **burst into** ～に飛び込む, 急に～する

☐ **bury** 動①埋葬する, 埋める ②覆い隠す

☐ **bush** 名低木の茂み

☐ **bushy** 形茂みのような, 毛がふさふさ[もじゃもじゃ]した

☐ **business** 名①職業, 仕事 ②商売 ③用事 ④出来事, やっかいなこと 形①職業の ②商売上の

☐ **bustle** 動①忙しく[せかせか]動く ②せき立てる 名せわしげな動き **hustle and bustle** 雑踏, 慌ただしさ

☐ **busy** 形①忙しい ②(電話で)話し中で ③にぎやかな, 交通が激しい

☐ **but** 接①でも, しかし ②～を除いて 前～を除いて, ～のほかは 副ただ, のみ, ほんの **anything but** ～のほかは何でも, 少しも～でない **have no choice but to** ～するしかない **not ～ but ...** ～ではなくて… **not only ～ but ...** ～だけでなく…もまた **nothing but** ただ～だけ, ～にすぎない, ～のほかは何も…ない

☐ **butt** 名①尻 ②(たばこの)吸いさし ③物笑いの種になる人 ④(武器・道具の)大きいほうの端 動①干渉する, 口を出す ②頭で突く

☐ **butter** 名バター 動バターを塗る, バターで味をつける

☐ **buy** 動買う, 獲得する 名購入, 買った[買える]物

☐ **by** 前①《位置》～のそばに[で] ②《手段・方法・行為者・基準》～によって, ～で ③《期限》～までには ④《通過・経由》～を経由して, ～を通って 副そばに, 通り過ぎて **by all means** なんとしても, ぜひとも **by chance** 偶然, たまたま **by heart** 暗記して **by name** ～という名の, 名前で, 名前だけは **by nature** 生まれつき **by no means** 決して～ではない **by the way** ところで, ついでに, 途中で **by this time** この時までに, もうすでに

C

☐ **cabin** 名(丸太作りの)小屋, 船室, キャビン

☐ **Caesar** 名ユリウス・カエサル《共和政ローマ末期の政務官, 文筆家。紀元前100年–紀元前44年》

☐ **caesarean section** 帝王切開

☐ **Caius** 名カイアス《ケント伯の変装名。リアに仕える》

☐ **Caliban** 名キャリバン《島に住む怪物》

☐ **call** 動①呼ぶ, 叫ぶ ②立ち寄る 名①呼び声, 叫び ②短い訪問 **call for** ～を求める, 訴える, ～を呼び求める, 呼び出す **call in** ～を呼ぶ, ～に立ち寄る **call on** 呼びかける, 招集する, 求める, 訪問する **call out** 叫ぶ, 呼び出す, 声を掛ける **call to** ～に声をかける **call upon** 求める, 頼む, 訪問する

☐ **calm** 形穏やかな, 落ち着いた 名静けさ, 落ち着き 動静まる, 静める **calm down** 静まる

☐ **calmly** 副落ち着いて, 静かに

☐ **came** 動come (来る)の過去

☐ **Camillo** 名カミロー《シチリア王の廷臣》

☐ **can** 助①～できる ②～してもよい ③～でありうる ④《否定文で》～のはずがない **as ～ as one can** できる限り～ **can hardly** とても～できない **Can I ～?** ～してもよいですか。 **Can you ～?** ～してくれますか。

☐ **cancel** 名取り消し, 使用中止 動取り消す, 中止する

☐ **candidate** 名①立候補者 ②学位取得希望者 ③志願者

☐ **candle** 名ろうそく

☐ **cannibal** 名カニバル, 人食い人種, 人食い部族

☐ **cannon** 名大砲

☐ **cannot ～ enough** いくら～してもしたりない

☐ **canopy** 名天蓋

☐ **cap** 名①(縁なしの)帽子 ②(瓶・万年筆など

の）ふた 動帽子［ふた］をかぶせる

□ **capable** 形 ①《be – of ～［～ing］》～の能力［資質］がある ②有能な

□ **captain** 名長, 船長, 首領, 主将 動キャプテン［指揮官］を務める

□ **captivate** 動魅了する, とりこにする

□ **capture** 動捕える 名捕えること, 捕獲（物）

□ **Capulet** 名キャピュレット《①ジュリエットの家の家名（ロミオとジュリエット） ②フローレンスの名家（終わりよければ全てよし）》

□ **care** 名 ①心配, 注意 ②世話, 介護 動 ①《通例否定文・疑問文で》気にする, 心配する ②世話をする **care for** ～の世話をする, ～を扱う, ～が好きである, ～を大事に思う **care to** ～したいと思う **take care** 気をつける, 注意する

□ **care-crazed** 形心配や苦悩で狂ったような

□ **careful** 形注意深い, 慎重な

□ **carefully** 副注意深く, 丹念に

□ **careless** 形不注意な, うかつな

□ **cargo** 名積み荷

□ **carriage** 名 ①馬車 ②乗り物, 車

□ **carrier** 名 ①運搬人, 配達人 ②（荷などをのせる）キャリアー ③（病原菌の）媒介（者, 体）

□ **carry** 動 ①運ぶ, 連れていく, 持ち歩く ②伝わる, 伝える **carry along** 持ち運ぶ **carry away** 運び去る **carry on** ①続ける ②持ち運ぶ **carry out** 外へ運び出す, ［計画を］実行する

□ **cart** 名荷馬車, 荷車 動運ぶ

□ **carving** 名彫刻, 彫刻作品

□ **case** 名 ①事件, 問題, 事柄 ②実例, 場合 ③実状, 状況, 症状 ④箱 **in case** ～だといけないので, 念のため, 万が一 **in that case** もしそうなら

□ **Cassio** 名キャシオー《オセローの副官》

□ **cast** 動 ①投げる ②役を与える 名 ①投げること ②配役 **cast away** 投げ捨てる **cast off** 絶縁する, 見捨てる

□ **castle** 名城, 大邸宅

□ **casually** 副何気なく, 軽い気持ちで, 偶然に

□ **cat** 名ネコ（猫）

□ **catch** 動 ①つかまえる ②追いつく ③（病気に）かかる 名つかまえること, 捕球

□ **caught** 動catch（つかまえる）の過去, 過去分詞

□ **cauldron** 名大釜

□ **cause** 名 ①原因, 理由, 動機 ②大義, 主張 動（～の）原因となる, 引き起こす

□ **caution** 名用心, 注意, 警告

□ **cave** 名洞穴, 洞窟

□ **cavern** 名（地下の）洞窟, 洞穴

□ **Cawdor** 名コーダー《地名》

□ **celebrate** 動 ①祝う, 祝福する ②祝典を開く

□ **celebrated** 形名高い, 有名な

□ **celebration** 名 ①祝賀 ②祝典, 儀式

□ **celestial** 形空［天空・天国・天上界］の, 非常に美しい

□ **Celia** 名シーリア《公爵の娘》

□ **center** 名 ①中心, 中央 ②中心地［人物］ 動集中する［させる］

□ **century** 名100年間, 1世紀

□ **ceremony** 名 ①儀式, 式典 ②礼儀, 作法, 形式ばること

□ **certain** 形 ①確実な, 必ず～する ②（人が）確信した ③ある ④いくらかの 代（～の中の）いくつか

□ **certainly** 副 ①確かに, 必ず ②《返答に用いて》もちろん, そのとおり, 承知しました

□ **certainty** 名確信, 確実性

□ **Cesario** 名シザーリオ《ヴァイオラの変装名》

□ **chain** 名 ①鎖 ②一続き 動 ①鎖でつなぐ ②束縛［拘束］する

□ **chair** 名 ①いす ②《the –》議長［会長］の席［職］

□ **challenge** 名 ①挑戦 ②難関 動挑む, 試す

□ **champion** 名優勝者, チャンピオン

□ **chance** 名 ①偶然, 運 ②好機 ③見込み 形偶然の, 思いがけない 動偶然見つける **by chance** 偶然, たまたま

□ **change** 動 ①変わる, 変える ②交換する ③両替する 名 ①変化, 変更 ②取り替え, 乗り換え ③つり銭, 小銭

□ **changed man** 別人

□ **changeling** 名すり替えられた子, 取り替えっ子

□ **chant** 名さえずり 動詠唱する

□ **chapel** 名礼拝堂

□ **character** 名 ①特性, 個性 ②（小説・劇などの）登場人物 ③文字, 記号 ④品性, 人格

□ **charge** 動①（代金を）請求する ②（～を…に）負わせる ③命じる 名 ①請求金額, 料金 ②責任 ③非難, 告発 **in charge of** ～を任されて, ～を担当して, ～の責任を負って

□ **Charles** 名チャールズ《レスリング選手》

□ **charm** 名 ①魅力, 魔力 ②まじない, お守り 動魅了する

□ **charmed** 形魔法［呪い］をかけられた，素晴らしく幸運な，強運な

□ **charming** 動charm（魅了する）現在分詞 形魅力的な，チャーミングな

□ **chase** 動①追跡する，追い［探し］求める ②追い立てる

□ **chat** 動おしゃべりをする，談笑する

□ **cheap** 形①（値段が）安い ②つまらない，質の悪い 副安っぽく

□ **check** 動①照合する，検査する ②阻止［妨害］する ③（所持品を）預ける 名①照合，検査 ②小切手 ③（突然の）停止，阻止（するもの） ④伝票，勘定書

□ **cheek** 名ほお

□ **cheer** 名①応援 ②気分，機嫌 動①元気づける ②かっさいを送る **cheer up** 元気になる，気分が引き立つ

□ **cheerful** 形上機嫌の，元気のよい，（人を）気持ちよくさせる

□ **cheerfully** 副陽気に，快活に

□ **cherish** 動①大切にする，（思い出などを）胸にしまっておく ②（アイデアなどを）温める ③（希望・イメージなどを）抱く

□ **cherry** 名サクランボ，桜

□ **chess** 名チェス《西洋将棋》

□ **chest** 名①大きな箱，戸棚，たんす ②金庫 ③胸，肺

□ **chicken** 名①ニワトリ（鶏） ②鶏肉，チキン 形臆病な

□ **chide** 動（悪い言動をした人を）叱る，たしなめる

□ **chief** 名頭，長，親分 形最高位の，第一の，主要な

□ **child** 名子ども

□ **childhood** 名幼年［子ども］時代

□ **children** 名child（子ども）の複数

□ **chilling** 形（冷気によって）薄ら寒い，肌寒い

□ **chin** 名あご

□ **chisel** 名のみ，たがね，彫刻刀 動のみで彫る，彫刻する

□ **choice** 名選択（の範囲・自由），えり好み，選ばれた人［物］ 形精選した **have no choice but to** ～するしかない

□ **choose** 動選ぶ，（～に）決める

□ **chooser** 名選択者

□ **chose** 動choose（選ぶ）の過去

□ **chosen** 動choose（選ぶ）の過去分詞 形選ばれた，精選された

□ **Christian** 名キリスト教徒，クリスチャン 形キリスト（教）の

□ **church** 名教会，礼拝（堂）

□ **churchyard** 名教会の境内，教会付属の墓地

□ **churn** 動①かくはんする，激しくかき回す ②激しく動く 名①かくはん（器） ②激動

□ **circumstance** 名①（周囲の）事情，状況，環境 ②《-s》（人の）境遇，生活状態

□ **citizen** 名①市民，国民 ②住民，民間人

□ **city** 名①都市，都会 ②《the－》（全）市民

□ **claim** 動①主張する ②要求する，請求する 名①主張，断言 ②要求，請求

□ **clamber** 動①よじ登る ②（はい）降りる

□ **clamor** 名騒がしい音，騒ぎ立てる声 動騒ぎ立てる

□ **Claudio** 名クローディオ《フローレンスの貴族》

□ **Claudius** 名クローディアス《デンマーク王，ハムレットの叔父》

□ **claw** 名鉤爪 動爪で引っかく

□ **clear** 形①はっきりした，明白な ②澄んだ ③（よく）晴れた 動①はっきりさせる ②片づける ③晴れる 副①はっきりと ②すっかり，完全に **clear up** きれいにする，片付ける，（疑問，問題を）解決する

□ **clearly** 副①明らかに，はっきりと ②《返答に用いて》そのとおり

□ **Cleomenes** 名クリオミニーズ《シチリア王の廷臣》

□ **clerk** 名事務員，店員

□ **clever** 形①頭のよい，利口な ②器用な，上手な

□ **cliff** 名断崖，絶壁

□ **clifftop** 名崖［断崖］の上

□ **climb** 動登る，徐々に上がる 名登ること，上昇 **climb over** ～を乗り越える

□ **cling** 動くっつく，しがみつく，執着する

□ **clink** 動（金属・ガラスなどを）チャリン［チリン・カチン］と鳴らす

□ **cloak** 名マント，袖なし外とう

□ **close** 形①近い ②親しい ③狭い 副①接近して ②密集して 動①閉まる，閉める ②終える，閉店する

□ **closed** 形閉じた，閉鎖した

□ **closely** 副①密接に ②念入りに，詳しく ③ぴったりと

□ **cloth** 名布（地），テーブルクロス，ふきん

□ **clothes** 名衣服，身につけるもの

□ **clothing** 名衣類, 衣料品
□ **cloud** 名 ①雲, 雲状のもの, 煙 ②大群 動曇る, 暗くなる
□ **clown** 名道化(役者), おどけ者
□ **clung** 動cling(くっつく)の過去, 過去分詞
□ **coast** 名海岸, 沿岸 動 ①滑降する ②(〜の)沿岸を航行する ③楽々とやり遂げる
□ **coat** 名 ①コート ②(動物の)毛 動 ①表面を覆う ②上着を着せる
□ **Cobweb** 名クモの巣《妖精》
□ **cock** 名 ①おんどり ②(水道の)栓, コック
□ **coffin** 名棺
□ **cold** 形 ①寒い, 冷たい ②冷淡な, 冷静な 名 ①寒さ, 冷たさ ②風邪
□ **cold-hearted** 形心の冷たい, 冷淡な, 冷酷な
□ **coldly** 副冷たく, よそよそしく
□ **collapse** 名崩壊, 倒壊 動崩壊する, 崩れる, 失敗する
□ **collect** 動 ①集める, 集金する ②まとめる 形着払いの
□ **color** 名 ①色, 色彩 ②絵の具 ③血色 動色をつける
□ **colorful** 形 ①カラフルな, 派手な ②生き生きとした
□ **combat** 名戦闘 動戦う, 効果がある
□ **come** 動 ①来る, 行く, 現れる ②(出来事が)起こる, 生じる ③〜になる ④comeの過去分詞 **come along** ①一緒に来る, ついて来る ②やって来る, 現れる ③うまくいく, よくなる, できあがる **come and** 〜しに行く **come away** 〜から離れて行く **come back** 戻る **come back to** 〜へ帰ってくる, 〜に戻る **come by** やって来る, 立ち寄る **come down** 下りて来る, 田舎へ来る **come for** 〜の目的で来る, 〜を取りに来る **come in** 中にはいる, やってくる, 出回る **come into** 〜に入ってくる **come off** 取れる, はずれる **come on** ①いいかげんにしろ, もうよせ, さあ来なさい ②(人)に偶然出合う **come out** 出てくる, 出掛ける, 姿を現す, 発行される **come out of** 〜から出てくる, 〜をうまく乗り越える **come over** やって来る, 〜の身にふりかかる **come true** 実現する **come up** 近づいてくる **come up with** 〜に追いつく, 〜を思いつく, 考え出す, 見つけ出す
□ **comedian** 名喜劇役者, コメディアン
□ **comedy** 名 ①喜劇 ②喜劇的場面
□ **comfort** 名 ①快適さ, 満足 ②慰め ③安楽 動心地よくする, ほっとさせる, 慰める
□ **comical** 形こっけいな, コミカルな
□ **coming** 形今度の, 来たるべき 名到来, 来ること
□ **command** 動命令する, 指揮する 名命令, 指揮(権) **at one's command** 思いのままに
□ **commander** 名司令官, 指揮官
□ **commend** 動推薦する, ほめる
□ **comment** 名論評, 解説, コメント 動論評する, 注解する, コメントする
□ **commercial** 形商業の, 営利的な 名コマーシャル
□ **commission** 名 ①委託, 委任(状) ②任務, 仕事 ③手数料, 歩合 動委任する, 依頼する
□ **commit** 動 ①委託する ②引き受ける ③(罪などを)犯す
□ **companion** 名 ①友, 仲間, 連れ ②添えもの, つきもの
□ **company** 名 ①会社 ②交際, 同席 ③友だち, 仲間, 一団, 人の集まり **in someone's company** (人)と一緒に
□ **compare** 動 ①比較する, 対照する ②たとえる
□ **comparison** 名比較, 対照
□ **compassion** 名思いやり, 深い同情
□ **compel** 動(人に)強制する, しいる, 〜させる
□ **complain** 動 ①不平[苦情]を言う, ぶつぶつ言う ②(病状などを)訴える
□ **complaint** 名不平, 不満(の種)
□ **complete** 形完全な, まったくの, 完成した 動完成させる
□ **completely** 副完全に, すっかり
□ **complexion** ①顔色, 肌の色 ②外観, 様子
□ **compliment** 名 ①賛辞, 敬意 ②《-s》あいさつ 動ほめる, お世辞を言う
□ **compose** 動 ①構成する, 《be -d of 〜》〜から成り立つ ②作曲する, (詩などを)書く
□ **comprehend** 動 ①よく理解する ②包含する
□ **conceal** 動隠す, 秘密にする
□ **concealed** 形隠れた, 隠し持っている
□ **conceive** 動思いつく, 心に抱く
□ **concentrate** 動一点に集める[集まる], 集中させる[する]
□ **concern** 動 ①関係する, 《be -ed in [with] 〜》〜に関係している ②心配させる, 《be -ed about [for] 〜》〜を心配する 名 ①関心事 ②関心, 心配 ③関係, 重要性
□ **conclude** 動 ①終える, 完結する ②結論を下す

□ **conclusion** 名結論, 結末
□ **condemn** 動①責める ②有罪と判決する
□ **condemned** 形有罪を宣告された
□ **condition** 名①(健康)状態, 境遇 ②《-s》状況, 様子 ③条件 動適応させる, 条件づける
□ **conduct** 名①行い, 振る舞い ②指導, 指揮 動①指導する ②実施する, 処理[処置]する
□ **confer** 動①(学位などを)与える, 授与する ②協議する
□ **confess** 動(隠し事などを)告白する, 打ち明ける, 白状する
□ **confession** 名告白, 自白
□ **confide** 動信頼する, 信用する, (秘密などを)打ち明ける
□ **confidence** 名自信, 確信, 信頼, 信用度
□ **confident** 形自信のある, 自信に満ちた
□ **confidently** 副確信して, 自信をもって, 大胆に
□ **confined** 形(〜の中に)閉じ込められた
□ **confirm** 動確かめる, 確かにする
□ **confiscate** 動没収する, 差し押さえる
□ **conflict** 名①不一致, 衝突 ②争い, 対立 ③論争 動衝突する, 矛盾する
□ **confused** 形困惑した, 混乱した
□ **confusion** 名混乱(状態)
□ **congratulate** 動祝う, 祝辞を述べる
□ **congratulation** 間《-s》おめでとう 名祝賀, 祝い, 《-s》祝いの言葉
□ **conjecture** 名推測, 憶測 動推測する
□ **conjure** 動魔法で呼び出す, (魔法のように)作り出す
□ **connect** 動つながる, つなぐ, 関係づける
□ **conquer** 動征服する, 制圧する
□ **conscience** 名良心
□ **consent** 動同意する, 承諾する 名同意, 承諾, 許可
□ **consequence** 名結果, 成り行き
□ **consider** 動①考慮する, 〜しようと思う ②(〜と)みなす ③気にかける, 思いやる
□ **considerate** 形思いやりのある
□ **consolation** 名慰め(となるもの)
□ **console** 動慰める, 元気づける 名制御盤, コンソール
□ **conspire** 動陰謀をたくらむ, 共謀する
□ **constant** 形①絶えない, 一定の, 不変の ②不屈の, 確固たる 名定数
□ **constantly** 副絶えず, いつも, 絶え間なく
□ **consult** 動①相談する ②(専門家に)意見を問う ③(参考書などを)調べる
□ **contain** 動①含む, 入っている ②(感情などを)抑える
□ **contempt** 名軽蔑, 侮辱, 軽視
□ **content** 名①《-s》中身, 内容, 目次 ②満足 形満足して 動満足する[させる] **be content with** 〜に満足している, 甘んじている
□ **contented** 形満足した
□ **continually** 副継続的に, 絶えず, ひっきりなしに
□ **continue** 動続く, 続ける, (中断後)再開する, (ある方向に)移動していく
□ **contract** 名契約(書), 協定 動①契約する ②縮小する
□ **contradict** 動矛盾する, 否定する, 反論する
□ **contrary** 形反対の, 逆の 名逆 副(〜に)反して, 逆らって
□ **contrast** 名対照, 対比 動対照させる, よい対象となる
□ **contrive** 動工夫する, 考案する, うまくやってのける
□ **control** 動①管理[支配]する ②抑制する, コントロールする 名①管理, 支配(力) ②抑制
□ **convenient** 形便利な, 好都合な
□ **convent** 名女子修道院
□ **conversation** 名会話, 会談
□ **converse** 動(打ち解けて)話す, 会話する 名①談話 ②正反対, 逆 形逆の, 正反対の
□ **convert** 動変える, 転換する, 改宗させる
□ **convince** 動納得させる, 確信させる
□ **convoy** 名①護送, 護衛 ②トラックなどの隊列 ③護衛隊, 護衛艦隊 動護送[護衛]する
□ **cook** 名料理女《兄ドローミオの妻》動料理する, (食物が)煮える **cook up** こしらえる
□ **cooked** 形加熱調理した
□ **cool** 形①涼しい, 冷えた ②冷静な ③かっこいい 動①涼しくなる, 冷える ②冷静になる 名涼しさ, 涼しい場所
□ **coolness** 名涼しさ, 冷淡
□ **copy** 名①コピー, 写し ②(書籍の)一部, 冊 ③広告文 動写す, まねる, コピーする
□ **coral** 名サンゴ(珊瑚) 形サンゴの
□ **Cordelia** 名コーデリア《リアの末娘》
□ **Corin** 名コーリン《羊飼い》
□ **corner** 名①曲がり角, 角 ②すみ, はずれ 動①窮地に追いやる ②買い占める ③角を曲

がる

□ **corn-field** 名トウモロコシ畑

□ **Cornwall** 名コーンウォール《地名》

□ **coronet** 小冠, 宝冠, (金や宝石で飾った女性の)頭飾り

□ **correct** 形正しい, 適切な, りっぱな 動(誤りを)訂正する, 直す

□ **correctly** 副正しく, 正確に

□ **correspond** 動①一致する, 対応する ②連絡する, 文通する

□ **cost** 名①値段, 費用 ②損失, 犠牲 動(金・費用が)かかる, (〜を)要する, (人に金額を)費やさせる

□ **cottage** 名小別荘, 小さな家

□ **could** 助①can(〜できる)の過去 ②《控え目な推量・可能性・願望などを表す》**could have done** 〜だったかもしれない《仮定法》**Could I 〜?** 〜してもよいですか。 **How could 〜?** 何だって〜なんてことがありえようか? **If**+《主語》+**could** 〜できればなあ《仮定法》

□ **council** 名会議, 評議会, 議会

□ **counsel** 名助言, 忠告 動忠告する, 勧める

□ **counselor** 名カウンセラー, 助言者, 相談役

□ **count** 動①数える ②(〜を…と)みなす ③重要[大切]である 名計算, 総計, 勘定

□ **countenance** 名①顔つき, 顔色 ②支持

□ **countess** 名伯爵夫人[令嬢], 女伯爵

□ **Countess of Roussillon** ロシリオン伯爵夫人《バートラムの母親》

□ **country** 名①国 ②《the –》田舎, 郊外 ③地域, 領域, 分野 形田舎の, 野暮な

□ **countryman** 名①田舎者 ②(ある土地の)出身者, 同郷人

□ **countrymen** 名countryman(同郷人)の複数形

□ **couple** 名①2つ, 対 ②夫婦, 一組 ③数個 動つなぐ, つながる, 関連させる **a couple of** 2, 3の

□ **courage** 名勇気, 度胸

□ **course** 名①進路, 方向 ②経過, 成り行き ③科目, 講座 ④策, 方策 **of course** もちろん, 当然

□ **court** 名①中庭, コート ②法廷, 裁判所 ③宮廷, 宮殿 動求愛する

□ **courteous** 形礼儀正しい, ていねいな

□ **courtesy** 名礼儀正しさ, ていねいさ, 好意

□ **courtier** 名廷臣

□ **courtly** 形宮廷風の, 優雅な

□ **courtship** 名求愛

□ **cousin** 名いとこ, よく似た人[物]

□ **cover** 動①覆う, 包む, 隠す ②扱う, (〜に)わたる, 及ぶ ③代わりを務める ④補う 名覆い, カバー

□ **coward** 名臆病者 形勇気のない, 臆病な

□ **cowardice** 名臆病

□ **cowardly** 形臆病な 副臆病に, 卑怯にも

□ **cowslip** 名キバナノクリンザクラ, リュウキンカ《植物》

□ **crab-apple** 名(小粒で酸味の強い)野生リンゴ

□ **crack** 名①割れ目, ひび ②(裂けるような)鋭い音 動①ひびが入る, ひびを入れる, 割れる, 割る ②鈍い音を出す

□ **craftsmen** 名craftsman(職人)の複数

□ **crazy** 形①狂気の, ばかげた, 無茶な ②夢中の, 熱狂的な

□ **cream** 名クリーム 形クリーム(入り)の, クリーム色の

□ **create** 動創造する, 生み出す, 引き起こす

□ **creature** 名(神の)創造物, 生物, 動物

□ **credit** 名①信用, 評判, 名声 ②掛け売り, 信用貸し 動信用する

□ **creep** 動①はう ②ゆっくり動く

□ **creeping** 形徐々に忍びよる

□ **crept** 動creep(はう)の過去, 過去分詞

□ **crew** 動crow((雄のニワトリなどが)大きな声で鳴く)の過去《crowedの古い形》

□ **crime** 名①(法律上の)罪, 犯罪 ②悪事, よくない行為

□ **criminal** 形犯罪の, 罪深い, 恥ずべき 名犯罪者, 犯人

□ **criticize** 動①非難する, あら探しをする ②酷評する ③批評する

□ **crouch** 動しゃがむ, うずくまる 名しゃがむこと

□ **crow** 名カラス(鳥) 動(雄のニワトリなどが)大きな声で鳴く

□ **crowbar** 名バール, かなてこ

□ **crowd** 動群がる, 混雑する 名群集, 雑踏, 多数, 聴衆

□ **crown** 名①冠 ②《the –》王位 ③頂, 頂上 動戴冠する[させる]

□ **crowned** 形王冠をいただいた, 王位についた

□ **cruel** 形残酷な, 厳しい

□ **cruelly** 副残酷に

□ **cruelty** 名残酷さ, 残酷な行為［言動・言葉］

□ **crust** 名 ①パン［パイ］の皮 ②堅い表面, 外皮 ③地殻

□ **cry** 動泣く, 叫ぶ, 大声を出す, 嘆く 名泣き声, 叫び, かっさい **cry out** 叫ぶ

□ **cuckoo** 名カッコウ（の鳴き声）

□ **cunning** 形ずるい, 狡猾な 名狡猾さ, ずるさ

□ **cunningly** 副ずるく, こうかつに

□ **curd** 名カスタード, カード《牛乳を乳酸菌で発酵させて固めたもの。チーズの原料》, 凝乳

□ **cure** 名治療, 治癒, 矯正 動治療する, 矯正する, 取り除く

□ **curiosity** 名 ①好奇心 ②珍しい物［存在］

□ **curious** 形好奇心の強い, 珍しい, 奇妙な, 知りたがる

□ **curl** 名巻き毛, 渦巻状のもの 動カールする, 巻きつく

□ **currently** 副今のところ, 現在

□ **curse** 動のろう, ののしる 名のろい（の言葉）, 悪態

□ **cursed** 形のろわれた, 忌まわしい

□ **curtain** 名 ①カーテン, （劇場の）幕 ②隠す［覆う］もの

□ **cushion** 名 ①クッション, 背［座］布団 ②衝撃を和らげるもの 動衝撃を和らげる

□ **custody** 名 ①管理, （未成年者の）保護, 監督 ②監禁, 留置

□ **custom** 名 ①習慣, 慣例, 風俗 ②顧客, ひいき, 得意先 ③《-s》関税, 《the -s》税関 形注文製の

□ **cut** 動 ①切る, 刈る ②短縮する, 削る ③cutの過去, 過去分詞 名 ①切ること, 切り傷 ②削除 **cut down** 切り倒す, 打ちのめす **cut off** 切断する, 切り離す

□ **cut-throat** 形殺人の, 凶暴な.

□ **cypress** 名イトスギ《植物》

□ **Cyprus** 名キプロス《島》

D

□ **dagger** 名短剣

□ **dairy** 名搾乳所, 酪農場, 乳製品販売［製造］所

□ **dairymaid** 名乳搾りの女

□ **daisy** 名ヒナギク（雛菊）, デージー

□ **damned** 形 ①非難された, 悪く評された ②ひどい, くそいまいましい 副ひどく, まったく

□ **dance** 動踊る, ダンスをする 名ダンス, ダンスパーティー

□ **dancing** 名ダンス, 舞踏

□ **Dane** 名デーン族, デーン族の人

□ **danger** 名危険, 障害, 脅威

□ **dangerous** 形危険な, 有害な

□ **Danish** 形デンマーク（人・語）の 名デンマーク語

□ **dappled** 形まだらの

□ **dare** 動《－to ～》思い切って［あえて］～する 助思い切って［あえて］～する 名挑戦 **How dare you ?!** よくも～できるね。

□ **dark** 形 ①暗い, 闇の ②（色が）濃い, （髪が）黒い ③陰うつな 名 ①《the－》暗がり, 闇 ②日暮れ, 夜 ③暗い色［影］

□ **darkness** 名暗さ, 暗やみ

□ **dark-skinned** 形浅黒い肌の

□ **darling** 名 ①最愛の人 ②あなた《呼びかけ》

□ **dash** 動 ①突進する, さっと過ぎ去る ②投げつける 名突進

□ **date** 名 ①日付, 年月日 ②デート 動 ①日付を記す ②デートする

□ **daughter** 名娘

□ **daughter-in-law** 名義理の娘, （姑にとっての）嫁

□ **daunt** 動（～を）威圧する, （～を）脅す

□ **dawn** 名 ①夜明け ②《the－》初め, きざし 動 ①（夜が）明ける ②（真実などが）わかり始める

□ **day** 名 ①日中, 昼間 ②日, 期日 ③《-s》時代, 生涯 **every day** 毎日 **in those days** あのころは, 当時は **one day**（過去の）ある日, （未来の）いつか **the other day** 先日 **these days** このごろ

□ **daybreak** 名夜明け

□ **daylight** 名 ①日光, 昼の明かり, 昼間 ②夜明け

□ **dazzle** 動 ①目をくらませる ②《be－d》目がくらむ 名まぶしい光

□ **de** 前 ～の《出身地を表す, 貴族の称号を表す》

□ **dead** 形 ①死んでいる, 活気のない, 枯れた ②まったくの 名《the－》死者たち, 故人 副完全に, まったく **in the dead of the night** 真夜中に

□ **deadly** 形命にかかわる, 痛烈な, 破壊的な 副ひどく, 極度に

□ **deaf** 形耳が聞こえない 名耳の聞こえない人

□ **deal** 動 ①分配する ②《－with［in］～》～を扱う 名 ①取引, 扱い ②（不特定の）量, 額 **a good［great］deal（of ～）** かなり［ずいぶん・

大量］(の〜), 多額(の〜)

□ **dear** 形いとしい, 親愛なる, 大事な 名ねえ, あなた《呼びかけ》間まあ, おや **dear to**（人）にとって大切な

□ **dearly** 副とても, 心から

□ **death** 名①死, 死ぬこと ②《the－》終えん, 消滅 **be put to death** 処刑される **bleeding to death** 失血死 **jaws of death** 死地 **on pain of death** 違反すると死刑に処す条件で **put to death** 処刑する **to death** 死ぬまで, 死ぬほど

□ **deathbed** 名死の床, 臨終

□ **death-like** 形死んだ［死人の］ような

□ **debt** 名①借金, 負債 ②恩義, 借り

□ **decay** 動腐る, 腐敗する［させる］名①腐敗, 衰え ②虫歯

□ **deceive** 動だます, あざむく

□ **decide** 動決定［決意］する, (〜しようと) 決める, 判決を下す

□ **decision** 名①決定, 決心 ②判決

□ **deck** 名(船の) デッキ, 甲板, 階, 床

□ **declaration** 名①宣言, 布告 ②告知, 発表

□ **declare** 動①宣言する ②断言する ③(税関で) 申告する

□ **decline** 動①断る ②傾く ③衰える 名①傾くこと ②下り坂, 衰え, 衰退

□ **deed** 名①行為, 行動 ②証書

□ **deem** 動(〜であると) 考える

□ **deep** 形①深い, 深さ〜の ②深遠な ③濃い 副深く

□ **deeply** 副深く, 非常に

□ **deer** 名シカ(鹿)

□ **defeat** 動①打ち破る, 負かす ②だめにする 名①敗北 ②挫折

□ **defend** 動防ぐ, 守る, 弁護する

□ **defense** 名①防御, 守備 ②国防 ③弁護, 弁明

□ **defile** 動(〜を) 汚す, (〜を) 冒涜する

□ **definitely** 副①限定的に, 明確に, 確実に ②まったくそのとおり

□ **defy** 動①拒む, 反抗する ②《－＋人＋to 〜》…に〜しろと挑む

□ **dejected** 形がっかりした, 落胆した

□ **delay** 動遅らせる, 延期する 名遅延, 延期, 猶予

□ **delicate** 形①繊細な, 壊れやすい ②淡い ③敏感な, きゃしゃな

□ **delicious** 形おいしい, うまい

□ **delight** 動喜ぶ, 喜ばす, 楽しむ, 楽しませる 名喜び, 愉快

□ **delighted** 形喜んでいる, うれしそうな

□ **delightful** 形楽しい, 愉快にさせる

□ **deliver** 動①配達する, 伝える ②達成する, 果たす

□ **deliverance** 名救出, 解放

□ **Delphi** 名デルファイ《古代ギリシャの神託所》

□ **demand** 動①要求する, 尋ねる ②必要とする 名①要求, 請求 ②需要

□ **Demetrius** 名ディミートリアス《イジーアスが決めたハーミアの許婚》

□ **Denmark** 名デンマーク《国名》

□ **deny** 動否定する, 断る, 受けつけない

□ **depart** 動①出発する ②(常道などから) はずれる

□ **departure** 名①出発, 発車 ②離脱

□ **depend** 動《－on［upon］〜》①〜を頼る, 〜をあてにする ②〜による

□ **dependence** 名依存, 頼ること

□ **dependent** 形頼っている, 〜次第である

□ **depose** 動退位させる, 権力の座から追放する

□ **depressed** 形がっかりした, 落胆した

□ **depression** 名①不景気, 不況 ②憂うつ, 意気消沈

□ **deprive** 動奪う, 取り上げる **deprive 〜 of ...** 〜から…を奪う

□ **deprived** 形恵まれない, 困窮している

□ **descend** 動①下りる ②減少する ③由来する, (子孫に) 伝わる ④《be -ed from》〜の子孫である, 〜に由来する

□ **descendant** 名子孫, 末えい, (祖先からの) 伝来物

□ **describe** 動(言葉で) 描写する, 特色を述べる, 説明する

□ **description** 名(言葉で) 記述(すること), 描写(すること)

□ **Desdemona** 名デズディモーナ《オセローの妻》

□ **desert** 名砂漠, 不毛の地 形砂漠の, 人の住まない 動見捨てる

□ **deserted** 形人影のない, さびれた

□ **deserve** 動(〜を) 受けるに足る, 値する, (〜して) 当然である

□ **design** 動設計する, 企てる 名デザイン, 設計(図)

□ **desire** 動強く望む, 欲する 名欲望, 欲求, 願望

- □ **despair** 動絶望する, あきらめる 名絶望, 自暴自棄
- □ **desperate** 形①絶望的な, 見込みのない ②ほしくてたまらない, 必死の
- □ **desperately** 副絶望的に, 必死になって
- □ **despise** 動軽蔑する
- □ **despised** 形軽蔑された, 侮蔑された
- □ **despite** 前～にもかかわらず
- □ **destroy** 動破壊する, 絶滅させる, 無効にする
- □ **destruction** 名破壊(行為・状態)
- □ **detail** 名①細部,《-s》詳細 ②《-s》個人情報 動詳しく述べる
- □ **detain** 動引き止める
- □ **detect** 動見つける
- □ **determination** 名決心, 決定
- □ **determined** 形決心した, 決然とした
- □ **develop** 動①発達する［させる］ ②開発する
- □ **devil** 名①悪魔(のような人) ②やっかいなこと ③《疑問詞を強調して》いったい全体
- □ **devilish** 形①悪魔のような ②のろわしい, 極悪な
- □ **devise** 動工夫する, 考案する
- □ **devote** 動①(～を…に)捧げる ②《– oneself to ～》～に専念する
- □ **devotion** 名献身, 没頭, 忠誠
- □ **dew** 名露
- □ **diamond** 名①ダイヤモンド ②ひし形
- □ **Diana** 名ダイアナ《未亡人の娘》
- □ **did** 動do (～をする)の過去 助doの過去
- □ **die** 動死ぬ, 消滅する **die down** 徐々にやむ **die of** ～がもとで死ぬ
- □ **differ** 動異なる, 違う, 意見が合わない
- □ **difference** 名違い, 相違, 差
- □ **different** 形異なった, 違った, 別の, さまざまな
- □ **difficult** 形困難な, むずかしい, 扱いにくい
- □ **difficulty** 名①むずかしさ ②難局, 支障, 苦情, 異議 ③《-ties》財政困難
- □ **digestion** 名消化, 理解
- □ **dignified** 形威厳のある, 尊厳のある
- □ **dignity** 名威厳, 品位, 尊さ, 敬意
- □ **dine** 動食事をする, ごちそうする
- □ **ding-dong** 名ディンドン《鐘の鳴る音》
- □ **dinner** 名①ディナー, 夕食 ②夕食［食事］会, 祝宴
- □ **Dion** 名ダイオン《シチリア王の廷臣》
- □ **direction** 名①方向, 方角 ②《-s》指示, 説明書 ③指導, 指揮
- □ **directly** 副①じかに ②まっすぐに ③ちょうど
- □ **dirty** 形①汚い, 汚れた ②卑劣な, 不正な 動汚す
- □ **disagree** 動異議を唱える, 反対する
- □ **disagreement** 名(意見の)不一致, 相違, 不適合
- □ **disappear** 動見えなくなる, 姿を消す, なくなる
- □ **disappoint** 動失望させる, がっかりさせる
- □ **disappointed** 形がっかりした, 失望した
- □ **disastrous** 形災害を引き起こす, 悲惨な
- □ **discharge** 動①解き放つ, 解放する ②解雇する ③荷揚げする, (乗客を)降ろす 名①解放, 免除 ②荷揚げ ③発砲, 発射
- □ **discipline** 名規律, しつけ 動訓練する, しつける
- □ **disclose** 動明らかにする, 暴露する
- □ **discontented** 形(現状などについて)不平［不満］のある
- □ **discourage** 動①やる気をそぐ, 失望させる ②(～するのを)阻止する, やめさせる
- □ **discover** 動発見する, 気づく
- □ **discovery** 名発見
- □ **discreet** 形慎重な, 思慮のある
- □ **discreetly** 副慎重に
- □ **discretion** 名①思慮, 分別, 慎重(な姿勢) ②判断［行動］の自由, 裁量
- □ **discuss** 動議論［検討］する
- □ **discussion** 名討議, 討論
- □ **disdain** 動さげすむ, 軽蔑する 名軽蔑
- □ **disease** 名①病気 ②(社会や精神の)不健全な状態
- □ **disgrace** 名不名誉 動名を汚す, ～の恥となる
- □ **disgraceful** 形恥ずべき, 不名誉な
- □ **disguise** 動変装させる, 隠す 名変装(すること), 見せかけ
- □ **disgusting** 形とてもいやな, うんざりさせる, 最低な
- □ **dish** 名①大皿 ②料理
- □ **dishonor** 名不名誉, 侮辱 動屈辱を与える
- □ **disinherit** 動(人から)相続権を奪う
- □ **dislike** 動嫌う 名反感, いや気

☐ **dismal** 形 気の滅入る, 陰気な
☐ **dismiss** 動 ①解散する ②解雇する ③捨てる ④却下する
☐ **disobedience** 名 不服従, 反抗
☐ **disobey** 動 服従しない, 違反する
☐ **disorder** 名 混乱, 無秩序, 乱雑 動 乱す
☐ **disown** 動 (～と)縁を切る
☐ **dispatch** 動 発送する, 派遣する, さっさと片づける 名 派遣, 急送
☐ **dispersal** 名 (分散による)消散, 散失
☐ **disperse** 動 追い散らす, 分散させる
☐ **displace** 動 ①置き換える, 取って代わる ②強制退去させる, 移す
☐ **display** 動 展示する, 示す 名 展示, 陳列, 表出
☐ **displease** 動 不快にする
☐ **displeasure** 名 不快, 不機嫌
☐ **disposal** 名 処分, 廃棄
☐ **disregard** 動 ①注意を払わない, 無視する ②軽視する, なおざりにする 名 無視, 軽視, 無関心
☐ **disrespect** 名 尊敬を欠くこと, 無礼
☐ **disrespectful** 形 失礼な, 無礼な
☐ **dissembler** 名 偽善者
☐ **distance** 名 距離, 隔たり, 遠方 **at a distance** 少し離れて
☐ **distant** 形 ①遠い, 隔たった ②よそよそしい, 距離のある
☐ **distinguish** 動 ①見分ける, 区別する ②特色づける ③相違を見分ける
☐ **distinguished** 形 顕著な, 優れた, 著名な, 気品のある
☐ **distracted** 形 気を散らされた, 取り乱した
☐ **distress** 名 悩み, 苦痛 動 悩ませる
☐ **distressed** 形 動揺して, 気が動転して
☐ **disturb** 動 かき乱す, 妨げる
☐ **disturbance** 名 ①乱すこと, 妨害(物), じゃま ②動揺, 不安
☐ **diversity** 名 多様性, 相違
☐ **divert** 動 そらす, 向きを変える, 転じる
☐ **divide** 動 分かれる, 分ける, 割れる, 割る **be divided into** 分けられる **divide into** ～に分かれる
☐ **divided** 形 分かれた, 分割[分断]された
☐ **divorce** 動 離婚する 名 離婚, 分離
☐ **divorced** 形 離婚した
☐ **do** 助 ①《ほかの動詞とともに用いて現在形の否定文・疑問文をつくる》②《同じ動詞を繰り返す代わりに用いる》③《動詞を強調するのに用いる》動 ～をする **do ～ good** ～のためになる
☐ **doctor** 名 医者, 博士(号)
☐ **Doctor Balthasar** バルサザー博士《ポーシャの変装名》
☐ **doe** 名 (シカ・ヤギ・ウサギなどの)雌
☐ **does** 動 do(～をする)の3人称単数現在 助 doの3人称単数現在
☐ **dog** 名 犬
☐ **doing** 名 ①すること, したこと ②《-s》行為, 出来事
☐ **domestic** 形 ①家庭の ②国内の, 自国の, 国産の
☐ **Don John** 名 ドン・ジョン《ドン・ペドロの異母弟》
☐ **Don Pedro** 名 ドン・ペドロ《アラゴン大公》
☐ **Donalbain** 名 ドナルベイン《ダンカンの次男》
☐ **done** 動 do(～をする)の過去分詞
☐ **donkey** 名 ロバ
☐ **doomed** 形 運の尽きた, 絶望的な
☐ **door** 名 ①ドア, 戸 ②一軒, 一戸
☐ **Doricles** 名 ドリクリーズ《フロリゼルが使った偽名》
☐ **dote** 動 溺愛する, (過度に)愛情を注ぐ
☐ **double** 形 ①2倍の, 二重の ②対の 副 ①2倍に ②対で 動 ①2倍になる[する] ②兼ねる **bend ～ double** ～を二つに折る **double meaning** 二重の意味
☐ **doubly** 副 二重に
☐ **doubt** 名 ①疑い, 不確かなこと ②未解決点, 困難 動 疑う **no doubt** きっと, たぶん
☐ **dove** 動 dive(飛び込む)の過去 名 ハト(鳩)
☐ **dove-feathered raven** 鳩の羽根を持つカラス《美しい外見とは裏腹に, 暗い本性を持つものを比喩的に表現》
☐ **Dover** 名 ドーバー《港町》
☐ **down** 副 ①下へ, 降りて, 低くなって ②倒れて 前 ～の下方へ, ～を下って 形 下方の, 下りの **calm down** 静まる **come down** 下りて来る, 田舎へ来る **cut down** 切り倒す, 打ちのめす **die down** 徐々にやむ **get down** 降りる, 着地する, 身をかがめる, ひざまずく **go down** 下に降りる **hang down** ぶら下がる **lie down** 横たわる, 横になる **look down** 見下ろす **push down** 押し倒す **run down** (液体が)流れ落ちる, 駆け下りる **run up and down** かけずり回る **throw down** 投げ出す, 放棄する **up and**

down 上がったり下がったり, 行ったり来たり, あちこちと **walk up and down** 行ったり来たりする

☐ **dowry** 名 持参金

☐ **doze** 動 まどろむ, うたた寝する, 居眠りする 名 まどろみ, 仮眠 **doze off** うとうととする, うたた寝する

☐ **drag** 動 ①引きずる ②のろのろ動く[動かす] 名 ①引きずること ②のろのろすること

☐ **dragon** 名 竜

☐ **draw** 動 ①引く, 引っ張る ②描く ③引き分けになる[する]

☐ **drawn** 動 draw (引く) の過去分詞

☐ **dread** 動 恐れる, こわがる 名 恐怖, 不安

☐ **dreadful** 形 恐ろしい

☐ **dream** 名 夢, 幻想 動 (〜の)夢を見る, 夢想[想像]する **dream of** 〜を夢見る

☐ **dreary** 形 荒涼とした, わびしい

☐ **drench** 動 ①ずぶぬれにする ②《be -ed》びしょぬれになる

☐ **dress** 名 ドレス, 衣服, 正装 動 ①服を着る[着せる] ②飾る

☐ **drew** 動 draw (引く) の過去

☐ **dried** 動 dry (乾燥する) の過去, 過去分詞 形 乾燥した

☐ **drift** 動 漂う 名 漂流

☐ **drink** 動 飲む, 飲酒する 名 飲み物, 酒, 1杯

☐ **drive** 動 ①車で行く, (車を) 運転する ②追いやる, (ある状態に) する 名 ドライブ

☐ **driven** 動 drive (車で行く) の過去分詞 **be driven from** 〜から追い出される

☐ **Dromio of Ephesus** 兄ドローミオ (エフェソスのドローミオ)《兄アンティフォラスに仕える》

☐ **Dromio of Syracuse** 弟ドローミオ (シラクサのドローミオ)《弟アンティフォラスに仕える》

☐ **drop** 動 ①(ぽたぽた) 落ちる, 落とす ②下がる, 下げる 名 しずく, 落下

☐ **drove** 動 drive (車で行く) の過去

☐ **drown** 動 ①おぼれる, 溺死する[させる] ②水浸しにする

☐ **drowned** 形 溺死した

☐ **drug** 名 薬, 麻薬, 麻酔薬

☐ **drum** 名 太鼓, ドラム 動 太鼓を鳴らす, ドラムを打つ

☐ **drunk** 動 drink (飲む) の過去分詞 形 (酒に) 酔った, 酔いしれた

☐ **drunken** 形 酔っ払った

☐ **ducat** 名 ダカット金貨

☐ **duchess** 名 公爵夫人, 女公爵

☐ **due** 形 予定された, 期日のきている, 支払われるべき 名 当然の権利 **due to** 〜によって, 〜が原因で

☐ **duel** 名 決闘

☐ **duke** 名 公爵

☐ **Duke of Albany** オルバニー公《ゴネリルの夫》

☐ **Duke of Burgundy** バーガンディー公《コーディリアの求婚者》

☐ **Duke of Cornwall** コーンウォール公《リーガンの夫》

☐ **Duke of Ephesus** エフェソス公《エフェソスの領主》

☐ **Duke of Florence** フローレンス公爵

☐ **Duke Senior** 前公爵《フレデリックの兄》

☐ **dukedom** 名 公爵の位

☐ **dull** 形 退屈な, 鈍い, くすんだ, ぼんやりした 動 鈍くなる[する]

☐ **duly** 副 正式に, 正当に

☐ **Duncan** 名 ダンカン王《スコットランド王》

☐ **Dunsinane** 名 ダンシネーン《地名》

☐ **during** 前 〜の間 (ずっと)

☐ **Dutch** 形 オランダの 名 オランダ人の

☐ **duteous** 形 本分を守る

☐ **dutiful** 形 義務を守る, 忠実な

☐ **dutifully** 副 従順に, 律義に

☐ **duty** 名 ①義務(感), 責任 ②職務, 任務, 関税 **out of duty** 義務感から

☐ **dwell** 動 ①住む ②存在する

☐ **dye** 動 染める, 染まる 名 染料

☐ **dyed** 形 染めた

☐ **dying** 動 die (死ぬ) の現在分詞 形 死にかかっている, 消えそうな

E

☐ **each** 形 それぞれの, 各自の 代 それぞれ, 各自 副 それぞれに **each one** 各自 **each other** お互いに

☐ **eager** 形 ①熱心な ②《be – for 〜》〜を切望している, 《be – to 〜》しきりに〜したがっている

☐ **eagerly** 副 熱心に, しきりに

□ **ear** 名 耳, 聴覚
□ **earl** 名 伯爵
□ **Earl of Gloucester** グロスター伯《エドマンドのこと》
□ **Earl of Kent** ケント伯《リアの忠臣》
□ **earldom** 名 伯爵の位
□ **early** 形 ①(時間や時期が) 早い ②初期の, 幼少の, 若い 副 ①早く, 早めに ②初期に, 初めのころに
□ **earnest** 名 ①熱心, 真剣 ②手付金, 保証金 ③(何かが起こる) 印, 証拠 形 熱心な, 真剣な, 重大な
□ **earnestly** 副 まじめに
□ **earth** 名 ①《the –》地球 ②大地, 陸地, 土 ③この世
□ **earth-bound** 形 (根などが) 地面にしっかりと付いた
□ **ease** 名 安心, 気楽 動 安心させる, 楽にする, ゆるめる
□ **easily** 副 ①容易に, たやすく, 苦もなく ②気楽に
□ **eastern** 形 ①東方の, 東向きの ②東洋の, 東洋風の
□ **easy** 形 ①やさしい, 簡単な ②気楽な, くつろいだ
□ **easy-going** 形 のんきな, 気楽な
□ **eat** 動 食べる, 食事する
□ **eaten** 動 eat (食べる) の過去分詞
□ **echo** 名 こだま, 反響 動 反響させる [する]
□ **Edgar** 名 エドガー《グロスター伯の嫡子》
□ **edge** 名 ①刃 ②端, 縁 動 ①刃をつける, 鋭くする ②縁どる, 縁に沿って進む
□ **Edmund** 名 エドマンド《グロスター伯の庶子》
□ **education** 名 教育, 教養
□ **effect** 名 ①影響, 効果, 結果 ②実施, 発効 動 もたらす, 達成する
□ **effectiveness** 名 有効性
□ **efficacy** 名 (薬などの) 効きめ, 効能
□ **effort** 名 努力 (の成果)
□ **Egeus** 名 イジーアス《ハーミアの父》
□ **eglantine** 名 エグランタイン, ノバラ《植物》
□ **Egyptian** 形 エジプト (人, 語) の 名 ①エジプト人 ②エジプト語
□ **eh** 間《略式》えっ (何ですか), もう一度言ってください《驚き・疑いを表したり, 相手に繰り返しを求める》
□ **eight** 名 8 (の数字), 8人 [個] 形 8の, 8人 [個] の
□ **eighteen** 名 18 (の数字), 18人 [個] 形 18の, 18人 [個] の
□ **eighty** 名 80 (の数字), 80人 [個] 形 80の, 80人 [個] の
□ **either** 形 ①(2つのうち) どちらかの ②どちらでも 代 どちらも, どちらでも 副 ①どちらか ②《否定文で》~もまた (…ない) 接《- ~ or …》~かまたは…か **either A or B** Aかそれとも B
□ **elder** 形 年上の, 年長の
□ **elderly** 形 かなり年配の, 初老の 名《the –》お年寄り
□ **eldest** 形 最年長の
□ **elegance** 名 優雅さ, 上品さ
□ **elegant** 形 上品な, 優雅な
□ **elegy** 名 哀歌, 挽歌
□ **element** 名 要素, 成分, 元素
□ **elephant** 名 象
□ **eleven** 名 ①11 (の数字), 11人 [個] ②11人のチーム, イレブン 形 11の, 11人 [個] の
□ **elf** 名 小妖精, 小人
□ **eloquence** 名 雄弁
□ **eloquent** 形 雄弁な, 表情豊かな
□ **eloquently** 副 雄弁に
□ **else** 副 ①そのほかに [の], 代わりに ②さもないと **anything else** ほかの何か
□ **Elsinore** 名 エルシノア《デンマークの城》
□ **elves** 名 elf (小妖精, 小人) の複数形
□ **embark** 動 乗船する, 着手する, 始める
□ **embrace** 動 抱き締める 名 抱擁
□ **embroidery** 名 刺しゅう
□ **emerge** 動 現れる, 浮かび上がる, 明らかになる
□ **emergency** 名 非常時, 緊急時 形 緊急の
□ **Emilia** 名 エミリア《①ポーライナの侍女 (冬物語) ②イアーゴーの妻, デズディモーナの侍女 (オセロー)》
□ **emperor** 名 皇帝, 天皇
□ **employ** 動 ①(人を) 雇う, 使う ②利用する 名 雇用, 職業
□ **empower** 動 ~する権限 [能力・機能] を与える
□ **empty** 形 ①空の, 空いている ②(心などが) ぼんやりした, 無意味な 動 空になる [する], 注ぐ
□ **enameled** 形 ほうろう [エナメル] 加工された

☐ **enchant** 動大いに喜ばせる，うっとりさせる，魔法をかける

☐ **enchanted** 形魅惑の，魅了するような

☐ **encounter** 動（思いがけなく）出会う，遭う 名遭遇，（思いがけない）出会い

☐ **encourage** 動①勇気づける ②促進する，助長する

☐ **encouraging** 形元気づける

☐ **end** 名①終わり，終末，死 ②果て，末，端 ③目的 動終わる，終える **at the end of** ～の終わりに **in the end** とうとう，結局，ついに **put an end to** ～に終止符を打つ，～を終わらせる，～に決着をつける

☐ **endearing** 形愛情［親しみ・親愛の情］のこもった，いとしさを感じさせる

☐ **endure** 動①我慢する，耐え忍ぶ ②持ちこたえる

☐ **enemy** 名敵

☐ **enforce** 動（法律などを）実行する，実施する，施行する

☐ **engage** 動①約束する，婚約する ②雇う，従事する［させる］，《be -d in》～に従事している

☐ **England** 名①イングランド ②英国

☐ **English** 名①英語 ②《the －》英国人 形①英語の ②英国（人）の

☐ **enjoy** 動楽しむ，享受する **enjoy doing** ～するのが好きだ，～するのを楽しむ

☐ **enjoyment** 名楽しむこと，喜び

☐ **enough** 形十分な，（～するに）足る 代十分（な量・数），たくさん 副（～できる）だけ，十分に，まったく **cannot ～ enough** いくら～してもしたりない **enough to do** ～するのに十分な **sure enough** 思ったとおり，確かに

☐ **enrage** 動（人を）激怒させる

☐ **enrich** 動豊かにする，充実させる

☐ **ensure** 動確実にする，保証する

☐ **enter** 動①入る，入会［入学］する［させる］②記入する ③（考えなどが）（心・頭に）浮かぶ **enter into** ～に入る

☐ **entertain** 動①もてなす，接待する ②楽しませる

☐ **entertainment** 名①楽しみ，娯楽 ②もてなし，歓待

☐ **enthusiastic** 形熱狂的な，熱烈な

☐ **entirely** 副完全に，まったく

☐ **entrance** 名①入り口，入場 ②開始

☐ **entreat** 動懇願する，請う

☐ **entreaty** 名懇願，嘆願

☐ **envelop** 動包む，くるむ

☐ **envious** 形うらやんで

☐ **envy** 名うらやましさ，嫉妬，羨望 動うらやましがる，嫉妬する

☐ **Ephesus** 名エフェソス《古代都市》

☐ **Epidamnum** 名エピダムヌス《古代都市》

☐ **equal** 形等しい，均等な，平等な 動匹敵する，等しい 名同等のもの［人］

☐ **equally** 副等しく，平等に

☐ **erase** 動①消える ②消去する，抹消する

☐ **erect** 形直立した，垂直の 動①直立させる ②建設する

☐ **error** 名誤り，間違い，過失

☐ **erupt** 動（火山が）噴火する，噴出する，爆発する，（戦争が）勃発する

☐ **escape** 動逃げる，免れる，もれる 名逃亡，脱出，もれ

☐ **especially** 副特別に，とりわけ

☐ **essence** 名①本質，真髄，最重要点 ②エッセンス，エキス

☐ **essential** 形本質的な，必須の 名本質，要点，必需品

☐ **established** 形（法律や習慣が）制定された，定着した

☐ **estate** 名不動産，財産，遺産，地所，土地

☐ **esteem** 動尊敬［尊重］する

☐ **esteemed** 形尊重［尊敬］されている，高く評価されている

☐ **evasive** 形回避的な，言い逃れの

☐ **even** 副①《強意》～でさえも，～ですら，いっそう，なおさら ②平等に 形①平らな，水平の ②等しい，均一の ③落ち着いた 動平らになる［する］，釣り合いがとれる **even if** たとえ～でも **even though** ～であるけれども，～にもかかわらず

☐ **evening** 名①夕方，晩 ②《the［one's］－》末期，晩年，衰退期

☐ **event** 名出来事，事件，イベント

☐ **eventful** 形重大な，出来事の多い

☐ **eventually** 副結局は

☐ **ever** 副①今までに，これまで，かつて，いつまでも ②《強意》いったい **ever since** それ以来ずっと **for ever** 永久に，長い間 **if ever** もし～ということがあれば

☐ **ever-faithful** 形常に忠実な

☐ **everlasting** 形永遠の，不朽の，永遠に続く 名永遠

☐ **every** 形①どの～も，すべての，あらゆる ②

毎～, ～ごとの **every day** 毎日 **every time** ～するときはいつも

□ **everybody** 代誰でも, 皆

□ **everyone** 代誰でも, 皆

□ **everything** 代すべてのこと[もの], 何でも, 何もかも

□ **everywhere** 副どこにいても, いたるところに

□ **evil** 形①邪悪な ②有害な, 不吉な 名①邪悪 ②害, わざわい, 不幸 副悪く

□ **ewe** 名雌羊

□ **exact** 形正確な, 厳密な, きちょうめんな

□ **exactly** 副①正確に, 厳密に, ちょうど ②まったくそのとおり

□ **examine** 動試験する, 調査[検査]する, 診察する

□ **example** 名例, 見本, 模範 **for example** たとえば

□ **excel** 動①ほかに勝る ②(～に)秀でる, 勝る

□ **excellence** 名優秀さ, 卓越, 長所

□ **excellent** 形優れた, 優秀な

□ **except** 前～を除いて, ～のほかは 接～ということを除いて

□ **excess** 名①超過, 過剰 ②不節制 形超過の, 過剰な, 余分の

□ **exchange** 動交換する, 両替する 名①交換, 両替 ②小切手, 為替

□ **exclaim** 動①(喜び・驚きなどで)声をあげる ②声高に激しく言う

□ **exclude** 動①排除する, 除く ②(～の)余地を与えない, 考慮しない

□ **excuse** 動①(～の)言い訳をする ②許す, 容赦する, 免除する 名①言い訳, 口実 ②免除 **excuse oneself** 辞退する

□ **execute** 動①実行する, 執行する ②死刑にする

□ **execution** 名①実行, 遂行 ②処刑

□ **exercise** 名①運動, 体操 ②練習 動①運動する, 練習する ②影響を及ぼす

□ **exert** 動①(力・知力・能力を)出す, 発揮する ②(権力を)行使する

□ **exhaust** 動①ひどく疲れさせる ②使い果たす ③排出する 名排気, 排出

□ **exhausted** 形疲れ切った, 消耗した

□ **exhaustion** 名①極度の疲労 ②消耗, 使い果たすこと

□ **exile** 名追放(者), 亡命(者) 動追放する

□ **exist** 動存在する, 生存する, ある, いる

□ **exit** 名出口, 退去 動退出する, 退去する

□ **expect** 動予期[予測]する, (当然のこととして)期待する

□ **expense** 名①出費, 費用 ②犠牲, 代価

□ **expensive** 形高価な, ぜいたくな

□ **experience** 名経験, 体験 動経験[体験]する

□ **expert** 名専門家, 熟練者, エキスパート 形熟練した, 専門の

□ **explain** 動説明する, 明らかにする, 釈明[弁明]する

□ **explanation** 名①説明, 解説, 釈明 ②解釈, 意味

□ **expose** 動①さらす, 露出する ②(秘密などを)暴露する ③商品を陳列する

□ **exposed** 形①雨風[光, 攻撃, 危険]にさらされた ②露出した, 無防備な ③露呈した, 発覚した

□ **express** 動表現する, 述べる 形①明白な ②急行の 名速達便, 急行列車 副速達で, 急行で

□ **expression** 名①表現, 表示, 表情 ②言い回し, 語句

□ **expressly** 副はっきりと, 明確に

□ **exquisite** 形この上なくすばらしい, 非常に美しい, 気品のある

□ **extend** 動①伸ばす, 延長[延期]する ②(範囲が)およぶ, 広がる, (期間などが)わたる

□ **extent** 名範囲, 程度, 広さ, 広がり

□ **extra** 形余分の, 臨時の 名①余分なもの ②エキストラ 副余分に

□ **extraordinary** 形異常な, 並はずれた, 驚くべき

□ **extreme** 形極端な, 極度の, いちばん端の 名極端

□ **eye** 名①目, 視力 ②眼識, 観察力 ③注目 **keep an eye on** ～から目を離さない

□ **eyebrow** 名まゆ(眉)

□ **eyelid** 名まぶた

F

□ **face** 名①顔, 顔つき ②外観, 外見 ③(時計の)文字盤, (建物の)正面 動直面する, 立ち向かう **make a face at** ～にしかめっ面をする

□ **face-to-face** 副面と向かって, 直接に

□ **fact** 名事実, 真相 **in fact** つまり, 実は, 要するに

□ **fade** 動①しぼむ, しおれる ②色あせる, 衰える

□ **fail** 動 ①失敗する, 落第する［させる］ ②《－to ～》～し損なう, ～できない ③失望させる 名 失敗, 落第点

□ **faint** 形 かすかな, 弱い, ぼんやりした 動 気絶する 名 気絶, 失神

□ **fair** 形 ①正しい, 公平［正当］な ②快晴の ③色白の, 金髪の ④かなりの ⑤《古》美しい 副 ①公平に, きれいに ②見事に

□ **fair-skinned** 形 色白の, 肌の白い

□ **fairy** 名 妖精 形 妖精の（ような）

□ **faith** 名 ①信念, 信仰 ②信頼, 信用

□ **faithful** 形 忠実な, 正確な

□ **faithfully** 副 忠実に, 正確に

□ **faithless** 形 不誠実な, 信念のない

□ **fake** 動 見せかける, でっち上げる, だます, 偽造する 名 にせもの 形 にせの

□ **fall** 動 ①落ちる, 倒れる ②（値段・温度が）下がる ③（ある状態に）急に陥る 名 ①落下, 墜落 ②滝 ③崩壊 ④秋 **fall asleep** 眠り込む, 寝入る **fall in love** 恋におちる **fall in love with** 恋におちる **fall into** ～に陥る, ～してしまう **fall off** 落ちる, 落ち込む, 下落する, 減る, 衰退する **fall on** ～に降りかかる **fall to pieces** ボロボロになる

□ **fallen** 動 fall（落ちる）の過去分詞 形 落ちた, 倒れた

□ **false** 形 うその, 間違った, にせの, 不誠実な 副 不誠実に

□ **falsely** 副 偽って, 不誠実に, 不当に

□ **fame** 名 評判, 名声

□ **familiar** 形 ①親しい, 親密な ②《be－with ～》～に精通している ③普通の, いつもの, おなじみの

□ **family** 名 家族, 家庭, 一門, 家柄

□ **famine** 名 飢え, 飢饉, 凶作

□ **famished** 形 空腹で

□ **famous** 形 有名な, 名高い

□ **fan** 名 ①愛好者 ②扇（状のもの）, うちわ 動 ①あおぐ, あおる ②（風などが）そよぐ

□ **fancy** 名 ①幻想, 空想 ②想像力 形 ①装飾的な, 見事な ②法外な, 高級な 動 ①心に描く,（～と）考える ②好む, 引かれる

□ **fantastic** 形 空想的な, 奇想天外な, 風変わりな, すばらしい

□ **far** 副 ①遠くに, はるかに, 離れて ②《比較級を強めて》ずっと, はるかに 形 遠い, 向こうの 名 遠方 **as far as** ～と同じくらい遠く, ～まで, ～する限り（では） **far away** 遠く離れて **far from** ～から遠い, ～どころか **far too** あまりにも～過ぎる **how far** どのくらいの距離か **so far** 今までのところ, これまでは

□ **fare** 名 運賃, 料金 動 元気である, 過ごしている

□ **farewell** 名 別れ, 別れのあいさつ, 送別会 間 さようなら, ごきげんよう

□ **fashion** 名 ①流行, 方法, はやり ②流行のもの（特に服装）

□ **fashionable** 形 ①流行の ②上流社会の

□ **fast** 形 ①（速度が）速い ②（時計が）進んでいる ③しっかりした 副 ①速く, 急いで ②（時計が）進んで ③しっかりと, ぐっすりと **fast asleep** ぐっすり眠っている

□ **fasten** 動 固定する, 結ぶ, 締まる

□ **fatal** 形 致命的な, 運命を決する

□ **fate** 名 ①《時にF-》運命, 宿命 ②破滅, 悲運 動（～の）運命にある

□ **father** 名 ①父親 ②先祖, 創始者 ③《F-》神 ④神父, 司祭

□ **father-in-law** 名 義父

□ **fatherly** 形 父親らしい, 父親にふさわしい

□ **fatigue** 名 疲労, 疲れ

□ **fault** 名 ①欠点, 短所 ②過失, 誤り 動 とがめる **find fault with** ～のあら探しをする

□ **favor** 名 ①好意, えこひいき ②格別のはからい 動 好意を示す, 賛成する **do ～ a favor** ～の願いを聞く

□ **favorable** 形 好意的な, 都合のよい

□ **favorably** 副 好意的に, 都合よく, 賛成して

□ **favorite** 名 お気に入り（の人［物］） 形 お気に入りの, ひいきの

□ **fawn** 名 ①子ジカ ②淡黄褐色《小ジカの色》 動 じゃれつく, 甘える

□ **fear** 名 ①恐れ ②心配, 不安 動 ①恐れる ②心配する **with fear** 怖がって

□ **feast** 名 ①饗宴, ごちそう ②（宗教上の）祝祭日 ③大きな楽しみ 動 ごちそうになる, もてなす

□ **feather** 名 羽, 羽毛

□ **feature** 名 ①特徴, 特色 ②顔の一部,《-s》顔立ち ③（ラジオ・テレビ・新聞などの）特集 動 ①（～の）特徴になる ②呼び物にする

□ **fed** 動 feed（食物を与える）の過去, 過去分詞

□ **fee** 名 謝礼, 料金

□ **feeble** 形 弱い, もろい

□ **feebly** 形 弱く

□ **feed** 動 ①食物を与える ②供給する 名 ①飼育, 食事 ②供給 **feed on** ～を餌にする

□ **feel** 動 感じる,（～と）思う **feel like** ～がほし

い, ～したい気がする, ～のような感じがする **feel sorry for** ～をかわいそうに思う

□**feeling** 名 ①感じ, 気持ち ②触感, 知覚 ③同情, 思いやり, 感受性 形 感じる, 感じやすい, 情け深い

□**feet** 名 ①foot(足)の複数 ②フィート《長さの単位。約30cm》

□**feign** 動 (～の)ふりをする, (～を)装う

□**fell** 動 fall(落ちる)の過去

□**fellow** 名 ①仲間, 同僚 ②人, やつ 形 仲間の, 同士の

□**felt** 動 feel(感じる)の過去, 過去分詞 名 フェルト 形 フェルト(製)の

□**female** 形 女性の, 婦人の, 雌の 名 婦人, 雌

□**fence** 名 囲み, さく 動 さくをめぐらす, 防御する

□**fencing** 名 フェンシング

□**Ferdinand** 名 ファーディナンド《ナポリ王子》

□**Feste** 名 フェステ《伯爵家の道化》

□**festival** 名 祭り, 祝日, ～祭

□**festivity** 名 祝祭(行事)

□**fetch** 動 行って取って[連れて]くる

□**fever** 名 ①熱, 熱狂 ②熱病 動 発熱させる, 熱狂させる

□**few** 形 ①ほとんどない, 少数の(～しかない) ②《a－》少数の, 少しはある 代 少数の人[物]

□**fiancé** 名 (女性から見た男性の)フィアンセ, 婚約者

□**fickleness** 名 不安定, 移り気

□**fictional** 形 架空の, 偽りの

□**fidelity** 名 誠実, 忠実, 貞節

□**field** 名 ①野原, 田畑, 広がり ②(研究)分野 ③競技場

□**fierce** 形 どう猛な, 荒々しい, すさまじい, 猛烈な

□**fiery** 形 ①火の, 燃えさかる ②火のように赤い

□**Fife** 名 ファイフ《地名》

□**fifteen** 名 15(の数字), 15人[個] 形 15の, 15人[個]の

□**fifty** 名 50(の数字), 50人[個] 形 50の, 50人[個]の

□**fight** 動 (～と)戦う, 争う 名 ①戦い, 争い, けんか ②闘志, ファイト **fight with** ～と戦う

□**fighting** 名 戦闘

□**figure** 名 ①人[物]の姿, 形 ②図(形) ③数字 動 ①描写する, 想像する ②計算する ③目立つ, (～として)現れる

□**filial** 形 子としての, 子としてふさわしい

□**fill** 動 ①満ちる, 満たす ②《be -ed with ～》～でいっぱいである

□**final** 形 最後の, 決定的な 名 ①最後のもの ②期末[最終]試験 ③《-s》決勝戦

□**finally** 副 最後に, ついに, 結局

□**finance** 名 ①財政, 財務 ②(銀行からの)資金, 融資 ③《-s》財政状態, 財源 動 資金を融通する

□**find** 動 ①見つける ②(～と)わかる, 気づく, ～と考える ③得る **find fault with** ～のあら探しをする **find one's way** たどり着く **find out** 見つけ出す, 気がつく, 知る, 調べる, 解明する

□**finding** 名 ①発見 ②《-s》発見物, 調査結果 ③《-s》認定, 決定, 答申

□**fine** 形 ①元気な ②美しい, りっぱな, 申し分ない, 結構な ③晴れた ④細かい, 微妙な 副 りっぱに, 申し分なく 動 罰金を科す 名 罰金

□**finery** 名 (特別な時に着用する)美しい衣服[装飾品]

□**finger** 名 (手の)指 動 指でさわる

□**finish** 動 終わる, 終える 名 終わり, 最後

□**fire** 名 ①火, 炎, 火事 ②砲火, 攻撃 動 ①発射する ②解雇する ③火をつける **set fire** 火をつける

□**fireplace** 名 暖炉

□**firmly** 副 しっかりと, 断固として

□**firmness** 名 堅さ, 断固とした態度

□**first** 名 最初, 第一(の人・物) 形 ①第一の, 最初の ②最も重要な 副 第一に, 最初に **at first** 最初は, 初めのうちは **at first sight** 一目見て **for the first time** 初めて

□**fish** 名 魚 動 釣りをする

□**fisherman** 名 漁師

□**fishermen** 名 fisherman(漁師)の複数形

□**fishing** 名 釣り, 魚業 形 釣りの, 漁業の

□**fishing boat** 漁船

□**fit** 形 ①適当な, 相応な ②体の調子がよい 動 合致[適合]する, 合致させる 名 発作, けいれん, 一時的興奮 **in a fit of** 発作的に **in a fit state** ～できる状態である

□**five** 名 5(の数字), 5人[個] 形 5の, 5人[個]の

□**fix** 動 ①固定する[させる] ②修理する ③決定する ④用意する, 整える **fix on** ～にくぎ付けになる

□**flatter** 動 こびへつらう, お世辞を言う, 喜ばせる, おだてる

□**flattering** 形 お世辞の, 喜ばせる

□ **flattery** 名へつらい, お世辞, おべっか
□ **Fleance** 名フリーアンス《バンクォーの息子》
□ **fled** 動flee (逃げる) の過去, 過去分詞
□ **fleet** 名艦隊, 船団 形 (動きが) 速い
□ **flesh** 名肉, 《the –》肉体
□ **flew** 動fly (飛ぶ) の過去
□ **flight** 名飛ぶこと, 飛行, (飛行機の) フライト
□ **flip** 動①(指先で) はじく ②(スイッチなどを) ぱちんとつける［消す］ ③(ファイルなどを) すばやくめくる
□ **flippant** 形不真面目な, 軽薄な, ふざけた
□ **flirt** 動①(異性と) いちゃつく ②もてあそぶ ③ひらひら飛ぶ 名浮気者
□ **float** 動①浮く, 浮かぶ ②漂流する ③(心に) 浮かぶ ④《be ～ing》(うわさなどが) 広まる 名浮くもの, いかだ
□ **flock** 名 (羊・鳥などの) 群れ, 群集 動集まる, 群がる
□ **flood** 名①洪水 ②殺到 動①氾濫する, 氾濫させる ②殺到する
□ **floor** 名床, 階
□ **floppy** 名フロッピー(ディスク) 形しまりのない
□ **Florence** 名フローレンス《イタリアの都市》
□ **Florizel** 名フロリゼル《ボヘミアの王子》
□ **flow** 動流れ出る, 流れる, あふれる 名①流出 ②流ちょう (なこと)
□ **flower** 名①花, 草花 ②満開 動花が咲く
□ **flowering** 形花の咲く 名開花, 全盛
□ **fly** 動①飛ぶ, 飛ばす ②(飛ぶように) 過ぎる, 急ぐ 名①飛行 ②ハエ **fly away** 飛び去る **fly off** 飛び去る **fly over** 飛び超える, 上空を飛ぶ
□ **focus** 名①焦点, ピント ②関心の的, 着眼点 ③中心 動①焦点を合わせる ②(関心・注意を) 集中させる
□ **fog** 名①濃霧, 煙 ②混乱, 当惑 動曇らせる, 当惑させる
□ **foil** 名(フェンシングの) フルーレ, フォイル《フェンシングで使用される剣》
□ **fold** 名折り目, ひだ 動①折りたたむ, 包む ②(手を) 組む
□ **follow** 動①ついていく, あとをたどる ②(～の) 結果として起こる ③(忠告などに) 従う ④理解できる **followed by** その後に～が続いて
□ **follower** 名信奉者, 追随者
□ **following** 形《the –》次の, 次に続く 名《the –》下記のもの, 以下に述べるもの
□ **folly** 名愚行, おろかさ
□ **fond** 形①《be – of ～》～が大好きである ②愛情の深い
□ **fondness** 名好み, 優しさ
□ **food** 名食物, えさ, 肥料
□ **fool** 名①ばか者, おろかな人 ②道化師 動ばかにする, だます, ふざける **make a fool of** ～をばかにする
□ **Fool** 名道化《リア付きの道化師》
□ **foolish** 形おろかな, ばかばかしい
□ **foolishly** 副おろかに
□ **foot** 名①足, 足取り ②(山などの) ふもと, (物の) 最下部, すそ ③フィート《長さの単位。約30cm》
□ **football** 名 (英国で) サッカー, (米国で) アメリカンフットボール 形卑劣な **base football player**「卑しい行為をする人物」の意
□ **footstep** 名足音, 歩み
□ **for** 前①《目的・原因・対象》～にとって, ～のために［の］, ～に対して ②《期間》～間 ③《代理》～の代わりに ④《方向》～へ (向かって) 接というわけは～, なぜなら～, だから **for a moment** 少しの間 **for a while** しばらくの間, 少しの間 **for all** ～にもかかわらず **for all the world** 絶対に, 断じて **for ever** 永久に, 長い間 **for example** たとえば **for long** 長い間 **for one's pains** 骨折ったかいもなく **for oneself** 独力で, 自分のために **for some reason** なんらかの理由で, どういうわけか **for some time** しばらくの間 **for the first time** 初めて **for the moment** 差し当たり, 当座は **for the rest of life** 死ぬまで **for ～ years** ～年間, ～年にわたって
□ **forbid** 動禁じる, 許さない
□ **force** 名力, 勢い 動①強制する, 力ずくで～する, 余儀なく～させる ②押しやる, 押し込む
□ **forced** 形強制された, 強制的な
□ **forehead** 名ひたい
□ **foreign** 形外国の, よその, 異質な
□ **foresight** 名先見の明, 将来への配慮
□ **forest** 名森林
□ **forever** 副永遠に, 絶えず
□ **forfeit** 動①失う ②剥奪される, 没収される 名①喪失 ②剥奪
□ **forgave** 動forgive (許す) の過去
□ **forget** 動忘れる, 置き忘れる
□ **forgetful** 形忘れっぽい, 無頓着な
□ **forgive** 動許す, 免除する
□ **forgiven** 動forgive (許す) の過去分詞

□ **forgiveness** 名許す(こと), 寛容
□ **forgot** 動forget(忘れる)の過去, 過去分詞
□ **forgotten** 動forget(忘れる)の過去分詞
□ **form** 名①形, 形式 ②書式 動形づくる
□ **former** 形①前の, 先の, 以前の ②《the ~》(二者のうち)前者の
□ **formidable** 形恐ろしい, 侮りがたい
□ **forsake** 動(~を)見捨てる
□ **forsaken** 動forsake((~を)見捨てる)の過去分詞形
□ **forth** 副前へ, 外へ **and so forth** など, その他 **set forth** 旅に出発する
□ **fortunate** 形幸運な, 幸運をもたらす
□ **fortune** 名①富, 財産 ②幸運, 繁栄, チャンス ③運命, 運勢
□ **fortune-teller** 名占い師, 易者
□ **forty** 名40(の数字), 40人[個] 形40の, 40人[個]の
□ **forward** 形①前方の, 前方へ向かう ②将来の ③先の 副①前方に ②将来に向けて ③先へ, 進んで 動①転送する ②進める **look forward to** ~を期待する
□ **fought** 動fight(戦う)の過去, 過去分詞
□ **foul** 形悪臭のある, 不潔な, 汚い, ひどい
□ **found** 動①find(見つける)の過去, 過去分詞 ②~の基礎を築く, ~を設立する
□ **foundation** 名①建設, 創設 ②基礎, 土台
□ **four** 名4(の数字), 4人[個] 形4の, 4人[個]の
□ **fourth** 名第4番目(の人・物), 4日 形第4番目の
□ **frame** 名骨組み, 構造, 額縁 動形づくる, 組み立てる **frame of mind** 考え方, 精神状態
□ **France** 名フランス《国名》
□ **frantic** 形半狂乱の, 死に物狂いの
□ **Frederick** 名フレデリック《公爵》
□ **free** 形①自由な, 開放された, 自由に~できる ②暇で, (物が)空いている, 使える ③無料の 副①自由に ②無料で 動自由にする, 解放する **set free** (人)を解放する, 釈放される, 自由の身になる
□ **freedom** 名①自由 ②束縛がないこと
□ **freely** 副自由に, 障害なしに
□ **French** 形フランス(人・語)の 名①フランス語 ②《the ~》フランス人
□ **frequent** 形ひんぱんな, よくある 動よく訪れる, 交際する
□ **frequently** 副頻繁に, しばしば
□ **fresh** 形①新鮮な, 生気のある ②さわやかな, 清純な ③新規の
□ **fret** 動いらいらさせる, 気をもむ 名いらだち, 焦燥
□ **friar** 名修道士
□ **Friar Francis** フランシス神父《修道士》
□ **Friar Lawrence** ロレンス神父《修道士》
□ **friend** 名友だち, 仲間
□ **friendless** 形友のない
□ **friendly** 形親しみのある, 親切な, 友情のこもった 副友好的に, 親切に
□ **friendship** 名友人であること, 友情
□ **frighten** 動驚かせる, びっくりさせる
□ **frightened** 形おびえた, びっくりした
□ **frog** 名カエル(蛙)
□ **from** 前①《出身・出発点・時間・順序・原料》~から ②《原因・理由》~がもとで **from now** 今から, これから **from that time on** あれから, あの時以来 **from time to time** ときどき
□ **front** 名正面, 前 形正面の, 前面の **in front of** ~の前に, ~の正面に
□ **frown** 動しかめ面をする, まゆを寄せる 名むずかしい顔つき, しかめ面, まゆを寄せること
□ **fruit** 名①果実, 実 ②《-s》成果, 利益 動実を結ぶ
□ **fruitless** 形成果のない, 実を結ばない, 不毛の
□ **fudge** 動(~を)ごまかす, (~を)でっち上げる
□ **fugitive** 形つかの間の, 変わりやすい 名逃亡者
□ **fulfilled** 形(条件などが)満たされている
□ **fulfillment** 名実現, 成就, 達成
□ **full** 形①満ちた, いっぱいの, 満期の ②完全な, 盛りの, 充実した 名全部 **be full of** ~で一杯である
□ **fully** 副十分に, 完全に, まるまる
□ **fun** 名楽しみ, 冗談, おもしろいこと 形楽しい, ゆかいな 動からかう, ふざける **make fun of** ~を物笑いの種にする, からかう
□ **funeral** 名葬式, 葬列 形葬式の
□ **funny** 形①おもしろい, こっけいな ②奇妙な, うさんくさい
□ **furious** 形怒り狂った, 激怒した, 激しい
□ **furnish** 動備える, 供給する, 家具をとりつける
□ **further** 形いっそう遠い, その上の, なおいっそうの 副いっそう遠く, その上に, もっと 動

促進する
□ **fury** 名激しさ, 激怒, 激情
□ **fuss** 名騒動, 空騒ぎ, 大騒ぎ 動大騒ぎする
□ **future** 名未来, 将来 形未来の, 将来の **in the future** 将来は

G

□ **gain** 動①得る, 増す ②進歩する, 進む 名①増加, 進歩 ②利益, 得ること, 獲得
□ **gambol** 名跳ね回る［飛び跳ねる］こと
□ **game** 名ゲーム, 試合, 遊び, 競技 動賭けごとをする
□ **Ganymede** 名ギャニミード《ロザリンドの変装名》
□ **garb** 名外観, 身なり, (職業などの特徴を表す) 服装
□ **garden** 名庭, 庭園 動園芸をする, 庭いじりをする
□ **garland** 名花冠
□ **garment** 名衣服, 《-s》衣料
□ **gasp** 動①あえぐ ②はっと息をのむ ③息が止まる 名①あえぎ ②息切れ ③息をのむこと
□ **gate** 名①門, 扉, 入り口 ②(空港・駅などの) ゲート
□ **gatecrash** 動乱入する, (パーティーなどに) 招待されていないのに出席する
□ **gather** 動①集まる, 集める ②生じる, 増す ③推測する
□ **gave** 動give (与える) の過去
□ **gaze** 名凝視, 注視 動凝視する
□ **general** 形①全体の, 一般の, 普通の ②おおよその ③(職位の) 高い, 上級の 名大将, 将軍
□ **generally** 副①一般に, だいたい ②たいてい
□ **generation** 名①同世代の人々 ②一世代 ③発生, 生成
□ **generosity** 名①寛大, 気前のよさ ②豊富さ
□ **generous** 形①寛大な, 気前のよい ②豊富な
□ **generously** 副十分に, たっぷりと
□ **gentle** 形①優しい, 温和な ②柔らかな
□ **gentleman** 名紳士
□ **gentlemen** 名gentleman (紳士) の複数
□ **gentleness** 名優しさ, 親切
□ **gentlewoman** 名上流婦人, 貴婦人
□ **gentlewomen** 名gentlewoman (上流婦人, 貴婦人) の複数形
□ **gently** 副親切に, 上品に, そっと, 優しく
□ **Gerard de Narbon** ジェラード・ド・ナーバン《有名な医者, ヘレナの父》
□ **German** 形ドイツ (人・語) の 名①ドイツ人 ②ドイツ語
□ **Germany** 名ドイツ《国名》
□ **Gertrude** 名ガートルード《デンマーク王妃, ハムレットの母》
□ **gesture** 名身振り, しぐさ, 意思表示 動身振り［手振り］で示す
□ **get** 動①得る, 手に入れる ②(ある状態に) なる, いたる ③わかる, 理解する ④〜させる, 〜を (…の状態に) する ⑤(ある場所に) 達する, 着く **get angry** 腹を立てる **get at** 届く, 入手する **get down** 降りる, 着地する, 身をかがめる, ひざまずく **get home** 家に着く［帰る］ **get in** 中に入る, 乗り込む **get into** 〜に入る, 入り込む, 〜に巻き込まれる **get on** (電車などに) 乗る, 気が合う **get ready** 用意［支度］をする **get rid of** 〜を取り除く **get there** そこに到着する, 目的を達成する, 成功する **get to do** 〜できるようになる, 〜できる機会を得る **get up** 起き上がる, 立ち上がる **get worse** 悪化する
□ **ghost** 名幽霊, 亡霊
□ **ghostly** 形幽霊のような, ぼんやりした
□ **giddy** 形目まいがする, 目の回るような
□ **gift** 名①贈り物 ②(天賦の) 才能 動授ける
□ **gilt** 動gild (金めっきする) の過去, 過去分詞 形金めっきした, 金をかぶせた
□ **girl** 名女の子, 少女
□ **give** 動①与える, 贈る ②伝える, 述べる ③(〜を) する **give away** ただで与える, 贈る, 譲歩する, 手放す **give back** (〜を) 返す **give birth** 出産する **give birth to** 〜を生む **give oneself up to** 〜に身を委ねる **give up** あきらめる, やめる, 引き渡す **give way** 道を譲る, 譲歩する, 負ける
□ **given** 動give (与える) の過去分詞 形与えられた
□ **glad** 形①うれしい, 喜ばしい ②《be – to 〜》〜してうれしい, 喜んで〜する
□ **gladly** 副喜んで, うれしそうに
□ **Glamis** 名グラミズ《地名》
□ **glass** 名①ガラス (状のもの), コップ, グラス ②鏡, 望遠鏡 ③《-es》めがね
□ **glide** 動滑る, 滑るように動く 名滑走, 滑空
□ **glimpse** 名ちらりと見ること 動ちらりと見る

□ **gloomy** 形 ①憂うつな，陰気な ②うす暗い

□ **Gloucester** 名 グロスター《地名》

□ **glove** 名 手袋，グローブ

□ **glowing** 動 glow（白熱して輝く）の現在分詞 形 白熱［赤熱］した，熱のこもった

□ **go** 動 ①行く，出かける ②動く ③進む，経過する，いたる ④（ある状態に）なる **be going to** ～するつもりである **go along** ～に沿って行く，（人）について行く **go along with** ～に同調する **go and** ～しに行く **go away** 立ち去る **go back to** ～に帰る［戻る］，～に遡る，（中断していた作業に）再び取り掛かる **go doing** ～をしに行く **go down** 下に降りる **go home** 帰宅する **go in** 中に入る，開始する **go into** ～に入る，（仕事）に就く **go mad** 発狂する **go off** ①出かける，去る，出発する ②始める，突然～しだす ③（電気が）消える **go on** 続く，続ける，進み続ける，起こる，発生する **go on to** ～に移る，～に取り掛かる **go out** 外出する，外へ出る **go over to** ～の前に［へ］行く，～に出向いて行く **go to bed** 床につく，寝る **go up** ①～に上がる，登る ②～に近づく，出かける **go up to** ～まで行く，近づく **go with** ～と一緒に行く，～と調和する，～にとても似合う **go without** ～なしですませる

□ **go-between** 名 仲介者，仲人

□ **goblin** 名（伝説上の）ゴブリン，小鬼

□ **god** 名 神 **God be with you.** 神のご加護がありますことを

□ **goddess** 名 女神

□ **gold** 名 金，金貨，金製品，金色 形 金の，金製の，金色の

□ **golden** 形 ①金色の ②金製の ③貴重な

□ **goldsmith** 名 金細工人《まちがって弟アンティフォラスに金ぐさりを渡す》

□ **gone** 動 go（行く）の過去分詞 形 去った，使い果たした，死んだ

□ **Goneril** 名 ゴネリル《リアの長女》

□ **Gonzago** 名 ゴンザーゴ《劇中劇に登場する人物》

□ **Gonzalo** 名 ゴンザーロー《ナポリ王の重臣》

□ **good** 形 ①よい，上手な，優れた，美しい ②（数量・程度が）かなりの，相当な 間 よかった，わかった，よろしい 名 ①善，徳，益，幸福 ②《-s》財産，品，物質 **as good as** ～も同然で，ほとんど～ **be good at** ～が得意だ **do ～ good** ～のためになる **have a good time** 楽しい時を過ごす

□ **good humor** 上機嫌，上手なユーモア

□ **goodbye** 間 さようなら 名 別れのあいさつ **say goodbye to** ～にさよならと言う

□ **good-looking** 形 顔立ちのよい，ハンサムな，きれいな

□ **good-natured** 形 気だてのよい，気さくな

□ **goodness** 名 ①善良さ，よいところ ②優秀 ③神《婉曲表現》

□ **goodnight** 間《就寝時・夜の別れのあいさつ》おやすみ

□ **goods** 名 ①商品，品物 ②財産，所有物

□ **good-tempered** 形 気立ての良い

□ **gorgeous** 形 華麗な，豪華な，華やかな，すばらしい

□ **gossip** 名 うわさ話，ゴシップ，うわさ好きな人 動 うわさ話をする，雑談する

□ **got** 動 get（得る）の過去，過去分詞 **have got** 持っている

□ **govern** 動 治める，管理する，支配する

□ **government** 名 政治，政府，支配

□ **governor** 名 ①知事 ②支配者，（学校・病院・官庁などの）長

□ **grab** 動 ①ふいにつかむ，ひったくる ②横取りする 名 ひっつかむこと，横取り

□ **grace** 名 ①優雅，気品がある ②好意，親切 ③《G-》閣下 ④猶予期間

□ **graceful** 形 優美な，上品な

□ **gracious** 形 ①親切な，ていねいな ②慈悲深い ③優雅な 間 おや！ まあ！

□ **graciously** 副（恩着せがましく）親切に，寛大に，快く

□ **gradually** 副 だんだんと

□ **grain** 名 ①穀物，穀類，（穀物の）粒 ②粒，極少量 動 粒にする

□ **grand** 形 雄大な，壮麗な

□ **granny** 名《略式》おばあちゃん

□ **grant** 動 ①許可する，承諾する ②授与する，譲渡する ③（なるほどと）認める 名 授与されたもの

□ **grape** 名 ブドウ

□ **grasp** 動 つかむ，握る，とらえる，理解する 名 把握，理解（力）

□ **grass** 名 草，牧草（地），芝生 動 草［芝生］で覆う［覆われる］

□ **grassy** 形 草で覆われた，草のような

□ **grateful** 形 感謝する，ありがたく思う

□ **Gratiano** 名 グラシアーノ《アントーニオとバサーニオの友人》

□ **gratitude** 名 感謝（の気持ち），報恩の念

□ **grave** 名 墓 形 重要な，厳粛な，落ち着いた

□ **gravely** 副 重大に，厳かに

□ **gray** 形 ①灰色の ②どんよりした, 憂うつな ③白髪の 名 灰色 動 灰色になる[する]

□ **great** 形 ①大きい, 広大な, (量や程度が)たいへんな ②偉大な, 優れた ③すばらしい, おもしろい

□ **greatly** 副 大いに

□ **greatness** 名 ①偉大さ ②大きいこと, 重要

□ **Greece** 名 ギリシア《国名》

□ **greedy** 形 どん欲である, 欲深い

□ **green** 形 ①緑色の, 青々とした ②未熟な, 若い ③生き生きした 名 ①緑色 ②草地, 芝生, 野菜

□ **green-eyed** 形 緑色の目をした

□ **greet** 動 ①あいさつする ②(喜んで)迎える

□ **greeting** 名 あいさつ(の言葉), あいさつ(状)

□ **grew** 動 grow(成長する)の過去

□ **grief** 名 (深い)悲しみ, 悲嘆

□ **grieve** 動 (深く)悲しむ, 悲しませる

□ **grim** 形 ①(表情などが)険しい, こわい ②厳しい, 残酷な

□ **groan** 動 ①うめく, うなる ②ぶうぶう言う 名 うめき声

□ **groom** 名 ①花婿, 新郎 ②宮内官 動 きれいに整える, 手入れをする

□ **ground** 名 地面, 土, 土地 動 ①基づかせる ②着陸する ③grind(ひく)の過去, 過去分詞 形 (粉に)ひいた, すった **kiss the ground** 平伏する **on the ground** 地面に

□ **groundless** 形 根拠のない, 事実無根の

□ **group** 名 集団, 群 動 集まる

□ **grow** 動 ①成長する, 育つ, 育てる ②増大する, 大きくなる, (次第に～に)なる **grow up** 成長する, 大人になる

□ **growl** 動 (～に向かって)うなる, 不平を言う, どなる 名 うなり声, ほえ声

□ **grown** 動 grow(成長する)の過去分詞 形 成長した, 成人した

□ **grub** 名 地虫

□ **grudge** 動 (物を)与えるのを惜しむ, 出ししぶる 名 うらみ

□ **grumble** 動 不平[不満]を言う, ゴロゴロ鳴る 名 不平, 苦情

□ **guarantee** 名 保証, 保証書, 保証人 動 保証する, 請け合う

□ **guarantor** 名 保証人

□ **guard** 名 ①警戒, 見張り ②番人 動 番をする, 監視する, 守る

□ **guardian** 名 保護者, 守護神

□ **guess** 動 ①推測する, 言い当てる ②(～と)思う 名 推定, 憶測 **guess at** ～を推測する

□ **guest** 名 客, ゲスト

□ **guide** 動 (道)案内する, 導く 名 ①ガイド, 手引き, 入門書 ②案内人

□ **guilt** 名 罪, 有罪, 犯罪

□ **guiltless** 形 罪のない, 潔白な

□ **guilty** 形 有罪の, やましい

□ **guise** 名 (変えた)外見, (偽りの)見せかけ

□ **gulp** 動 (液体など)ぐいぐい飲む, (がつがつ)急いで食べる

□ **gum** 名 樹脂, 樹液

H

□ **haberdasher** 名 (特に男性向けの)雑貨小間物商人

□ **habit** 名 習慣, 癖, 気質

□ **habitation** 名 居住(地), 住まい

□ **had** 動 have(持つ)の過去, 過去分詞 助 have の過去《過去完了の文をつくる》

□ **hag** 名 くそばばあ

□ **ha-ha** 間 あはは!, はは!

□ **hail** 動 ①歓呼して迎える, 歓迎する ②合図をおくる 名 ①あいさつ, 歓迎 ②ひょう, あられ

□ **hair** 名 髪, 毛

□ **hairbreadth** 形 間一髪の, 危機一髪の

□ **hairy** 形 毛むくじゃらの, 毛製の

□ **half** 名 半分 形 半分の, 不完全な 副 半分, なかば, 不十分に

□ **half-brother** 名 腹違いの兄(弟)

□ **half-crazed** 形 ちょっと気が狂った

□ **halfway** 副 中間[中途]で, 不完全に 形 中間[中途]の, 不完全な

□ **hall** 名 公会堂, ホール, 大広間, 玄関

□ **halves** 名 half(半分)の複数

□ **Hamlet** 名 ハムレット《デンマーク王国の後継者》

□ **hand** 名 ①手 ②(時計の)針 ③援助の手, 助け 動 手渡す **hand in** 差し出す, 提出する **on the other hand** 一方, 他方では

□ **handful** 名 一握り, 少量

□ **handkerchief** 名 ハンカチ

□ **handle** 名 取っ手, 握り 動 ①手を触れる ②操縦する, 取り扱う

□ **handsome** 形 端正な(顔立ちの), りっぱな,

(男性が)ハンサムな

□ **hand writing** ①手書き, 肉筆 ②筆跡, 書体

□ **hang** 動かかる, かける, つるす, ぶら下がる 名①かかり具合 ②《the –》扱い方, こつ **hang back** ためらう **hang down** ぶら下がる **hang on** ～につかまる, しがみつく, がんばる, (電話を)切らずに待つ

□ **hanging** 名(つるしてある)カーテン, タペストリー

□ **happen** 動①(出来事が)起こる, 生じる ②偶然[たまたま]～する **happen to** たまたま～する, 偶然～する

□ **happening** 名出来事, 事件

□ **happily** 副幸福に, 楽しく, うまく, 幸いにも

□ **happiness** 名幸せ, 喜び

□ **happy** 形幸せな, うれしい, 幸運な, 満足して **be happy to do** ～してうれしい, 喜んで～する

□ **harbor** 名港, 停泊所, 隠れ場 動かくまう

□ **hard** 形①堅い ②激しい, むずかしい ③熱心な, 勤勉な ④無情な, 耐えがたい, 厳しい, きつい 副①一生懸命に ②激しく ③堅く

□ **hard-hearted** 形冷酷な, 無情な, むごい

□ **hardly** 副①ほとんど～でない, わずかに ②厳しく, かろうじて **can hardly** とても～できない

□ **hardship** 名(耐えがたい)苦難, 辛苦

□ **harm** 名害, 損害, 危害 動傷つける, 損なう

□ **harmless** 形無害の, 安全な

□ **harmony** 名調和, 一致, ハーモニー

□ **harsh** 形厳しい, とげとげしい, 不快な

□ **harshly** 副過酷に, 荒々しく

□ **has** 動have(持つ)の3人称単数現在 助haveの3人称単数現在《現在完了の文をつくる》

□ **haste** 名急ぐこと, あわてること **in haste** 急いで

□ **hasten** 動急がせる, 急ぐ, 早める

□ **hastily** 副急いで, 軽率に

□ **hasty** 形①急ぎの, あわただしい ②早まった, 軽率な

□ **hat** 名(縁のある)帽子

□ **hate** 動嫌う, 憎む, (～するのを)いやがる 名憎しみ

□ **hatred** 名憎しみ, 毛嫌い

□ **haughty** 形横柄な, 高慢な, 傲慢な

□ **haunt** 動よく行く, 出没する, つきまとう

□ **have** 動①持つ, 持っている, 抱く ②(～が)ある, いる ③食べる, 飲む ④経験する, (病気に)かかる ⑤催す, 開く ⑥(人に) ～させる **have to** ～しなければならない 助《〈have + 過去分詞〉の形で現在完了の文をつくる》～した, ～したことがある, ずっと～している **could have done** ～だったかもしれない《仮定法》 **have a good time** 楽しい時を過ごす **have a headache** 頭痛がする **have been to** ～へ行ったことがある **have got** 持っている **have never been to** ～に行ったことがない **have no choice but to** ～するしかない **have no idea** わからない **have power over** ～を思いのままに操る力を持っている **have something made** ～を作らせる **have to do with** ～と関係がある **should have done** ～すべきだった(のにしなかった)《仮定法》**would have ... if ～** もし～だったとしたら…しただろう

□ **hawk** 名タカ(鷹)

□ **hawthorn** 名サンザシ《植物》

□ **he** 代彼は[が]

□ **head** 名①頭 ②先頭 ③長, 指導者 動向かう, 向ける **head of** ～の長

□ **headache** 名頭痛 **have a headache** 頭痛がする

□ **headstrong** 形頑固な, 強情な

□ **heal** 動いえる, いやす, 治る, 治す

□ **health** 名健康(状態), 衛生, 保健

□ **healthy** 形健康な, 健全な, 健康によい

□ **hear** 動聞く, 聞こえる **hear about** ～について聞く **hear from** ～から手紙[電話・返事]をもらう **hear of** ～について聞く

□ **heard** 動hear(聞く)の過去, 過去分詞

□ **hearing** 名①聞くこと, 聴取, 聴力 ②聴聞会

□ **heart** 名①心臓, 胸 ②心, 感情, ハート ③中心, 本質 **by heart** 暗記して **take ～ to heart** ～を深く悲しむ **with all one's heart** 心から

□ **heartbroken** 形悲しみに打ちひしがれた

□ **heartily** 副心から, 十分に

□ **heat** 名①熱, 暑さ ②熱気, 熱意, 激情 動熱する, 暖める

□ **heath** 名荒野, 荒れ地

□ **heaven** 名①天国 ②天国のようなところ[状態], 楽園 ③空 ④《H-》神

□ **heavenly** 形①天の, 天国のような ②すばらしい

□ **heavy** 形重い, 激しい, つらい

□ **Hecuba** 名ヘカベー《トロイアの王妃》

□ **hedge** 名生け垣, 垣根 動①生け垣で囲う, 取り囲む ②分散してリスクを避ける

□ **hedge sparrow** ヨーロッパカヤクグリ《鳥》

□ **hedgehog** 名ハリネズミ, ヤマアラシ

□ **hee-haw** 名ロバの鳴き声, ばか笑い, アッハッハ, ガハハ

□ **heigh ho** リズムや音として, 歌ったり口ずさむような軽快さを表したもの

□ **height** 名①高さ, 身長 ②《the –》絶頂, 真っ盛り ③高台, 丘

□ **heir** 名相続人, 後継者

□ **heiress** 名女相続人

□ **held** 動hold (つかむ) の過去, 過去分詞

□ **Helena** 名ヘレナ《①伯爵夫人の侍女(終わりよければ全てよし) ②ハーミアの友人(夏の夜の夢)》

□ **hell** 名地獄, 地獄のようなところ［状態］

□ **hell-hound** 名悪魔のような人, 地獄の番犬

□ **helmet** 名ヘルメット, かぶと

□ **help** 動①助ける, 手伝う ②給仕する 名助け, 手伝い **help ~ to ...** ～が…するのを助ける **help ~ with ...** …を～の面で手伝う

□ **helper** 名助手, 助けになるもの

□ **helpless** 形無力の, 自分ではどうすることもできない

□ **hemlock** 名毒ニンジン《植物》, 毒ニンジンから採った毒薬

□ **henbane** 名ヒヨス《植物》, ヒヨスから採った毒

□ **her** 代①彼女を［に］ ②彼女の

□ **herald** 名①使者, 伝達者, 報道者 ②先駆者 動先触れとなる

□ **herb** 名薬草, 香草, ハーブ

□ **herd** 名(大型動物の) 一群, 群集, 民衆

□ **here** 副①ここに［で］ ②《- is［are］～》ここに～がある ③さあ, そら 名ここ **Here it is.** はい, どうぞ。 **here are ~** こちらは～です。 **here is ~** こちらは～です。 **over here** こっちへ［に］; ほら, さあ《人の注意を引く》

□ **Hermia** 名ハーミア《ライサンダーの想い人》

□ **Hermione** 名ハーマイオニー《リオンティーズの妃》

□ **hermit** 名隠者, 世捨て人

□ **hero** 名英雄, ヒーロー

□ **Hero** 名ヒーロー《レオナートの娘》

□ **hers** 代彼女のもの

□ **herself** 代彼女自身

□ **hesitate** 動ためらう, ちゅうちょする

□ **hidden** 動hide(隠れる)の過去分詞 形隠れた, 秘密の

□ **hide** 動隠れる, 隠す, 隠れて見えない, 秘密にする

□ **hideous** 形ひどくみにくい, ぞっとする

□ **hiding** 形隠す［隠れる］こと

□ **high** 形①高い ②気高い, 高価な 副①高く ②ぜいたくに 名高い所

□ **high-born** 形高貴の生まれの

□ **highly** 副①大いに, 非常に ②高度に, 高位に ③高く評価して, 高価で

□ **highness** 名《H-》殿下

□ **high-spirited** 形元気のよい, 活発な, 威勢がいい

□ **hill** 名丘, 塚

□ **him** 代彼を［に］

□ **himself** 代彼自身

□ **hindrance** 名妨害, じゃま, 障害物

□ **hint** 名暗示, ヒント, 気配 動暗示する, ほのめかす

□ **hire** 動雇う, 賃借りする 名雇用, 賃借り, 使用料

□ **his** 代①彼の ②彼のもの

□ **history** 名歴史, 経歴

□ **hit** 動①打つ, なぐる ②ぶつける, ぶつかる ③命中する ④(天災などが) 襲う, 打撃を与える ⑤hitの過去, 過去分詞 名①打撃 ②命中 ③大成功

□ **hmm** 間ふむ, ううむ《熟考・疑問・ためらいなどを表す》

□ **ho** 間《驚き・喜びなどを表して》ほう, 《注意を引く呼びかけとして》おーい, 《笑い声を表して》ほっほっ

□ **hoard** 名蓄え, 貯蔵, 蓄積 動(ひそかに) 貯蔵する, 買いだめする

□ **hold** 動①つかむ, 持つ, 抱く ②保つ, 持ちこたえる ③収納できる, 入れることができる ④(会などを) 開く 名①つかむこと, 保有 ②支配［理解］力 **hold in** (動かないように) 押さえる **hold on** しっかりつかまる **hold out** ①差し出す, (腕を) 伸ばす ②持ちこたえる, 粘る, 耐える **take hold of** ～をつかむ, 捕らえる, 制する

□ **hollow** 名①へこみ ②空白 形うつろな, くぼんだ

□ **holy** 形聖なる, 神聖な

□ **home** 名①家, 自国, 故郷, 家庭 ②収容所 副家に, 自国へ 形家の, 家庭の, 地元の **bring home** 家に持ってくる **bring ~ home to someone** (人) に～をはっきりと認識させる **get home** 家に着く［帰る］ **go home** 帰宅する **on one's way home** 帰り道で **take someone home** (人) を家まで送る

□ **homesick** 形家を恋しがる，故郷を慕う，ホームシックの

□ **honest** 形①正直な，誠実な，心からの ②公正な，感心な

□ **honestly** 副正直に

□ **honesty** 名正直，誠実

□ **honey** 名①蜂蜜（のように甘いもの） ②《呼びかけ》かわいい人

□ **honey-bag** 名みつ袋

□ **honeysuckle** 名スイカズラ《植物》

□ **honor** 名①名誉，光栄，信用 ②節操，自尊心 動尊敬する，栄誉を与える **honor of doing** 〜する光栄［栄誉］

□ **honorable** 形①尊敬すべき，立派な ②名誉ある ③高貴な

□ **hood** 名①フード，ずきん ②（車の）ボンネット

□ **hoot** 動①やじる ②（フクロウが）ホーホーと鳴く 名①やじ ②フクロウの鳴き声

□ **hop** 動①（片足で）ぴょんと飛ぶ，飛び越える，飛び乗る ②飛行機で行く，短い旅行をする 名ぴょんと飛ぶこと，跳躍

□ **hope** 名希望，期待，見込み 動望む，（〜であるようにと）思う **in the hope of** 〜を望んで［期待して］

□ **hopeless** 形①希望のない，絶望的な ②勝ち目のない

□ **Horatio** 名ホレイショー《ハムレットの親友》

□ **horrible** 形恐ろしい，ひどい

□ **horrid** 形恐ろしい，忌まわしい

□ **horrified** 形怖がって，恐怖に襲われて

□ **horror** 名①恐怖，ぞっとすること ②嫌悪

□ **horse** 名馬

□ **horseback** 名馬の背

□ **Hortensio** 名ホーテンシオ《ペトルーチオの古い友人》

□ **hospitable** 形もてなしのよい，親切な

□ **hospitality** 名歓待，温かいもてなし

□ **host** 名①客をもてなす主人 ②（テレビなどの）司会者

□ **hostess** 名女主人，女性司会者

□ **hot** 形①暑い，熱い ②できたての，新しい ③からい，強烈な，熱中した 副①熱く ②激しく

□ **hotly** 副熱く，暑く，激しく

□ **hound** 名猟犬

□ **hour** 名1時間，時間

□ **hourly** 形1時間ごとの，絶え間ない，たびたびの

□ **house** 名①家，家庭 ②（特定の目的のための）建物，小屋

□ **household** 名家族，世帯 形家族の

□ **hovel** 名家畜小屋，掘っ建て小屋

□ **how** 副①どうやって，どれくらい，どんなふうに ②なんて（〜だろう） ③《関係副詞》〜する方法 **How could 〜?** 何だって〜なんてことがありえようか？ **How dare you ?!** よくも〜できるね。 **how far** どのくらいの距離か **how often** 何回〜ですか **how to** 〜する方法 **show 〜 how to ...** 〜に…のやり方を示す

□ **however** 副たとえ〜でも 接けれども，だが

□ **howl** 動①遠ぼえする，うなる ②（苦痛・怒りなどで）うなる，うめく 名遠ぼえ，うなり（声・音）

□ **huge** 形巨大な，ばく大な

□ **human** 形人間の，人の 名人間 **human being** 人，人間

□ **humble** 形つつましい，粗末な 動卑しめる，謙虚にさせる

□ **humbly** 副謙虚に

□ **humor** 名おかしみ，面白さ，ユーモア **good humor** 上機嫌，上手なユーモア

□ **hundred** 名①100（の数字），100人［個］ ②《-s》何百，多数 形①100の，100人［個］の ②多数の

□ **hung** 動hang（かかる）の過去，過去分詞

□ **hunger** 名①空腹，飢え ②（〜への）欲 動①飢える ②熱望する

□ **hungry** 形①空腹の，飢えた ②渇望して ③不毛の

□ **hunting** 名狩り，狩猟，ハンティング，捜索 形狩猟の

□ **hurry** 動急ぐ，急がせる，あわてる 名急ぐこと，急ぐ必要 **in a hurry** 急いで，あわてて

□ **hurt** 動傷つける，痛む，害する 名傷，けが，苦痛，害

□ **husband** 名夫

□ **husk** 名殻，外皮 動①殻をとる，皮をむく ②しゃがれた声で言う

□ **hustle** 動①乱暴に押す，急がせる，急ぐ ②張り切る，ハッスルする 名精力的な活動，ハッスル **hustle and bustle** 雑踏，慌ただしさ

□ **hymn** 名賛美歌，聖歌

I

□ **I** 代私は［が］

□ **Iago** 名 イアーゴー《オセローの旗手》

□ **ice** 名 ①氷 ②氷菓子 動 凍る, 凍らす, 氷で冷やす

□ **idea** 名 考え, 意見, アイデア, 計画 **have no idea** わからない

□ **identical** 形 まったく同じ, 等しい, 同一の

□ **idiot** 名 ばか, まぬけ

□ **idle** 形 ①暇な ②怠けている, ぶらぶらしている ③つまらない, むだな 動 怠けてすごす, ぶらぶらする

□ **idly** 副 何もしないで, 無為に, 怠けて

□ **if** 接 もし〜ならば, たとえ〜でも, 〜かどうか 名 疑問, 条件, 仮定 **as if** あたかも〜のように, まるで〜みたいに **ask 〜 if** 〜かどうか尋ねる **even if** たとえ〜でも **If +《主語》+ could** 〜できればなあ《仮定法》 **if any** もしあれば, あったとしても **if ever** もし〜ということがあれば **if only** 〜でありさえすれば **see if** 〜かどうかを確かめる **would have ... if 〜** もし〜だったとしたら…しただろう

□ **ignorant** 形 ①無知な, 無学な ②知らないで, 気づかないで

□ **ignore** 動 無視する, 怠る

□ **ill** 形 ①病気の, 不健康な ②悪い 副 悪く, 不完全に

□ **illegitimate** 形 非嫡出の, 私生の

□ **illness** 名 病気

□ **ill-usage** 名 虐待, 酷使

□ **illusion** 名 ①錯覚, 幻想 ②勘違い, 見間違い

□ **Illyria** 名 イリリア《架空の国》

□ **Illyrian** 名 イリリア人《登場人物たちの住む国の住民》

□ **image** 名 ①印象, 姿 ②画像, 映像 動 心に描く, 想像する

□ **imagination** 名 想像(力), 空想

□ **imagine** 動 想像する, 心に思い描く

□ **imitate** 動 まねる, 模造する

□ **immediate** 形 さっそくの, 即座の, 直接の

□ **immediately** 副 すぐに, 〜するやいなや

□ **immortal** 形 ①死ぬことのない, 不死の ②不滅の 名 不死の人

□ **impart** 動 (情報・秘密などを)伝える, 知らせる, 開示する

□ **impatiently** 副 我慢できずに, いらいらして

□ **imperfect** 形 不完全な, 未完成な

□ **impersonate** 動 (だますために人に)成りすます

□ **implore** 動 懇願する

□ **importance** 名 重要性, 大切さ

□ **important** 形 重要な, 大切な, 有力な

□ **impossible** 形 不可能な, できない, あり[起こり]えない

□ **impostor** 名 詐称者, 偽者, 替え玉

□ **impress** 動 印象づける, 感銘させる 名 刻印, 痕跡

□ **impression** 名 ①印象, 感想 ②感動

□ **imprison** 動 投獄する, 閉じ込める

□ **improper** 形 不適切な, 妥当でない

□ **in** 前 ①《場所・位置・所属》〜(の中)に[で・の] ②《時》〜(の時)に[の・で], 〜後(に), 〜の間(に) ③《方法・手段》〜で ④〜を身につけて, 〜を着て ⑤〜に関して, 〜について ⑥《状態》〜の状態で 副 中へ[に], 内へ[に] **in a fit of** 発作的に **in a hurry** 急いで, あわてて **in a sense** ある意味では **in a way** ある意味では **in answer to** 〜に応じて **in any way** 決して, 多少なりとも **in case** 〜だといけないので, 念のため, 万が一 **in charge of** 〜を任されて, 〜を担当して, 〜の責任を負って **in fact** つまり, 実は, 要するに **in front of** 〜の前に, 〜の正面に **in haste** 急いで **in line** 一列に **in memory of** 〜の記念として **in need** 必要で, 困って **in no time** すぐに, 一瞬で **in no way** 決して〜でない **in order** きちんと(整理されて), 順序正しく **in order to** 〜するために, 〜しようと **in other words** すなわち, 言い換えれば **in particular** 特に, とりわけ **in peace** 平和のうちに, 安心して **in person** (本人)自ら, 自身で **in progress** 進行中で **in question** 問題の, 論争中の **in return** お返しとして **in respect** 〜であるという点で **in search of** 〜を探し求めて **in silence** 黙って, 沈黙のうちに **in some way** 何とかして, 何らかの方法で **in someone's company** (人)と一緒に **in spite of** 〜にもかかわらず **in sport** 冗談で **in store** 蓄えて, 用意されて **in tears** 涙を流しながら **in terms of** 〜の言葉で言えば, 〜の点から **in that case** もしそうなら **in the dead of the night** 真夜中に **in the end** とうとう, 結局, ついに **in the future** 将来は **in the hope of** 〜を望んで[期待して] **in the meantime** それまでは, 当分は **in the middle of** 〜の真ん中[中ほど]に **in the presence of** 〜の面前で **in the shape of** 〜の形をした **in the world** 世界で **in this way** このようにして **in those days** あのころは, 当時は **in time** 間に合って, やがて **in vain** むだに, むなしく

□ **inability** 名 できないこと, 不能, 無力

□ **inadvertently** 副 不注意で, うっかりして

□ **incident** 名 出来事, 事故, 事変, 紛争 形 ①起こりがちな ②付随する

□ **incline** 動 ①傾ける, 傾く, 曲げる ②(心などを)傾ける, (~の)傾向がある
□ **included** 形 含まれた
□ **including** 前 ~を含めて, 込みで
□ **inconvenient** 形 不便な, 不自由な
□ **increase** 動 増加[増強]する, 増やす, 増える 名 増加(量), 増大
□ **increasing** 形 増加する, 拡大する
□ **incredible** 形 ①信じられない, 信用できない ②すばらしい, とてつもない
□ **incurable** 形 不治の, 治療不能の
□ **indebted** 形 借金がある, 恩を受けている
□ **indecent** 形 わいせつな, みだらな, 下品な
□ **indeed** 副 ①実際, 本当に ②《強意》まったく 間 本当に, まさか
□ **independent** 形 独立した, 自立した
□ **India** 名 インド《国名》
□ **indicate** 動 ①指す, 示す, (道などを)教える ②それとなく言う ③きざしがある
□ **indignation** 名 憤り, 憤慨
□ **indignity** 名 侮辱
□ **indiscretion** 名 無分別, 軽率さ
□ **inequality** 名 ①不平等, 不均衡 ②《-ties》起伏, (表面の)荒いこと ③(天候・温度の)変動 ④不等式
□ **inexperienced** 形 経験のない, 不慣れな
□ **infallible** 形 完全無欠な, 絶対確実な
□ **infancy** 名 ①幼少, 幼年期 ②初期
□ **infant** 名 ①幼児 ②初心者, 入門者
□ **infernal** 形 地獄[悪魔]の(ような)
□ **infidelity** 名 不貞, 不義
□ **influence** 名 影響, 勢力 動 影響をおよぼす
□ **inform** 動 ①告げる, 知らせる ②密告する
□ **infuse** 形 (強い感情や熱意を)注ぐ, 注入する
□ **ingratitude** 名 恩知らず
□ **ingredient** 名 成分, 原料, 材料
□ **inhabitant** 名 居住者, 住民
□ **inherit** 動 相続する, 受け継ぐ
□ **inhuman** 形 人間味のない, 冷酷な
□ **inhumanity** 名 残酷(な行為)
□ **injure** 動 痛める, 傷つける
□ **injured** 形 負傷した, (名誉・感情などを)損ねられた
□ **injury** 名 ①けが ②侮辱, 無礼
□ **injustice** 名 不当, 不正(行為)
□ **inn** 名 宿屋, 居酒屋
□ **innocence** 名 ①無邪気, 純真 ②無罪, 潔白
□ **innocent** 名 無邪気な人, 罪のない人 形 無邪気な, 無実の
□ **innocently** 副 無邪気に, 何食わぬ顔で
□ **inquire** 動 尋ねる, 問う
□ **inside** 名 内部, 内側 形 内部[内側]にある 副 内部[内側]に 前 ~の内部[内側]に
□ **insist** 動 ①主張する, 断言する ②要求する
□ **insistence** 名 主張, 無理強い
□ **instance** 名 ①例 ②場合, 事実
□ **instant** 形 即時の, 緊急の, 即席の 名 瞬間, 寸時
□ **instantly** 副 すぐに, 即座に
□ **instead** 副 その代わりに **instead of** ~の代わりに, ~をしないで
□ **instruct** 動 ①教える, 教育する ②指図[命令]する
□ **instruction** 名 教えること, 指示, 助言
□ **instrument** 名 ①道具, 器具, 器械 ②楽器 ③手段
□ **insult** 動 侮辱する, ばかにする 名 侮辱, 無礼な言動
□ **integrity** 名 完全性, 高潔
□ **intelligent** 形 頭のよい, 聡明な
□ **intend** 動《– to ~》~しようと思う, ~するつもりである
□ **intended** 形 故意の, 意図された
□ **intent** 形 ①専念した, 熱心な ②《be – on ~》~するつもりである 名 意図, 意向
□ **intention** 名 ①意図, (~する)つもり ②心構え
□ **interest** 名 ①興味, 関心 ②利害(関係), 利益 ③利子, 利息 動 興味を起こさせる
□ **interested** 形 興味を持った, 関心のある **be interested in** ~に興味[関心]がある
□ **interesting** 形 おもしろい, 興味を起こさせる
□ **interference** 名 ①妨害, 干渉 ②雑音, 電波障害
□ **international** 形 国際(間)の
□ **interrupt** 動 さえぎる, 妨害する, 口をはさむ
□ **interval** 名 間隔, 距離, 合間
□ **intervention** 名 介入, 仲裁, 調停, 干渉
□ **into** 前 ①《動作・運動の方向》~の中へ[に] ②《変化》~に[へ] **be divided into** 分けられる **burst into** ~に飛び込む, 急に~する **come**

into ～に入ってくる **divide into** ～に分かれる **enter into** ～に入る **fall into** ～に陥る, ～してしまう **get into** ～に入る, 入り込む, ～に巻き込まれる **go into** ～に入る, (仕事)に就く **jump into** ～に飛び込む **look into** ①～を検討する, ～を研究する ②～の中を見る, ～をのぞき込む **put ～ into ...** ～を…の状態にする, ～を…に突っ込む **run into** (思いがけず) ～に出会う, ～に駆け込む, ～の中に走って入る **rush into** ～に突入する, ～に駆けつける, ～に駆け込む **take into** 手につかむ, 中に取り入れる **turn into** ～に変わる

□ **intoxicated** 形 (酒・麻薬などに)酔って, 酩酊して

□ **introduce** 動 紹介する, 採り入れる, 導入する

□ **intruding** 形 邪魔をする, 無礼な

□ **invent** 動 ①発明[考案]する ②ねつ造する

□ **invest** 動 投資する, (金・精力などを)注ぐ

□ **invisible** 名 目に見えないもの 形 目に見えない, 表に出ない

□ **invitation** 名 招待(状), 案内(状)

□ **invite** 動 ①招待する, 招く ②勧める, 誘う ③～をもたらす

□ **involve** 動 ①含む, 伴う ②巻き込む, かかわらせる

□ **involved** 形 ①巻き込まれている, 関連する ②入り組んだ, 込み入っている

□ **inward** 形 内部(へ)の, 内側(へ)の 副 内部[内側]へ

□ **Ireland** 名 アイルランド《国名》

□ **iron** 名 ①鉄, 鉄製のもの ②アイロン 形 鉄の, 鉄製の 動 アイロンをかける

□ **irritated** 形 イライラした, 怒った

□ **is** 動 be (～である)の3人称単数現在

□ **island** 名 島

□ **issue** 名 ①問題, 論点 ②発行物 ③出口, 流出 動 ①(～から)出る, 生じる ②発行する **issue of** 単一争点の, 一つの問題だけに焦点をしぼった

□ **it** 代 ①それは[が], それを[に] ②《天候・日時・距離・寒暖などを示す》 **It is ～ for someone to ...** (人)が…するのは～だ **It takes someone ～ to ...** (人)が…するのに～(時間など)がかかる

□ **Italian** 形 イタリア(人・語)の 名 ①イタリア人 ②イタリア語

□ **Italy** 名 イタリア《国名》

□ **item** 名 ①項目, 品目 ②(新聞などの)記事

□ **its** 代 それの, あれの

□ **itself** 代 それ自体, それ自身

J

□ **jailer** 名 看守

□ **James the Sixth of Scotland and the First of England** スコットランド王ジェームズ6世及びイングランド王ジェームズ1世

□ **Jaques le Grand, St.** 名 聖ジャック・ル・グラン《守護聖人》

□ **jaw** 名 ①あご ②《-s》あご状のもの **jaws of death** 死地

□ **jay** 名 カケス《鳥》

□ **jealous** 形 嫉妬して, 嫉妬深い, うらやんで

□ **jealousy** 名 嫉妬, ねたみ

□ **jeer** 動 あざける, ひやかす

□ **jest** 名 冗談, ふざけ 動 冗談を言う, からかう

□ **jester** 名 (中世の王侯や貴族に仕えた)道化師

□ **Jew** 名 ユダヤ人

□ **jewel** 名 宝石, 貴重な人[物] 動 宝石で飾る

□ **jeweler** 名 宝石商[職人]

□ **jewelry** 名 宝石, 宝飾品類

□ **Jewish** 形 ユダヤ人の, ユダヤ教の

□ **jingle** 名 チリンチリンと鳴る音

□ **join** 動 ①一緒になる, 参加する ②連結[結合]する, つなぐ 名 結合 **join in** 加わる, 参加する

□ **jointly** 副 合同で, 一緒に, 連帯して

□ **joke** 名 冗談, ジョーク 動 冗談を言う, ふざける, からかう **practical joke** 悪ふざけ, いたずら

□ **journey** 名 ①(遠い目的地への)旅 ②行程

□ **joy** 名 喜び, 楽しみ

□ **joyful** 形 楽しませる, 喜びに満ちた

□ **joyfully** 副 うれしそうに, 喜んで

□ **joyous** 形 うれしい, 喜びに満ちた

□ **judge** 動 判決を下す, 裁く, 判断する, 評価する 名 裁判官, 判事, 審査員

□ **judgment** 名 ①判断, 意見 ②裁判, 判決

□ **juice** 名 ジュース, 液, 汁

□ **Juliet** 名 ジュリエット《主人公。キャピュレットの娘》

□ **Julio Romano** 名 ジュリオ・ロマーノ《イタリアの建築家》

□ **jump** 動 ①跳ぶ, 跳躍する, 飛び越える, 飛びかかる ②(～を)熱心にやり始める 名 ①跳躍

②急騰, 急転 **jump around** 跳び回る **jump into** ～に飛び込む

□ **Jupiter** 名 ジュピター《ローマ神話の神》

□ **just** 形 正しい, もっともな, 当然な 副 ①まさに, ちょうど, (～した)ばかり ②ほんの, 単に, ただ～だけ ③ちょっと **just as** (ちょうど)であろうとおり **just in time** いよいよというときに, すんでのところで, やっと間に合って **just then** そのとたんに

□ **justice** 名 ①公平, 公正, 正当, 正義 ②司法, 裁判(官)

□ **jutting** 形 突き出た

K

□ **Kate** 名 ケイト《キャサリンの別名》

□ **Kate the Cursed** 呪われたケイト

□ **Katharine** 名 キャサリン《バプティスタの長女, じゃじゃ馬》

□ **Katharine the Shrew** じゃじゃ馬キャサリン

□ **keen** 形 ①鋭い, 鋭敏な ②熱心な **be keen to** ～したがる

□ **keep** 動 ①とっておく, 保つ, 続ける ②(～を…に)しておく ③飼う, 養う ④経営する ⑤守る **keep an eye on** ～から目を離さない **keep one's promise** 約束を守る **keep pace with** ～と歩調をそろえる **keep safe** 守護する **keep to** ～から離れない, ～を守る **keep up** 続ける, 続く, 維持する, (遅れないで)ついていく, 上げたままにしておく

□ **keeper** 名 保護者, 後見人

□ **Kent** 名 ケント《地名》

□ **kept** 動 keep(とっておく)の過去, 過去分詞

□ **kick** 動 ける, キックする 名 けること

□ **kill** 動 殺す, 消す, 枯らす 名 殺すこと

□ **killing** 名 殺害, 殺人 形 ①人を殺す, 植物を枯らす ②死ぬほどくたびれる

□ **kilometer** 名 キロメートル《長さの単位》

□ **kind** 形 親切な, 優しい 名 種類 **all kinds of** さまざまな, あらゆる種類の **be kind to** ～に親切である **be very kind of you** ～してくださってありがとう **kind of** ある程度, いくらか, ～のようなもの[人]

□ **kind-hearted** 形 心の優しい[温かい], 思いやりのある

□ **kindly** 形 ①親切な, 情け深い, 思いやりのある ②(気候などの)温和な, 快い 副 親切に, 優しく

□ **kindness** 名 親切(な行為), 優しさ

□ **king** 名 王, 国王

□ **King Hamlet** 名 先王ハムレット《先代のデンマーク王。ハムレットの父》

□ **King of France** 名 フランス王

□ **kingdom** 名 王国

□ **kiss** 名 キス 動 キスする **kiss the ground** 平伏する

□ **kitchen** 名 台所, 調理場

□ **knee** 名 ひざ

□ **kneel** 動 ひざまずく, ひざをつく

□ **knelt** 動 kneel(ひざまずく)の過去, 過去分詞

□ **knew** 動 know(知っている)の過去

□ **knife** 名 ナイフ, 小刀, 包丁, 短剣

□ **knight** 名 騎士, ナイト爵位の人

□ **knit** 動 編む, 編み物をする **knit one's brow** 眉を寄せる

□ **knitter** 名 編む人

□ **knock** 動 ノックする, たたく, ぶつける 名 打つこと, 戸をたたくこと[音]

□ **know** 動 ①知っている, 知る, (～が)わかる, 理解している ②知り合いである **as you know** ご存知のとおり **know no bounds** 際限がない **know of** ～について知っている **you know** ご存知のとおり, そうでしょう

□ **knowledge** 名 知識, 理解, 学問

□ **known** 動 know(知っている)の過去分詞 形 知られた **be known as** ～として知られている **be known to** ～に知られている

L

□ **labor** 名 労働, 骨折り 動 ①働く, 努力する, 骨折る ②苦しむ, 悩む **manual labor** 肉体労働

□ **lack** 動 不足している, 欠けている 名 不足, 欠乏

□ **lacking** 形 不足している, 欠けている **be lacking in** ～が足りない

□ **ladder** 名 はしご, はしご状のもの

□ **lady** 名 婦人, 夫人, 淑女, 奥さん

□ **Lady Capulet** キャピュレット夫人《キャピュレットの妻》

□ **Lady Montague** モンタギュー夫人《モンタギューの妻》

□ **lady-in-waiting** 名 (女王の)女官

□ **Laertes** 名 レアティーズ《オフィーリアの兄》

□ **Lafeu** 名ラフュー《老貴族》
□ **laid** 動lay（置く）の過去，過去分詞
□ **lamb** 名①子羊（の肉）②おとなしい人
□ **lament** 動嘆き悲しむ 名悲嘆
□ **lamentable** 形悲しむべき，嘆かわしい
□ **land** 名①陸地，土地 ②国，領域 動上陸する，着地する
□ **landing** 名①上陸，着陸 ②荷揚げ（場）③（階段の）踊り場
□ **language** 名言語，言葉，国語，～語，専門語
□ **lantern** 名手提げランプ，ランタン
□ **large** 形①大きい，広い ②大勢の，多量の 副①大きく ②自慢して
□ **lark** 名①ヒバリ（雲雀）《鳥》②浮かれ，たわむれ，冗談 動たわむれる，ふざける
□ **last** 形①《the –》最後の ②この前の，先～ ③最新の 副①最後に ②この前 名《the –》最後（のもの），終わり 動続く，持ちこたえる **at last** ついに，とうとう **at long last** やっとのことで
□ **late** 形①遅い，後期の ②最近の ③《the –》故～ 副①遅れて，遅く ②最近まで，以前
□ **late Earl of Gloucester** 故グロスター伯《エドガーとエドマンドの父》
□ **lately** 副近ごろ，最近
□ **later** 形もっと遅い，もっと後の 副後で，後ほど
□ **latest** 形①最新の，最近の ②最も遅い 副最も遅く，最後に
□ **Latin** 名①ラテン語 ②ラテン系民族の人 形ラテン（語・系）の
□ **laugh** 動笑う **laugh at** ～を見て［聞いて］笑う **make someone laugh**（人）を笑わせる 名笑い（声）
□ **laughter** 名笑い（声）
□ **launch** 動①（ロケットなどを）打ち上げる，発射する ②進水させる ③（事業などを）始める
□ **law** 名①法，法律 ②弁護士業，訴訟
□ **lawful** 形合法な
□ **lawfully** 副合法的に，適法に
□ **lawyer** 名弁護士，法律家
□ **lay** 動①置く，横たえる，敷く ②整える ③卵を産む ④lie（横たわる）の過去
□ **lazy** 形怠惰な，無精な
□ **le** 冠フランス語で「男性名詞の単数形」を表す定冠詞
□ **lead** 動①導く，案内する ②（生活を）送る 名①鉛 ②先導，指導 **lead someone by the nose**（人）を思うままに操る **lead to** ～に至る，～に通じる，～を引き起こす
□ **leader** 名指導者，リーダー
□ **leaf** 名葉
□ **leant** 動lean（もたれる）の過去，過去分詞
□ **leap** 動①跳ぶ ②跳び越える 名跳ぶこと
□ **leapt** 動leap（跳ぶ）の過去，過去分詞
□ **Lear** 名リア王《ブリテン王》
□ **learn** 動学ぶ，習う，教わる，知識［経験］を得る
□ **least** 形いちばん小さい，最も少ない 副いちばん小さく，最も少なく 名最小，最少 **at least** 少なくとも
□ **leather** 名皮革，皮製品
□ **leave** 動①出発する，去る ②残す，置き忘れる ③（～を…の）ままにしておく ④ゆだねる 名①休暇 ②許可 ③別れ **leave behind** あとにする，～を置き去りにする **leave in** ～をそのままにしておく **leave out** 抜かす，除外する **leave ～ alone** ～をそっとしておく **leave ～ for ...** …を～のために残しておく **make someone leave** 退校［職］させる
□ **leaves** 名leaf（葉）の複数 動leave（出発する）の3人称単数現在
□ **led** 動lead（導く）の過去，過去分詞
□ **left** 名《the –》左，左側 形左の，左側の 副左に，左側に 動leave（去る，～をあとに残す）の過去，過去分詞
□ **leg** 名①脚，すね ②支柱
□ **legacy** 名遺産，遺贈品
□ **legal** 形法律（上）の，正当な
□ **leisure** 名余暇 形余暇の **at leisure** 暇で，ゆっくり
□ **lend** 動貸す，貸し出す **lend out** 貸し出す
□ **length** 名長さ，縦，たけ，距離 **at length** ついに，長々と，詳しく
□ **lengthy** 形非常に長い，長ったらしい
□ **lenient** 形（犯罪などに対して）情け深い，大目に見る
□ **lent** 動lend（貸す）の過去，過去分詞
□ **Leonato** 名レオナート《メッシーナの知事》
□ **Leontes** 名レオンティーズ《シチリア王》
□ **less** 形～より小さい［少ない］ 副～より少なく，～ほどでなく **much less** まして～でない
□ **lesser** 形小さいほうの，劣ったほうの 副より少なく
□ **let** 動（人に～）させる，（～するのを）許す，（～をある状態に）する **Let me see.** ええと。

let us どうか私たちに～させてください

□ **letter** 名 ①手紙 ②文字 ③文学, 文筆業

□ **level** 名 ①水平, 平面 ②水準 形 ①水平の, 平たい ②同等［同位］の 動 ①水平にする ②平等にする

□ **levy** 名 徴収, (税金などの)取りたて

□ **liar** 名 うそつき

□ **liberty** 名 ①自由, 解放 ②《-ties》特権, 特典 ③《-ties》勝手な振る舞い

□ **lid** 名 (箱, なべなどの)ふた

□ **lie** 動 ①うそをつく ②横たわる, 寝る ③(ある状態に)ある, 存在する 名 うそ, 詐欺 **lie down** 横たわる, 横になる **tell a lie** うそをつく

□ **lieutenant** 名 ①中尉, 少尉 ②代理, 副官

□ **life** 名 ①生命, 生物 ②一生, 生涯, 人生 ③生活, 暮らし, 世の中 **for the rest of life** 死ぬまで **way of life** 生き様, 生き方, 暮らし方

□ **lifeboat** 名 ①救命ボート ②援助基金

□ **lifeless** 形 ①生物の住まない ②生命のない ③活力のない

□ **lift** 動 ①持ち上げる, 上がる ②取り除く, 撤廃する 名 ①持ち上げること ②エレベーター, リフト

□ **light** 名 光, 明かり 動 火をつける, 照らす, 明るくする 形 ①明るい ②(色が)薄い, 淡い ③軽い, 容易な ④(頭などが)ボーッとした, ぼんやりした 副 軽く, 容易に

□ **light-hearted** 形 気楽な, 快活な

□ **lightly** 副 ①軽く, そっと ②軽率に

□ **lightning** 名 電光, 雷, 稲妻

□ **like** 動 好む, 好きである 前 ～に似ている, ～のような 形 似ている, ～のような 接 あたかも～のように **feel like** ～がほしい, ～したい気がする, ～のような感じがする **like this** このような, こんなふうに **look like** ～のように見える, ～に似ている **rather like** ～に似ている, きらいはでない **sound like** ～のように聞こえる **would like** ～がほしい **would like to** ～したいと思う **Would you like ～?** ～はいかがですか。

□ **likely** 形 ①ありそうな, (～)しそうな ②適当な 副 たぶん, おそらく

□ **likeness** 名 (～に)よく似ていること

□ **liking** 名 好み, 趣味

□ **limb** 名 ①手足, 四肢 ②大枝

□ **limp** 動 ①足を引きずって歩く ②のろのろ進む 名 足を引きずって歩くこと 形 ①ぐにゃぐにゃした ②弱々しい

□ **line** 名 ①線, 糸, 電話線 ②(字の)行 ③列, (電車の)～線 動 ①線を引く ②整列する **in line** 一列に **line of** ～の系統, 血筋

□ **link** 名 ①(鎖の)輪 ②リンク ③相互［因果］関係 動 連結する, つながる

□ **lion** 名 ライオン

□ **lioness** 名 雌ライオン

□ **lip** 名 唇, 《-s》口

□ **liquid** 名 液体 形 ①液体(状)の, 流動する ②流ちょうな ③澄んだ ④不安定な

□ **list** 名 名簿, 目録, 一覧表 動 名簿［目録］に記入する

□ **listen** 動 《－to ～》～を聞く, ～に耳を傾ける

□ **little** 形 ①小さい, 幼い ②少しの, 短い ③ほとんど～ない, 《a－》少しはある 名 少し(しか), 少量 副 全然～ない, 《a－》少しはある

□ **live** 動 住む, 暮らす, 生きている 形 生きている, 生きた **Long live ～!** ～万歳! **there lived ～.** ～が住んでいました。

□ **lively** 形 ①元気のよい, 活発な ②鮮やかな, 強烈な, 真に迫った

□ **lives** 名 life(生命)の複数

□ **living** 名 生計, 生活 形 ①生きている, 現存の ②使用されている ③そっくりの

□ **lizard** 名 トカゲ(蜥蜴)

□ **load** 名 (重い)荷, 積荷, (心の)重荷 動 (荷を)積む

□ **loathe** 動 大嫌いである, ひどく嫌う

□ **local** 形 ①地方の, ある場所［土地］の, 部分的な ②各駅停車の 名 ある特定の地方のもの

□ **location** 名 位置, 場所

□ **lock** 名 錠(前) 動 錠を下ろす, 閉じ込める, 動けなくする **lock up** ～を閉じ込める

□ **lodge** 名 ①番小屋 ②山小屋 動 泊まる, 泊める, 下宿する［させる］

□ **log** 名 ①丸太 ②(航海)日誌 動 ①伐採する ②記録する

□ **log-carrying** 形 丸太運び

□ **log-man** 名 丸太運び人

□ **long** 形 ①長い, 長期の ②《長さ・距離・時間などを示す語句を伴って》～の長さ［距離・時間］の 副 長い間, ずっと 名 長い期間 動 切望する, 思い焦がれる **as long as** ～する以上は, ～である限りは **at long last** やっとのことで **before long** やがて, まもなく **for long** 長い間 **long ago** ずっと前に, 昔 **Long live ～!** ～万歳! **no longer** もはや～でない［～しない］ **so long as** ～する限りは **wait a long time** 長時間待つ

□ **long-lost** 形 長い間行方不明だった

□ **long-separated** 形 長い間離れていた

□ **longstanding** 形 長く続いている

□ **long-suffering** 形（人が苦痛などに耐え続けて）我慢［辛抱］強い

□ **look** 動 ①見る ②（～に）見える，（～の）顔つきをする ③注意する ④《間投詞のように》ほら，ねえ 名 ①一見，目つき ②外観，外見，様子 **look after** ～の世話をする，～に気をつける **look around** まわりを見回す **look back at** ～に視線を戻す，～を振り返って見る **look down** 見下ろす **look for** ～を探す **look forward to** ～を期待する **look into** ①～を検討する，～を研究する ②～の中を見る，～をのぞき込む **look like** ～のように見える，～に似ている **look on** 傍観する，眺める **look out** ①外を見る ②気をつける，注意する **look out of**（窓などから）外を見る **look over** ～越しに見る，～を見渡す **look up** 見上げる，調べる **look up to** ～を仰ぎ見る **look upon** ～を見る，見つめる

□ **loose** 形 自由な，ゆるんだ，あいまいな 動 ほどく，解き放つ **break loose**（人が監禁状態から）逃げ出す

□ **loosen** 動 ①ゆるめる，ほどく ②解き放つ

□ **lord** 名 首長，主人，領主，貴族，上院議員

□ **Lord Capulet** キャピュレット卿《キャピュレット家の家長》

□ **Lord Montague** モンタギュー卿《モンタギュー家の家長》

□ **lordship** 名 ①君主の地位，領地 ②《L-》閣下

□ **Lorenzo** 名 ロレンゾ《シャイロックの娘の夫でアントーニオの友人》

□ **lose** 動 ①失う，迷う，忘れる ②負ける，失敗する **lose one's way** 道に迷う **lose sight of** ～を見失う

□ **loss** 名 ①損失（額・物），損害，浪費 ②失敗，敗北

□ **lost** 動 lose（失う）の過去，過去分詞 形 ①失った，負けた ②道に迷った，困った ③没頭している

□ **lot** 名 ①くじ，運 ②地所，区画 ③たくさん，たいへん，《a – of ～ / -s of ～》たくさんの～ ④やつ，連中

□ **loud** 形 大声の，騒がしい 副 大声に［で］

□ **loudly** 副 大声で，騒がしく

□ **love** 名 愛，愛情，思いやり 動 愛する，恋する，大好きである **be in love with** ～に恋して，～に心を奪われて **fall in love** 恋におちる **fall in love with** 恋におちる

□ **love-charm** 名 恋の魔法

□ **Love-in-Idleness** 名 野生の3色スミレ《植物》

□ **love-juice** 名 愛の汁

□ **lovely** 形 愛らしい，美しい，すばらしい

□ **lover** 名 ①愛人，恋人 ②愛好者

□ **lovesick** 形 恋に悩む

□ **love-song** 名 恋歌

□ **loving** 形 愛する，愛情のこもった

□ **low** 形 ①低い，弱い ②低級の，劣等な 副 低く 名 ①低い水準［点］ ②低速ギア

□ **low-born** 形 生まれの卑しい

□ **lowly** 形 卑しい

□ **loyal** 形 忠実な，誠実な 名 忠実，愛国者

□ **loyalty** 名 忠義，忠誠

□ **Lucentio** 名 ルーセンシオ《ビアンカの求婚者》

□ **Luciana** 名 ルシアーナ《エイドリアーナの妹》

□ **Lucianus** 名 ルシアーナス《劇中劇に登場する人物》

□ **luck** 名 運，幸運，めぐり合わせ

□ **luckily** 副 運よく，幸いにも

□ **lucky** 形 幸運な，運のよい，縁起のよい

□ **lulla** 名 詩のリズムを作るために使われる言葉

□ **lullaby** 名 子守歌

□ **lunacy** 名 ①狂気，精神錯乱 ②目に余る愚かさ，ひどく軽率な行為，暴挙

□ **lunatic** 形 ①（ひどく）愚かな ②気の狂った，狂気の

□ **lute** 名 リュート《楽器》

□ **lying** 動 lie（うそをつく・横たわる）の現在分詞 形 ①うそをつく，虚偽の ②横になっている 名 ①うそをつくこと，虚言，虚偽 ②横たわること

□ **Lysander** 名 ライサンダー《ハーミアの恋人》

M

□ **Macbeth** 名 マクベス《ダンカン王の臣下で，スコットランドの将軍》

□ **Macduff** 名 マクダフ《スコットランドの貴族，ファイフの領主》

□ **mad** 形 ①気の狂った ②逆上した，理性をなくした ③ばかげた ④（～に）熱狂［熱中］して，夢中の **go mad** 発狂する

□ **madam** 名《ていねいな呼びかけ》奥様，お嬢様

□ **made** 動 make（作る）の過去，過去分詞 形 作った，作られた **be made of** ～でできて［作られて］いる **have something made** ～を作らせる

☐ **madman** 名 ①狂人 ②常軌を逸した人
☐ **madness** 名 狂気, 熱中
☐ **magic** 名 ①魔法, 手品 ②魔力 形 魔法の, 魔力のある
☐ **magical** 形 ①魔法の力による ②魅惑的な
☐ **magician** 名 魔法使い, 奇術師, マジシャン
☐ **magistrate** 名 判事
☐ **maid** 名 お手伝い, メイド
☐ **maid-of-honor** 名 (女王・王女に仕える未婚の) 女官
☐ **main** 形 主な, 主要な
☐ **majesty** 名 ①威厳, 壮麗さ ②《M-》陛下
☐ **major** 形 ①大きいほうの, 主な, 一流の ②年長[古参]の 名 ①陸軍少佐 ②専攻科目 動 専攻する
☐ **make** 動 ①作る, 得る ②行う, (〜に) なる ③(〜を…に) する, (〜を…) させる **make a face at** 〜にしかめっ面をする **make a fool of** 〜をばかにする **make a mistake** 間違いをする **make a mouth at** 〜に向かってしかめっ面をする **make a speech** 演説をする **make a vow** 誓いを立てる **make amends** 償いをする **make fun of** 〜を物笑いの種にする, からかう **make it** 実現する **make one's way** 進む, 行く, 成功する **make 〜 out of ...** 〜を…から作る **make someone laugh** (人) を笑わせる **make someone leave** 退校[職] させる **make sure** 確かめる, 確認する **make way** 道を譲る[あける], 前進する
☐ **malady** 名 病気, 弊害
☐ **Malcolm** 名 マルカム《ダンカンの長男》
☐ **male** 形 男の, 雄の 名 男, 雄
☐ **malice** 名 悪意, 敵意
☐ **Mamillius** 名 マミリアス《レオンティーズとハーマイオニーの息子》
☐ **man** 名 男性, 人, 人類 **changed man** 別人
☐ **manage** 動 ①動かす, うまく処理する ②経営[管理]する, 支配する ③どうにか〜する
☐ **management** 名 ①経営, 取り扱い ②運営, 管理 (側)
☐ **man-eater** 名 人食い人種
☐ **manliness** 名 男らしさ
☐ **manly** 形 ①男らしい, 断固とした ②男のような
☐ **manner** 名 ①方法, やり方 ②態度, 様子 ③《-s》行儀, 作法, 生活様式
☐ **mansion** 名 ①大邸宅 ②《〜 M-s》〜アパート, 〜マンション
☐ **Mantua** 名 マントヴァ《イタリアの都市》
☐ **Mantuan** 名 マントヴァの
☐ **manual** 形 肉体の, 手作業の **manual labor** 肉体労働
☐ **many** 形 多数の, たくさんの 代 多数(の人・物) **so many** 非常に多くの
☐ **map** 名 地図 動 ①地図を作る ②計画を立てる
☐ **marble-hearted** 形 (人の心が) 大理石 (marble) のように冷たい, 冷酷な
☐ **march** 名 ①行進 ②《M-》3月 動 行進する[させる], 進展する
☐ **Margaret** 名 マーガレット《ヒーローの侍女》
☐ **mark** 名 ①印, 記号, 跡 ②点数 ③特色 ④マルク《お金の単位》 動 ①印[記号]をつける ②採点する ③目立たせる
☐ **market** 名 市場, マーケット, 取引, 需要 動 市場に出す
☐ **marriage** 名 ①結婚 (生活・式) ②結合, 融合, (吸収) 合併
☐ **married** 形 結婚した, 既婚の
☐ **marry** 動 結婚する
☐ **Mars** 名 マルス《ローマ神話の神》
☐ **mask** 名 面, マスク 動 マスクをつける
☐ **masked** 形 マスク[仮面・覆面]をかぶった
☐ **mast** 名 マスト, 帆柱 動 マストをつける
☐ **master** 名 主人, 雇い主, 師, 名匠 動 ①修得する ②〜の主となる
☐ **match** 名 ①試合, 勝負 ②相手, 釣り合うもの ③マッチ (棒) ④縁談, 結婚相手 動 ①〜に匹敵する ②調和する, 釣り合う ③(〜を…と) 勝負させる
☐ **matchless** 形 無比の, 比類のない
☐ **matrimony** 名 結婚式
☐ **matter** 名 物, 事, 事件, 問題 動《主に疑問文・否定文で》重要である **a matter of** 〜の問題
☐ **may** 助 ①〜かもしれない ②〜してもよい, 〜できる 名《M-》5月 **May I 〜?** 〜してもよいですか。
☐ **maybe** 副 たぶん, おそらく
☐ **me** 代 私を[に] **Let me see.** ええと。
☐ **meal** 名 ①食事 ②ひいた粉, あらびき粉
☐ **mean** 動 ①意味する ②(〜のつもりで) 言う, 意図する ③〜するつもりである 形 ①卑怯な, けちな, 意地悪な ②中間の 名 中間, 中位
☐ **meaning** 名 ①意味, 趣旨 ②重要性 **double meaning** 二重の意味
☐ **meaningless** 形 無意味な, つまらない
☐ **means** 名 ①方法, 手段 ②資力, 財力 **by all**

means なんとしても，ぜひとも **by no means** 決して～ではない **means of** ～する手段

□ **meant** 動 mean（意味する）の過去，過去分詞

□ **meantime** 名 合間，その間 副 その間に **in the meantime** それまでは，当分は

□ **meanwhile** 副 それまでの間，一方では

□ **measure** 動 ①測る，（～の）寸法がある ②評価する 名 ①寸法，測定，計量，単位 ②程度，基準 **measure out** 測り分ける

□ **meat** 名 ①肉 ②要点，内容

□ **meddling** 形 おせっかいな，邪魔をする

□ **mediate** 動 調停［仲裁］をする

□ **mediation** 名 調停

□ **medicine** 名 ①薬 ②医学，内科

□ **meditate** 動 深く考える，瞑想する

□ **Mediterranean** 形 地中海（沿岸）の 名《the M-》地中海

□ **meek** 形 ①おとなしい，従順な ②意気地のない

□ **meekly** 副 おとなしく，柔順に，素直に

□ **meet** 動 ①会う，知り合いになる ②合流する，交わる ③（条件などに）達する，合う **meet with** ～に出会う

□ **meeting** 名 ①集まり，ミーティング，面会 ②競技会

□ **melancholy** 形 もの悲しい，憂うつな，ふさぎ込んだ 形 哀愁，憂うつ，うつ病

□ **melodious** 形（声や音が）耳に心地良い

□ **melt** 動 ①溶ける，溶かす ②（感情が）和らぐ，次第に消え去る

□ **member** 名 一員，メンバー

□ **memory** 名 記憶（力），思い出 **in memory of** ～の記念として

□ **men** 名 man（男性）の複数

□ **Menaphon** 名 メナフォン公《有名な軍人。エフェソス公のおじ》

□ **mental** 形 ①心の，精神の ②知能［知性］の

□ **mention** 動（～について）述べる，言及する 名 言及，陳述

□ **merchant** 名 商人，貿易商

□ **merciful** 形 慈悲深い

□ **merciless** 形 無慈悲な

□ **mercury** 名 ①水銀，水銀柱 ②《M-》水星

□ **Mercutio** 名 マーキューシオ《ロミオの友人》

□ **mercy** 名 ①情け，哀れみ，慈悲 ②ありがたいこと，幸運 **at one's mercy** ～のなすがままになって

□ **mere** 形 単なる，ほんの，まったく～にすぎない

□ **merely** 副 単に，たかが～に過ぎない

□ **merit** 名 価値，長所，メリット 動 値する，価値がある

□ **merrily** 副 楽しく，愉快に，陽気に

□ **merry** 形 陽気な，愉快な，快活な

□ **message** 名 伝言，（作品などに込められた）メッセージ 動 メッセージで送る，伝える

□ **Messaline** 名 メサリーン《架空の国》

□ **messenger** 名 使者，（伝言・小包などの）配達人，伝達者

□ **Messina** 名 メッシーナ《イタリアの都市》

□ **messy** 形 散らかった，汚い

□ **met** 動 meet（会う）の過去，過去分詞

□ **Mexico** 名 メキシコ《国名》

□ **Michael Cassio** マイケル・キャシオー《オセローの副官》

□ **middle** 名 中間，最中 形 中間の，中央の **in the middle of** ～の真ん中［中ほど］に

□ **midnight** 名 夜の12時，真夜中，暗黒 形 真夜中の，真っ暗な

□ **midst** 名 真ん中，中央

□ **midsummer** 名 ①真夏 ②夏至

□ **might** 助《mayの過去》①～かもしれない ②～してもよい，～できる 名 力，権力

□ **mighty** 形 強力な，権勢のある

□ **Milan** 名 ミラノ《イタリアの都市》

□ **mild** 形 柔和な，温和な，口あたりのよい，穏やかな

□ **mildly** 副 ①優しく，穏やかに ②少し

□ **mildness** 名 温和，温厚

□ **mile** 名 ①マイル《長さの単位。1,609m》②《-s》かなりの距離

□ **military** 形 軍隊［軍人］の，軍事の 名《the –》軍，軍部

□ **milk** 名 牛乳，ミルク 動 乳をしぼる

□ **mind** 名 ①心，精神，考え ②知性 動 ①気にする，いやがる ②気をつける，用心する **frame of mind** 考え方，精神状態

□ **mine** 代 私のもの 名 鉱山 動 採掘する，坑道を掘る

□ **minister** 名 ①大臣，閣僚，公使 ②聖職者

□ **minute** 名 ①（時間の）分 ②ちょっとの間 形 ごく小さい，細心の

□ **miracle** 名 奇跡（的な出来事），不思議なこと

□ **miraculously** 副 驚異的に，奇跡的に

□ **Miranda** 名ミランダ《プロスペローの娘》
□ **mirth** 名陽気, 浮かれ騒ぎ
□ **mischief** 名いたずら, (損)害
□ **mischief-maker** 名人の仲を裂く人
□ **mischievous** 形いたずらな
□ **miserable** 形みじめな, 哀れな
□ **misery** 名①悲惨, みじめさ ②苦痛, 不幸, 苦難
□ **misfortune** 名不運, 不幸, 災難
□ **miss** 動①失敗する, 免れる, ～を見逃す, (目標を)はずす ②(～が)ないのに気づく, (人が)いなくてさびしく思う 名①はずれ, 失敗 ②《M-》《女性に対して》～さん, ～先生
□ **missing** 形欠けている, 行方不明の 名《the –》行方不明者
□ **mission** 名①使命, 任務 ②使節団, 代表団, 派遣団 ③伝道, 布教
□ **mistake** 名誤り, 誤解, 間違い 動間違える, 誤解する **make a mistake** 間違いをする
□ **mistaken** 動mistake (間違える) の過去分詞 形誤った
□ **mistakenly** 副間違って, 誤解して
□ **mistress** 名①愛人, 恋人 ②女主人, 女性の支配者, 女性の先生
□ **misty** 形霧の(深い), かすんだ
□ **misunderstanding** 名考え違い, 誤解
□ **mix** 動①混ざる, 混ぜる ②(～を)一緒にする 名混合(物) **mix in** 混入する, よく混ぜ合わせる
□ **mixed** 形①混合の, 混ざった ②男女共学の
□ **moan** 名うめき声, 不平 動うめき声を出す
□ **mock** 動①あざける, まねをしてからかう ②だます, 無効にする 形うわべの, まがいの, 模擬の
□ **modest** 形控えめな, 謙虚な
□ **modesty** 名謙遜, 謙虚さ, つつましさ, しとやかさ
□ **mold** 名①型, 鋳型 ②特徴 ③かび 動①型に入れて作る, 形成する ②かびさせる, かびる
□ **moment** 名①瞬間, ちょっとの間 ②(特定の)時, 時期 **at any moment** 今すぐにも **at that moment** その時に, その瞬間に **for a moment** 少しの間 **for the moment** 差し当たり, 当座は **one moment** ちょっとの間
□ **monarch** 名君主
□ **monastery** 名修道院, 僧院
□ **money** 名金, 通貨
□ **money-lender** 名(高利)金貸し
□ **money-lending** 名(高利)金貸し
□ **monkey** 名サル(猿) 動ふざける, いたずらをする
□ **monster** 名怪物
□ **Montague** 名モンタギュー《ロミオの家の家名》
□ **Montano** 名モンターノ《将校》
□ **month** 名月, 1カ月
□ **monument** 名記念碑, 記念物
□ **mood** 名気分, 機嫌, 雰囲気, 憂うつ
□ **moon** 名月, 月光
□ **moonlight** 名月明かり, 月光
□ **moor** 名原野, 沼地 動停泊する［させる］
□ **more** 形①もっと多くの ②それ以上の, 余分の 副もっと, さらに多く, いっそう **more of** ～よりもっと **more than** ～以上 **no more** もう～ない **no more than** ただの～にすぎない **not ～ any more** もう［これ以上］～ない **once more** もう一度 **the more ～ the more …** ～すればするほどますます…
□ **moreover** 副その上, さらに
□ **morning** 名朝, 午前 **one morning** ある朝
□ **morsel** 名(食物の)ひと口, 一片
□ **mortal** 形①死ぬ運命にある ②人間の ③致命的な 名①死すべきもの ②人間
□ **moss** 名コケ《植物》
□ **most** 形①最も多い ②たいていの, 大部分の 代①大部分, ほとんど ②最多数, 最大限 副最も(多く)
□ **mostly** 副主として, 多くは, ほとんど
□ **Moth** 名蛾《妖精》
□ **mother** 名母, 母親
□ **mother-in-law** 名義母
□ **motion** 名①運動, 移動 ②身振り, 動作 ③(機械の)運転 動身振りで合図する
□ **motive** 名動機, 目的, モチーフ
□ **mountain** 名①山 ②《the ～ M-s》～山脈 ③山のようなもの, 多量
□ **mourn** 動悲しむ, 悼む, 喪に服す
□ **mournful** 形悲しい, 哀れを誘う, 陰気な
□ **mourning** 名①悲嘆, 哀悼 ②服喪, 哀悼の意を表すこと
□ **mousetrap** 名ネズミ捕り
□ **mouth** 名①口 ②言葉, 発言 **make a mouth at** ～に向かってしかめっ面をする
□ **move** 動①動く, 動かす ②感動させる ③引っ越す, 移動する 名①動き, 運動 ②転居, 移動

move on 先に進む **move someone to pity** (人)の哀れみを誘う **move to** ～に引っ越す

□ **moved** 形 感動[感激・感銘]する **be moved** 感激する, 感銘する

□ **moving** 形 ①動いている ②感動させる

□ **Mr.** 名《男性に対して》～さん, ～氏, ～先生

□ **much** 形 (量・程度が)多くの, 多量の 副 ①とても, たいへん ②《比較級・最上級を修飾して》ずっと, はるかに **as much as** ～と同じだけ **much less** まして～でない **too much** 過度の

□ **mud** 名 ①泥, ぬかるみ ②つまらぬもの

□ **muddy** 形 泥だらけの, ぬかるみの 動 泥まみれにする, 濁らせる

□ **mummy** 名 ①ママ, お母さん ②ミイラ

□ **murder** 名 人殺し, 殺害, 殺人事件 動 殺す

□ **murderer** 名 殺人犯

□ **murderous** 形 人殺しの, 凶悪な

□ **murmur** 動 囁く, ぶつぶつ言う 名 つぶやき, かすかな音

□ **music** 名 音楽, 楽曲

□ **musician** 名 音楽家

□ **musk-rose** 名 マスクローズ《植物》

□ **must** 助 ①～しなければならない ②～に違いない 名 絶対に必要なこと[もの]

□ **Mustardseed** 名 カラシの実《妖精》

□ **mutton** 名 羊肉, マトン

□ **mutual** 形 相互の, 共通の

□ **mutually** 副 相互に, 互いに

□ **my** 代 私の

□ **myself** 代 私自身

□ **mysterious** 形 神秘的な, 謎めいた

□ **mystery** 名 ①神秘, 不可思議 ②推理小説, ミステリー

N

□ **name** 名 ①名前 ②名声 ③《-s》悪口 動 ①名前をつける ②名指しする **by name** ～という名の, 名前で, 名前だけは

□ **nap** 名 昼寝, うたた寝 動 昼寝する, うたた寝する

□ **Naples** 名 ナポリ《イタリアの都市》

□ **nation** 名 国, 国家, 《the –》国民

□ **native** 形 ①出生(地)の, 自国の ②(～に)固有の, 生まれつきの, 天然の 名 (ある土地に)生まれた人

□ **natural** 形 ①自然の, 天然の ②生まれつきの, 天性の ③当然な

□ **naturally** 副 生まれつき, 自然に, 当然

□ **nature** 名 ①自然(界) ②天性, 性質 ③自然のまま, 実物 ④本質 **by nature** 生まれつき

□ **naughty** 形 (子どもが)いたずらな, 言うことを聞かない, わんぱくな

□ **near** 前 ～の近くに, ～のそばに 形 近い, 親しい 副 近くに, 親密で

□ **nearby** 形 近くの, 間近の 副 近くで, 間近で

□ **nearly** 副 ①近くに, 親しく ②ほとんど, あやうく

□ **neat** 形 きちんとした, きれいな

□ **necessary** 形 必要な, 必然の 名《-s》必要品, 必需品

□ **neck** 名 首, (衣服の)えり

□ **need** 動 (～を)必要とする, 必要である 助 ～する必要がある 名 ①必要(性), 《-s》必要なもの ②まさかの時 **in need** 必要で, 困って

□ **needle** 名 針, 針状のもの 動 針で縫う, 突き通す

□ **needless** 形 不必要な

□ **negative** 形 ①否定的な, 消極的な ②負の, マイナスの, (写真が)ネガの 名 ①否定, 反対 ②ネガ, 陰画, 負数, マイナス

□ **neglect** 動 ①無視する, 怠る ②放置する, 軽視する 名 無視, 軽視, 怠慢

□ **neglected** 形 おろそかにされた, 無視された

□ **negotiate** 動 交渉[協議]する

□ **neighborhood** 名 近所(の人々), 付近

□ **neighing** 形 いななく

□ **neither** 形 どちらの～も…でない 代 (2者のうち)どちらも～でない 副《否定文に続いて》～も…しない **neither ～ nor ...** ～も…もない

□ **nephew** 名 おい(甥)

□ **Nerissa** 名 ネリッサ《ポーシャの侍女》

□ **nest** 名 ①巣 ②居心地よい場所, 休憩所, 隠れ家 動 (鳥が)巣を作る

□ **net** 名 ①網, 網状のもの ②わな ③正味, 純益 形 正味の, 純益の 動 ①網でつかまえる ②純益を上げる

□ **nettle** 名 イラクサ《植物》

□ **never** 副 決して[少しも]～ない, 一度も[二度と]～ない **have never been to** ～に行ったことがない

□ **new** 形 ①新しい, 新規の ②新鮮な, できたての

□ **newly** 副 再び, 最近, 新たに

□ **newly-arrived** 形新入, 近着, 新着の

□ **newly-married** 形新婚の

□ **newly-weds** 名新婚夫婦

□ **news** 名報道, ニュース, 便り, 知らせ **breaking news** 最新ニュース, ニュース速報

□ **newt** 名イモリ

□ **next** 形①次の, 翌〜 ②隣の 副①次に ②隣に **next time** 次回に **next to** 〜のとなりに, 〜の次に

□ **nice** 形すてきな, よい, きれいな, 親切な

□ **niece** 名めい(姪)

□ **night** 名夜, 晩 **in the dead of the night** 真夜中に **the night before** 前の晩

□ **nightingale** 名①ナイチンゲール《鳥》②美しい声で歌う人

□ **nightmare** 名悪夢

□ **night-wandering** 形夜な夜な彷徨う

□ **nine** 名9(の数字), 9人[個] 形9の, 9人[個]の

□ **nip** 動①摘み取る, はさみで切り取る ②急いで行く 名ひとひねり, ひとつまみ

□ **no** 副①いいえ, いや ②少しも〜ない 形〜がない, 少しも〜ない, 〜どころでない, 〜禁止 名否定, 拒否 **be no bigger than** 〜ほどの大きさだ **by no means** 決して〜ではない **have no choice but to** 〜するしかない **have no idea** わからない **in no time** すぐに, 一瞬で **in no way** 決して〜でない **no doubt** きっと, たぶん **no longer** もはや〜でない[〜しない] **no more** もう〜ない **no more than** ただの〜にすぎない **no one** 誰も[一人も]〜ない **no sooner** 〜するや否や **there is no way** 〜する見込みはない

□ **nobility** 名①高貴さ ②《the –》貴族

□ **noble** 形気高い, 高貴な, りっぱな, 高貴な 名貴族

□ **nobleman** 名貴族, 高貴の生まれの人

□ **noble-spirited** 形気高い性格の

□ **nobly** 副立派に, 気高く

□ **nobody** 代誰も[1人も]〜ない

□ **nod** 動①うなずく, うなずいて〜を示す ②居眠りする 名①うなずき ②居眠り

□ **noise** 名騒音, 騒ぎ, 物音

□ **noisy** 形①騒々しい, やかましい ②けばけばしい

□ **none** 代(〜の)何も[誰も・少しも]…ない

□ **nonsense** 名ばかげたこと, ナンセンス

□ **non-stop** 形ノンストップの, (列車・飛行機などが)直通[直行]の, 休みなしの 名直通[直行]便, 直通列車[飛行機]　　副

□ **noon** 名①正午, 真昼 ②《the –》全盛期

□ **no-one** 代だれも…ない

□ **nor** 接〜もまたない **neither 〜 nor ...** 〜も…もない

□ **normal** 形普通の, 平均の, 標準的な 名平常, 標準, 典型

□ **north** 名《the –》北, 北部 形北の, 北からの 副北へ[に], 北から

□ **northern** 形北の, 北向きの, 北からの

□ **Norwegian** 形ノルウェー(人, 語)の 名①ノルウェー人 ②ノルウェー語

□ **nose** 名鼻, 嗅覚, におい **lead someone by the nose** (人)を思うままに操る

□ **not** 副〜でない, 〜しない **not always** 必ずしも〜であるとは限らない **not 〜 any more** もう[これ以上]〜ない **not at all** 少しも〜でない **not 〜 at all** 少しも[全然]〜ない **not 〜 but ...** 〜ではなくて… **not in any way** 少しも[全く]〜ない **not only 〜 but ...** 〜だけでなく…もまた **not quite** まったく〜だというわけではない **not yet** まだ〜してない **whether or not** 〜かどうか

□ **notable** 名著名人, 著名な事物 形注目に値する, 著名な, 重要な

□ **note** 名①メモ, 覚え書き ②注釈 ③注意, 注目 ④手形 動①書き留める ②注意[注目]する

□ **nothing** 代何も〜ない[しない] **nothing but** ただ〜だけ, 〜にすぎない, 〜のほかは何も…ない

□ **notice** 名①注意 ②通知 ③公告 動①気づく, 認める ②通告する

□ **nourish** 動栄養を与える, 養う

□ **novelty** 名①目新しさ, 新奇 ②目新しいもの, 新型商品

□ **now** 副①今(では), 現在 ②今すぐに ③では, さて 名今, 現在 形今の, 現在の **from now** 今から, これから **now that** 今や〜だから, 〜からには **right now** 今すぐに, たった今

□ **nowhere** 副どこにも〜ない

□ **number** 名①数, 数字, 番号 ②〜号, 〜番 ③《-s》多数 動番号をつける, 数える **a number of** いくつかの〜, 多くの〜

□ **nun** 名修道女, 尼僧

□ **nunnery** 名女子修道院

□ **nurse** 名①看護師[人] ②乳母 動①看病する ②あやす

□ **nut** 名木の実, ナッツ

O

□ **oath** 名 宣誓, 誓い

□ **obedience** 名 服従, 従順

□ **obedient** 形 従順な, 孝行な

□ **Oberon** 名 オーベロン《妖精の王》

□ **obey** 動 服従する, (命令などに) 従う

□ **object** 名 ①物, 事物 ②目的物, 対象 動 反対する, 異議を唱える

□ **obliging** 形 好意的な, 愛想のいい

□ **observation** 名 観察(力), 注目

□ **observe** 動 ①観察[観測]する, 監視[注視]する ②気づく ③守る, 遵守する

□ **observer** 名 観察者, オブザーバー

□ **obstinate** 形 強情な, 頑固な

□ **obtain** 動 ①得る, 獲得する ②一般に通用している

□ **obvious** 形 明らかな, 明白な

□ **obviously** 副 明らかに, はっきりと

□ **occasion** 名 ①場合, (特定の) 時 ②機会, 好機 ③理由, 根拠

□ **occupation** 名 ①職業, 仕事, 就業 ②占有, 居住, 占領

□ **occur** 動 (事が) 起こる, 生じる, (考えなどが) 浮かぶ

□ **ocean** 名 海, 大洋, 《the ~ O-》~洋

□ **o'clock** 副 ~時

□ **odd** 形 ①奇妙な ②奇数の ③(一対のうちの) 片方の

□ **of** 前 ①《所有・所属・部分》~の, ~に属する ②《性質・特徴・材料》~の, ~製の ③《部分》~のうち ④《分離・除去》~から **of one's own** 自分自身の **of which** ~の中で

□ **of course** もちろん, 当然

□ **off** 副 ①離れて ②はずれて ③止まって ④休んで 形 ①離れて ②季節はずれの ③休みの 前 ~を離れて, ~をはずれて, (値段が) ~引きの **come off** 取れる, はずれる **cut off** 切断する, 切り離す **doze off** うとうととする, うたた寝する **fall off** 落ちる, 落ち込む, 下落する, 減る, 衰退する **fly off** 飛び去る **go off** ①出かける, 去る, 出発する ②始める, 突然~しだす ③(電気が) 消える **pay off** ①支払う ②期待の成果をあげる, (大) もうけになる **put off** ~から逃れる, 延期する, 要求をそらす, 不快にさせる, やめさせる **run off** 走り去る, 逃げ去る **set off** 出発する, 発射する **take off** (衣服を) 脱ぐ, 取り去る, ~を取り除く, 離陸する, 出発する **tell off** (人) をしかりつける **throw off** 脱ぎ捨てる

□ **offense** 名 ①違反, 犯罪 ②感情を傷つけること, 気にさわること, 不快

□ **offer** 動 申し出る, 申し込む, 提供する 名 提案, 提供

□ **office** 名 ①会社, 事務所, 職場, 役所, 局 ②官職, 地位, 役

□ **officer** 名 役人, 公務員, 警察官

□ **official** 形 ①公式の, 正式の ②職務上の, 公の 名 公務員, 役人, 職員

□ **often** 副 しばしば, たびたび **how often** 何回~ですか

□ **oh** 間 ああ, おや, まあ

□ **old** 形 ①年取った, 老いた ②~歳の ③古い, 昔の 名 昔, 老人 **old age** 老後

□ **Oliver** 名 オリバー《ド・ボイズ家の長男》

□ **Olivia** 名 オリヴィア《イリリアの伯爵令嬢》

□ **omen** 名 前兆, 兆し

□ **on** 前 ①《場所・接触》~(の上) に ②《日・時》~に, ~と同時に, ~のすぐ後で ③《関係・従事》~に関して, ~について, ~して 副 ①身につけて, 上に ②前へ, 続けて **on behalf of** ~のために, ~に代わって **on board** (乗り物などに) 乗って, 搭乗して **on one's own** 自力で **on one's way** 途中で **on one's way home** 帰り道で **on one's way to** ~に行く途中で **on pain of death** 違反すると死刑に処す条件で **on purpose** わざと, 故意に **on shore** 陸に, 上陸して **on someone's account** (人) のために **on the ground** 地面に **on the other hand** 一方, 他方では **on ~ terms with ...** …と~な仲である **on the way** 途中で **on the way to** ~へ行く途中で **pass on** ①通り過ぎる ②(情報などを他者に) 伝える

□ **once** 副 ①一度, 1回 ②かつて 名 一度, 1回 接 いったん~すると **at once** すぐに, 同時に **once more** もう一度 **once upon a time** むかしむかし

□ **one** 名 1(の数字), 1人[個] 形 ①1の, 1人[個]の ②ある~ ③《the –》唯一の 代 ①(一般の) 人, ある物 ②一方, 片方 ③~なもの **no one** 誰も[一人も] ~ない **one another** お互い **one day** (過去の) ある日, (未来の) いつか **one moment** ちょっとの間 **one morning** ある朝 **one of** ~の1つ[人] **one side** 片側 **this one** これ, こちら

□ **oneself** 代 自分自身 **excuse oneself** 辞退する **for oneself** 独力で, 自分のために **give oneself up to** ~に身を委ねる **say to oneself** ひとり言を言う, 心に思う

□ **onion** 名 タマネギ(玉葱)

□ **only** 形 唯一の 副 ①単に, ~にすぎない, ただ~だけ ②やっと 接 ただし, だがしかし **if only** ~でありさえすれば **not only ~ but ...** ~だけ

でなく…もまた

□ **onto** 前 ～の上へ［に］

□ **open** 形 ①開いた，広々とした ②公開された 動 ①開く，始まる ②広がる，広げる ③打ち明ける **break open**（金庫などを）こじ開ける **open air** 戸外，野外

□ **openly** 副 率直に，公然と

□ **operation** 名 ①操作，作業，動作 ②経営，運営 ③手術 ④作戦，軍事行動

□ **Ophelia** 名 オフィーリア《ハムレットの恋人，ポローニアスの娘》

□ **opinion** 名 意見，見識，世論，評判

□ **opponent** 形 敵対する，反対する 名 競争相手，敵，反対者

□ **opportunity** 名 好機，適当な時期［状況］

□ **oppose** 動 反対する，敵対する

□ **opposite** 形 反対の，向こう側の 前 ～の向こう側に 名 反対の人［物］

□ **or** 接 ①～か…，または ②さもないと ③すなわち，言い換えると

□ **oracle** 名 ①神託神殿［所］ ②神官，巫女 ③神託，託宣

□ **orange** 名 オレンジ 形 オレンジ色の

□ **orchard** 名 果樹園

□ **ordain** 動（法律などによって～を）定める，規定する，制定する

□ **order** 名 ①順序 ②整理，整頓 ③命令，注文（品） 動 ①（～するよう）命じる，注文する ②整頓する，整理する **in order** きちんと（整理されて），順序正しく **in order to** ～するために，～しようと

□ **ordinary** 形 ①普通の，通常の ②並の，平凡な

□ **organize** 動 組織する

□ **original** 形 ①始めの，元の，本来の ②独創的な 名 原型，原文

□ **Orlando** 名 オーランドー《ド・ボイズ家の末っ子》

□ **Orsino** 名 オーシーノ公爵《イリリアの公爵。オリヴィアに求婚》

□ **Othello** 名 オセロー《ヴェニスの軍人でムーア人》

□ **other** 形 ①ほかの，異なった ②（2つのうち）もう一方の，（3つ以上のうち）残りの 代 ①ほかの人［物］ ②《the－》残りの1つ 副 そうでなく，別に **each other** お互いに **in other words** すなわち，言い換えれば **on the other hand** 一方，他方では **the other day** 先日

□ **otherwise** 副 さもないと，そうでなければ

□ **ought** 助《－to ～》当然～すべきである，きっと～するはずである

□ **our** 代 私たちの

□ **ourselves** 代 私たち自身

□ **out** 副 ①外へ［に］，不在で，離れて ②世に出て ③消えて ④すっかり 形 ①外の，遠く離れた ②公表された 前 ～から外へ［に］ 動 ①追い出す ②露見する **as it turned out** 後でわかったことだが **be out** 外出している **break out** 発生する，急に起こる，（戦争が）勃発する **bring out**（物）をとりだす，引き出す，（新製品など）を出す **burn out** 燃え尽きる **call out** 叫ぶ，呼び出す，声を掛ける **carry out** 外へ運び出す，［計画を］実行する **come out** 出てくる，出掛ける，姿を現す，発行される **come out of** ～から出てくる，～をうまく乗り越える **cry out** 叫ぶ **find out** 見つけ出す，気がつく，知る，調べる，解明する **go out** 外出する，外へ出る **hold out** ①差し出す，（腕を）伸ばす ②持ちこたえる，粘る，耐える **leave out** 抜かす，除外する **lend out** 貸し出す **look out** ①外を見る ②気をつける，注意する **look out of**（窓などから）外を見る **make ～ out of ...** ～を…から作る **measure out** 測り分ける **out of** ①～から外へ，～から抜け出して ②～から作り出して，～を材料として ③～の範囲外に，～から離れて ④（ある数）の中から **out of duty** 義務感から **out of sight** 見えないところに **pick out** 拾い出す，えり抜く，選び出す **point out** 指し示す，指摘する，目を向ける，目を向けさせる **pour out** どっと出てくる，～に注ぎだす，吐き出す **put out** ①外に出す，（手など）を（差し）出す ②（明かり・火を）消す **read out** 声を出して読む，読み上げる **rush out of** 急いで～から出てくる **send out** 使いに出す，派遣する，発送する **set out** ①出発する，置く ②配置する **set out on** ～に出発する **sort out** ～を整理［解決］する **step out of** ～から出る **throw out** 放り出す **turn out** ①～と判明する，（結局～に）なる ②（照明などを）消す ③養成する ④出かける，集まる ⑤外側に向く，ひっくり返す **turn out to be** ～という結果になる **way out of** ～から抜け出る道 **worn out** 擦り切れた

□ **outburst** 名 爆発，噴出

□ **outcome** 名 結果，結末

□ **outdo** 動（～に）勝る

□ **outdone** 動 outdo（（～に）勝る）の過去分詞 形 **be outdone by** ～に負ける，～より劣っている

□ **outside** 名 外部，外側 形 外部の，外側の 副 外へ，外側に 前 ～の外に［で・の・へ］，～の範囲を越えて

□ **over** 前 ①～の上の［に］，～を一面に覆って ②～を越えて，～以上に，～よりまさって ③

～の向こう側の［に］ ④～の間 副上に，一面に，ずっと 形①上部の，上位の，過多の ②終わって，すんで **all over** ～中で，全体に亘って，～の至る所で **be over** 終わる **climb over** ～を乗り越える **come over** やって来る，～の身にふりかかる **fly over** 飛び超える，上空を飛ぶ **go over to** ～の前に［へ］行く，～に出向いて行く **have power over** ～を思いのままに操る力を持っている **look over** ～越しに見る，～を見渡す **over all** 全体にわたって **over here** こっちへ［に］；ほら，さあ《人の注意を引く》 **over there** あそこに **take over** 引き継ぐ，支配する，乗っ取る **win over** 説得する，口説き落とす

□ **overcame** 動 overcome（勝つ）の過去

□ **overcome** 動勝つ，打ち勝つ，克服する **be overcome with** ～に圧倒される，～にやられる

□ **overhear** 動ふと耳にする，立ち聞きする

□ **overheard** 動 overhear（ふと耳にする）の過去，過去分詞

□ **overjoyed** 形大喜びの

□ **overlook** 動①見落とす，（チャンスなどを）逃す ②見渡す ③大目に見る 名見晴らし

□ **overruling** 形却下する，覆す

□ **overseas** 形海外の，外国の 副海外へ 名国外

□ **overtook** 動 overtake（追いつく）の過去

□ **overwhelmed** 形圧倒された，手に負えなくなった

□ **owe** 動①（～を）負う，（～を人の）お陰とする ②（金を）借りている，（人に対して～の）義務がある

□ **owl** 名①フクロウ（梟），ミミズク ②利口ぶった人，夜更かしの人

□ **own** 形自身の 動持っている，所有する **of one's own** 自分自身の **on one's own** 自力で

□ **owner** 名持ち主，オーナー

P

□ **pace** 名歩調，速度 動ゆっくり歩く，行ったり来たりする **keep pace with** ～と歩調をそろえる

□ **Padua** 名パドヴァ《イタリアの都市》

□ **page** 名①ページ ②（ホテルなどの）ボーイ ③（中世の貴族の）小姓 動（ボーイや放送で）呼び出す

□ **paid** 動 pay（払う）の過去，過去分詞 形有給の，支払い済みの

□ **pain** 名①痛み，苦悩 ②《-s》骨折り，苦労 動苦痛を与える，痛む **for one's pains** 骨折ったかいもなく **on pain of death** 違反すると死刑に処す条件で

□ **paint** 動①ペンキを塗る ②（絵の具などで）描く 名塗料，ペンキ，絵の具

□ **painted board** 罪状書きの書かれた板

□ **pair** 名（2つから成る）一対，一組，ペア 動対になる［する］

□ **palace** 名宮殿，大邸宅

□ **pale** 形①（顔色・人が）青ざめた，青白い ②（色が）薄い，（光が）薄暗い 動①青ざめる，青ざめさせる ②淡くなる［する］，色あせる

□ **paleness** 名蒼白

□ **palm** 名手のひら（状のもの）

□ **paltry** 形無価値の，微々たる，取るに足りない

□ **pansy** 名パンジー，三色スミレ

□ **paper** 名①紙 ②新聞，論文，答案 ③《-s》書類 ④紙幣，手形

□ **parade** 名①パレード，行列 ②見せびらかし 動①行進する ②見せびらかす

□ **pardon** 名許し，容赦 動許す，容赦する **I beg your pardon.** ごめんなさい。失礼ですが。もう一度言ってください。

□ **parent** 名《-s》両親

□ **parentage** 名家系，生まれ

□ **Paris** 名①パリ《フランスの首都》 ②パリス伯爵《貴族の青年》

□ **parlor** 名①パーラー，店 ②客間 ③休憩室

□ **part** 名①部分，割合 ②役目 動分ける，分かれる，別れる **part with** ～を手放す **take part in** ～に参加する

□ **partake** 動（出されたものを）食べる，飲む

□ **particular** 形①特別の ②詳細な 名事項，細部，《-s》詳細 **in particular** 特に，とりわけ

□ **particularly** 副特に，とりわけ

□ **parting** 動 part（分ける）の現在分詞 名別離，別れ，分離

□ **partly** 副一部分は，ある程度は

□ **partner** 名配偶者，仲間，同僚 動（～と）組む，提携する

□ **party** 名①パーティー，会，集まり ②派，一行，隊，一味

□ **pass** 動①過ぎる，通る ②（年月が）たつ ③（試験に）合格する ④手渡す 名①通過 ②入場券，通行許可 ③合格，パス **pass as** ～として通す **pass away** 過ぎ去る，終わる，死ぬ **pass by** ～のそばを通る［通り過ぎる］ **pass for** ～で通る **pass on** ①通り過ぎる ②（情報などを他者に）伝える **pass through** ～を通る，通行する

□ **passenger** 名乗客，旅客

□ **passing** 形通り過ぎる, 一時的な 名①通行, 通過 ②合格, 及第

□ **passion** 名情熱, (～への)熱中, 激怒

□ **passionate** 形情熱的な, (感情が)激しい, 短気な

□ **past** 形過去の, この前の 名過去(の出来事) 前《時間・場所》～を過ぎて, ～を越して 副通り越して, 過ぎて

□ **pastime** 名気晴らし, 娯楽

□ **patch** 名継ぎはぎ, 継ぎ, 傷当て 動継ぎを当てる, 一時的に繕う

□ **path** 名①(踏まれてできた)小道, 歩道 ②進路, 通路

□ **patience** 名我慢, 忍耐(力), 根気

□ **patient** 形我慢[忍耐]強い, 根気のある 名病人, 患者

□ **patiently** 副我慢強く, 根気よく

□ **patrimony** 名世襲財産

□ **patron** 名後援者, パトロン

□ **Paulina** 名ポーライナ《ハーマイオニーの友人, アンティゴナスの妻》

□ **pay** 動①支払う, 払う, 報いる, 償う ②割に合う, ペイする 名給料, 報い **pay off** ①支払う ②期待の成果をあげる, (大)もうけになる

□ **payment** 名支払い, 払い込み

□ **pea** 名エンドウ(豆)

□ **peace** 名①平和, 和解,《the －》治安 ②平穏, 静けさ **in peace** 平和のうちに, 安心して

□ **peacefully** 副平和に, 穏やかに

□ **pearl** 名真珠

□ **Peaseblossom** 名エンドウの花《妖精》

□ **peculiar** 形①奇妙な, 変な ②特有の, 固有の

□ **peddler** 名行商人

□ **pedestal** 名台座

□ **penalty** 名刑罰, 罰, ペナルティー

□ **penitence** 名(宗教的な罪に対する)後悔

□ **penitent** 形(宗教的な罪を)後悔している 名(宗教的な罪の)悔悟者

□ **pension** 名①年金, 恩給 ②下宿屋, ペンション 動年金を支給する

□ **people** 名①(一般に)人々 ②民衆, 世界の人々, 国民, 民族 ③人間 動(～を人などで)一杯にする

□ **perceive** 動気づく, 感知する

□ **percentage** 名パーセンテージ, 割合, 比率

□ **Perdita** 名パーディタ《ハーマイオニーとレオンティーズの娘》

□ **perfect** 形①完璧な, 完全な ②純然たる 動完成する, 改良[改善]する

□ **perfection** 名完全, 完成

□ **perfectly** 副完全に, 申し分なく

□ **perform** 動①(任務などを)行う, 果たす, 実行する ②演じる, 演奏する

□ **performance** 名①実行, 行為 ②成績, できばえ, 業績 ③演劇, 演奏, 見世物

□ **perhaps** 副たぶん, ことによると

□ **peril** 名(差し迫った)危険

□ **period** 名①期, 期間, 時代 ②ピリオド, 終わり

□ **perish** 動滅びる, 死ぬ

□ **permission** 名許可, 免許

□ **permit** 動①許可する ②(物・事が)可能にする 名許可(証), 免許

□ **perplexed** 形当惑した, まごついた

□ **perplexity** 名困惑, 難題

□ **persist** 動①固執する, 主張する ②続く, 存続する

□ **persistence** 名固執, がんばり

□ **person** 名①人 ②人格, 人柄 **in person** (本人)自ら, 自身で

□ **personality** 名人格, 個性

□ **personally** 副個人的には, 自分で

□ **persuade** 動説得する, 促して～させる

□ **persuasion** 名①説得(力) ②信念, 信仰

□ **persuasive** 形説得力のある

□ **pet** 名ペット, お気に入り 形お気に入りの, 愛がんの 動かわいがる

□ **petition** 名請願(書), 嘆願

□ **Petruchio** 名ペトルーチオ《キャサリンの求婚者》

□ **physician** 名医師, 医者

□ **pick** 動①(花・果実などを)摘む, もぐ ②選ぶ, 精選する ③つつく, つついて穴をあける, ほじくり出す ④(～を)摘み取る 名①《the －》精選したもの ②選択(権) ③つつくもの, つるはし **pick out** 拾い出す, えり抜く, 選び出す **pick up** 拾い上げる, 車で迎えに行く, 習得する, 再開する, 回復する

□ **pickax** 名つるはし

□ **picture** 名①絵, 写真,《-s》映画 ②イメージ, 事態, 状況, 全体像 動描く, 想像する

□ **pie** 名パイ

□ **piece** 名①一片, 部分 ②1個, 1本 ③作品 **bits and pieces** こまごました物 **fall to pieces** ボロボロになる

- □ **pierce** 動 ①突き刺す, 貫く, ～に穴をあける ②身にしみる ③見抜く
- □ **pig** 名 ブタ(豚)
- □ **pile** 名 積み重ね, (～の)山 動 積み重ねる, 積もる **pile up** 積み重ねる
- □ **pilgrim** 名 ①巡礼者, 旅人 ②最初の移住者
- □ **pilgrimage** 名 巡礼の旅
- □ **pill** 名 錠剤, ピル
- □ **pillow** 名 まくら
- □ **pin** 動 留める, 固定する
- □ **pinch** 動 ①つまむ, はさむ ②ピンチに陥れる 名 ①つまむこと ②ひとつまみ ③ピンチ, 窮地
- □ **pine** 名 マツ(松), マツ材 動 (渇望のあまり)やつれる、痩せ衰える **pine away** やつれる
- □ **pirate** 名 海賊 動 海賊行為を働く
- □ **Pisa** 名 ピサ《イタリアの都市》
- □ **pitiable** 形 哀れな, かわいそうな
- □ **pitiful** 形 ①哀れな, 痛々しい ②浅ましい
- □ **pity** 名 哀れみ, 同情, 残念なこと 動 気の毒に思う, 哀れむ **move someone to pity** (人)の哀れみを誘う **take pity on** ～に同情を示す, ～を哀れむ
- □ **place** 名 ①場所, 建物 ②余地, 空間 ③《one's -》家, 部屋 動 ①置く, 配置する ②任命する, 任じる **take one's place** (人と)交代する, (人)の代わりをする, 後任になる **take place** 行われる, 起こる
- □ **plain** 形 ①明白な, はっきりした ②簡素な ③平らな ④不細工な, 平凡な 副 はっきりと, まったく 名 高原, 草原
- □ **plainly** 副 はっきりと, 明らかに
- □ **plainness** 名 質実, 平易, 明瞭
- □ **plan** 名 計画, 設計(図), 案 動 計画する
- □ **plant** 名 ①植物, 草木 ②設備, プラント, 工場 動 植えつける, すえつける
- □ **play** 動 ①遊ぶ, 競技する ②(楽器を)演奏する, (役を)演じる 名 遊び, 競技, 劇 **play tricks** 策をろうする **play with** ～で遊ぶ, ～と一緒に遊ぶ
- □ **player** 名 ①競技者, 選手, 演奏者, 俳優 ②演奏装置
- □ **playful** 形 ふざけた, 陽気な
- □ **plea** 名 嘆願
- □ **plead** 動 ①嘆願する, 訴える ②弁護する, 弁解する
- □ **pleasant** 形 ①(物事が)楽しい, 心地よい ②快活な, 愛想のよい
- □ **pleasantly** 副 楽しく, 心地よく
- □ **pleasant-spirited** 形 気さくで陽気な
- □ **please** 動 喜ばす, 満足させる 間 どうぞ, お願いします
- □ **pleased** 形 喜んだ, 気に入った **be pleased to do** ～してうれしい **be pleased with** ～が気に入る
- □ **pleasure** 名 喜び, 楽しみ, 満足, 娯楽
- □ **plenty** 名 十分, たくさん, 豊富
- □ **plight** 名 ひどい状態[状況・ありさま]
- □ **plot** 名 構想, 筋立て, プロット, 策略 動 構想を練る, たくらむ
- □ **pluck** 動 ぐいと引っ張る, 引き抜く, むしる
- □ **plunge** 動 ①飛び込む, 突入する ②(ある状態に)陥れる 名 突入, 突進
- □ **ply** 動 ①(仕事に)精を出す ②(定期的に)往復する 名 層, 重ね **ply someone with** ～をしつこく人に勧める
- □ **pocket** 名 ①ポケット, 袋 ②所持金 動 ①ポケットに入れる ②着服する 形 携帯用の, 小型の
- □ **poem** 名 詩
- □ **poetic** 形 詩の, 詩的な
- □ **poetry** 名 詩歌, 詩を書くこと
- □ **point** 名 ①先, 先端 ②点 ③地点, 時点, 箇所 ④《the -》要点 動 ①(～を)指す, 向ける ②とがらせる **point out** 指し示す, 指摘する, 目を向ける, 目を向けさせる **to the point** 要領を得た
- □ **poison** 名 ①毒, 毒薬 ②害になるもの 動 毒を盛る, 毒する
- □ **poisonous** 形 有毒な, 有害な
- □ **politely** 副 ていねいに, 上品に
- □ **Polixenes** 名 ポリクシニーズ《ボヘミア王》
- □ **Polonius** 名 ポローニアス《デンマーク国王の重臣。オフィーリアとレアティーズの父》
- □ **pomp** 名 壮麗さ, 荘厳さ, 尊大さ
- □ **ponder** 動 じっくり考える, 熟考する
- □ **poor** 形 ①貧しい, 乏しい, 粗末な, 貧弱な ②劣った, へたな ③不幸な, 哀れな, 気の毒な
- □ **popular** 形 ①人気のある, 流行の ②一般的な, 一般向きの
- □ **port** 名 ①港, 港町, 空港 ②ポートワイン
- □ **Portia** 名 ポーシャ《裕福な貴婦人》
- □ **portion** 名 一部, 分け前 動 分配する
- □ **portrait** 名 肖像画
- □ **pose** 名 ①姿勢, 態度, ポーズ ②気取った様子 動 ①ポーズをとる[とらせる] ②気取る, 見せかける ③引き起こす

□ **position** 名 ①位置, 場所, 姿勢 ②地位, 身分, 職 ③立場, 状況 動 置く, 配置する

□ **positive** 形 ①前向きな, 肯定的な, 好意的な ②明確な, 明白な, 確信している ③プラスの 名 ①正数, プラス, 陽極 ②ポジ, 陽画

□ **possess** 動 ①持つ, 所有する ②(心などを)保つ, 制御する

□ **possession** 名 ①所有(物) ②財産, 領土

□ **possibility** 名 可能性, 見込み, 将来性

□ **possible** 形 ①可能な ②ありうる, 起こりうる **as ~ as possible** できるだけ~

□ **possibly** 副 ①あるいは, たぶん ②《否定文, 疑問文で》どうしても, できる限り, とても, なんとか

□ **posterity** 名 子孫

□ **postpone** 動 延期する

□ **posture** 名 ①姿勢 ②(気取った)態度 ③状況 動 ①ポーズをとる[とらせる] ②気取る

□ **potion** 名 (薬の)一服

□ **pound** 名 ①ポンド《英国の通貨単位》 ②ポンド《重量の単位。453.6g》 動 どんどんたたく, 打ち砕く

□ **pour** 動 ①注ぐ, 浴びせる ②流れ出る, 流れ込む ③ざあざあ降る **pour out** どっと出てくる, ~に注ぎだす, 吐き出す

□ **poverty** 名 貧乏, 貧困, 欠乏, 不足

□ **power** 名 力, 能力, 才能, 勢力, 権力 **have power over** ~を思いのままに操る力を持っている

□ **powerful** 形 力強い, 実力のある, 影響力のある

□ **powerless** 形 力のない, 頼りない, 弱い

□ **practical** 形 ①実際的な, 実用的な, 役に立つ ②経験を積んだ **practical joke** 悪ふざけ, いたずら

□ **practice** 名 ①実行, 実践 ②練習 ③慣習 ④(医者・弁護士などの)業務 ⑤やり方, 方法 動 実行する, 練習[訓練]する

□ **praise** 動 ほめる, 賞賛する 名 賞賛

□ **prank** 名 (悪意のない)いたずら, 悪ふざけ 動 ~を派手に飾る, めかしこむ

□ **pray** 動 祈る, 懇願する **pray for** ~のために祈る

□ **prayer** 名 ①祈り, 祈願(文) ②祈る人

□ **precious** 形 ①貴重な, 高価な ②かわいい, 大事な

□ **prediction** 名 予言, 予報, 予測

□ **prefer** 動 (~のほうを)好む, (~のほうが)よいと思う

□ **pregnant** 形 妊娠している

□ **preparation** 名 ①準備, したく ②心構え

□ **prepare** 動 ①準備[用意]をする ②覚悟する[させる] **prepare for** ~の準備をする

□ **prepared** 形 準備[用意]のできた

□ **preposterous** 形 本末転倒の, 不合理な, 非常識な, ばかげた

□ **presence** 名 ①存在すること ②出席, 態度 **in the presence of** ~の面前で

□ **present** 形 ①出席している, ある, いる ②現在の 名 ①《the –》現在 ②贈り物, プレゼント 動 ①紹介する ②現れる ③与える ④提出する, 述べる, 示す **at present** 今のところ, 現在は, 目下

□ **presentation** 名 ①提出, 提示 ②実演, プレゼンテーション

□ **presently** 副 ①やがて, じき ②今, 目下

□ **preserve** 動 保存[保護]する, 保つ

□ **preserver** 名 保存者, 保護者.

□ **press** 動 ①圧する, 押す, プレスする ②強要する, 迫る 名 ①圧迫, 押し, 切迫 ②出版物[社], 新聞

□ **presumably** 副 おそらく

□ **pretend** 動 ①ふりをする, 装う ②あえて~しようとする

□ **pretense** 名 口実, 言い訳, 見せかけ

□ **pretty** 形 ①かわいい, きれいな ②相当な 副 かなり, 相当, 非常に

□ **prevail** 動 ①普及する ②勝つ, 圧倒する

□ **prevent** 動 ①妨げる, じゃまする ②予防する, 守る, 《– ~ from …》~が…できない[しない]ようにする

□ **previously** 副 あらかじめ, 以前に[は]

□ **prey** 名 えじき, 犠牲, 食いもの

□ **Priam** 名 プリアモス《トロイア王》

□ **prick** 動 刺す, 穴をあける

□ **pricking** 名 刺すような感覚

□ **prickly** 形 とげだらけの, ちくちく傷む

□ **pride** 名 誇り, 自慢, 自尊心 動《– oneself》誇る, 自慢する

□ **priest** 名 聖職者, 牧師, 僧侶

□ **priestess** 名 巫女, 女性の祭司

□ **prince** 名 王子, プリンス

□ **Prince** 名 ヴェローナの太守

□ **princess** 名 王女

□ **principal** 形 主な, 第一の, 主要な, 重要な 名 ①長, 社長, 校長 ②主役, 主犯, 本人

□ **principle** 名 ①原理, 原則 ②道義, 正道
□ **prison** 名 ①刑務所, 監獄 ②監禁
□ **prisoner** 名 囚人, 捕虜
□ **private** 形 ①私的な, 個人の ②民間の, 私立の ③内密の, 人里離れた
□ **privilege** 名 ①特権, 特典, 格別の光栄 ②(基本的) 人権
□ **prize** 名 ①賞, 賞品, 賞金 ②戦利品, 捕獲物 動 高く評価する, 重んじる
□ **probability** 名 見込み, 可能性
□ **probably** 副 たぶん, あるいは
□ **problem** 名 問題, 難問
□ **proceed** 動 進む, 進展する, 続ける 名《-s》①結果 ②収益, 所得, 売却代金
□ **process** 名 ①過程, 経過, 進行 ②手順, 方法, 製法, 加工
□ **procession** 名 行進, 行列
□ **proclaim** 動 宣言[布告]する
□ **produce** 動 ①生産する, 製造する ②生じる, 引き起こす 名 ①生産額[物] ②結果
□ **profess** 動 公言する
□ **profession** 名 職業, 専門職
□ **profit** 名 利益, 利潤, ため 動 利益になる, (人の) ためになる, 役立つ
□ **progress** 名 ①進歩, 前進 ②成り行き, 経過 動 前進する, 上達する **in progress** 進行中で
□ **project** 名 ①計画, プロジェクト ②研究課題 動 ①投影する, 映写する ②計画[企画]する ③描く, 予測する, 見積もる
□ **promise** 名 ①約束 ②有望 動 ①約束する ②見込みがある **keep one's promise** 約束を守る
□ **promising** 形 有望な, 見込みのある
□ **promote** 動 促進する, 昇進[昇級]させる
□ **promotion** 名 ①昇進 ②促進 ③宣伝販売
□ **pronounce** 動 ①発音する ②宣言する
□ **proof** 名 ①証拠, 証明 ②試し, 吟味 ③《-s》校正刷り, ゲラ
□ **proper** 形 ①適した, 適切な, 正しい ②固有の
□ **properly** 副 適切に, きっちりと
□ **prophecy** 名 予言
□ **prophetic** 形 予言的な
□ **proportion** 名 ①割合, 比率, 分け前 ②釣り合い, 比例
□ **proposal** 名 ①提案, 計画 ②プロポーズ
□ **propose** 動 ①申し込む, 提案する ②結婚を申し込む
□ **prospect** 名 見込み, 見通し, 眺め 動 調査する
□ **prosperity** 名 繁栄, 繁盛, 成功
□ **Prospero** 名 プロスペロー《前ミラノ大公》
□ **prosperous** 形 繁栄している
□ **protect** 動 保護する, 防ぐ
□ **protection** 名 保護, 保護するもの[人]
□ **protest** 動 ①主張[断言]する ②抗議する, 反対する 名 抗議(書), 不服
□ **protestation** 名 断言, 強い主張
□ **proud** 形 ①自慢の, 誇った, 自尊心のある ②高慢な, 尊大な **be proud of** ～を自慢に思う
□ **prove** 動 ①証明する ②(～であることが) わかる, (～と) なる
□ **provide** 動 ①供給する, 用意する, (～に) 備える ②規定する
□ **Providence** 名 神意, 摂理, 神の導き
□ **provision** 名 ①用意, 対策 ②食糧 ③規定, 条項 動 食糧を供給する
□ **provoke** 動 ①怒らせる ②刺激して～させる ③引き起こす
□ **prudent** 形 分別のある, 慎重な
□ **prune** 動 (～を) 切り取る, 刈り取る, 刈り込む
□ **public** 名 一般の人々, 大衆 形 公の, 公開の
□ **Puck** 名 パック《いたずら好きの妖精》
□ **pudding** 名 プディング
□ **pull** 動 ①引く, 引っ張る ②引きつける 名 ①引くこと ②縁故, こね
□ **pulse** 名 ①脈拍 ②律動, 拍子 動 脈打つ, 鼓動する
□ **punishment** 名 ①罰, 処罰 ②罰を受けること
□ **pure** 形 ①純粋な, 混じりけのない ②罪のない, 清い
□ **purgatory** 名 煉獄, 苦行, 苦難(の場)
□ **purple** 形 紫色の 名 紫色
□ **purpose** 名 目的, 意図, 決意 動 もくろむ, 企てる **on purpose** わざと, 故意に
□ **purse** 名 ①財布, 小銭入れ ②小物入れ
□ **pursue** 動 ①追う, つきまとう ②追求する, 従事する
□ **pursuit** 名 追跡, 追求
□ **push** 動 ①押す, 押し進む, 押し進める ②進む, 突き出る 名 押し, 突進, 後援 **push away** 押しのける, 押しやる **push down** 押し倒す

□ **put** 動①置く, のせる ②入れる, つける ③(ある状態に)する ④putの過去, 過去分詞 **be put to death** 処刑される **put an end to** ～に終止符を打つ, ～を終わらせる, ～に決着をつける **put away** 片づける, 取っておく **put back** (もとの場所に)戻す, 返す **put in** ～の中に入れる **put ～ into ...** ～を…の状態にする, ～を…に突っ込む **put off** ～から逃れる, 延期する, 要求をそらす, 不快にさせる, やめさせる **put on** ①～を身につける, 着る ②～を…の上に置く **put out** ①外に出す, (手など)を(差し)出す ②(明かり・火を)消す **put to death** 処刑する

Q

□ **quality** 名①質, 性質, 品質 ②特性 ③良質

□ **quarrel** 名けんか, 争論, 不和 動けんかする, 口論する

□ **quarrelsome** 形怒りっぽい, けんか好きの

□ **quarry** 名採石場 動採石する, 石を切り出す

□ **queen** 名女王, 王妃

□ **quench** 動(火・光などを)消す

□ **question** 名質問, 疑問, 問題 動①質問する ②調査する ③疑う **in question** 問題の, 論争中の

□ **questioning** 名質問, 尋問

□ **quick** 形(動作が)速い, すばやい 副速く, 急いで, すぐに

□ **quickly** 副敏速に, 急いで

□ **quiet** 形①静かな, 穏やかな, じっとした ②おとなしい, 無口な, 目立たない 名静寂, 平穏 動静まる, 静める

□ **quieten** 動(～を)静かにさせる, 静める

□ **quietly** 副①静かに ②平穏に, 控えめに

□ **quill** 名羽軸, (ヤマアラシなどの)針

□ **quite** 副①まったく, すっかり, 完全に ②かなり, ずいぶん ③ほとんど **not quite** まったく～だというわけではない

R

□ **rabble** 名暴徒, やじ馬

□ **race** 名①競争, 競走 ②人種, 種族 動①競争[競走]する ②疾走する

□ **radiant** 形光[熱]を放つ, きらきらと輝く 名光[熱]を放つ点[物体]

□ **rage** 名激怒, 猛威, 熱狂

□ **raging** 形①(痛みなどが)ひどい ②荒れ狂う

□ **rail** 名①横木, 手すり ②レール, 鉄道

□ **railing** 名罵り, 悪口

□ **rain** 名雨, 降雨 動①雨が降る ②雨のように降る[降らせる]

□ **raise** 動①上げる, 高める ②起こす ③～を育てる ④(資金を)調達する 名高める[上げる]こと, 昇給

□ **ran** 動run(走る)の過去

□ **rank** 名①列 ②階級, 位 動①並ぶ, 並べる ②分類する

□ **ransom** 名身代金, 賠償金 動(身代金を払って)取り戻す

□ **rapidly** 副速く, 急速, すばやく, 迅速に

□ **rare** 形①まれな, 珍しい, 逸品の ②希薄な ③(肉が)生焼けの, レアの

□ **rash** 名発疹, 吹き出物

□ **rat** 名①ネズミ(鼠) ②裏切り者

□ **rather** 副①むしろ, かえって ②かなり, いくぶん, やや ③それどころか逆に **rather like** ～に似ている, きらいはでない **rather than** ～よりむしろ **would rather** ～する方がよい **would rather ～ than ...** …よりむしろ～したい

□ **rattlebrain** 名頭の空っぽな人

□ **raven** 名ワタリガラス, オオガラス **dove-feathered raven** 鳩の羽根を持つカラス《美しい外見とは裏腹に, 暗い本性を持つものを比喩的に表現》

□ **reach** 動①着く, 到着する, 届く ②手を伸ばして取る 名手を伸ばすこと, (手の)届く範囲 **reach in** 手を突っ込む

□ **react** 動反応する, 対処する

□ **reaction** 名反応, 反動, 反抗, 影響

□ **read** 動読む, 読書する **read out** 声を出して読む, 読み上げる

□ **readily** 副①すぐに, さっそく ②快く, 進んで

□ **ready** 形用意[準備]ができた, まさに～しようとする, 今にも～せんばかりの 動用意[準備]する **be ready to** すぐに[いつでも]～できる, ～する構えで **get ready** 用意[支度]をする

□ **real** 形実際の, 実在する, 本物の 副本当に

□ **reality** 名現実, 実在, 真実(性)

□ **realize** 動理解する, 実現する

□ **really** 副本当に, 実際に, 確かに

□ **realm** 名①領域, 範囲 ②王国, 領土

□ **reason** 名①理由 ②理性, 道理 動①推論する ②説き伏せる **for some reason** なんらかの理由で, どういうわけか **reason for** ～の理由

□ **rebel** 名反逆者, 反抗者, 謀反人 動反抗する, 反逆する
□ **rebellion** 名反乱, 反抗, 謀反, 暴動
□ **rebuke** 名叱責, 避難 動叱る, 叱責する
□ **recall** 動思い出す, 思い出させる, 呼び戻す, 回収する 名呼び戻し, リコール
□ **receive** 動①受け取る, 受領する ②迎える, 迎え入れる
□ **recent** 形近ごろの, 近代の
□ **recently** 副近ごろ, 最近
□ **reception** 名もてなし, 接待, 宴会, 受付
□ **reciprocate** 動報いる, 返礼する
□ **reckon** 動①数える ②(～と)みなす, 推測する
□ **recognize** 動認める, 認識[承認]する
□ **recollection** 名①思い出, 記憶(力) ②平静
□ **recommend** 動①推薦する ②勧告する, 忠告する
□ **reconcile** 動和解させる, 調和させる
□ **reconciliation** 名和解, 仲直り, 調停
□ **reconsider** 動考え直す, 再検討する
□ **recount** 動①詳しく話す ②数え直す, 列挙する 名(票などの)数え直し
□ **recover** 動①取り戻す, ばん回する ②回復する
□ **recovery** 名回復, 復旧, 立ち直り
□ **recreation** 名気晴らし, 休養, 娯楽
□ **red** 形赤い 名赤, 赤色
□ **reduce** 動①減じる ②しいて～させる, (～の)状態にする
□ **refer** 動①《–to ～》～に言及する, ～と呼ぶ ②～を参照する, ～に問い合わせる
□ **referee** 名審判員, レフェリー
□ **reformation** 名①矯正, 改心, 改良, 改善 ②《R-》宗教改革
□ **reformed** 形改良された, 改心した
□ **refrain** 名(詩歌の)リフレイン, 反復句 動差し控える, 自制する
□ **refreshment** 名①気分をすっきりさせること ②軽い食事[飲み物], お茶菓子
□ **refuge** 名避難, 保護, 避難所 動避難する **take refuge** 避難する, 逃げ込む
□ **refusal** 名拒絶
□ **refuse** 動拒絶する, 断る 名くず, 廃物
□ **regain** 動取り戻す, (～に)戻る
□ **Regan** 名リーガン《リアの次女》
□ **regard** 動①(～を…と)見なす ②尊敬する, 重きを置く ③関係がある 名①注意, 関心 ②尊敬, 好感 ③《-s》(手紙などで)よろしくというあいさつ **with regard to** ～に関しては
□ **regarding** 前～に関しては, ～について
□ **regardless** 形無頓着な, 注意しない 副それにもかかわらず, それでも
□ **regret** 動後悔する, 残念ながら～する 名遺憾, 後悔, (～に対する)悲しみ
□ **regular** 形①規則的な, 秩序のある ②定期的な, 一定の, 習慣的
□ **reign** 名①治世 ②君臨, 支配 動君臨する, 支配する
□ **reject** 動①拒絶する, 断る ②(法案など)否決する
□ **rejected** 形却下された, 除外された
□ **rejection** 名拒絶, 不採用
□ **rejoice** 動喜ぶ
□ **relate** 動①関連がある, かかわる, うまく折り合う ②物語る
□ **related** 形①関係のある, 関連した ②姻戚の
□ **relation** 名①(利害)関係, 間柄 ②親戚
□ **relationship** 名関係, 関連, 血縁関係
□ **relative** 形関係のある, 相対的な 名親戚, 同族
□ **release** 動①解き放す, 釈放する ②免除する ③発表する, リリースする 名解放, 釈放
□ **relief** 名(苦痛・心配などの)除去, 軽減, 安心, 気晴らし
□ **relieved** 形安心した, ほっとした
□ **relight** 動(～に)再び火がつける
□ **religion** 名宗教, ～教, 信条
□ **religious** 形①宗教の ②信心深い
□ **relit** 動relight((～に)再び火がつける)の過去, 過去分詞
□ **reluctance** 名気乗りしないこと, いやがること
□ **reluctant** 形気乗りしない, しぶしぶの
□ **reluctantly** 副いやいやながら, 仕方なく
□ **rely** 動(人が…に)頼る, 当てにする
□ **remain** 動①残っている, 残る ②(～の)ままである[いる] 名《-s》①残り(もの) ②遺跡
□ **remainder** 名残り(の人々), 残り物, 余り
□ **remaining** 形残った, 残りの
□ **remark** 名①注意, 注目, 観察 ②意見, 記事, 批評 動①注目する ②述べる, 批評する
□ **remedy** 名治療(薬), 改善(案) 動治療する,

(状況を)改善する
□ **remember** 動思い出す, 覚えている, 忘れないでいる
□ **remembrance** 名記憶, 記念品
□ **remind** 動思い出させる, 気づかせる
□ **remnant** 名(～の)残り, なごり
□ **remorse** 名(深い)後悔, 良心の呵責
□ **remote** 形①(距離・時間的に)遠い, 遠隔の ②人里離れた ③よそよそしい
□ **remove** 動①取り去る, 除去する ②(衣類を)脱ぐ ③(～を)移動させる
□ **render** 動(～を…に)する, 与える
□ **renew** 動新しくする, 更新する, 回復する, 再開する
□ **renown** 名名声, 有名
□ **renowned** 形有名な, 高名な
□ **repay** 動①払い戻す, 返金する ②報いる, 恩返しする
□ **repeat** 動繰り返す 名繰り返し, 反復, 再演
□ **repeatedly** 副繰り返して, たびたび
□ **repent** 動悔やむ, 後悔する
□ **repentance** 名良心の呵責, 後悔
□ **repentant** 形後悔している, ざんげする
□ **replace** 動①取り替える, 差し替える ②元に戻す
□ **reply** 動答える, 返事をする, 応答する 名答え, 返事, 応答
□ **report** 動①報告[通知・発表]する ②記録する, 記事を書く 名①報告, レポート ②(新聞の)記事, 報道
□ **reprehend** 動(～を)しかる, とがめる
□ **represent** 動①表現する ②意味する ③代表する
□ **reproach** 動非難する, 叱る 名非難, 叱責
□ **reprove** 動しかる, 叱責する
□ **reputation** 名評判, 名声, 世評
□ **repute** 名評判, 世評
□ **request** 名願い, 要求(物), 需要 動求める, 申し込む
□ **require** 動①必要とする, 要する ②命じる, 請求する
□ **rescue** 動救う 名救助, 救出
□ **reseal** 動再び封じる
□ **resemblance** 名類似(点), 似ていること
□ **resemble** 動似ている
□ **resentment** 名怒り, 立腹, うらみ
□ **reservation** 名①留保, 制限 ②予約, 指定
□ **reserve** 動①とっておく, 備えておく ②予約する ③留保する 名①蓄え, 備え ②準備[積立]金 ③遠慮 形予備の
□ **resident** 名居住者, 在住者
□ **resignation** 名①辞任, 辞表 ②あきらめ
□ **resist** 動抵抗[反抗・反撃]する, 耐える
□ **resolution** 名①決定, 決議 ②決心, 決断 ③解決
□ **resolve** 動決心する, 解決する 名決心, 決意
□ **respect** 名①尊敬, 尊重 ②注意, 考慮 動尊敬[尊重]する **in respect** ～であるという点で
□ **respective** 形それぞれの, 個別の
□ **responsible** 形責任のある, 信頼できる, 確実な
□ **rest** 名①休息 ②安静 ③休止, 停止 ④《the –》残り 動①休む, 眠る ②休止する, 静止する ③(～に)基づいている ④(～の)ままである **for the rest of life** 死ぬまで **rest on** ～の上に載っている **take a rest** 休息する
□ **restore** 動元に戻す, 復活させる
□ **restrain** 動①(人・動物の行動を)制する, 抑制する ②こらえる ③拘束する
□ **result** 名結果, 成り行き, 成績 動(結果として)起こる, 生じる, 結局～になる **as a result** その結果(として) **as a result of** ～の結果(として)
□ **retire** 動引き下がる, 退職[引退]する
□ **return** 動帰る, 戻る, 返す 名①帰還, 返却 ②返答, 報告(書), 申告 形①帰りの, 往復の ②お返しの **in return** お返しとして **return to** ～に戻る, ～に帰る
□ **reunion** 名①再結合 ②再会, 同窓会
□ **reunite** 動再結合する, 再会させる
□ **reveal** 動明らかにする, 暴露する, もらす
□ **revelation** 名①明らかになること, 発覚, 暴露(されたもの), 新事実 ②啓示
□ **revenge** 名復讐 動復讐する
□ **revenue** 名所得, 収入, 利益, (国の)歳入
□ **reverence** 名尊敬, 崇拝
□ **revert** 動(前の状態に)戻る, 復帰する
□ **revive** 動生き返る, 生き返らせる, 復活する[させる]
□ **revoke** 動(～を)無効にする, (～を)取り消す《法律》
□ **revolt** 動そむく, 反乱を起こす
□ **reward** 名報酬, 償い, 応報 動報いる, 報酬を与える
□ **Rialto** 名リアルト橋《ヴェニスの橋》

□ **riband** 名装飾用のリボン

□ **rich** 形①富んだ，金持ちの ②豊かな，濃い，深い 名裕福な人

□ **richness** 名豊富であること，金持ちであること

□ **rid** 動取り除く **get rid of** ～を取り除く

□ **riddle** 名謎

□ **ridicule** 動あざ笑う，笑いものにする，からかう 名あざけり，からかい

□ **ridiculous** 形ばかげた，おかしい

□ **right** 形①正しい ②適切な ③健全な ④右(側)の 副①まっすぐに，すぐに ②右(側)に ③ちょうど，正確に 名①正しいこと ②権利 ③《the－》右，ライト **right away** すぐに **right now** 今すぐに，たった今

□ **rightful** 形正当な，当然の

□ **right-hand** 形右(側)の，右手(用)の

□ **ring** 名①輪，円形，指輪 ②競技場，リング 動①輪で取り囲む ②鳴る，鳴らす ③電話をかける

□ **riot** 名暴動，騒動

□ **risen** 動rise(昇る)の過去分詞 形上がった，起こった

□ **risk** 名危険 動危険にさらす，賭ける，危険をおかす **at the risk of** ～の危険をおかして

□ **rite** 名(宗教的な)儀式

□ **rival** 名競争相手，匹敵する人 動競争する

□ **road** 名①道路，道，通り ②手段，方法

□ **roasted** 形(肉などがじか火で)焼かれた

□ **rob** 動奪う，金品を盗む，襲う **rob ～ of ...** ～から…を奪う

□ **robe** 名①ローブ，化粧着，部屋着 ②《-s》式服，法衣

□ **Robin Goodfellow** ロビン・グッドフェロー《パックの別名》

□ **Robin Hood of England** ロビン・フッド《イギリスの伝説的な盗賊》

□ **rock** 名①岩，岸壁，岩石 ②揺れること，動揺 動揺れる，揺らす

□ **rocky** 形①岩の多い ②ぐらぐら揺れる，ぐらつく

□ **rode** 動ride(乗る)の過去

□ **role** 名①(劇などの)役 ②役割，任務

□ **roll** 動①転がる，転がす ②(波などが)うねる，横揺れする ③(時が)たつ 名①一巻き ②名簿，目録

□ **rolling** 形(目が)ぎょろつく.

□ **Roman** 形ローマ(人)の 名①ローマ人[市民] ②(ローマ)カトリック教

□ **romance** 名恋愛(関係・感情)，恋愛[空想・冒険]小説

□ **romantic** 形ロマンチックな，空想的な 名ロマンチックな人

□ **Rome** 名①ローマ《イタリアの首都》 ②古代ローマ(帝国)

□ **Romeo** 名ロミオ《主人公。モンタギューの息子》

□ **roof** 名屋根(のようなもの)，住居 動屋根をつける

□ **rooftop** 名屋上 形屋上の

□ **room** 名①部屋 ②空間，余地

□ **root** 名①根，根元 ②根源，原因 ③《-s》先祖，ルーツ 動根づかせる，根づく

□ **rope** 名綱，なわ，ロープ 動なわで縛る

□ **Rosalind** 名ロザリンド《前公爵の娘》

□ **Rosaline** 名ロザライン《ロミオが最初に恋する女性》

□ **rose** 名①バラ(の花) ②バラ色 形バラ色の 動rise(昇る)の過去

□ **rotten** 形①腐った，堕落した ②不快な

□ **rough** 形①(手触りが)粗い ②荒々しい，未加工の

□ **roughly** 副①おおよそ，概略的に，大ざっぱに ②手荒く，粗雑に

□ **roughneck** 名不作法者，乱暴者

□ **round** 形①丸い，円形の ②ちょうど 副①回って ②周りに 名①円，球，輪 ②回転 前①～を回って ②～の周囲に 動①丸くなる[する] ②回る

□ **rouse** 動目を覚まさせる，奮起させる

□ **Roussillon** 名ロシリオン《フランスの地名》

□ **Rowland de Boys** ローランド・ド・ボイズ《オリバーとオーランドーの父》

□ **royal** 形王の，女王の，国立の

□ **royalty** 名①著作権使用料，印税 ②特権階級，王位

□ **rude** 形粗野な，無作法な，失礼な

□ **rudely** 副無礼に，手荒く

□ **ruff** 名ひだ襟

□ **rule** 名①規則，ルール ②支配 動支配する

□ **run** 動①走る ②運行する ③(川が)流れる ④経営する 名①走ること，競走 ②連続，続き ③得点 **run after** ～を追いかける **run away** 走り去る，逃げ出す **run away from** ～から逃れる **run down** (液体が)流れ落ちる，駆け下りる **run into** (思いがけず) ～に出会う，～に駆

け込む, ～の中に走って入る **run off** 走り去る, 逃げ去る **run through** 走り抜ける **run up** ～に走り寄る **run up and down** かけずり回る

□ **runaway** 名逃亡者, 家出 形逃げた, 手に負えない

□ **rung** 動ring（鳴る）の過去分詞

□ **rural** 形田舎の, 地方の

□ **rush** 動突進する, せき立てる 名突進, 突撃, 殺到 **rush in** ～に突入する, ～に駆けつける **rush into** ～に突入する, ～に駆けつける, ～に駆け込む **rush out of** 急いで～から出てくる

□ **rustic** 形田舎風の, 素朴な, 田舎くさい 名田舎者

S

□ **sacred** 形神聖な, 厳粛な

□ **sacrifice** 動（～に）生け贄をささげる, （～のために）犠牲になる

□ **sad** 形①悲しい, 悲しげな ②惨めな, 不運な

□ **saddle** 名（自転車などの）サドル, （馬などの）鞍

□ **sadly** 副悲しそうに, 不幸にも

□ **sadness** 名悲しみ, 悲哀

□ **safe** 形①安全な, 危険のない ②用心深い, 慎重な 名金庫 **keep safe** 守護する

□ **safely** 副安全に, 間違いなく

□ **safety** 名安全, 無事, 確実

□ **saga** 名武勇談, 冒険談

□ **said** 動say（言う）の過去, 過去分詞

□ **sail** 名①帆, 帆船 ②帆走, 航海 動①帆走する, 航海する, 出航する ②滑らかに飛ぶ

□ **sailing** 名帆走, セーリング, ヨット競技

□ **sailing ship** 帆船

□ **sailor** 名船員, （ヨットの）乗組員

□ **saint** 名聖人, 聖徒

□ **sake** 名（～の）ため, 利益, 目的

□ **salute** 名敬礼, あいさつ 動敬礼する, あいさつする

□ **same** 形①同じ, 同様の ②前述の 代《the –》同一の人［物］ 副《the –》同様に **the same ～ as ...** …と同じ（ような）～

□ **sanctify** 動神聖にする

□ **sang** 動sing（歌う）の過去

□ **sank** 動sink（沈む）の過去

□ **sarcastic** 形皮肉な, いやみな

□ **sat** 動sit（座る）の過去, 過去分詞

□ **satisfied** 形満足した

□ **sauce** 名ソース

□ **savage** 形どう猛な, 残忍な 名野蛮人, 不作法者 動ひどく攻撃する, 暴れてかみつく

□ **save** 動①救う, 守る ②とっておく, 節約する

□ **saw** 動①see（見る）の過去 ②のこぎりで切る, のこぎりを使う 名のこぎり

□ **say** 動言う, 口に出す 名言うこと, 言い分 間さあ, まあ **say goodbye to** ～にさよならと言う **say to oneself** ひとり言を言う, 心に思う

□ **saying** 名ことわざ, 格言, 発言

□ **scale** 名①目盛り ②規模, 割合, 程度, スケール ③うろこ（鱗） ④てんびん, はかり 動はかりにかける, はかる

□ **scar** 名傷跡

□ **scarcely** 副かろうじて, やっと, まさか［ほとんど］～しない

□ **scare** 動こわがらせる, おびえる 名恐れ, 不安

□ **scared** 形おびえた, びっくりした

□ **scarf** 名スカーフ

□ **scarves** 名scarf（スカーフ）の複数

□ **scene** 名①光景, 風景 ②（劇の）場, 一幕 ③（事件の）現場

□ **scheduled** 形計画的な, 予定された

□ **scheme** 名計画, スキーム, たくらみ, 仕組み, 枠組み 動たくらむ

□ **scholar** 名学者

□ **school** 名①学校, 校舎, 授業（時間） ②教習所, 学部 ③流派 ④群れ

□ **schooldays** 名学生時代

□ **schoolmate** 名学友, 同じ学校の友達

□ **scolding** 動scold（叱る）の現在分詞 名叱ること, 小言

□ **scorn** 名軽蔑, 冷笑 動軽蔑する, さげすむ

□ **scornful** 形軽蔑した, さげすむ

□ **Scotland** 名スコットランド《英国の北部地方》

□ **Scottish** 形スコットランドの, スコットランド人の

□ **scrap** 名①切れ端, くず, スクラップ ②（新聞などの）切り抜き 動①くずとして捨てる ②（計画などを）やめる

□ **scratch** 動ひっかく, 傷をつける, はがし取る 名ひっかき傷, かくこと

□ **scream** 名金切り声, 絶叫 動叫ぶ, 金切り声を出す

□ **scuffle** 名取っ組み合い, もみ合い, 小競り合い 動取っ組み合う, 乱闘する

□ **sculptor** 名彫刻家

□ **sea** 名海, 《the ~ S-, the S- of ~》~海

□ **sea fight** (戦艦同士の)海戦

□ **sea voyage** 海洋航海

□ **seal** 名①印, 封印 ②アザラシ, アシカ 動印を押す, ふたをする, 密閉する

□ **sealed** 形密封された, 封印された

□ **sea-monster** 名海の怪獣, 海坊主

□ **search** 動捜し求める, 調べる 名捜査, 探索, 調査 **in search of** ~を探し求めて

□ **seated** 形座っている, 着席[着座]した

□ **seawater** 名海水

□ **Sebastian** 名セバスチャン《ヴァイオラの双子の兄》

□ **second** 名①第2(の人[物]) ②(時間の)秒, 瞬時 形第2の, 2番の 副第2に 動後援する, 支持する **second wind** 回復した元気

□ **secret** 形①秘密の, 隠れた ②神秘の, 不思議な 名秘密, 神秘

□ **secretly** 副秘密に, 内緒で

□ **section** 名①断片 ②区分, 区域 ③部門, 課 動区分する

□ **seduce** 動誘惑する, そそのかす, くどく

□ **see** 動①見る, 見える, 見物する ②(~と)わかる, 認識する, 経験する ③会う ④考える, 確かめる, 調べる ⑤気をつける **Let me see.** ええと。 **see ~ as ...** ~を…と考える **see if** ~かどうかを確かめる **you see** あのね, いいですか

□ **seek** 動捜し求める, 求める

□ **seem** 動(~に)見える, (~のように)思われる **seem to be** ~であるように思われる

□ **seen** 動see(見る)の過去分詞

□ **seize** 動①ぐっとつかむ, 捕らえる ②襲う

□ **seldom** 副まれに, めったに~ない

□ **select** 動選択する, 選ぶ 形選んだ, 一流の, えり抜きの

□ **self** 名①自己, ~そのもの ②私利, 私欲, 利己主義 ③自我

□ **sell** 動売る, 売っている, 売れる

□ **senate** 名①《the S-》(米・仏などの)上院 ②《the –》(古代ローマの)元老院 ③(大学などの)評議会

□ **senator** 名上院議員, 元老院議員, (大学の)評議員

□ **send** 動①送る, 届ける ②手紙を出す ③(人を~に)行かせる ④《– + 人[物など] + ~ing》~を(ある状態に)する **send away** 追い払う, 送り出す, ~を呼び寄せる **send for** ~を呼びにやる, ~を呼び寄せる **send out** 使いに出す, 派遣する, 発送する **send someone on** (人)を~に送り出す

□ **senior** 形年長の, 年上の, 古参の, 上級の 名年長者, 先輩, 先任者

□ **sense** 名①感覚, 感じ ②《-s》意識, 正気, 本性 ③常識, 分別, センス ④意味 動感じる, 気づく **in a sense** ある意味では

□ **sent** 動send(送る)の過去, 過去分詞

□ **sentence** 名①文 ②判決, 宣告 動判決を下す, 宣告する

□ **separate** 動①分ける, 分かれる, 隔てる ②別れる, 別れさせる 形分かれた, 別れた, 別々の

□ **serenade** 動(~に)セレナーデを歌う

□ **serious** 形①まじめな, 真剣な ②重大な, 深刻な, (病気などが)重い

□ **seriously** 副①真剣に, まじめに ②重大に

□ **sermon** 名(教会などでの)説教

□ **serpent** 名①ヘビ(蛇) ②陰険な人

□ **servant** 名①召使, 使用人, しもべ ②公務員, (公共事業の)従業員

□ **serve** 動①仕える, 奉仕する ②(客の)応対をする, 給仕する, 食事[飲み物]を出す ③(役目を)果たす, 務める, 役に立つ ④(球技で)サーブをする 名(球技で)サーブ(権)

□ **service** 名①勤務, 業務 ②公益事業 ③点検, 修理 ④奉仕, 貢献 動保守点検する, (点検)修理をする

□ **set** 動①置く, 当てる, つける ②整える, 設定する ③(太陽・月などが)沈む ④(~を…の状態に)する, させる ⑤setの過去, 過去分詞 形①決められた, 固定した ②断固とした ③準備のできた 名①一そろい, セット ②舞台装置, セット **set about** ~に取り掛かる **set fire** 火をつける **set forth** 旅に出発する **set free** (人)を解放する, 釈放される, 自由の身になる **set off** 出発する, 発射する **set out** ①出発する, 置く ②配置する **set out on** ~に出発する **set to** ~へ向かう, ~に着手する, けんかを始める, 食べ始める, 本気で始める

□ **settle** 動①安定する[させる], 落ち着く, 落ち着かせる ②《- in ~》~に移り住む, 定住する

□ **settled** 動settle(安定する)の過去, 過去分詞 形固定した, 落ち着いた, 解決した

□ **seven** 名7(の数字), 7人[個] 形7の, 7人[個]の

□ **several** 形 ①いくつかの ②めいめいの 代 いくつかのもの，数人，数個

□ **severe** 形 厳しい，深刻な，激しい

□ **severely** 副 厳しく，簡素に

□ **severity** 名 厳しさ，過酷さ

□ **shade** 名 ①陰，日陰 ②日よけ ③色合い 動 ①陰にする，暗くする，陰影をつける ②次第に変わる［変える］

□ **shadow** 名 ①影，暗がり ②亡霊 動 ①陰にする，暗くする ②尾行する

□ **shady** 形 日陰の，陰をなす

□ **shake** 動 ①振る，揺れる，揺さぶる，震える ②動揺させる 名 ①振ること ②ミルクセーキ

□ **shaken** 動 shake（振る）の過去分詞

□ **shall** 助 ①《Iが主語で》～するだろう，～だろう ②《I以外が主語で》(…に) ～させよう，(…は)～することになるだろう **Shall I ～?**（私が）～しましょうか。 **Shall we ～?**（一緒に）～しましょうか。

□ **shame** 名 ①恥，恥辱 ②恥ずべきこと，ひどいこと 動 恥をかかせる，侮辱する

□ **shameful** 形 恥ずべき，下品な

□ **shape** 名 ①形，姿，型 ②状態，調子 動 形づくる，具体化する **in the shape of** ～の形をした

□ **share** 名 ①分け前，分担 ②株 動 分配する，共有する

□ **shark** 名 サメ（鮫）

□ **sharp** 形 ①鋭い，とがった ②刺すような，きつい ③鋭敏な ④急な 副 ①鋭く，急に ②（時間が）ちょうど

□ **sharpen** 動 ①鋭くする，鋭くなる，とぐ ②厳しくする ③敏感になる

□ **sharply** 副 鋭く，激しく，はっきりと

□ **she** 代 彼女は［が］

□ **sheathe** 動（剣を）さやに納める

□ **shed** 名 小屋，倉庫 動 ①（涙・血を）流す ②（服・皮・殻などを）脱ぎすてる，脱皮［脱毛，落葉］する ③捨てる，解雇する

□ **sheep** 名 羊

□ **sheep-hook** 名 羊飼いの杖《羊飼いは低い社会階級に属していたために，低い社会階級や粗野な人物を連想させた》

□ **sheep-shearing** 名 羊毛刈り

□ **sheet** 名 ①シーツ ②（紙などの）1枚

□ **shelf** 名 棚

□ **shell** 名 ①貝がら，（木の実・卵などの）から ②（建物の）骨組み

□ **shellfish** 名 貝，甲殻類《カニ，エビなど》

□ **shelter** 名 ①避難所，隠れ家 ②保護，避難 動 避難する，隠れる

□ **shelves** 名 shelf（棚）の複数

□ **shepherd** 名 ①羊飼い ②牧師 動（羊の）番をする，導く

□ **shepherdess** 名 女性の羊飼い

□ **shine** 動 ①光る，輝く ②光らせる，磨く 名 光，輝き

□ **ship** 名 船，飛行船 動 ①船に積む，運送する ②乗船する

□ **shipwreck** 名 難破（船） 動 難破させる

□ **shock** 名 衝撃，ショック 動 ショックを与える

□ **shocked** 形 ～にショックを受けて，憤慨して

□ **shocking** 形 衝撃的な，ショッキングな

□ **shone** 動 shine（光る）の過去，過去分詞

□ **shook** 動 shake（振る）の過去

□ **shop** 名 ①店，小売り店 ②仕事場 動 買い物をする

□ **shore** 名 岸，海岸，陸 **on shore** 陸に，上陸して

□ **short** 形 ①短い ②背の低い ③不足している 副 ①手短に，簡単に ②不足して 名 ①《the –》要点 ②短編映画 ③（野球で）ショート

□ **shortly** 副 まもなく，すぐに

□ **should** 助 ～すべきである，～したほうがよい **should have done** ～すべきだった（のにしなかった）《仮定法》

□ **shoulder** 名 肩 動 肩にかつぐ，肩で押し分けて進む

□ **shout** 動 叫ぶ，大声で言う，どなりつける 名 叫び，大声，悲鳴

□ **show** 動 ①見せる，示す，見える ②明らかにする，教える ③案内する 名 ①表示，見世物，ショー ②外見，様子 **show ～ around** ～を案内して回る **show ～ how to ...** ～に…のやり方を示す

□ **shower** 名 ①にわか雨，夕立 ②《a – of ～》たくさんの～ 動 にわか雨が降る，雨のように注ぐ

□ **shown** 動 show（見せる）の過去分詞

□ **shrank** 動 shrink（縮む）の過去

□ **shrew** 名《軽蔑的・やや古》口やかましい［ガミガミ］女

□ **shrewd** 形 抜け目のない，敏感な

□ **shrewish** 形《軽蔑的・やや古》（女性が）口やかましい［うるさい］

- □ **shrine** 名廟, 聖堂, 神社
- □ **shrink** 動①縮む, 縮小する ②尻込みする, ひるむ
- □ **shroud** 名①経かたびら《死体に着せる白衣》②覆うもの, とばり 動(死体に)経かたびらを着せる, 覆い隠す
- □ **shrug** 動(肩を)すくめる
- □ **shut** 動①閉まる, 閉める, 閉じる ②たたむ ③閉じ込める ④shutの過去, 過去分詞 **shut in** ～に閉じ込める
- □ **Shylock** 名シャイロック《ユダヤ人の金貸し》
- □ **shyness** 名内気
- □ **Sicilian** 名シチリア人
- □ **Sicily** 名シチリア《イタリアの島》
- □ **sick** 形①病気の ②むかついて, いや気がさして
- □ **sicken** 動①吐き気がする, うんざりさせる ②病気になる[させる]
- □ **sickness** 名病気
- □ **side** 名側, 横, そば, 斜面 形①側面の, 横の ②副次的な 動(～の)側につく, 賛成する **one side** 片側
- □ **siege** 名包囲攻撃
- □ **sigh** 動ため息をつく, ため息をついて言う 名ため息
- □ **sight** 名①見ること, 視力, 視界 ②光景, 眺め ③見解 **at first sight** 一目見て **at the sight of** ～を見るとすぐに **lose sight of** ～を見失う **out of sight** 見えないところに
- □ **sign** 名①きざし, 徴候 ②跡 ③記号 ④身振り, 合図, 看板 動①署名する, サインする ②合図する
- □ **signor** 名～殿, ～様《イタリア語》
- □ **silence** 名沈黙, 無言, 静寂 動沈黙させる, 静める **in silence** 黙って, 沈黙のうちに
- □ **silent** 形①無言の, 黙っている ②静かな, 音を立てない ③活動しない
- □ **silk** 名絹(布), 生糸 形絹の, 絹製の
- □ **silken** 形①絹の(ような) ②柔らかくてつやつやした ③上品な
- □ **silkworm** 名カイコ《昆虫》
- □ **silly** 形おろかな, 思慮のない
- □ **silver** 名銀, 銀貨, 銀色 形銀製の
- □ **similar** 形同じような, 類似した, 相似の
- □ **similarity** 名類似(点), 相似
- □ **simple** 形①単純な, 簡単な, 質素な ②単一の, 単独の ③普通の, ただの
- □ **simply** 副①簡単に ②単に, ただ ③まったく, 完全に
- □ **sin** 名(道徳・宗教上の)罪
- □ **since** 接①～以来 ②～だから 前～以来 副それ以来 **ever since** それ以来ずっと
- □ **sincere** 形誠実な, まじめな
- □ **sincerely** 副真心をこめて
- □ **sincerity** 名正直, 誠実
- □ **sing** 動①(歌を)歌う ②さえずる
- □ **singing** 名歌うこと, 歌声 形歌う, さえずる
- □ **single** 形①たった1つの ②1人用の, それぞれの ③独身の ④片道の 名①片道乗車券 ②(ホテルなどの)1人用の部屋 ③《-s》(テニスなどの)シングルス
- □ **sink** 動沈む, 沈める, 落ち込む 名(台所の)流し
- □ **sir** 名①あなた, 先生《目上の男性, 客などに対する呼びかけ》②拝啓《手紙の書き出し》
- □ **sister** 名①姉妹, 姉, 妹 ②修道女
- □ **sister-in-law** 名義理の姉[妹]
- □ **sit** 動①座る, 腰掛ける ②止まる ③位置する **sit on** ～の上に乗る, ～の上に乗って動けないようにする
- □ **situate** 動(ある場所に)置く, 位置づける
- □ **situation** 名①場所, 位置 ②状況, 境遇, 立場
- □ **six** 名6(の数字), 6人[個] 形6の, 6人[個]の
- □ **sixteen** 名16, 16個
- □ **sixth** 名第6番目(の人・物), 6日 形第6番目の
- □ **size** 名大きさ, 寸法, サイズ 動(大きさに従って)分類する, 測る
- □ **skill** 名①技能, 技術 ②上手, 熟練
- □ **skillful** 形熟練した, 腕のいい
- □ **skillfully** 副上手に, 熟練して
- □ **skim** 動①すくい取る ②かすめて飛ぶ ③ざっと読む 名すくい取ること
- □ **skin** 名皮膚, 皮, 革(製品) 動皮をはぐ, すりむく
- □ **sky** 名①空, 天空, 大空 ②天気, 空模様, 気候
- □ **slain** 形殺された, 殺害された
- □ **slander** 名名誉毀損, 中傷, 悪口 動中傷する
- □ **slash** 動サッと切りつけること
- □ **slaughter** 動虐殺する, 打ち負かす 名大虐殺, 完敗
- □ **slave** 名奴隷 動(奴隷のように)あくせく働く

□ **slavery** 名奴隷制度, 奴隷状態

□ **sleep** 動①眠る, 寝る ②活動しない 名①睡眠, 冬眠 ②静止, 不活動 **sleep in** 寝床に入る, 朝寝坊する, 住み込む

□ **sleeping** 形眠っている, 休止している 名睡眠(状態), 不活動

□ **sleeve** 名袖, たもと, スリーブ

□ **slender** 形①ほっそりとした ②わずかな

□ **slept** 動sleep(眠る)の過去, 過去分詞

□ **slight** 形①わずかな ②ほっそりして ③とるに足らない

□ **slip** 動滑る, 滑らせる, 滑って転ぶ 名滑ること

□ **slow** 形遅い 副遅く, ゆっくりと 動遅くする, 速度を落とす

□ **slowly** 副遅く, ゆっくり

□ **sly** 形ずる賢い, いたずらっぽい

□ **small** 形①小さい, 少ない ②取るに足りない 副小さく, 細かく

□ **smart** 形①利口な, 抜け目のない ②きちんとした, 洗練された ③激しい, ずきずきする 動ひりひり[ずきずき]痛む

□ **smash** 動①粉砕する, 強打する ②撃破する 名①粉砕(音), 強打, 衝突 ②破滅, 破産

□ **smell** 動①(～の)においがする ②においをかぐ ③かぎつける, 感づく 名①嗅覚 ②におい, 香り

□ **smile** 動微笑する, にっこり笑う 名微笑, ほほえみ **smile at** ～に微笑みかける

□ **smiling** 形微笑する, にこにこした

□ **snake** 名ヘビ(蛇) 動(体を)くねらす, 蛇行する

□ **snakeskin** 名ヘビ革

□ **snap** 動①ぽきっと折る, ぷつんと切る ②ぱたんと閉じる[閉まる] 名①ぱちっ[ぴしっ]という音, ぽきっと折れること ②留め金, スナップ

□ **snatch** 動①ひったくる ②(睡眠・食事などを)急いで取る 名ひったくり

□ **snip** 動(はさみで)ちょんと切る品 名ちょんと切ること, 切れ端

□ **snore** 名いびき 動いびきをかく

□ **snowy** 形雪の多い, 雪のように白い

□ **so** 副①とても ②同様に, ～もまた ③《先行する句・節の代用》そのように, そう 接①だから, それで ②では, さて **and so** そこで, それだから, それで **and so forth** など, その他 **so ～ as to ...** …するほど～で **so far** 今までのところ, これまでは **so long as** ～する限りは **so many** 非常に多くの **so that** ～するために, それで, ～できるように **so ～ that ...** 非常に～なので…

□ **sober** 形①しらふの, 酒を飲んでいない ②冷静な, まじめな

□ **society** 名社会, 世間

□ **soft** 形①柔らかい, 手ざわり[口あたり]のよい ②温和な, 落ち着いた ③(処分などが)厳しくない, 手ぬるい, 甘い

□ **soften** 動柔らかくなる[する], 和らぐ

□ **softly** 副柔らかに, 優しく, そっと

□ **soil** 名土, 土地 動汚す

□ **sold** 動sell(売る)の過去, 過去分詞

□ **soldier** 名兵士, 兵卒

□ **sole** 形唯一の, 単独の 名足の裏, 靴底

□ **solemn** 形まじめな, おごそかな, 神聖な

□ **solid** 形①固体[固形]の ②頑丈な ③信頼できる 名固体, 固形物

□ **solitary** 形ひとりの, 孤独な, 人里離れた

□ **solve** 動解く, 解決する

□ **some** 形①いくつかの, 多少の ②ある, 誰か, 何か 副約, およそ 代①いくつか ②ある人[物]たち **for some reason** なんらかの理由で, どういうわけか **for some time** しばらくの間 **in some way** 何とかして, 何らかの方法で **some time** いつか, そのうち

□ **somehow** 副①どうにかこうにか, ともかく, 何とかして ②どういうわけか

□ **someone** 代ある人, 誰か

□ **something** 代①ある物, 何か ②いくぶん, 多少

□ **sometimes** 副時々, 時たま

□ **somewhat** 副いくらか, やや, 多少

□ **somewhere** 副①どこかへ[に] ②いつか, およそ

□ **son** 名息子, 子弟, ～の子

□ **song** 名歌, 詩歌, 鳴き声

□ **son-in-law** 名義理の息子

□ **sonnet** 名ソネット, 14行詩

□ **soon** 副まもなく, すぐに, すみやかに **as soon as** ～するとすぐ, ～するや否や **no sooner** ～するや否や

□ **soothe** 動なだめる, 慰める

□ **sorcerer** 名魔法使い, 魔術師

□ **sorceress** 名魔女

□ **sorely** 形(感情などの程度が)非常に, ひどく, 激しく

□ **sorrow** 名悲しみ, 後悔

□ **sorrowfully** 副悲しそうに, 悲しんで

□ **sorry** 形気の毒に[申し訳なく]思う, 残念な **feel sorry for** ～をかわいそうに思う

□ **sort** 名種類, 品質 動分類する **a sort of** ～のようなもの, 一種の～ **sort out** ～を整理[解決]する

□ **sought** 動seek(捜し求める)の過去, 過去分詞

□ **soul** 名①魂 ②精神, 心

□ **sound** 名音, 騒音, 響き, サウンド 動①音がする, 鳴る ②(～のように)思われる, (～と)聞こえる 形①健全な ②妥当な ③(睡眠が)ぐっすりの 副(睡眠を)ぐっすりと, 十分に **sound like** ～のように聞こえる

□ **soundly** 副①こっぴどく, 激しく ②(睡眠などが)ぐっすりと

□ **south** 名《the –》南, 南方, 南部 形南の, 南方[南部]の

□ **spade** 名①鋤, 踏みぐわ ②(トランプの)スペード 動鋤で掘り起こす, 耕す

□ **spaniel** 名スパニエル犬

□ **Spanish** 形スペイン(人・語)の 名①スペイン人 ②スペイン語

□ **spare** 動①取っておく ②(～を)惜しむ, 節約する 形暇の, 予備の 名予備品, スペア

□ **sparrow** 名スズメ(雀)

□ **speak** 動話す, 言う, 演説する **speak about** ～について話す **speak of** ～を口にする **speak to** ～と話す

□ **speaking** 形話す, ものを言う 名話すこと, 談話, 演説

□ **special** 形①特別の, 特殊の, 臨時の ②専門の

□ **specially** 副特別に

□ **specific** 形明確な, はっきりした, 具体的な

□ **spectator** 名観客, 見物人

□ **speech** 名演説, 言語, 語 **make a speech** 演説をする

□ **speechless** 形無言の, 口がきけない

□ **speed** 名速力, 速度 動①急ぐ, 急がせる ②制限速度以上で走る, スピード違反をする

□ **speedy** 形速い, 迅速な

□ **spell** 動①(語を)つづる, つづりを言う ②呪文にかける 名①一続き, ひとしきり ②呪文, まじない

□ **spend** 動①(金などを)使う, 消費[浪費]する ②(時を)過ごす

□ **spent** 動spend(使う)の過去, 過去分詞 形使い果たした, 疲れ切った

□ **spill** 動こぼす, まき散らす 名こぼすこと, 流出

□ **spinster** 名糸紡ぎ女

□ **spirit** 名①霊 ②精神, 気力

□ **spirited** 形活発な, 元気のいい, 威勢のいい

□ **spit** 動吐く, つばを吐く 名つば(を吐くこと)

□ **spite** 名悪意, うらみ **in spite of** ～にもかかわらず

□ **splendid** 形見事な, 壮麗な, 堂々とした

□ **splendor** 名壮観, 豪華, 輝き

□ **split** 動裂く, 裂ける, 割る, 割れる, 分裂させる[する] 名①裂くこと, 割れること ②裂け目, 割れ目

□ **spoil** 動①台なしにする, だめになる ②甘やかす

□ **spoiled** 形(食べ物が)腐った

□ **spoiler** 名ネタバレ

□ **spoke** 動speak(話す)の過去

□ **spoken** 動speak(話す)の過去分詞 形口語の

□ **sport** 名①スポーツ ②気晴らし, 娯楽 **in sport** 冗談で

□ **spot** 名①地点, 場所, 立場 ②斑点, しみ 動①～を見つける ②点を打つ, しみをつける

□ **spotted** 形斑点のある, まだらの, ぶちの

□ **spout** 動①噴き出る, 噴き出す ②べらべらしゃべる 名注ぎ口, 蛇口, 噴出

□ **spread** 動①広がる, 広げる, 伸びる, 伸ばす ②塗る, まく, 散布する 名広がり, 拡大

□ **spring** 名①春 ②泉, 源 ③ばね, ぜんまい 動跳ねる, 跳ぶ

□ **sprite** 名妖精

□ **spurn** 動拒絶する, 突っぱねる

□ **spy** 名スパイ 動ひそかに見張る, スパイする

□ **squirrel** 名リス

□ **St. Jaques le Grand** 聖ジャック・ル・グラン《守護聖人》

□ **stab** 名刺し傷, 突き傷 動①(突き)刺す ②中傷する

□ **stable** 形安定した, 堅固な, 分解しにくい 名馬小屋, 厩舎

□ **stage** 名①舞台 ②段階 動上演する

□ **stagger** 動よろめく, ぐらつかせる

□ **stain** 動①(～に)染みを付ける, (～を)汚す ②(評判などを)傷つける, おとしめる

□ **stamp** 名①印 ②切手 動①印を押す ②踏

みつける

□ **stand** 動 ①立つ, 立たせる, 立っている, ある ②耐える, 立ち向かう 名 ①台, 屋台, スタンド ②《the -s》観覧席 ③立つこと **stand by** そばに立つ, 傍観する, 待機する **stand for** ～を意味する, ～を支持する, ～を我慢する, ～をこらえる **stand up to** ～に耐える

□ **star** 名 ①星, 星形の物 ②人気者 形 星形の

□ **star-crossed** 形 星回りの悪い, 薄幸な

□ **stare** 動 じっと[じろじろ]見る 名 じっと見ること, 凝視

□ **start** 動 ①出発する, 始まる, 始める ②生じる, 生じさせる 名 出発, 開始 **start doing** ～し始める **start to do** ～し始める

□ **startled** 形 びっくりして, あっと驚いて

□ **starve** 動 ①餓死する, 飢えさせる ②熱望する

□ **starved** 形 (食べ物に)飢えた

□ **state** 名 ①あり様, 状態 ②国家, (アメリカなどの)州 ③階層, 地位 動 述べる, 表明する **affairs of state** 政務 **in a fit state** ～できる状態である

□ **stately** 形 堂々とした, 威厳のある

□ **station** 名 ①駅 ②署, 局, 本部, 部署 動 部署につかせる, 配置する

□ **statue** 名 像

□ **status** 名 ①(社会的な)地位, 身分, 立場 ②状態

□ **stay** 動 ①とどまる, 泊まる, 滞在する ②持続する, (～の)ままでいる 名 滞在 **stay at** (場所)に泊まる **stay away from** ～から離れている **stay in** 家にいる, (場所)に泊まる, 滞在する **stay with** ～の所に泊まる

□ **steady** 形 ①しっかりした, 安定した, 落ち着いた ②堅実な, まじめな

□ **steal** 動 ①盗む ②こっそりと手に入れる, こっそりと～する 名 盗み, 盗品 **steal away** ～をこっそり盗み去る **steal up** 忍び寄る

□ **steel** 名 鋼, 鋼鉄(製の物) 形 鋼鉄の, 堅い

□ **step** 名 ①歩み, 1歩(の距離) ②段階 ③踏み段, 階段 動 歩む, 踏む **step out of** ～から出る

□ **stern** 形 厳格な, 厳しい

□ **sternly** 副 厳格に, 厳しく

□ **steward** 名 家令, 執事

□ **stifle** 動 ①窒息させる, 息の根を止める ②鎮圧する

□ **still** 副 ①まだ, 今でも ②それでも(なお) 形 静止した, 静かな

□ **stimulate** 動 ①刺激する ②促す, 活性化させる ③元気づける

□ **sting** 動 刺す, ひりひりさせる 名 ①(昆虫などの)針, とげ ②刺すこと, 刺されること

□ **stir** 動 動かす, かき回す 名 動き, かき回すこと **stir up** 荒立てる, 引き起こす

□ **stock** 名 ①貯蔵 ②仕入れ品, 在庫品 ③株式 動 仕入れる, 蓄える

□ **stocks** 名 (刑罰道具の)ストック, 足かせ

□ **stole** 動 steal (盗む)の過去

□ **stolen** 動 steal (盗む)の過去分詞

□ **stone** 名 ①石, 小石 ②宝石 形 石の, 石製の

□ **stood** 動 stand (立つ)の過去, 過去分詞

□ **stool** 名 腰掛け, 踏み台

□ **stoop** 動 ①かがむ, 猫背である ②落ちぶれて～する 名 かがむこと, 猫背

□ **stop** 動 ①やめる, やめさせる, 止める, 止まる ②立ち止まる 名 ①停止 ②停留所, 駅 **stop by** 途中で立ち寄る, ちょっと訪ねる **stop doing** ～するのをやめる

□ **store** 名 ①店 ②蓄え ③貯蔵庫, 倉庫 動 蓄える, 貯蔵する **in store** 蓄えて, 用意されて

□ **storm** 名 ①嵐, 暴風雨 ②強襲 動 ①襲撃[強襲]する ②嵐が吹く ③突入する

□ **story** 名 ①物語, 話 ②(建物の)階

□ **storyteller** 名 ①物語をする人, 物語作家 ②うそつき

□ **straight** 形 ①一直線の, まっすぐな, 直立[垂直]の ②率直な, 整然とした 副 ①一直線に, まっすぐに, 垂直に ②率直に 名 一直線, ストレート

□ **strange** 形 ①知らない, 見[聞き]慣れない ②奇妙な, 変わった

□ **strangely** 副 奇妙に, 変に, 不思議なことに, 不慣れに

□ **stranger** 名 ①見知らぬ人, 他人 ②不案内[不慣れ]な人

□ **stratagem** 名 策略

□ **straw** 名 麦わら, ストロー

□ **strawberry** 名 イチゴ(苺)

□ **streaked** 形 縞入りの

□ **stream** 名 ①小川, 流れ ②風潮 動 流れ出る, 流れる, なびく

□ **street** 名 ①街路 ②《S-》～通り

□ **strength** 名 ①力, 体力 ②長所, 強み ③強度, 濃度

□ **strewn** 動 strew (まき散らす)の過去分詞 形 散らかった, 散らばった

□ **strict** 形 厳しい, 厳密な

□ **strictly** 副厳しく, 厳密に

□ **strife** 名争い, 不和

□ **strike** 動①打つ, ぶつかる ②(災害などが)急に襲う 名①ストライキ ②打つこと, 打撃

□ **stroke** 名①一撃, 一打ち ②一動作 ③一なで, 一さすり 動なでる, さする

□ **strong** 形①強い, 堅固な, 強烈な ②濃い ③得意な 副強く, 猛烈に

□ **strongly** 副強く, 頑丈に, 猛烈に, 熱心に

□ **strong-willed** 形意志の強い, 断固とした

□ **struck** 動strike (打つ) の過去, 過去分詞

□ **struggle** 動もがく, 奮闘する 名もがき, 奮闘

□ **strut** 動気取って歩く

□ **stubborn** 形頑固な, 強情な

□ **stuck** 動stick (刺さる) の過去, 過去分詞

□ **student** 名学生, 生徒

□ **study** 動①勉強する, 研究する ②調べる 名①勉強, 研究 ②書斎

□ **stuff** 名①材料, 原料 ②もの, 持ち物 動詰める, 詰め込む

□ **stumble** 動①よろめく, つまずく ②偶然出会う 名つまずき

□ **stun** 動①あ然とさせる, びっくりさせる ②衝撃を与える, 気絶させる

□ **stung** 動sting (刺す) の過去, 過去分詞

□ **stupid** 形ばかな, おもしろくない

□ **style** 名やり方, 流儀, 様式, スタイル

□ **subdue** 動征服する, 抑える

□ **subject** 名①話題, 議題, 主題 ②学科 ③題材, 対象 形①支配を受ける, 従属している ②(〜を)受けやすい, (〜を)必要とする 動服従させる

□ **submit** 動①服従する, 服従させる ②提出する

□ **subtle** 形微妙な, かすかな, 繊細な, 敏感な, 器用な

□ **succeed** 動①成功する ②(〜の)跡を継ぐ **succeed in doing** 〜する事に成功する

□ **success** 名成功, 幸運, 上首尾

□ **successful** 形成功した, うまくいった

□ **successive** 形連続する, 続く

□ **successor** 名後継者, 相続人, 後任者

□ **such** 形①そのような, このような ②そんなに, とても, 非常に 代そのような人[物] **as such** 〜など **such a** そのような **such as** たとえば〜, 〜のような **such 〜 as ...** …のような〜 **such 〜 that ...** 非常に〜なので…

□ **suck** 動吸う, しゃぶる 名吸うこと

□ **sudden** 形突然の, 急な

□ **suddenly** 副突然, 急に

□ **suffer** 動①(苦痛・損害などを)受ける, こうむる ②(病気に)なる, 苦しむ, 悩む

□ **sufficient** 形十分な, 足りる

□ **suggest** 動①提案する ②示唆する

□ **suggestion** 名①提案, 忠告 ②気配, 暗示

□ **suit** 名①スーツ, 背広 ②訴訟 ③ひとそろい, 一組 動①適合する[させる] ②似合う

□ **suitable** 形適当な, 似合う, ふさわしい

□ **suite** 名①(ホテルなどの)スイートルーム, 家具のセット, ひとそろい ②(音楽で)組曲 ③随行員, 側近

□ **suitor** 名求婚者《女性と結婚したがっている男性》

□ **sullenly** 副不機嫌に, ふてくされた様子で

□ **sum** 名①総計 ②金額 動①合計する ②要約する

□ **summer** 名夏

□ **summon** 動呼び出す, 要求する

□ **sun** 名《the –》太陽, 日

□ **Sunday** 名日曜日

□ **sung** 動sing (歌う) の過去分詞

□ **sunk** 動sink (沈む) の過去分詞

□ **sunny** 形①日当たりのよい, 日のさす ②陽気な, 快活な

□ **sunset** 名日没, 夕焼け

□ **super-dainty** 形超可憐な

□ **superior** 形優れた, 優秀な, 上方の 名優れた人, 目上(の人)

□ **supper** 名夕食, 晩さん, 夕飯

□ **suppertime** 名夕食時

□ **supply** 動供給[配給]する, 補充する 名供給(品), 給与, 補充

□ **support** 動①支える, 支持する ②養う, 援助する 名①支え, 支持 ②援助, 扶養

□ **suppose** 動①仮定する, 推測する ②《be -d to 〜》〜することになっている, 〜するものである

□ **supposed** 形仮定された, 想定されている, 思われている **be supposed to** 〜することになっている, 〜するはずである

□ **supremacy** 名優位, 主権, 至高

□ **sure** 形確かな, 確実な, 《be – to 〜》必ず[きっと]〜する, 確信して 副確かに, まったく, 本当に **be sure to do** 必ず〜する **make sure**

確かめる，確認する **sure enough** 思ったとおり，確かに
- □ **surely** 副確かに，きっと
- □ **surprise** 動驚かす，不意に襲う 名驚き，不意打ち
- □ **surprised** 形驚いた **be surprised at** ～に驚く **be surprised to do** ～して驚く
- □ **surprising** 形驚くべき，意外な
- □ **surround** 動囲む，包囲する
- □ **survive** 動①生き残る，存続する，なんとかなる ②長生きする，切り抜ける
- □ **suspect** 動疑う，(～ではないかと)思う 名容疑者，注意人物
- □ **suspense** 名①(映画・小説などの)サスペンス ②宙ぶらりんの状態，不安
- □ **suspicion** 名①容疑，疑い ②感づくこと
- □ **suspicious** 形あやしい，疑い深い
- □ **suspiciously** 副疑い深く，あやしそうに
- □ **swallow** 名ツバメ(燕) 動①飲み込む ②うのみにする
- □ **swan** 名ハクチョウ(白鳥)
- □ **swear** 動①誓う，断言する ②口汚くののしる
- □ **sweet** 形①甘い ②快い ③親切な ④かわいい，魅力的な 名①《-s》甘い菓子 ②甘い味[香り]，甘いもの ③いとしい人，《my -》あなた《呼びかけ》
- □ **sweetly** 副甘く，優しく
- □ **sweetness** 名①甘さ ②優しさ，美しさ
- □ **sweet-smelling** 形香りのよい
- □ **swell** 動①ふくらむ，ふくらませる ②増加する，増やす 名膨張，増大
- □ **swept** 動sweep(掃く)の過去，過去分詞
- □ **swift** 形速い，迅速な
- □ **swim** 動泳ぐ 名泳ぎ
- □ **switch** 名スイッチ 動①スイッチを入れる[切る] ②切り替える，切り替わる
- □ **swoon** 名(ショックなどによる)気絶，卒倒
- □ **sword** 名①剣，刀 ②武力
- □ **swordfight** 名剣戟
- □ **swordsman** 名剣士
- □ **swordsmen** 名swordsman(剣士)の複数形
- □ **swore** 動swear(誓う)の過去
- □ **sworn** 動swear(誓う)の過去分詞
- □ **sycamore** 名プラタナス，西洋スズカケノキ
- □ **Sycorax** 名シコラックス《魔女》
- □ **sympathetic** 形同情する，思いやりのある
- □ **Syracuse** 名シラクサ《古代都市》
- □ **Syracusian** 形シラクサの

T

- □ **table** 名①テーブル，食卓，台 ②一覧表 動卓上に置く，棚上げにする
- □ **tablet** 名①錠剤，タブレット ②便箋，メモ帳 ③銘板
- □ **tailor** 名仕立屋，テーラー 動(服を)仕立てる，注文で作る
- □ **take** 動①取る，持つ ②持って[連れて]いく，捕らえる ③乗る ④(時間・労力を)費やす，必要とする ⑤(ある動作を)する ⑥飲む ⑦耐える，受け入れる **It takes someone ～ to ...** (人)が…するのに～(時間など)がかかる **take a rest** 休息する **take advantage of** ～を利用する，～につけ込む **take away** ①連れ去る ②取り上げる，奪い去る ③取り除く **take back** ①取り戻す ②(言葉，約束を)取り消す，撤回する **take care** 気をつける，注意する **take hold of** ～をつかむ，捕らえる，制する **take in** 取り入れる，取り込む，(作物・金などを)集める **take into** 手につかむ，中に取り入れる **take off** (衣服を)脱ぐ，取り去る，～を取り除く，離陸する，出発する **take on** 雇う，(仕事などを)引き受ける **take one's place** (人と)交代する，(人)の代わりをする，後任になる **take over** 引き継ぐ，支配する，乗っ取る **take part in** ～に参加する **take pity on** ～に同情を示す，～を哀れむ **take place** 行われる，起こる **take refuge** 避難する，逃げ込む **take someone away** (人)を連れ出す **take someone home** (人)を家まで送る **take ～ to ...** ～を…に連れて行く **take ～ to heart** ～を深く悲しむ
- □ **taken** 動take(取る)の過去分詞
- □ **tale** 名①話，物語 ②うわさ，悪口
- □ **talk** 動話す，語る，相談する 名①話，おしゃべり ②演説 ③《the –》話題 **talk of** ～のことを話す
- □ **talkative** 形話し好きな，おしゃべりな
- □ **tall** 形高い，背の高い
- □ **tame** 形管理された，飼いならされた 動飼いならす，従わせる
- □ **taming** 名飼いならし
- □ **tankard** 名タンカード《取っ手とふたのついた金属・陶器製の大コップ》.
- □ **tart** 名タルト《菓子》
- □ **tartness** 名酸味

□ **task** 名（やるべき）仕事, 職務, 課題 動仕事を課す, 負担をかける

□ **taste** 名 ①味, 風味 ②好み, 趣味 動味がする, 味わう

□ **taunt** 動あざける, からかう

□ **teach** 動教える

□ **tear** 名 ①涙 ②裂け目 動裂く, 破る, 引き離す **in tears** 涙を流しながら **tear at** ～を引き裂こうとする

□ **teardrop** 名涙, 涙のしずく

□ **tease** 動いじめる, からかう, 悩ます

□ **tedious** 形うんざりするような, 退屈な

□ **teenage** 形ティーンエイジャーの, 10代の

□ **teeth** 名tooth（歯）の複数

□ **tell** 動 ①話す, 言う, 語る ②教える, 知らせる, 伝える ③わかる, 見分ける **tell a lie** うそをつく **tell of** ～について話す［説明する］ **tell off**（人）をしかりつける **tell ～ to ...** ～に…するように言う **to tell the truth** 実は, 実を言えば

□ **temper** 名 ①気質, 気性, 気分 ②短気 動 ①～の厳しさを和らげる, ～を調節する ②鍛える

□ **temperament** 名気質, 気性

□ **tempest** 名嵐, 暴風雨

□ **temple** 名 ①寺, 神殿 ②こめかみ

□ **temporary** 形一時的な, 仮の

□ **tempt** 動誘う, 誘惑する, 導く, 心を引きつける

□ **ten** 名10（の数字）, 10人［個］ 形10の, 10人［個］の

□ **tend** 動 ①（～の）傾向がある,（～）しがちである ②面倒を見る, 手入れをする

□ **tender** 形柔らかい, もろい, 弱い, 優しい

□ **tenderly** 副優しく, そっと

□ **tenderness** 名柔らかさ, もろさ, 優しさ

□ **term** 名 ①期間, 期限 ②語, 用語 ③《-s》条件 ④《-s》関係, 仲 **in terms of** ～の言葉で言えば, ～の点から **on ～ terms with ...** …と～な仲である

□ **terrible** 形恐ろしい, ひどい, ものすごい, つらい

□ **terribly** 副ひどく

□ **terrified** 形おびえた, こわがった

□ **terror** 名 ①恐怖 ②恐ろしい人［物］

□ **test** 名試験, テスト, 検査 動試みる, 試験する

□ **than** 接 ～よりも, ～以上に **be no bigger than** ～ほどの大きさだ **more than** ～以上 **no more than** ただの～にすぎない **rather than** ～よりむしろ **would rather ～ than ...** …よりむしろ～したい

□ **thane** 名（スコットランドの）氏族の長, 領主

□ **thane of Cawdor** コーダーの領主《マクベス》

□ **thane of Fife** ファイフの領主《マクダフ》

□ **thane of Glamis** グラミズの領主《マクベス》

□ **thank** 動感謝する, 礼を言う 名《-s》感謝, 謝意 **thank ～ for** ～に対して礼を言う **thanks to** ～のおかげで, ～の結果

□ **thankless** 形感謝知らずの, 恩知らずの

□ **that** 形その, あの 代 ①それ, あれ, その［あの］人［物］ ②《関係代名詞》～である… 接 ～ということ, ～なので, ～だから 副そんなに, それほど **after that** その後 **at that moment** その時に, その瞬間に **at that time** その時 **from that time on** あれから, あの時以来 **in that case** もしそうなら **now that** 今や～だから, ～からには **so that** ～するために, それで, ～できるように **so ～ that ...** 非常に～なので… **such ～ that ...** 非常に～なので… **those that** それらの物

□ **the** 冠 ①その, あの ②《形容詞の前で》～な人々 副《－＋比較級, －＋比較級》～すればするほど…

□ **thee** 代汝を, 汝は

□ **their** 代彼（女）らの, それらの

□ **theirs** 代彼（女）らのもの, それらのもの

□ **them** 代彼（女）らを［に］, それらを［に］

□ **theme** 名主題, テーマ, 作文

□ **themselves** 代彼（女）ら自身, それら自身

□ **then** 副その時（に・は）, それから, 次に 名その時 形その当時の **just then** そのとたんに

□ **there** 副 ①そこに［で・の］, そこへ, あそこへ ②《－is［are］～》～がある［いる］ 名そこ **get there** そこに到着する, 目的を達成する, 成功する **over there** あそこに **there is no way** ～する見込みはない **there lived ～.** ～が住んでいました。

□ **therefore** 副したがって, それゆえ, その結果

□ **these** 代これら, これ 形これらの, この **these days** このごろ

□ **Theseus** 名シーシアス《アテネの領主》

□ **they** 代 ①彼（女）らは［が］, それらは［が］ ②（一般の）人々は［が］

□ **thick** 形厚い, 密集した, 濃厚な 副厚く, 濃く 名最も厚い［強い・濃い］部分

□ **thief** 名泥棒, 強盗

□ **thieves** 名thief（泥棒）の複数

□ **thin** 形薄い, 細い, やせた, まばらな 副薄く 動薄く[細く]なる, 薄くする

□ **thing** 名①物, 事 ②《-s》事情, 事柄 ③《one's -s》持ち物, 身の回り品 ④人, やつ

□ **think** 動思う, 考える **think of** ～のことを考える, ～を思いつく, 考え出す

□ **third** 名第3(の人[物]) 形第3の, 3番の

□ **this** 形①この, こちらの, これを ②今の, 現在の 代①これ, この人[物] ②今, ここ **by this time** この時までに, もうすでに **in this way** このようにして **like this** このような, こんなふうに **this one** これ, こちら **this way** このように

□ **thistle** 名アザミ(薊)

□ **thorn** 名とげ, とげのある植物, いばら

□ **those** 形それらの, あれらの 代それら[あれら]の人[物] **in those days** あのころは, 当時は **those that** それらの物 **those who** ～する人々

□ **thou** 代汝, そなた《主格のyouに当たる》

□ **though** 接①～にもかかわらず, ～だが ②たとえ～でも 副しかし **as though** あたかも～のように, まるで～みたいに **even though** ～であるけれども, ～にもかかわらず

□ **thought** 動think(思う)の過去, 過去分詞 名考え, 意見

□ **thousand** 名①1000(の数字), 1000人[個] ②《－s》何千, 多数 形①1000の, 1000人[個]の ②多数の

□ **threat** 名おどし, 脅迫

□ **threaten** 動脅かす, おびやかす, 脅迫する

□ **three** 名3(の数字), 3人[個] 形3の, 3人[個]の

□ **three-legged** 形3脚の, 3本足の

□ **threw** 動throw(投げる)の過去

□ **thrilled** 形ぞくぞく, わくわくして 動thrill の過去, 過去分詞

□ **throat** 名のど, 気管

□ **throb** 動①鼓動する, 脈が打つ, ずきずきする ②感動する 名①動悸, 鼓動, 脈拍 ②興奮, 感動

□ **throne** 名王座, 王権

□ **through** 前～を通して, ～中を[に], ～中 副①通して ②終わりまで, まったく, すっかり **break through** ～を打ち破る **pass through** ～を通る, 通行する **run through** 走り抜ける

□ **throughout** 前①～中, ～を通じて ②～のいたるところに 副初めから終わりまで, ずっと

□ **throw** 動投げる, 浴びせる, ひっかける 名投げること, 投球 **throw away** ～を捨てる；～を無駄に費やす, 浪費する **throw down** 投げ出す, 放棄する **throw off** 脱ぎ捨てる **throw out** 放り出す

□ **thrower-out** 名捨てる人

□ **thrown** 動throw(投げる)の過去分詞

□ **thrust** 動①強く押す, 押しつける, 突き刺す ②張り出す, 突き出る 名①ぐいと押すこと, 突き刺すこと ②《the －》要点

□ **thumb** 名親指

□ **thunder** 名雷, 雷鳴 動雷が鳴る, どなる

□ **Thursday** 名木曜日

□ **thwart** 動(計画や目的などを)阻止する, 妨害する

□ **thy** 代汝の, そなたの

□ **thyme** 名ジャコウソウ

□ **tickle** 動①くすぐる ②喜ばす

□ **tie** 動結ぶ, 束縛する 名①結び(目) ②ネクタイ ③《-s》縁, きずな **tie up** ひもで縛る, 縛り上げる, つなぐ, 拘束する, 提携させる

□ **tiff** 名ちょっとした口論[口げんか]

□ **tight** 形堅い, きつい, ぴんと張った 副堅く, しっかりと

□ **till** 前～まで(ずっと) 接～(する)まで

□ **time** 名①時, 時間, 歳月 ②時期 ③期間 ④時代 ⑤回, 倍 動時刻を決める, 時間を計る **all the time** ずっと, いつも, その間ずっと **any time** いつでも **at a time** 一度に, 続けざまに **at another time** 別の折に **at that time** その時 **at the time** そのころ, 当時は **at times** 時には **by this time** この時までに, もうすでに **every time** ～するときはいつも **for some time** しばらくの間 **for the first time** 初めて **from that time on** あれから, あの時以来 **from time to time** ときどき **have a good time** 楽しい時を過ごす **in no time** すぐに, 一瞬で **in time** 間に合って, やがて **just in time** いよいよというときに, すんでのところで, やっと間に合って **next time** 次回に **once upon a time** むかしむかし **some time** いつか, そのうち **wait a long time** 長時間待つ

□ **timidly** 副こわごわ, 臆病に

□ **tinge** 名淡い色, 色合い, 気味 動淡く着色する

□ **tiny** 形ちっぽけな, とても小さい

□ **tip** 名①チップ, 心づけ ②先端, 頂点 動①チップをやる ②先端につける

□ **tiptoe** 名つま先 動つま先で歩く

□ **tired** 形①疲れた, くたびれた ②あきた, うんざりした **be tired from** ～で疲れる

□ **tiring** 形①疲れる, 骨の折れる ②退屈させる

□ **Titania** 名ティターニア《妖精の女王》

□ **title** 名 ①題名, タイトル ②肩書, 称号 ③権利, 資格 動 題をつける, 肩書を与える

□ **to** 前 ①《方向・変化》～へ, ～に, ～の方へ ②《程度・時間》～まで ③《適合・付加・所属》～に ④《－＋動詞の原形》～するために[の], ～する, ～すること **to tell the truth** 実は, 実を言えば **to the point** 要領を得た

□ **toad** 名 ヒキガエル

□ **toast** 名 ①トースト ②乾杯 動 ①(パンなどが)焼ける, 焼く, トーストにする ②(火で)暖める ③乾杯する

□ **today** 名 今日 副 今日(で)は

□ **toe** 名 足指, つま先

□ **together** 副 ①一緒に, ともに ②同時に

□ **token** 名 ①しるし, 形見 ②トークン, 代用コイン

□ **told** 動 tell(話す)の過去, 過去分詞

□ **Tom** 名 トム《幽霊の名》

□ **tomb** 名 墓穴, 墓石, 納骨堂

□ **tomorrow** 名 明日 副 明日は

□ **tone** 名 音, 音色, 調子 動 調和する[させる]

□ **tongue** 名 ①舌 ②弁舌 ③言語

□ **tongue-in-cheek** 形 不真面目な, ふざけた

□ **tonight** 名 今夜, 今晩 副 今夜は

□ **too** 副 ①～も(また) ②あまりに～すぎる, とても～ **far too** あまりにも～過ぎる **too much** 過度の **too well** 十二分に **too ～ to ...** …するには～すぎる

□ **took** 動 take(取る)の過去

□ **tooth** 名 歯, 歯状のもの

□ **top** 名 ①頂上, 首位 ②こま 形 いちばん上の 動 ①頂上を覆う ②首位を占める ③(～より)優れる

□ **topic** 名 話題, 見出し

□ **topple** 動 つんのめる, 倒れる

□ **torch** 名 たいまつ, 光明

□ **tore** 動 tear(裂く)の過去

□ **torment** 動 困らせる, 苦しめる 名 苦痛, 苦悩, 苦労の種

□ **torn** 動 tear(裂く)の過去分詞

□ **torture** 名 (肉体的な)苦痛を与えること, 拷問 動 拷問にかける, ひどく苦しめる

□ **toss** 動 投げる, 放り上げる, 上下に動く 名 投げ上げ, トス

□ **totally** 副 全体的に, すっかり

□ **touch** 動 ①触れる, さわる, ～を触れさせる ②接触する ③感動させる 名 ①接触, 手ざわり ②手法

□ **tough** 形 堅い, 丈夫な, たくましい, 骨の折れる, 困難な

□ **toward** 前 ①《運動の方向・位置》～の方へ, ～に向かって ②《目的》～のために

□ **to-who** 副 フクロウの鳴き声の擬声語

□ **town** 名 町, 都会, 都市

□ **track** 名 ①通った跡 ②競走路, 軌道, トラック 動 追跡する

□ **trade** 名 取引, 貿易, 商業 動 取引する, 貿易する, 商売する

□ **tragedy** 名 悲劇, 惨劇

□ **tragic** 形 悲劇の, 痛ましい

□ **train** 名 ①列車, 電車 ②(～の)列, 連続 動 訓練する, 仕立てる

□ **traitor** 名 反逆者, 裏切り者

□ **trance** 名 恍惚状態, 催眠状態

□ **transform** 動 (～の状態・形・外観などを)変える

□ **trap** 名 わな, 策略 動 わなを仕掛ける, わなで捕らえる

□ **travel** 動 ①旅行する ②進む, 移動する[させる], 伝わる 名 旅行, 運行 **travel on** 旅を続ける

□ **traveler** 名 旅行者

□ **traveling** 名 旅行

□ **treacherous** 形 裏切りの, あてにならない

□ **treachery** 名 裏切り(行為), 背信, 謀反

□ **treason** 名 裏切り[反逆]行為, 背信

□ **treasure** 名 財宝, 貴重品, 宝物 動 秘蔵する

□ **treat** 動 ①扱う ②治療する ③おごる 名 ①おごり, もてなし, ごちそう ②楽しみ

□ **treatment** 名 ①取り扱い, 待遇 ②治療(法)

□ **tree** 名 ①木, 樹木, 木製のもの ②系図

□ **tremble** 動 ①震える, おののく ②(地面が)揺れる 名 震え, 身震い

□ **trembling** 形 震える, 震えおののく

□ **trial** 名 ①試み, 試験 ②試練, 苦難 ③裁判 形 試みの, 試験の

□ **tribute** 名 ①貢ぎ物, 捧げ物, 贈り物 ②賛辞, 感謝の言葉

□ **trick** 名 ①策略 ②いたずら, 冗談 ③手品, 錯覚 動 だます **play tricks** 策をろうする

□ **tricky** 形 油断のならない, 扱いにくい, ずるい

□ **tried** 動 try(試みる)の過去, 過去分詞 形 試験済みの, 信頼できる

□ **trifle** 名 くだらないこと, つまらないもの 動 いい加減に扱う, もてあそぶ, 浪費する

□ **trip** 名 ①(短い)旅行, 遠征, 遠足, 出張 ②幻覚体験, トリップ 動つまずく, しくじる **trip up**(人を)つまづかせる, (人の)足をすくう

□ **Tripoli** 名トリポリ《都市》

□ **triumph** 名(大)勝利, 大成功, 勝利の喜び 動勝利をおさめる, 成功する

□ **triumphal** 形勝利の, 祝勝の

□ **triumphant** 形勝利を得た, 勝ち誇った

□ **trivial** 形 ①ささいな ②平凡な

□ **troop** 名群れ, 隊 動ぞろぞろ歩く, 群れ[列]をなして進む

□ **trouble** 名 ①困難, 迷惑 ②心配, 苦労 ③もめごと 動 ①悩ます, 心配させる ②迷惑をかける

□ **trouble-free** 形支障のない, 問題のない, 円滑な

□ **troupe** 名一座, 一行

□ **Troy** 名トロイア《古代都市》

□ **truant** 形怠ける, 怠惰な

□ **true** 形 ①本当の, 本物の, 真の ②誠実な, 確かな 副本当に, 心から **come true** 実現する

□ **truly** 副 ①全く, 本当に, 真に ②心から, 誠実に

□ **trunk** 名 ①幹, 胴 ②本体, 主要部分 ③トランク, 旅行かばん

□ **trust** 動信用[信頼]する, 委託する 名信用, 信頼, 委託

□ **truth** 名 ①真理, 事実, 本当 ②誠実, 忠実さ **to tell the truth** 実は, 実を言えば

□ **truthful** 形正直な, 真実の

□ **try** 動 ①やってみる, 試みる ②努力する, 努める 名試み, 試し

□ **tune** 名 ①曲, 節 ②正しい調子[旋律] 動 ①(ラジオ・テレビなどを)合わせる ②(楽器の)調子を合わせる

□ **Turk** 名トルコ, トルコ人

□ **Turkish** 形トルコ(人・語)の 名トルコ語

□ **turn** 動 ①ひっくり返す, 回転する[させる], 曲がる, 曲げる, 向かう, 向ける ②(～に)なる, (～に)変える 名 ①回転, 曲がり ②順番 ③変化, 転換 **as it turned out** 後でわかったことだが **turn away** 向こうへ行く, 追い払う, (顔を)そむける, 横を向く **turn back** 元に戻る **turn into** ～に変わる **turn on** ①～の方を向く ②(スイッチなどを)ひねってつける, 出す **turn out** ①～と判明する, (結局～に)なる ②(照明などを)消す ③養成する ④出かける, 集まる ⑤外側に向く, ひっくり返す **turn out to be** ～という結果になる **turn to** ～の方を向く, ～に頼る, ～に変わる **turn white** 青ざめる, 血の気が引く

□ **tu-whit** 副フクロウの鳴き声の擬声語

□ **twelfth** 名第12(の人・物) 形第12の, 12番の

□ **twelve** 名12(の数字), 12人[個] 形12の, 12人[個]の

□ **twenty** 名20(の数字), 20人[個] 形 ①20の, 20人[個]の ②非常に多くの, 数えきれないほどの《誇張》

□ **twice** 副2倍, 2度, 2回

□ **twin** 名双子の一方, 双生児, よく似た1対の人の一方 形双子の, 1対の

□ **twist** 動 ①ねじる, よれる ②～を巻く ③身をよじる 名ねじれ, より合わせること

□ **two** 名2(の数字), 2人[個] 形2の, 2人[個]の

□ **Tybalt** 名ティボルト《ジュリエットの従兄》

□ **type** 名 ①型, タイプ, 様式 ②見本, 模様, 典型 動 ①典型となる ②タイプで打つ

□ **tyrant** 名暴君, 専制君主

U

□ **ugly** 形 ①醜い, ぶかっこうな ②いやな, 不快な, 険悪な

□ **unable** 形《be – to ～》～することができない

□ **unattractive** 形魅力のない, 人目を引かない

□ **unaware** 形無意識の, 気づかない

□ **unbelievable** 形信じられない(ほどの), 度のはずれた

□ **unbelievably** 副信じられないほど

□ **unbeliever** 名不信心者

□ **uncertain** 形不確かな, 確信がない

□ **uncertainty** 名不確かさ, 不安

□ **uncle** 名おじ

□ **unconscious** 形無意識の, 気絶した

□ **uncontrollable** 形制御できない

□ **uncontrolled** 形制御されていない

□ **uncovered** 形カバー[覆い]を取られた, 覆いのない

□ **uncrown** 動(王を)退位させる

□ **under** 前 ①《位置》～の下[に] ②《状態》～で, ～を受けて, ～のもと ③《数量》～以下[未満]の, ～より下の 形下の, 下部の 副下に[で], 従属[服従]して

□ **underdog** 名《the -》①(政治・社会的)犠牲者, 負け犬 ②(試合などで)勝ち目のない人
□ **underneath** 前 ～の下に, ～真下に 副下に[を], 根底は 名《the –》底部
□ **understand** 動理解する, わかる, ～を聞いて知っている
□ **understood** 動 understand(理解する)の過去, 過去分詞
□ **undertake** 動 ①引き受ける ②始める, 企てる
□ **underway** 形航行[進行]中の
□ **undone** 動 undo(ほどく)の過去分詞 形 ①解かれた, ほどけた ②未完成の
□ **uneasy** 形不安な, 焦って
□ **uneducated** 形教養のない, 無学の
□ **unexpected** 形思いがけない, 予期しない
□ **unfaithful** 形不誠実な, 不貞な
□ **unfit** 形向いていない, 適さない
□ **unfold** 動展開する, ～を開く[広げる]
□ **unfortunate** 形不運な, あいにくな, 不適切な
□ **unfortunately** 副不幸にも, 運悪く
□ **ungraciously** 形無礼に, 不作法に
□ **ungrateful** 形感謝しない, 恩知らずの
□ **unhappily** 副不幸に, 運悪く, 不愉快そうに
□ **unhappy** 形不運な, 不幸な
□ **unintended** 形予想外の
□ **unite** 動 ①1つにする[なる], 合わせる, 結ぶ ②結束する, 団結する
□ **university** 名(総合)大学
□ **unjust** 形不公平な, 不当な
□ **unkind** 形不親切な, 意地の悪い
□ **unkindly** 形不親切な, 意地悪な
□ **unkindness** 名不親切
□ **unknowingly** 副知らないで, 知らず知らず, 無意識のうちに
□ **unknown** 形知られていない, 不明の
□ **unlawful** 形 ①違法の, 非合法の ②不道徳な, 背徳の
□ **unless** 接もし～でなければ, ～しなければ
□ **unlike** 形似ていない, 違った 前 ～と違って
□ **unlikely** 形ありそうもない, 考えられない
□ **unlucky** 形 ①不運な ②不吉な, 縁起の悪い
□ **unmoved** 形不動の, 動じない
□ **unnatural** 形不自然な, 異常な
□ **unnecessary** 形不必要な, 余分な, 必要以上の
□ **unnoticed** 形気づかれない, 注目されない
□ **unpleasant** 形不愉快な, 気にさわる, いやな, 不快な
□ **unquiet** 形落ち着かない, そわそわした
□ **unraveling** 名白紙に戻ること
□ **unreasonable** 形理屈にあわない, 理性のない
□ **unrequited** 形(愛が)報われない, 一方的な
□ **unseen** 形目に見えない
□ **unsettled** 形不安定な, 不穏な
□ **unsheathe** 動(刀・ナイフなどを)鞘から抜く
□ **unsuccessful** 形失敗の, 不成功の
□ **untainted** 形染まっていない
□ **untaught** 形無教育の
□ **until** 前 ～まで(ずっと) 接 ～の時まで, ～するまで
□ **untrue** 形真実でない, 事実に反する
□ **untutored** 形教養のない, 無教養な
□ **unusual** 形普通でない, 珍しい, 見[聞き]慣れない
□ **unusually** 形異常に, 珍しく
□ **unweeded** 形除草していない
□ **unwelcome** 形歓迎されない
□ **unwell** 形気分[体調]が優れない, 具合の悪い
□ **unwilling** 形気が進まない, 不本意の
□ **unwillingly** 副不本意に, いやいや
□ **unwisely** 形愚かにも, よく考えずに, 無分別に
□ **unworthy** 形値しない, ふさわしくない
□ **up** 副 ①上へ, 上がって, 北へ ②立って, 近づいて ③向上して, 増して 前 ①～の上(の方)へ, 高い方へ ②(道)に沿って 形上向きの, 上りの 名上昇, 向上, 値上がり **be up to** ～する力がある, ～しようとしている, ～の責任[義務]である **bear up** 耐える, 持ちこたえる **blow up** 破裂する[させる] **break up** ばらばらになる, 解散させる **cheer up** 元気になる, 気分が引き立つ **clear up** きれいにする, 片付ける, (疑問, 問題を)解決する **come up** 近づいてくる **come up with** ～に追いつく, ～を思いつく, 考え出す, 見つけ出す **cook up** こしらえる **get up** 起き上がる, 立ち上がる **give oneself up to** ～に身を委ねる **give up** あきらめる, やめる, 引き渡す **go up** ①～に上がる, 登る ②～に近づく, 出かける **go up to** ～まで行く, 近づく **grow up** 成長する, 大人になる **keep up** 続ける, 続く,

維持する, (遅れないで) ついていく, 上げたままにしておく **lock up** ～を閉じ込める **look up** 見上げる, 調べる **look up to** ～を仰ぎ見る **pick up** 拾い上げる, 車で迎えに行く, 習得する, 再開する, 回復する **pile up** 積み重ねる **run up** ～に走り寄る **run up and down** かけずり回る **stand up to** ～に耐える **steal up** 忍び寄る **stir up** 荒立てる, 引き起こす **tie up** ひもで縛る, 縛り上げる, つなぐ, 拘束する, 提携させる **trip up** (人を) つまずかせる, (人の) 足をすくう **up and down** 上がったり下がったり, 行ったり来たり, あちこちと **up to** ～まで, ～に至るまで, ～に匹敵して **use up** ～を使い果たす **wake up** 起きる, 目を覚ます **wake up to** ～に気付く, ～で目を覚ます **walk up** 歩み寄る, 歩いて上る **walk up and down** 行ったり来たりする

□ **update** 動 最新にする, アップデートする 名 最新情報, 最新のもの

□ **upon** 前 ①《場所・接触》～(の上) に ②《日・時》～に ③《関係・従事》～に関して, ～について, ～して 副 前へ, 続けて **call upon** 求める, 頼む, 訪問する **look upon** ～を見る, 見つめる **once upon a time** むかしむかし

□ **upright** 形 ①まっすく立った, 直立した ②公正な, 正義の 名 まっすぐな状態

□ **uproar** 名 大騒ぎ, わあわあいう声

□ **upset** 形 憤慨して, 動揺して 動 気を悪くさせる, (心・神経など) をかき乱す

□ **upstairs** 副 2階へ[に], 階上へ 形 2階の, 階上の 名 2階, 階上

□ **urge** 動 ①せき立てる, 強力に推し進める, かりたてる ②《- … to ～》…に～するよう熱心に勧める 名 衝動, かりたてられるような気持ち

□ **urgent** 形 緊急の, 差し迫った

□ **Ursula** 名 アースラ《ヒーローの侍女》

□ **us** 代 私たちを[に] **let us** どうか私たちに～させてください

□ **use** 動 ①使う, 用いる ②費やす 名 使用, 用途 **use up** ～を使い果たす

□ **used** 動 ①use (使う) の過去, 過去分詞 ②《– to》よく～したものだ, 以前は～であった 形 ①慣れている, 《get [become] – to》～に慣れてくる ②使われた, 中古の

□ **useful** 形 役に立つ, 有効な, 有益な

□ **useless** 形 役に立たない, 無益な

□ **usual** 形 通常の, いつもの, 平常の, 普通の **as usual** いつものように, 相変わらず

□ **usurp** 動 (他人の権利・土地・地位などを) 奪う

□ **usurper** 名 (権力・地位の) 強奪者

□ **utmost** 形 最大限の, 極度の 名《the –》最大限, 極度

□ **utter** 形 完全な, まったくの 動 (声・言葉を) 発する

V

□ **vacant** 形 空いている, 使用されていない

□ **vaguely** 副 ぼんやりと, あいまいに

□ **vain** 形 ①無益の, むだな ②うぬぼれが強い **in vain** むだに, むなしく

□ **valiant** 形 (人が) 勇気ある, 勇敢な

□ **valor** 名 (特に戦闘における) 勇気, 武勇

□ **valuable** 形 貴重な, 価値のある, 役に立つ

□ **value** 名 価値, 値打ち, 価格 動 評価する, 値をつける, 大切にする

□ **valued** 形 高く評価された, 貴重な

□ **vanish** 動 姿を消す, 消える, ゼロになる

□ **various** 形 変化に富んだ, さまざまの, たくさんの

□ **vast** 形 広大な, 巨大な, ばく大な

□ **vault** 名 ①地下金庫室, 地下貯蔵室 [納骨堂] ②アーチ形天井 動 飛び越える, 跳躍する

□ **veil** 名 ベール, 覆い隠す物

□ **veiled** 形 ベールで隠された

□ **vein** 名 静脈, 血管

□ **venerable** 形 尊敬すべき, 立派な

□ **Venetian** 名 ヴェニス市民 形 ヴェニス (市民) の, ヴェニス風の

□ **vengeance** 名 復讐, あだ討ち

□ **Venice** 名 ヴェネチア, ヴェニス《イタリアの都市》

□ **venison** 名 鹿の肉

□ **venomous** ①有毒な, 毒を持つ ②悪意に満ちた, 毒のある

□ **venture** 動 思い切って～する, 危険にさらす 名 冒険 (的事業), 危険

□ **Verona** 名 ヴェローナ《イタリアの都市》

□ **very** 副 とても, 非常に, まったく 形 本当の, きわめて, まさしくその **be very kind of you** ～してくださってありがとう **very well** 結構, よろしい

□ **vessel** 名 ① (大型の) 船 ②器, 容器 ③管, 脈管

□ **via** 前 ～経由で, ～によって

□ **victim** 名 犠牲者, 被害者

☐ **victorious** 形勝利を得た, 勝った
☐ **Vienna** 名ウィーン《オーストリアの首都》
☐ **view** 名①眺め, 景色, 見晴らし ②考え方, 意見 動眺める
☐ **vile** 形ひどい, とても悪い
☐ **village** 名村, 村落
☐ **villager** 名村人, 田舎の人
☐ **villain** 名悪党, 悪者, 罪人
☐ **villainy** 名悪事, 極悪, 非道
☐ **Vincentio** 名ヴィンセンシオ《ルーセンシオの父》
☐ **Viola** 名ヴァイオラ《主人公》
☐ **violence** 名①暴力, 乱暴 ②激しさ
☐ **violent** 形暴力的な, 激しい
☐ **violet** 名①スミレ(菫) ②スミレ色, バイオレット
☐ **virgin** 名①処女, バージン, 童貞 ②《the V-(Mary)》処女[聖母]マリア 形処女の, 人跡未踏の, 初めての
☐ **virtue** 名①徳, 高潔 ②美点, 長所 ③効力, 効き目
☐ **virtuous** 形①有徳の, 高潔な ②偽善的な
☐ **visible** 形目に見える, 明らかな
☐ **vision** 名①視力 ②先見, 洞察力
☐ **visit** 動訪問する 名訪問
☐ **visitor** 名訪問客
☐ **vividly** 副生き生きと, 鮮やかに
☐ **voice** 名①声, 音声 ②意見, 発言権 動声に出す, 言い表す
☐ **void** 形無効の, 欠けている 名①《the –》空虚, 空間 ②むなしさ 動無効にする
☐ **volcano** 名火山, 噴火口
☐ **voluntary** 形自発的な, ボランティアの
☐ **vouch** 動(個人的に)保証する, 請け合う, (人の)保証人となる
☐ **vow** 名誓い, 誓約 動誓う **make a vow** 誓いを立てる
☐ **voyage** 名航海, 航行, 空の旅 動航海する, 空の旅をする

W

☐ **wager** 名賭け, 賭け金
☐ **wait** 動①待つ,《– for ~》~を待つ ②延ばす, 延ばせる, 遅らせる ③《– on [upon] ~》~に仕える, 給仕をする **wait a long time** 長時間待つ **wait for** ~を待つ
☐ **wake** 動①目がさめる, 起きる, 起こす ②奮起する **wake up** 起きる, 目を覚ます **wake up to** ~に気付く, ~で目を覚ます
☐ **walk** 動歩く, 歩かせる, 散歩する 名歩くこと, 散歩 **walk about** 歩き回る **walk around** 歩き回る, ぶらぶら歩く **walk away** 立ち去る, 遠ざかる **walk up** 歩み寄る, 歩いて上る **walk up and down** 行ったり来たりする
☐ **walking** 名歩行, 歩くこと 形徒歩の, 歩行用の
☐ **wall** 名①壁, 塀 ②障壁 動壁[塀]で囲む, ふさぐ
☐ **walnut** 名クルミ(胡桃)
☐ **wand** 名杖, 指揮棒
☐ **wander** 動①さまよう, 放浪する, 横道へそれる ②放心する
☐ **wanderer** 名放浪者
☐ **want** 動ほしい, 望む, ~したい, ~してほしい 名欠乏, 不足
☐ **war** 名戦争(状態), 闘争, 不和
☐ **warhorse** 名軍馬
☐ **warm** 形①暖かい, 温暖な ②思いやりのある, 愛情のある 動暖まる, 暖める
☐ **warmly** 副温かく, 親切に
☐ **warmth** 名暖かさ, 思いやり
☐ **warn** 動警告する, 用心させる
☐ **warning** 名警告, 警報
☐ **warrior** 名戦士, 軍人
☐ **was** 動《beの第1・第3人称単数現在am, isの過去》~であった, (~に)いた[あった]
☐ **wash** 動①洗う, 洗濯する ②押し流す[される] 名洗うこと
☐ **waste** 動浪費する, 消耗する 形①むだな, 余分な ②不毛の, 荒涼とした 名①浪費, 消耗 ②くず, 廃物 ③荒地
☐ **watch** 動①じっと見る, 見物する ②注意[用心]する, 監視する 名①警戒, 見張り ②腕時計
☐ **watchman** 名夜警
☐ **watchmen** 名watchman(夜警)の複数
☐ **water** 名①水 ②(川・湖・海などの)多量の水 動水を飲ませる, (植物に)水をやる
☐ **wave** 名①波 ②(手などを)振ること 動①揺れる, 揺らす, 波立つ ②(手などを振って)合図する
☐ **way** 名①道, 通り道 ②方向, 距離 ③方法, 手段 ④習慣 **all the way** ずっと, はるばる, いろいろと **by the way** ところで, ついでに, 途中で **find one's way** たどり着く **give way** 道を譲る,

譲歩する，負ける **in a way** ある意味では **in any way** 決して，多少なりとも **in no way** 決して～でない **in some way** 何とかして，何らかの方法で **in this way** このようにして **lose one's way** 道に迷う **make one's way** 進む，行く，成功する **make way** 道を譲る［あける］，前進する **not in any way** 少しも［全く］～ない **on one's way** 途中で **on one's way home** 帰り道で **on one's way to** ～に行く途中で **on the way** 途中で **on the way to** ～へ行く途中で **one's way to** （～への）途中で **there is no way** ～する見込みはない **this way** このように **way of** ～する方法 **way of life** 生き様，生き方，暮らし方 **way out of** ～から抜け出る道 **way to** ～する方法

□ **we** 代 私たちは［が］ **Shall we ～?** （一緒に）～しましょうか。

□ **weak** 形 ①弱い，力のない，病弱な ②劣った，へたな，苦手な

□ **weaken** 動 弱くなる，弱める

□ **weakness** 名 ①弱さ，もろさ ②欠点，弱点

□ **wealth** 名 ①富，財産 ②豊富，多量

□ **wealthy** 形 裕福な，金持ちの

□ **weapon** 名 武器，兵器 動 武装させる，武器を供給する

□ **wear** 動 ①着る，着ている，身につける ②疲れる，消耗する，すり切れる 名 ①着用 ②衣類

□ **wearily** 形 疲れて

□ **weary** 形 とても疲れた，あきあきした

□ **weaver** 名 織り手

□ **wedding** 名 結婚式，婚礼

□ **wedding day** 結婚式の日

□ **wedding feast** 結婚披露宴

□ **Wednesday** 名 水曜日

□ **weed** 名 雑草 動 草取りをする，（不要なものを）取り除く

□ **week** 名 週，1週間

□ **weep** 動 ①しくしく泣く，嘆き悲しむ ②しずくが垂れる

□ **weeping** 名 涙を流す，泣く

□ **weigh** 動 ①（重さを）はかる ②重さが～ある ③圧迫する，重荷である

□ **weight** 名 ①重さ，重力，体重 ②重荷，負担 ③重大さ，勢力 動 ①重みをつける ②重荷を負わせる

□ **weird** 形 変わった，妙な，奇妙な

□ **welcome** 間 ようこそ 名 歓迎 動 歓迎する 形 歓迎される，自由に～してよい

□ **welfare** 名 ①福祉 ②福祉手当［事業］，失業手当

□ **well** 副 ①うまく，上手に ②十分に，よく，かなり 間 へえ，まあ，ええと 形 健康な，適当な，申し分ない 名 井戸 **as well** なお，その上，同様に **as well as** ～と同様に **be well -ed** よく［十分に］～された **do well** 成績が良い，成功する **too well** 十二分に **very well** 結構，よろしい **well done** うまくやった

□ **well-behaved** 形 行儀のよい

□ **well-bred** 形 育ちのよい，行儀のよい，上品な

□ **well-dressed** 形 身なりのよい，りっぱな服を着た

□ **well-earned** 形 自分の力でかち得た

□ **well-educated** 形 高学歴の

□ **well-meant** 形 （結果はともかく）善意から出た

□ **well-proved** 形 十分に証明された

□ **went** 動 go（行く）の過去

□ **wept** 動 weep（しくしく泣く）の過去，過去分詞

□ **were** 動 《beの2人称単数・複数の過去》～であった，（～に）いた［あった］ **I wish ～ were ...** 私が～なら…なのに。《仮定法過去》

□ **west** 名 《the –》西，西部，西方，《the W-》西洋 形 西の，西方［西部］の，西向きの 副 西へ，西方へ

□ **wet** 形 ぬれた，湿った，雨の 動 ぬらす，ぬれる

□ **what** 代 ①何が［を・に］ ②《関係代名詞》～するところのもの［こと］ 形 ①何の，どんな ②なんと ③～するだけの 副 いかに，どれほど **what ... for** どんな目的で **What's the matter?** どうしたんですか。

□ **whatever** 代 ①《関係代名詞》～するものは何でも ②どんなこと［もの］が～とも 形 ①どんな～でも ②《否定文・疑問文で》少しの～も，何らかの

□ **when** 副 ①いつ ②《関係副詞》～するところの，～するとその時，～するとき 接 ～の時，～するとき 代 いつ

□ **whenever** 接 ①～するときはいつでも，～するたびに ②いつ～しても

□ **where** 副 ①どこに［で］ ②《関係副詞》～するところの，そしてそこで，～するところ 接 ～なところに［へ］，～するところに［へ］ 代 ①どこ，どの点 ②～するところの **where to** どこで～すべきか

□ **wherever** 接 どこでも，どこへ［で］～するとも 副 いったいどこへ［に・で］

□ **whether** 接 ～かどうか，～かまたは…，～で

あろうとなかろうと **whether or not** ～かどうか

□ **which** 形 ①どちらの，どの，どれでも ②どんな～でも，そしてこの 代 ①どちら，どれ，どの人［物］ ②《関係代名詞》～するところの **of which** ～の中で

□ **while** 接 ①～の間（に），～する間（に） ②一方，～なのに 名 しばらくの間，一定の時 **after a while** しばらくして **for a while** しばらくの間，少しの間

□ **whim** 名 気まぐれ，思い付き

□ **whip** 動 ①むちうつ ②急に動く［動かす］ 名 むち

□ **whisper** 動 ささやく，小声で話す 名 ささやき，ひそひそ話，うわさ

□ **white** 形 ①白い，（顔色などが）青ざめた ②白人の 名 白，白色 **turn white** 青ざめる，血の気が引く

□ **whiteness** 名 白さ，純白，潔白

□ **who** 代 ①誰が［は］，どの人 ②《関係代名詞》～するところの（人） **those who** ～する人々

□ **whole** 形 全体の，すべての，完全な，満～，丸～ 名《the –》全体，全部

□ **whom** 代 ①誰を［に］ ②《関係代名詞》～するところの人，そしてその人を

□ **whose** 代 ①誰の ②《関係代名詞》（～の）…するところの

□ **why** 副 ①なぜ，どうして ②《関係副詞》～するところの（理由） 間 ①おや，まあ ②もちろん，なんだって ③ええと **Why don't you ～?** ～したらどうだい，～しませんか。

□ **wicked** 形 悪い，不道徳な

□ **wickedness** 名 邪悪

□ **wide** 形 幅の広い，広範囲の，幅が～ある 副 広く，大きく開いて

□ **widely** 副 広く，広範囲にわたって

□ **widow** 名 未亡人，やもめ

□ **widowed** 形 夫［妻］を亡くした，夫［妻］と死別した

□ **widower** 名 妻を亡くした［妻と死別した］男性，寡夫

□ **wife** 名 妻，夫人

□ **wig** 名 かつら

□ **wild** 形 ①野生の ②荒涼として ③荒っぽい ④奇抜な

□ **wilderness** 名 荒野，荒れ地

□ **wildly** 副 荒々しく，乱暴に，むやみに

□ **wildness** 名 野生，荒廃，無謀

□ **will** 助 ～だろう，～しよう，する（つもりだ） 名 決意，意図 **Will you ～?** ～してくれませんか。

□ **willing** 形 ①喜んで～する，～しても構わない，いとわない ②自分から進んで行う

□ **willingly** 副 喜んで，快く

□ **willow** 名 ヤナギ（柳）

□ **win** 動 勝つ，獲得する，達する 名 勝利，成功 **win over** 説得する，口説き落とす

□ **wind** 名 ①風 ②うねり，一巻き 動 巻く，からみつく，うねる **second wind** 回復した元気

□ **window** 名 窓，窓ガラス

□ **wine** 名 ワイン，ぶどう酒

□ **wing** 名 翼，羽

□ **winged** 形 翼のある，有翼の

□ **wink** 名 まばたき，ウインク，きらめき 動 ウインクする，まばたきする

□ **winter** 名 冬 動 冬を過ごす

□ **wintry** 形 冬の，冬のように寒い

□ **wipe** 動 ～をふく，ぬぐう，ふきとる 名 ふくこと

□ **wisdom** 名 知恵，賢明（さ）

□ **wise** 形 賢明な，聡明な，博学の

□ **wisely** 副 賢明に

□ **wish** 動 望む，願う，（～であればよいと）思う 名（心からの）願い **I wish ～ were ...** 私が～なら…なのに。《仮定法過去》 **wish for** 所望する

□ **wit** 名 ①機知，ウィット ②才能，理解力

□ **witch** 名 魔法使い，魔女

□ **witchcraft** 名 魔法，魔術，魔力

□ **witches** 名（3人の）魔女《マクベスとバンクォーに予言をする》

□ **with** 前 ①《同伴・付随・所属》～と一緒に，～を身につけて，～とともに ②《様態》～（の状態）で，～して ③《手段・道具》～で，～を使って **agree with**（人）に同意する **along with** ～と一緒に **be content with** ～に満足している，甘んじている **be filled with** ～でいっぱいになる **be in love with** ～に恋して，～に心を奪われて **be overcome with** ～に圧倒される，～にやられる **be pleased with** ～が気に入る **be wrong with**（～にとって）よくない，～が故障している **come up with** ～に追いつく，～を思いつく，考え出す，見つけ出す **do with** ～を処理する **fall in love with** 恋におちる **fight with** ～と戦う **find fault with** ～のあら探しをする **go along with** ～に同調する **go with** ～と一緒に行く，～と調和する，～にとても似合う **God be with you.** 神のご加護があらんことを **have to do with** ～と関係がある **help ～ with ...** …を～の面で手伝う **keep pace with** ～と歩

調をそろえる **meet with** ～に出会う **on ～ terms with ...** …と～な仲である **part with** ～を手放す **play with** ～で遊ぶ, ～と一緒に遊ぶ **stay with** ～の所に泊まる **with all** ～がありながら **with all one's heart** 心から **with fear** 怖がって **with regard to** ～に関しては

□ **wither** 動 しぼむ, しおれる, しおれさせる, 枯れる, 衰える

□ **withered** 形 しぼんだ, 干からびた

□ **within** 前 ①～の中[内]に, ～の内部に ②～以内で, ～を越えないで 副 中[内]へ[に], 内部に 名 内部

□ **without** 前 ～なしで, ～がなく, ～しないで **go without** ～なしですませる

□ **witness** 名 ①証拠, 証言 ②目撃者 動 ①目撃する ②証言する

□ **Wittenberg University** 名 ヴィッテンベルク大学《ハムレットが学んだ大学》

□ **witty** 形 機知に富んだ, 気のきいた

□ **wives** 名 wife (妻) の複数

□ **woe** 名 悲哀, 悲痛

□ **woke** 動 wake (目が覚める) の過去

□ **woken** 動 wake (目が覚める) の過去分詞

□ **wolf** 名 オオカミ (狼)

□ **wolves** 名 wolf (オオカミ) の複数

□ **woman** 名 (成人した) 女性, 婦人

□ **womanly** 形 女性らしい, 女性にふさわしい

□ **women** 名 woman (女性) の複数

□ **won** 動 win (勝つ) の過去, 過去分詞

□ **wonder** 動 ①不思議に思う, (～に) 驚く ②(～かしらと) 思う 名 驚き (の念), 不思議なもの **wonder about** ～について知りたがる

□ **wonderful** 形 驚くべき, すばらしい, すてきな

□ **wonderfully** 副 不思議なほど, すばらしく

□ **won't** will notの短縮形

□ **woo** 動 (女性に) 求婚する, 求愛する

□ **wood** 名 ①《しばしば-s》森, 林 ②木材, まき

□ **woodbine** 名 ウッドバイン, ニオイエンドウ《植物》

□ **wooden** 形 木製の, 木でできた

□ **wool** 名 羊毛, 毛糸, 織物, ウール

□ **word** 名 ①語, 単語 ②ひと言 ③《one's –》約束 **in other words** すなわち, 言い換えれば

□ **wore** 動 wear (着ている) の過去

□ **work** 動 ①働く, 勉強する, 取り組む ②機能[作用]する, うまくいく 名 ①仕事, 勉強 ②職 ③作品 **work in** ～の分野で働く, ～に入り込む **work of** ～の仕業 **work on** ～で働く, ～に取り組む, ～を説得する, ～に効く

□ **workmanship** 名 (職人の) 手腕, 優れた技術

□ **world** 名《the –》世界, ～界 **brave new world** 素晴らしい新世界 **for all the world** 絶対に, 断じて **in the world** 世界で **world of** 大量の, 無数の

□ **worn** 動 wear (着ている) の過去分詞 形 ①すり切れた, 使い古した ②やつれた, 疲れた **worn out** すり切れた

□ **worried** 形 心配そうな, 不安げな **be worried about** (～のことで) 心配している, ～が気になる[かかる]

□ **worry** 動 悩む, 悩ませる, 心配する[させる] 名 苦労, 心配 **worry about** ～のことを心配する

□ **worse** 形 いっそう悪い, より劣った, よりひどい 副 いっそう悪く **get worse** 悪化する

□ **worship** 名 崇拝, 礼拝, 参拝 動 崇拝する, 礼拝[参拝]する, 拝む

□ **worst** 形《the –》最も悪い, いちばんひどい 副 最も悪く, いちばんひどく 名《the –》最悪の事態[人・物]

□ **worth** 形 (～の) 価値がある, (～) しがいがある 名 価値, 値打ち

□ **worthy** 形 価値のある, 立派な

□ **would** 助《willの過去》①～するだろう, ～するつもりだ ②～したものだ **would have ... if ～** もし～だったとしたら…しただろう **would like** ～がほしい **would like to** ～したいと思う **would rather** ～する方がよい **would rather ～ than ...** …よりむしろ～したい **Would you like ～?** ～はいかがですか。 **Would you ～?** ～してくださいませんか。

□ **wound** 名 傷 動 ①負傷させる, (感情を) 害する ②wind (巻く) の過去, 過去分詞

□ **wrap** 動 包む, 巻く, くるむ, 覆い隠す 名 包み

□ **wrestle** 動 取っ組み合う, 格闘する

□ **wrestler** 名 レスリング選手

□ **wrestling** 名 レスリング

□ **wretch** 名 みじめな[哀れな]人

□ **wretched** 形 哀れな, 困った, みじめな, ひどい

□ **wrinkled** 形 しわの寄った, しわくちゃの

□ **wrist** 名 手首, リスト

□ **write** 動 書く, 手紙を書く **write to** ～に手紙を書く

□ **written** 動 write (書く) の過去分詞 形 文書の, 書かれた

☐ **wrong** 形 ①間違った，（道徳上）悪い ②調子が悪い，故障した 副 間違って 名 不正，悪事 **be wrong with**（～にとって）よくない，～が故障している

☐ **wrongly** 副 誤って，間違って

☐ **wrote** 動 write（書く）の過去

Y

☐ **year** 名 ①年，1年 ②学年，年度 ③～歳 **for ~ years** ～年間，～年にわたって

☐ **year-old** 尾 ～歳

☐ **yes** 副 はい，そうです 名 肯定の言葉［返事］

☐ **yesterday** 名 ①昨日 ②過ぎし日，昨今 副 昨日（は）

☐ **yet** 副 ①《否定文で》まだ～（ない［しない］）②《疑問文で》もう ③《肯定文で》まだ，今もなお 接 それにもかかわらず，しかし，けれども **and yet** それなのに，それにもかかわらず **not yet** まだ～してない **yet another** さらにもう一つの

☐ **yew** 名 イチイ《植物》

☐ **yield** 動 ①生じる，産出する ②譲る，明け渡す 名 ①産出（物，高），収穫（量）②利回り，利益

☐ **you** 代 ①あなた（方）は［が］，あなた（方）を［に］②（一般に）人は **you know** ご存知のとおり，そうでしょう **you see** あのね，いいですか

☐ **young** 形 若い，幼い，青年の

☐ **your** 代 あなた（方）の

☐ **yours** 代 あなた（方）のもの

☐ **yourself** 代 あなた自身

☐ **youth** 名 若さ，元気，若者

☐ **youthful** 形 若々しい

英語で読む
シェイクスピア珠玉の15篇

2024年 5 月 5 日　第1刷発行

原著者　チャールズ・ラム
　　　　メアリー・ラム

リライト　ステュウット ヴァーナム－アットキン

発行者　賀川　洋

発行所　IBCパブリッシング株式会社
〒162-0804 東京都新宿区中里町29番3号 菱秀神楽坂ビル
Tel. 03-3513-4511　Fax. 03-3513-4512
www.ibcpub.co.jp

印刷所　株式会社シナノパブリッシングプレス

ISBN978-4-7946-0812-3